EARLY URBANISM ON THE SYRIAN EUPHRATES

EARLY URBANISM ON THE SYRIAN EUPHRATES

Lisa Cooper

Routledge
Taylor & Francis Group

NEW YORK AND LONDON

First published 2006
by Routledge
270 Madison Ave, New York NY 10016

Simultaneously published in the UK
by Routledge
2 Park Square, Milton Park, Abingdon, Oxon, OX14 4RN

Routledge is an imprint of the Taylor & Francis Group, an informa business

Transferred to Digital Printing 2008

© 2006 Lisa Cooper

Typeset in Garamond 3 by
RefineCatch Limited, Bungay, Suffolk

British Library Cataloguing in Publication Data
A catalogue record for this book is available from the British Library

Library of Congress Cataloging in Publication Data
Cooper, Lisa, 1963–
Early urbanism on the Syrian Euphrates / Lisa Cooper.
p. cm.
Includes bibliographical references and index.
ISBN 0-415-35351-3 (hardback : alk. paper) 1. Cities and
towns, Ancient—Syria. 2. Cities and towns, Ancient—Euphrates
Valley. 3. Syria—History—To 333 B.C. 4. Euphrates Valley—
History. I. Title.

DS96.C56 2006
939′43009732—dc22   2005029935

ISBN10: 0-415-35351-3 (hbk)
ISBN10: 0-415-48720-X (pbk)
ISBN10: 0-203-30672-4 (ebk)

ISBN13: 978-0-415-35351-9 (hbk)
ISBN13: 978-0-415-48720-7 (pbk)
ISBN13: 978-0-203-30672-7 (ebk)

CONTENTS

ILLUSTRATIONS

ILLUSTRATIONS

TABLES

PREFACE AND ACKNOWLEDGEMENTS

This book was written to fill the need for a synthetic presentation of the rich and diverse array of Early Bronze archaeological remains brought to light in the Euphrates River of northern Syria region in the recent past. Until now, much of this archaeological material has only been published in reports of a preliminary nature or in studies concerning one site or one class of artifacts. By bringing all material bearing on the northern Euphrates of the third millennium BC together in one place, I have endeavoured to produce a clear overview of the most salient characteristics of this pivotal era of antiquity. I consider also the prevalent scholarly interpretations of the archaeological remains of this period, highlighting especially those pertaining to the rise and persistence of urban life among settlements of the Euphrates River Valley, and factors that contributed to Euphrates cities' distinctive and complex character.

My interest in the ancient Euphrates River Valley first arose out of doctoral research on pottery and the chronology of the Middle Bronze Age of northern Syria. While working on this project, I frequently found myself drawn to archaeological reports describing the ancient remains of the earlier Early Bronze Age of the Euphrates Valley. Not only was the EB period represented by a wealth of funerary remains, it had well-built, densely inhabited settlements that testified to a flourishing riverine culture from a very early period of urban society in the Near East. It seemed that a broad, yet comprehensive investigation of the Syrian Euphrates during this period might yield interesting patterns regarding settlement complexity and urbanism that could serve as valuable points of comparison with ancient complex societies of other regions of the Near East such as southern Mesopotamia, the Khabur Plains of northeastern Syria and the Levant. With this project in mind, my research focus slowly shifted backward in time, first with a concentration on the elusive 'dark age' and collapse of complex societies at the end of the third millennium BC, and subsequently with a review of the principal remains of Early Bronze Age settlements in the centuries before this urban decline.

My engagement with the EB (Early Bronze Age) Euphrates was further heightened by my participation in archaeological projects in northern Syria on the Euphrates, at Tell Banat in 1995 and 1997, Tell Amarna in 1998 and at Tell es-Sweyhat in 2000. I wish to thank directors Tom McClellan and Anne Porter, Onhan Tunça, and Richard Zettler, for inviting me to share in their exciting field seasons, and encouraging my research on their archaeological material, especially their pottery. My conversations and deliberations with these individuals and members of their teams were tremendously stimulating. Overall, I do not believe that this book could have been written without the opportunity I had to listen to and learn from the talented and experienced archaeologists that I met and worked with in Syria. I am also grateful to my Syrian colleagues and friends, whose generosity and hospitality ensured that all of my seasons in the field were thoroughly enjoyable and productive.

My participation in conferences and workshops pertaining to the archaeology of the Syrian Early Bronze Age provided other useful venues for the collection of data. The Barcelona Conference of 1998, organized by Gregorio del Olmo Lete, which presented early results of excavations in the Tishreen Dam region of the Euphrates, provided many summaries of recent archaeological projects. The workshop on the Carchemish Region at the ICAANE congress in Berlin, 2004, organized by Edgar Peltenburg, endeavoured to bring together recent research of sites in the region both to the north and south of the ancient city of Carchemish. The meetings of the EB-MB workshop in Blaubeuren, which I attended in 2002 and 2005, helped me to understand more fully the material culture of the late third millennium, and how individual sites should correspond with one another temporally and culturally. My special thanks goes to Uwe Finkbeiner for organizing these meetings, and to all of those who participated in and contributed to these productive and colleagial workshops.

I am grateful to Marie-Claude Boileau, Giacchino Falsone, Alice Petty, Edgar Peltenburg, Anne Porter, Paola Sconzo, Jill Weber and Tony Wilkinson, for providing me with copies of their research reports or book manuscripts in advance of their publication. I would also like to thank Rudolph Dornemann, Michel Fortin, Renate Gut, Ralph Hempelmann, Thomas McClellan, the late Nina Pons, Anne Porter, Ferhan Sakal and Glenn Schwartz for offering me useful advice or opinions on issues pertaining to the EB Syrian Euphrates, or referring me to important and relevant sources of published information. Grant Frame and Douglas Frayne of the Royal Inscriptions of Mesopotamia Project at the University of Toronto generously made their archives available to me during my research visits to Toronto. I am indebted to colleagues who have supplied me with illustrations or have given their permission to use them: Luc Bachelot, Gregorio del Olmo Lete, Uwe Finkbeiner, Thomas Holland, Thomas McClellan, Diederik Meijer, Winfried Orthmann, Edgar Peltenburg, Peter Pfälzner, Anne Porter, Kemal Sertok, Eva Strommenger, Carmen Valdés Pereiro, Peter Werner and Richard Zettler.

At the University of British Columbia, I gratefully acknowledge the talent and dedication of my student Anthony Russell who assisted in the preparation of the majority of illustrations in this book. Julia Armstrong also contributed to the production and final layout of two of the figures. I had the great fortune of enlisting the talents of Amanda Peters, who provided lovely line drawings of several tombs, kilns and artifacts.

A research stipend for Early Career Scholars provided by the Peter Wall Institute of the University of British Columbia provided me with the funding necessary to purchase computer equipment and software, and to employ student research assistants. Additional funding provided by two HSS Small Research Grants from the University of British Columbia, and a Travel Research Grant from the British School of Archaeology in Iraq, enabled me to travel to and research in Toronto, Milwaukee, Philadelphia and Syria.

The steadfast support of my colleagues in the Department of Classical, Near Eastern and Religious Studies at the University of British Columbia ensured that I had a productive environment in which to conduct my research. I am particularly grateful to Rob Cousland and Anthony Barrett for reading early drafts of sections of this book. My greatest thanks goes to my colleague Shirley Sullivan. Not only did she read the entire manuscript several times, offering countless editorial comments and corrections, she was a unending source of moral support and encouragement.

A special thanks must go to my professor and mentor, the late T. Cuyler Young Jr., formerly of the Royal Ontario Museum and the University of Toronto. A superb lecturer, a talented field archaeologist and a gentleman, Cuyler will always be a major source of inspiration to me in my life and work.

My fiancé Richard Ritson read most of my manuscript with great interest, and made many valuable comments. I also thank him for his cheerful support and companionship during what was a busy time for me.

My deepest expression of gratitude goes to my parents, Reed and Jane Cooper. It was their love of travel and curiosity for the ancient world that sparked my interest in Near Eastern archaeology in the first place, and their continuing support for my academic progress through the years helped me to get to where I am today. This book is dedicated to them, with admiration and affection.

1

INTRODUCTION

The majestic presence of the river in the midst of uncultivated lands, which, with the help of its waters, would need so little labour to make them productive, takes a singular hold on the imagination. I do not believe that the east bank has always been so thinly peopled . . . it is probable that there was once a continuous belt of villages, their site being still marked by mounds.

(Gertrude Bell, 1910: 518)

We have had no rain since we came to Carchemish, but generally sun, with often after midday a gale from the North that drives the workmen off the top of the mound, and tosses up the dust of our diggings . . . If one can struggle up to the top of the mound and hold on one can look over all the plain of the river valley up to Biredjik and down to Tell Ahmar, and over it all the only things to show out of the dust clouds are the hills and tops of the tells.

(T.E. Lawrence, quoted in Garnett 1938: 98–9)[1]

The striking landscape and rich archaeological potential of the northern Euphrates Valley could not fail to affect even Gertrude Bell and T.E. Lawrence, two individuals who were to figure prominently in the shaping of the modern Middle East.

In the recent past, many more than a few travellers and casual archaeologists have turned their attention to the antiquity of the land of Syria, including the Euphrates River Valley. Especially in recent decades, Syria has become the major focus of many investigations, when archaeologists, no longer able to access the antiquity of countries such as Iraq and Iran, shifted their focus to the heritage of Syria and its rich array of ancient architectural remains and artifacts. Their investigations have proven tremendously significant. They have demonstrated that we can no longer regard the ancient land of Mesopotamia, defined by the alluvial valley of the Tigris and Euphrates

1

Rivers of southern Iraq, as the sole source of the great cultural transformations taking place at the dawn of history. Now we must realize that Syria too partook in many of these radical major changes.

Especially important were developments taking place in ancient Syria during the third millennium BC. This time period, often referred to as the Early Bronze Age, was witness to a dynamic growth of complex societies and the rise of urbanism. These new advancements had a major impact on human populations, bringing about dramatic changes to their political systems, and radically reorganizing their social and economic structures. Many of these pivotal developments are now well attested in the archaeological record. Investigations have shown, for example, that in the northeastern corner of Syria, along the banks and tributaries of the Khabur River, large and densely populated cities, supported by the agricultural produce of vast tracts of fertile fields, began to spring up all over the landscape. Settlements such as Tell Leilan, grew as large as 100 ha by 2600 BC, truly attesting to the early success of urban growth in this region. The discovery of an administrative archive of cuneiform tablets at the site of Tell Beydar, confirming that people of the Khabur region were literate, lends further support to this picture of urban progress. Cities also emerged in western Syria, in the agriculturally rich Orontes River Valley and the dry farming plains to the south of Aleppo. Here, the most well-known of ancient Syrian cities, Ebla, is renowned not only for its immense and rambling palace but for its archive rooms, found full of thousands of inscribed cuneiform tablets describing all the political activities and economic accounts of the powerful Eblaite king and his numerous officials.

In light of such discoveries in Syrian archaeology, the land of southern Mesopotamia must now be seen as but one of many regions in the Near East where early civilizations arose. More importantly still, ancient Syria's urban transformation should not be regarded as having derived solely from its contact with Mesopotamia, its cultural achievements being but pale imitations of the truly monumental advances engendered in the south. As the archaeological evidence has proven, many aspects of Syrian cities are original and distinctive, and they attest to the vibrant, independent character of their people and culture.

The northern Euphrates River Valley perhaps stands out as one of the most remarkable areas in which early urbanism evolved in Syria (Figure 1.1). This riverine region, stretching for about 100 km from the modern border of Turkey and Syria down to the area around the ancient site of Emar, supported several flourishing settlements during the third millennium BC. Settlements were established near the banks of the river and on the higher terraces. Here they were able to take advantage of the agricultural potential of the alluvial valley and commercial traffic of the river itself, as well as the pastoral and hunting opportunities provided by the vast upland steppe plateau that rises up on either side of the river valley. For several centuries populations increased

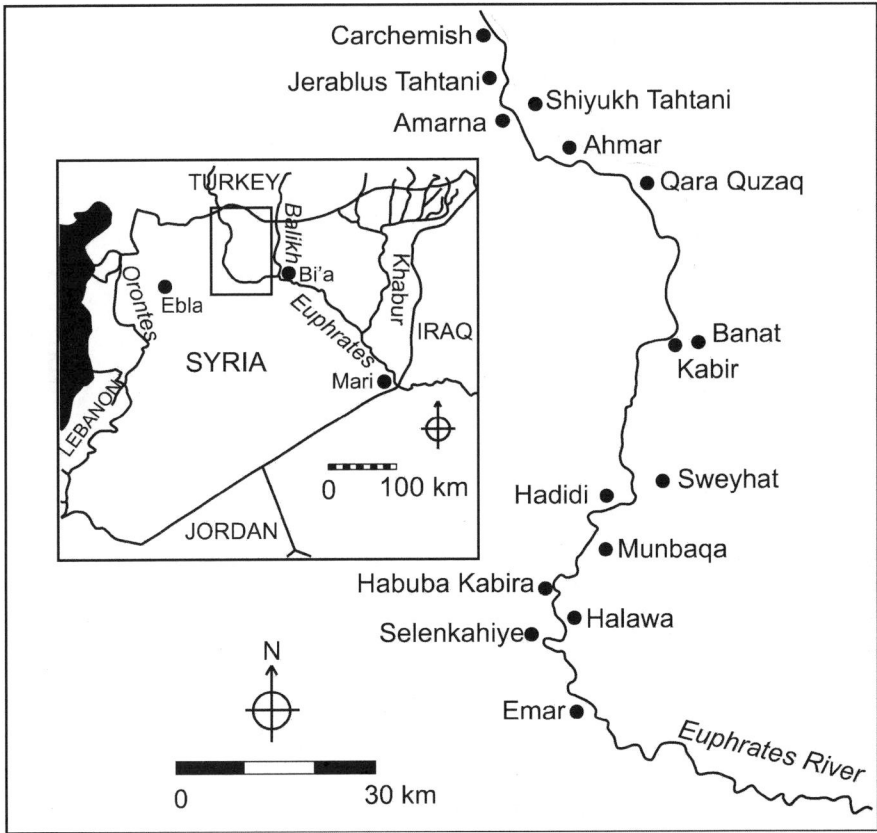

Figure 1.1 Locator map of Syria (left), and map of Euphrates River, with principal EB sites (right).

and flourished, and settlements grew into substantial centres featuring many urban trappings.

Such settlements were well defended by monumental defensive systems. They had communal places of worship, usually in the form of large temple structures surrounded by sacred enclosures. Some settlements featured lavish, multi-roomed buildings, which probably functioned as the residences and administrative headquarters of wealthy or prominent elites. An array of fine copper and bronze metalwork and other manufactured goods such as pottery demonstrates that craft specialists with well-developed skills were present. Extensive sectors of housing, well spaced out and accessible by straight, interconnecting streets, grew up in these third millennium towns. Associated with these living communities were large cemeteries for the dead, containing impressive rock-cut graves and grand stone-built tombs, many filled with rich assemblages of precious or rare grave offerings. Finally, monumental

3

funerary tumuli, towering high above the river valley, provided an important focus of community identity. Together, this evidence demonstrates that the northern Euphrates River Valley was not merely a backwater of simple farming and pastoral villages. It also had a sophisticated, thriving culture, characterized by many of the same urban attributes as its Mesopotamian and Syrian neighbours.

On the other hand, several notable differences serve to distinguish settlements that grew in the northern Euphrates Valley from those found elsewhere. Although some settlements grew considerably in size, supporting fairly large populations, their scale was modest compared to that of the cities of southern Mesopotamia or even the Khabur Plains of northeastern Syria. The largest northern Euphrates city in Syria expanded to no more 56 ha during the third millennium BC, only half the size of some of the cities of the Khabur Plains, and only a small fraction of the grand urban centres of the south. Other northern Euphrates settlements were even smaller, most being less than 10 ha in area.

Another striking difference from the south was the absence of rigid settlement hierarchies and the associated presence of city-states in the northern Euphrates Valley, a development that marks many urban societies elsewhere in Greater Mesopotamia. While it is possible to identify clusters of settlements of varying sizes in some parts of the region, these site aggregations do not appear to exhibit rigid hierarchical structures. They are not defined by central or core cities that possessed all the administrative and organizational apparatus to govern and control the political, economic and religious affairs of the smaller, simpler, agro-pastoral communities that surrounded them. On the contrary, what we see in the Euphrates region is a more evenly dispersed arrangement of political, economic and religious authority, such that even the smallest settlements exhibited significant displays of complexity. These smaller riverine communities were characterized, for example, by impressively rich tombs and monumental temples. Because of these unexpected features and the unusual settlement configurations they reflect, it is not appropriate to use the term 'city-state' to refer to any settlement cluster within the northern Euphrates region. This designation suggests too many notions of a central-place political ascendancy and economic domination that are simply not well attested.

As the evidence will show, however, it is impossible to deny the existence of local elites and some degree of social stratification in the northern Euphrates Valley. Yet, we submit that there existed at the same time a contrasting or opposing dynamic that appears strongly to have constrained the degree to which elite power and authority could take hold and grow. Few powerful individuals or families appear to have risen to such a level of authority that they could control the entire economic base and administrative systems of the community in which they lived. This situation is reflected by the rarity of palatial complexes or public buildings from which such pre-eminent authority would have emanated. Such architectural complexes have only been found at a few sites and appear to have existed only towards the very end of the third millennium BC. In contrast to these complexes, most of the evidence from the northern Euphrates River Valley appears to reflect a more heterarchically structured society, in which there existed several coexisting and overlapping sources of power and political-economic control.

Although archaeological manifestations of such heterarchical organization are more difficult to identify than the physical markers of social stratification and elite control, they are nonetheless apparent in some contexts. We find, for example, a kind of group-centred ideology existing at the remarkable mortuary centre of Tell Banat. At this site, monuments in the form of towering tumuli and their accompanying burial rites reflect corporate notions of inclusion in which all markers of individual social status and personal wealth were extinguished (Porter 2002b: 166). But nonetheless, in contrast, these ideals of corporate belonging do not stand alone at Tell Banat. The presence of well-built, lavishly furnished tombs at this site and elsewhere undoubtedly mark the burial places of wealthy, elite members of society. Our evidence suggests, therefore, that the society of the northern Euphrates was varied. It seems inappropriate to characterize it as either a 'corporate' or a hierarchically structured society. Rather, we must acknowledge the presence of both systems, sometimes existing in tension and opposition to one another, while at other times coexisting in a state of mutual interdependence and complementarity (Porter 2002b: 169).

All the differences we have outlined suggest that we should regard the Syrian Euphrates Valley as a unique place. On the one hand, it is defined by many of the same urban attributes that may be observed in other regions of the Near East. On the other hand, it developed distinctive social, political and economic structures differing significantly from examples of ancient urbanism observed elsewhere. In the chapters that follow, we will discuss a variety of factors that, in our view, contribute to this region's unique character. We will suggest how these factors contributed not only to long settlement life and cultural continuity but how they enabled the region to withstand socio-political and environmental stresses at the end of the third millennium.

The archaeological heritage of the Euphrates Valley of Syria has been known for well over a hundred years. Early twentieth-century investigations at the site of Carchemish by British archaeologists, and at Tell Ahmar by the French, confirmed that the third millennium was an important period of settlement in this region (Thureau-Dangin and Dunand 1936; Woolley and Barnett 1952). Not until the last few decades of the twentieth century, however, were serious, systematic attempts made to explore this region's antiquity. The greatest strides came with the archaeological salvage work initiated prior to the construction of two large dams across the Euphrates. These dams led to the formation of massive lakes that submerged the majority of ancient sites located in the river valley. Before completion of the first dam at Tabqa in 1973, surveys and archaeological salvage work were conducted in the southern section of the region, from el-Qitar in the north, extending well below the site of Meskene/Emar in the south (Van Loon 1967; Freedman 1979). The more recent Tishreen hydroelectric dam prompted investigations of the northern-most stretch of the Euphrates in Syria, from just below the site of Jerablus and the ancient site of Carchemish in the north, to the site of el-Qitar in the south (McClellan and Porter in press). The bulk of information presented in this book derives from the archaeological reports produced by the archaeological teams carrying out salvage operations in these Tishreen and Tabqa Dam regions.

CHRONOLOGY

The time period that we present in this book covers over 1,000 years of human settlement in Syria. It not only spans all of the third millennium BC but it also includes the last centuries of the fourth millennium and the first 100 years of the second millennium (c. 3200–1900 BC). For absolute dates in this book we have followed the so-called 'middle' chronology, which reckons all developments backward in time from the fall of Babylon in 1595 BC (Akkermans and Schwartz 2003: 13). It is possible that the 'low' chronology advocated by several scholars in the recent past may eventually prove to be more accurate (Gasche *et al.* 1998). Nevertheless, since the majority of archaeologists working in the northern Euphrates Valley up to this point have used the 'middle' chronology, we do not wish to cause confusion by deviating from this conventional practice.

One of the biggest dilemmas facing scholars investigating the material remains of the northern Euphrates region of Syria is the terminology used to describe the passage of time during the third millennium BC. The general designation 'Early Bronze Age' is almost universally applied to this region, but given that this age covers over 1,000 years, a periodization that divides this time into smaller phases is needed to chronicle the more precise socio-political changes and cultural transformations taking place.

Several chronological terminologies exist, but few are appropriate. The third millennium BC of southern Mesopotamia is divided according to historical developments that chronicle the establishment of the Sumerian Early Dynastic city-states and the subsequent rise and fall of the Old Akkadian and Ur III empires (ED I, II, III, Akkadian and Ur III periods). Although the Syrian Euphrates is contemporary with these developments and shares some cultural features with southern Mesopotamia, its abundant differences cannot justify the adoption of this southern chronological sequence. The lack of perfect synchronisms between the two regions, gleaned primarily from inscriptional evidence, further urges against the use of the southern Mesopotamian chronology.

The sequence devised for the Amuq plain of southern Turkey (phases G–K) (Braidwood and Braidwood 1960), the Levantine sequence, which applies principally to Palestine and Jordan (EBI–IV), and even the recently devised Early Jezireh periodization, which pertains to the area of northeastern Syria (Early Jezireh I–IV) (Pfälzner 1998), are equally inapplicable to the Syrian Euphrates. This region shares many cultural features with the other areas, and indeed, several important chronological synchronisms have been established through correlations with these places' cultural assemblages. Nonetheless, the northern Euphrates' distinctive, singular cultural developments through time necessitate the establishment of its own chronological sequence.

Within the Syrian Euphrates, several superb efforts have been made to formulate a relative chronological sequence based principally on changes observed in the form and fabric of pottery through time. Rudolph Dornenmann's detailed examination of the pottery from successive strata at Tell Hadidi represents the first serious attempt to formulate a chronological sequence that divides the Early Bronze Age into smaller sub-phases, these being reckoned roughly according to the Palestinian sequence (Dornemann 1979, 1988, 1990). Andrew Jamieson also made important strides when he attempted to build a chronological sequence for the Euphrates Valley based on pottery obtained from the entire region, not just one site (Jamieson 1993). Jamieson's division of the Early Bronze Age into successive ceramic 'horizons' included many important observations about ceramic developments through time. Since his publication, however, the appearance of new stratified ceramic material from sites such as Tell es-Sweyhat, Qara Quzaq, Tell Banat and Tell Kabir has required some adjustments to his sequence. In particular, Jamieson's final third millennium horizon, 2B, can now be further subdivided into two smaller phases, each marked by significant ceramic developments.

Tony Wilkinson, well aware of the shortcomings of earlier chronologies and the problems of using other regions' sequences, has often used general terms such as 'Early Early Bronze Age', 'Middle-Late Bronze Age' and 'Late Early Bronze Age' to denote the passage of time in the Euphrates region (Wilkinson 2004: 83–92). As straightforward as this chronological scheme may sound, its threefold periodization does not account for important changes in the ceramic assemblages that correlate with significant developments in settlement structure, urban growth and regional collapse over the course of the third millennium BC.

Anne Porter's own attempt to establish a regional chronology represents the most recent effort to establish a northern Euphrates sequence (Porter in press). It is an improvement over others in that it is based almost exclusively on Early Bronze pottery assemblages from the Syrian Euphrates itself rather than material from areas further to the north in Anatolia or from the west and east. Porter's periodization, which consists of six separate ceramic phases

(Phases 1–6), has been specifically designed to mark the passage of time in the Euphrates River Valley of Syria, and its terminology is separate and distinct from that of other Near Eastern regional chronologies.

Rather than generating any further confusion by devising yet another chronological sequence to compete with the myriad of those already in existence, we have decided to adopt Porter's six-phase sequence for the Early Bronze Age. A few slight adjustments have been made to the dating of the phases to conform to recent radiocarbon determinations. Moreover, a few different diagnostic ceramic types have been presented for each phase, but essentially this is Porter's sequence:

Phases 1 and 2: 3200–2600 BC
Phase 3: 2600–2450 BC
Phase 4: 2450–2300 BC
Phase 5: 2300–2100 BC
Phase 6: 2100–1900 BC (also referred to as the EB-MB transitional period)

Before describing some principal ceramic traits of each of these phases, it is important to note that the entire Early Bronze Age sequence is marked by strong continuity. Invariably, diagnostic vessel types are representative not only of one Early Bronze Age phase but rather appear over the course of several phases. As Porter notes, the overall ceramic sequence displays a 'series of gradual additions and deletions of types' (Porter in press). In light of this continuity, the best way to document the passage of time is not simply to register the presence or absence of various pot types, but rather to consider their frequency relative to other types within the overall assemblage and the rise and fall in their abundance through successive strata. A vessel form that has reached a high frequency proportionate to other vessel types can be said to be diagnostic of the phase in which it occurs. It is challenging to determine vessel frequencies given the unquantified nature of many ceramic reports. Nonetheless, by carefully considering pots' relationships to other vessel types within the assemblage and carefully considering the ways in which the assemblages are described by the excavators, one can frequently ascertain important ceramic developments through time.

Phases 1 and 2 (3200–2600 BC)[2]

A great deal of ceramic continuity exists between Phases 1 and 2, and the precise differences that distinguishes one from the other is still a matter of debate. It has been pointed out that Late Uruk vessels no longer appear in assemblages belonging to Phase 2, which probably began sometime after 2900 BC (Dornemann 1988: 16; Porter in press). Since Uruk wares, however, are not documented in every site's pottery sequence, we cannot confirm that their presence or absence is always an issue pertaining to progress through time. Others have suggested that the replacement of the sinuous-sided cup with the so-called *cyma recta* cup form marks the beginning of Phase 2, but this is problematic in that some assemblages do not feature *cyma recta* cups at all (Wilkinson 2004: 90). Furthermore, sinuous-sided cups have now been shown to have extended well into Phase 2 and possibly even later (Porter in press). It is clear that further fine-tuning of the ceramic sequence still needs to be done for these early phases of the Early Bronze Age. For this reason, we are treating the two phases together in this study and will proceed to describe and illustrate vessel forms which are largely representative of the two phases as a whole.

The beginning of the Early Bronze Age can be traced back to the earlier fourth millennium. Although originally believed to begin around 3100 BC at the earliest, recent radiocarbon dates from the site of Hajji Ibrahim, whose pottery is most distinctly Early Bronze in character, suggest that the EB should be pushed back even earlier, perhaps to 3300 or 3200 BC (Danti 2000: 159; Wilkinson 2004: 89 n. 57). The beginning of the Early Bronze Age probably overlapped with the end of the earlier Late Uruk period (3500–3100 BC), whose material culture, which is distinguished by features that have a strong southern Mesopotamian orientation and includes such vessels as bevelled-rim bowls, contrasts sharply to the local Euphrates assemblage. At some sites like Tell Hadidi, both Uruk and EB ceramic assemblages occur in abundance in the same strata (Str. 1, Dornemann 1988: 16). At the majority of sites, however, the local EB forms overshadow those of Late Uruk appearance, the latter of which may only appear as a few scattered sherds. At settlements with such assemblages, we may surmise that we are witnessing the tail end of the Late Uruk culture, whose southern Mesopotamian presence and influence is withdrawing from this region and is becoming completely replaced by a culture of local origin and inspiration.

Phases 1 and 2 of the Early Bronze Age sequence are characterized by key pottery types which appear at a number of sites along the length of the northern Euphrates Valley of Syria. All of these pots are distinguished by mineral inclusions. Their relatively well-finished, symmetrical appearance was achieved by their partial forming or finishing on a rotative device. The most diagnostic vessel of this early period are plain bowls with simple, tapered rims (Figure 1.2a–c). These bowls are documented at many sites throughout the region, although their frequency appears to diminish as one travels to the north. Sometimes these bowls have incised 'potter's' marks on their exterior walls. Unfortunately, the precise meaning of these markings remains uncertain.

Distinctive sinuous-sided bowls are quite common, and as we have already reported, they appear throughout Phases 1 and 2 (Figure 1.2d–e). One sees an increase, however, of the somewhat similarly shaped *cyma recta* cup during the latter part of this period (Figure 1.2f–g). Such cups, which seem to have a

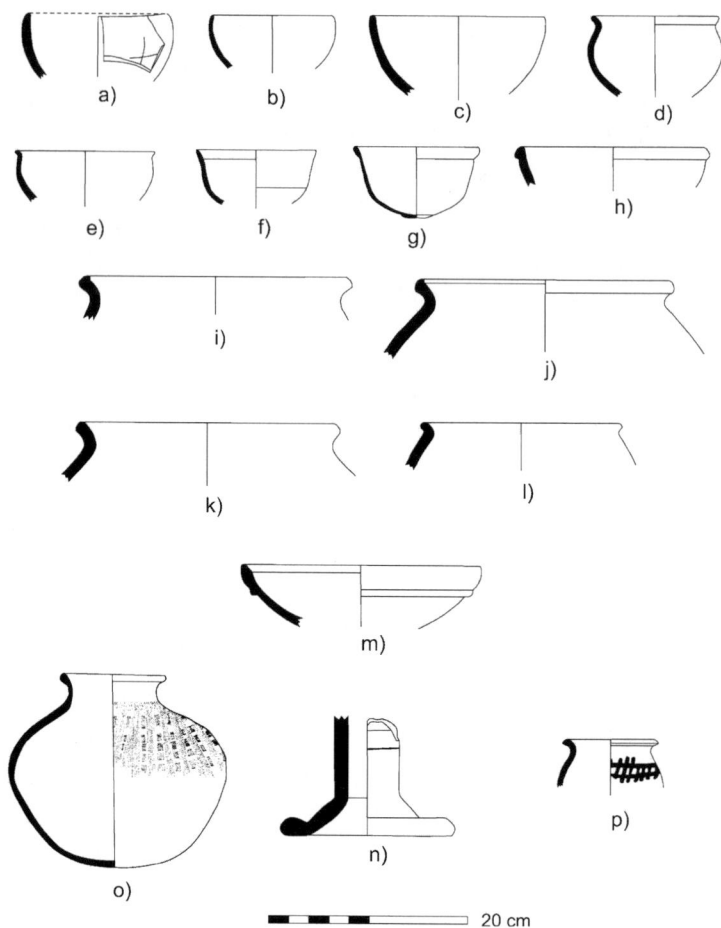

Figure 1.2 Phase 1–2 pottery.

fairly wide distribution covering much of southern Turkey and western Syria, are distinguished by their thin, out-flared sinuous profiles, and also by small ring bases (Dornemann 1988: 17; Jamieson 1993: 46). For the most part, *cyma recta* cups are diagnostic of the northern stretch of the Syrian Euphrates, while further to the south below Tell Hadidi, they are much rarer. At Halawa Tell B, a variant of a *cyma recta* cup is distinguished by the absence of a small ring base.

Medium-sized, hemispherical bowls with exterior thickened rims appear in Phases 1 and 2 of the Early Bronze Age (Figure 1.2h). Like the *cyma recta* cups, they appear to be concentrated in the northern part of the Euphrates. On the other hand, restricted necked jars, characterized by out-turned thickened rims and interior rim indentations, seem more frequent in the southern part of the region, occurring at sites such as Tell es-Sweyhat, Tell Hadidi and Halawa Tell B (Figure 1.2i–j). Nonetheless, a few of such jars are attested at the more northerly site of Tell Ahmar.

More diagnostic of the entire northern Euphrates are restricted neck jars with out-turned thickened rims, but which have no visible interior rim indentation (Figure 1.2k–l). These occur with great frequency. Other wide-mouthed neckless jars, featuring short, slightly out-turned rims, are also well attested. At least a few of these forms, bearing a rather coarse fabric and rough, handmade appearance, represent cooking pots.

Still other vessel forms are diagnostic of the Phases 1 and 2 of the Early Bronze Age, although their presence is less frequent and they may have a more restricted distribution than some of the vessel types described above. Most distinctive are large bowls with plain flaring rims, whose carination below the rim is frequently emphasized by a protruding ridge (Figure 1.2m). These bowls invariably stood on long, stems with wide flaring bases and raised, rounded lips (Figure 1.2n) (Falsone 1998: 29). Encountered first in Early Bronze Age tombs at Carchemish at the northern end of the region, such so-called 'champagne vases' have now been encountered at the sites of Shiyukh Tahtani, Jerablus Tahtani, and Qara Quzaq, as well as further north along the Euphrates in Turkey, at sites such as the Birecik Dam Cemetery (Woolley and Barnett 1952: 219–22; Sertok and Ergeç 1999: 92). It has been suggested that their frequent or almost exclusive association with tombs is reflective of their function as ceremonial drinking containers in feasts associated with burial rites (Peltenburg in press a). The majority of these vessels occurs at sites located north of Tell Banat, signifying that they may have been part of a northern funerary tradition that was not shared by all of the inhabitants of the region.

Another northern diagnostic vessel type, referred to as Late Reserved-Slip Ware is distinguished by its decoration, which features a light-coloured slip applied to the upper body of the vessel and then partially wiped off in oblique radial lines to expose the darker clay body beneath (Figure 1.2o) (Jamieson 1993: 43). This type of decoration occurs on a variety of cup and bowls, but is most frequent on restricted necked jars with externally thickened, out-turned rims (Jamieson 1993: 43).

Finally, there are a few vessel groups having a very narrow distribution that occur at only one or a few sites. There is, for example, a unique group of red painted pots which have only been recorded at Qara Quzaq (Figure 1.2p) (Valdés Pereiro 1994: 63). Within the Tell es-Sweyhat embayment, still other local wares have been reported, these including jars with squared rims or hollowed tops, and jars with grooved, exterior rims (Wilkinson 2004: 90). Such locally distinctive features indicate that while Euphrates settlements belonged to the same cultural horizon overall, they nonetheless possessed distinctive local traditions which found expression in several aspects of their material culture, including pottery.

Phase 3 (2600–2450 BC)[3]

Although several vessel types appearing in Phases 1 and 2 continue into Phase 3, this phase is also distinguished by several new vessel forms and wares. Of particular note is the introduction of a class of fine wares in the Euphrates region. These wares have received considerable discussion in the literature, being variously referred to as Metallic Ware, Euphrates Banded Ware, Red Banded Ware and Orange Spiral Burnished Ware. None of these designations is entirely satisfactory. The term Metallic Ware is problematic because it is often confused with the Metallic Ware of the Khabur region of northeastern Syria, appearing around the same time period. This latter pottery, which is also referred to as Stone Ware, features a dense, highly vitrified fabric with few visible inclusions, whose sherds make a 'metallic' clinky sound when they are struck together (Schneider 1989; Akkermans and Schwartz 2003: 254). Fine Euphrates pottery, in contrast, comprises an altogether different fabric, range of fired colours, and set of vessel shapes. Nevertheless, most of the Euphrates specimens of this ware consist of well-made vessels, sometimes featuring eggshell-thin walls which are uniformly highly fired and well finished, and therefore their designation as fine ware seems appropriate.

Euphrates Fine Ware is usually decorated. It commonly features fine, horizontal striations or corrugations, especially on the upper section of a vessel's exterior. This surface decoration may be accompanied by spiral bands of horizontal burnishing. This decoration was produced when a thin tool was applied to the exterior of the vessel as it was being turned on a rotative device (Porter in press). The ware is also sometimes decorated with thin concentric bands of red paint.

Several vessel forms belong to the class of Euphrates Fine Wares. Common are medium-sized jars with long, straight necks and very pronounced everted rims (Figure 1.3a–b). Thin bands of red paint are found frequently on the upper bodies and necks of these vessels. The bases of these jars are usually distinguished by ring bases. Sometimes the foot ring encircles a convex base which extends beyond the ring itself, producing a vessel that could not have stood upright. Porter has observed that some jar examples have the remnants of a criss-cross string bag on their exterior surfaces, suggesting that they were frequently suspended (Porter 1995a: 20).

Other Euphrates Fine Ware vessel types include bottle-necked jars with flaring and inverted rims, round bodies and ring bases (Figure 1.3c). Open bowls with thickened, usually out-turned, rims, are also included among these fine wares (Figure 1.3d). They often have thin, graceful walls and fine spiral burnishing. One deep, fine-walled bowl found in Tomb 5 at Tell es-Sweyhat was supported by three attached tubular feet (Figure 1.3h).

A version of the 'champagne' cup or 'fruit-stand' exists in Euphrates Fine Ware. The majority of these have pronounced corrugations on the

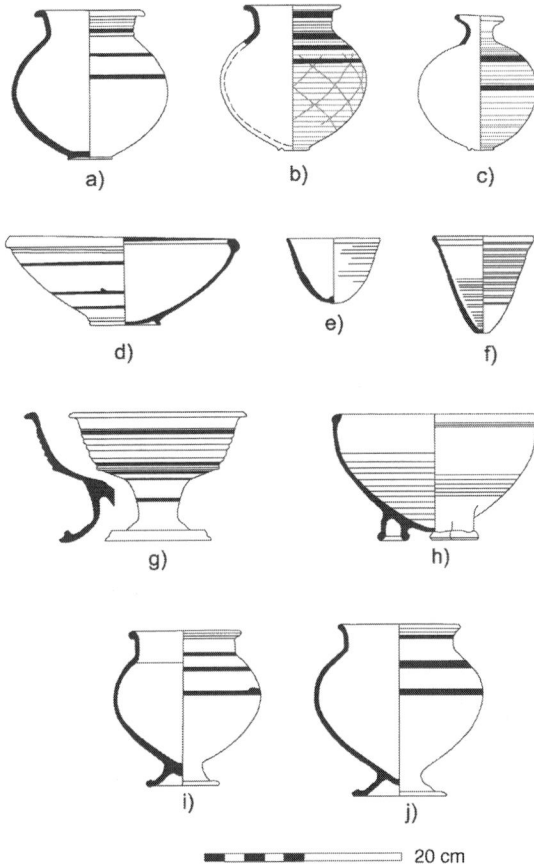

Figure 1.3 Phase 3 pottery: Euphrates fine wares.

body, sometimes ending in a prominent ridge (Figure 1.3g). Some are also decorated with horizontal bands of red paint.

Vessels or 'chalices' with short necks, globular bodies and pedestal bases first appear in the Euphrates Fine Ware assemblages of Phase 3 and then persist into the subsequent Phase 4. The majority of vessels feature red painted bands on their upper bodies and necks (Figure 1.3i–j). At one site, fine ware types known as 'sugar-loaf' beakers, which are small corrugated conical cups with convex, almost pointed bases and tapered, sometimes everted rims, were found inside the red banded chalices described above (Figure 1.3e–f) (Sconzo in press b). Their co-occurrence suggests that they formed a type of luxury drinking set. Moreover, since these vessels generally existed in burial contexts, it is possible that they served a funerary function (Sconzo in press b).

Besides the presence of Euphrates Fine Wares, Phase 3 has many vessel types that can be classified as Plain Simple Ware. Particularly diagnostic of

13

this period are small, round-based straight-sided cups with rounded, tapered or squared rims (Figure 1.4c–d). The fact that many of these cups were found inside or in the immediate vicinity of large jars in Tomb 1 at Tell Banat may suggest that they functioned as dippers (Porter 1995a: 19). Also representative of this phase are bowls with rounded sides and thickened rims, usually on the exterior (Figure 1.4a–b, e). They often have round bases. The largest of the bowls are quite deep, and frequently curve slightly inwards towards the rim. These bowls are most common at sites located to the south of Qara Quzaq. They are particularly abundant at Tell Banat, where thousands of fragments have been found in association with the pottery manufacturing zone of Area D. This is probably where many of the bowls were mass manufactured (Porter and McClellan 1998: 21).

A slight variant of the bowl just described features perforated lug handles

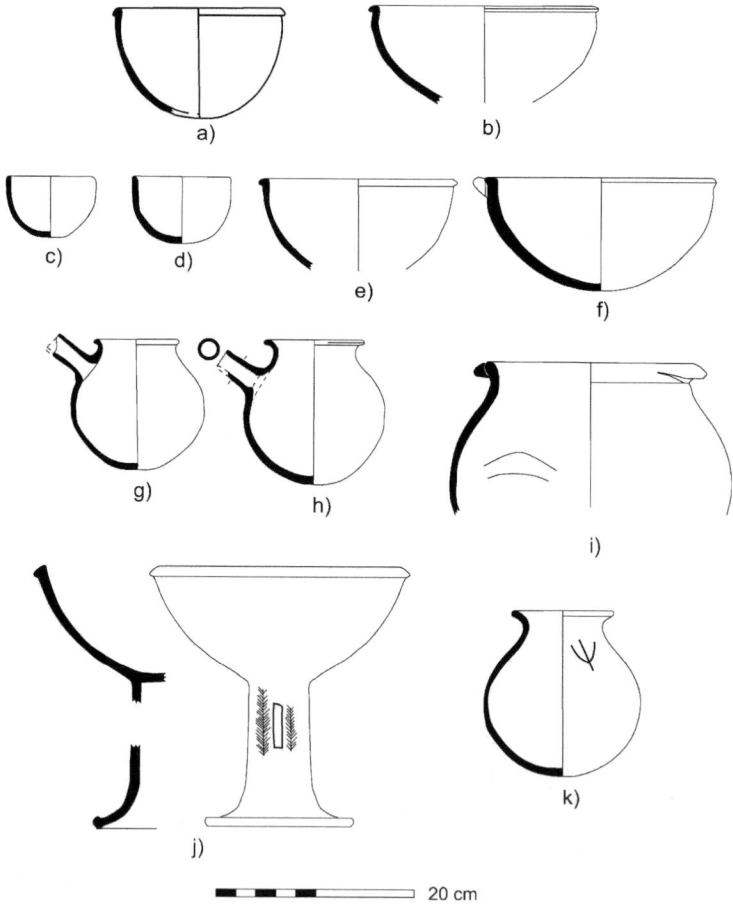

Figure 1.4 Phase 3 pottery: plain simple wares.

14

(Figure 1.4f). These bowls' association with tomb contexts suggests that they were part of funerary assemblages. Other funerary vessels include 'champagne' bowls in Plain Simple Ware. Vessels from Tomb 1 at Tell Banat have thickened triangular rims, and some also have fenestrated and incised tubular stems (Figure 1.4j). Two pedestalled 'champagne' vases from Halawa Tell A and Tomb 5 at Tell es-Sweyhat probably also belong to this same class of vessels.

Spouted jars stand out as another diagnostic vessel type of Phase 3 (Figure 1.4g–h). These vessels, commonly dubbed 'teapots', have round bases. All feature a single straight spout extending from the upper shoulder of the jar, below a simple everted rim. Other medium-sized jars do not appear with spouts. They are either short or long-necked, but they invariably have rounded bases and plain everted rims. A few of these types of jars are additionally distinguished by potter's marks on the shoulders (Figure 1.4k). Last, Phase 3 includes large, restricted necked jars with round bases. These have short, flaring rims which are often thickened on the exterior. Many bear an interior rim indentation, a distinctive feature that was introduced in Phase 2 (Porter and McClellan 1998: 21).

Triangular lugged cooking pots replace the earlier Cooking Pot Ware of Phases 1 and 2 (Figure 1.4i). Like their predecessors, these hand-made vessels are globular, only now they are distinguished by applied triangular handles or lugs which are attached to the top of the rim (Jamieson 1993: 48). The domestic, utilitarian function of these vessels is supported by their infrequent appearance in tomb contexts.

Phase 4 (2450–2300 BC)[4]

Phase 4 marks an important period in the Syrian Euphrates. Many sites experienced significant expansions and urban transformations during this time, reflected by increases in the size, monumentality and complexity of secular residences, temples and fortifications. One also sees greater regional homogeneity in the material culture during this period. A growing number of tomb structures, for example, share similar plans, construction materials and techniques. This period also marks the widespread appearance of the so-called temples *in antis*. These long-roomed temples are not only present at several Euphrates sites, they appear throughout northern Mesopotamia (see Chapter 7). The reason for such growing homogeneity in architectural styles, in our view, is related to the increase in trade and exchange within the Euphrates region and beyond, and the desire of many inhabitants to emulate the styles and technology of their neighbours.

The increased cultural homogeneity attested in architecture during Phase 4 is also manifested in the pottery of this time period. Many of the same vessel types occur throughout the northern Euphrates Valley. Unlike earlier phases of the Early Bronze Age, it is usually difficult to speak of northern and southern pottery collections (Porter in press). In spite of this wider trend towards homogeneity, however, slight variations in the form and decoration of pots within each general vessel type can be discerned at the local level. We suspect that this local variability can be ascribed to the presence of workshops dispersed throughout the region whose potters were producing vessels according to the tastes of consumers in their own local areas. In sum, although a increase in communication and exchange throughout the Euphrates Valley generated an overall homogeneous pottery repertoire, the concurrent presence of well-organized, locally-based craft workshops resulted in slight differences in vessel styles from one settlement to the next.

Euphrates Fine Wares continue to be manufactured and consumed during Phase 4. As with the earlier Phase 3, these fine wares have been recovered primarily from funerary contexts (Porter 1999: 313). Of the common forms, tall-necked globular jars painted with red horizontal bands and spiral burnishing continue to appear, although greater variations now exist. Whereas in Phase 3, such jars invariably featured pronounced everted rims, now one sees several different rim forms, including thickened rims, or double and multiple grooved rims (Figure 1.5a–b). A jar from Wreide has a potter's mark, as have some of the jars from the Tawi cemetery. Another Wreide jar features vertical, as opposed to, horizontal burnishing on the neck. The overall impression conveyed by these differently decorated jars is that while the tradition of Euphrates Fine Ware is well-known among all sites during this period, there is a tendency for local variability.

As already reported, 'chalices' with short necks, globular bodies and pedestal bases continue to appear in Phase 4 (Figure 1.5c). As in Phase 3, the majority of these vessels have red painted bands on their necks and upper bodies as well as spiral burnishing.

There are a few new additions to the Fine Euphrates Ware repertoire in Phase 4. Like the older fine ware pots, these new vessels are hard, highly fired, and are frequently decorated with spiral burnishing and corrugations. Their noteworthy distinction is that they have a dark grey colour. These types of vessels are sometimes referred to as Grey Spiral Burnished Ware (Van Loon 2001: 5A.233) or Black Euphrates Banded Ware (Porter in press). Of this grey ware, one of the most prominent vessel types appearing in frequency in Phase 4 is the so-called 'Syrian bottle'. This is a small jar or bottle, distinguished by a long bag-shaped or globular body and a very narrow neck that flares out to a wider rim (Figure 1.5d). The long body of the bottle rounds to a slightly pointed base (Porter in press). These distinctive vessels have been found throughout the Syrian Euphrates, usually in tomb contexts. One wonders about their specific function. Given their small size, narrow bodies and restricted necks, it is possible that they contained some kind of precious perfumed resin or oil that was used in funerary celebrations.

Also included among the Grey Fine Euphrates Wares are a variety of small, short necked jars with wide, rounded shoulders that taper to a rounded, flat or ring base (Figure 1.5e–f) (Porter in press). The majority are also decorated

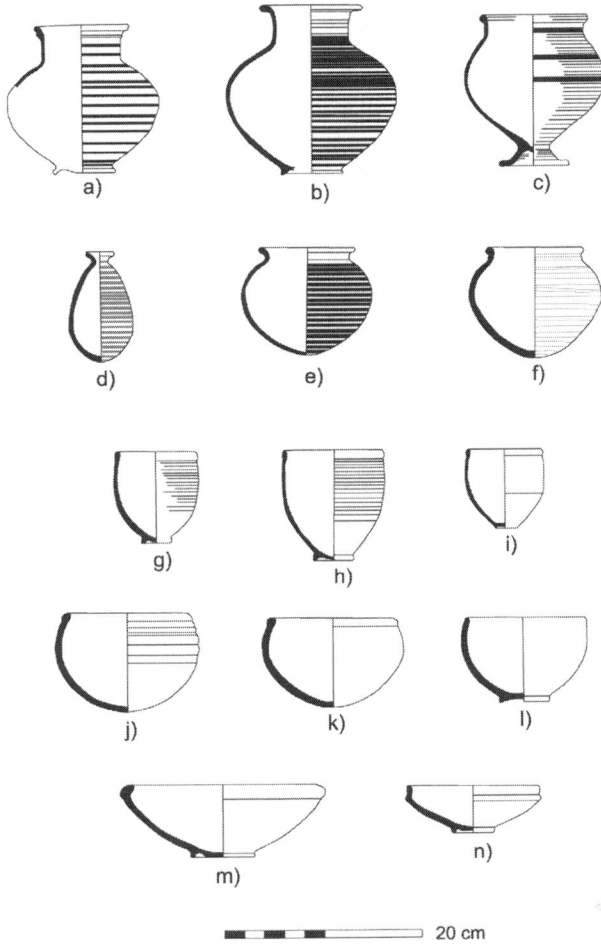

Figure 1.5 Phase 4 pottery: fine and plain simple wares.

with spiral burnishing across the length of their bodies and necks. At a few sites such as Selenkahiye, Tell Banat and Tell Ahmar, these vessels are additionally characterized by perforated handles or lugs on the sides (Thureau-Dangin and Dunand 1936: Figure 31, lower left corner; Van Loon 2001: 5A.24: f and i; Porter in press).

Vessels classified as Plain Simple Wares continue to constitute an important part of the Phase 4 Euphrates repertoire. Many of these pots are highly fired, thin-walled and smooth, sometimes attaining the quality of the Euphates Fine Ware (Peltenburg *et al.* 1996: 19; Porter 1999: 313). The difference, however, is that such vessels are not distinguished by painted decoration or spiral burnishing.

The hallmark of Phase 4 is the corrugated goblet or beaker (Figure 1.5g–h). Such goblets are well-known throughout Syria, appearing most abundantly in the EB assemblages of Tell Mardikh (Ebla) and Hama to the west (Heinrich *et al.* 1970: 79–80). They are frequently referred to as 'Hama goblets' and are said to constitute a major element of the highly urbanized 'caliciform' culture of western Syria (Mazzoni 1985: 14–15). Goblets found in the Euphrates region appear to represent a regional variety of these 'Hama goblets'. Overall, the vessel is characterized by a barrel shape, ring base, and corrugated exterior surface (Jamieson 1993: 52). Rims appear in a variety of forms, being simply tapered, beaded or slightly thickened. The goblets are found at most Euphrates sites occupied during Phase 4. Because their presence is not confined to burials, it is likely that they functioned as a kind of all-purpose drinking cup. Closely related to the corrugated goblet is the plain goblet, which shares the same form but has few or no distinctive corrugations or ridges on its exterior walls (Figure 1.5i).

Small beaded rim cups or bowls occur abundantly in Phase 4. At Tell Banat they are particularly frequent (Figure 1.5j–k) (Porter and McClellan 1998: 29). These vessels are deeper and wider than the goblets just described, and usually have a round or flat base. Other types of small cups with rounded sides and simple rims also exist in Phase 4 (Figure 1.5l).

Among the most common bowl types are hemispherical bowls with externally thickened rims which sometimes turn inwards at the top (Figure 1.5m). There are also bowls featuring lips that turn slightly inward at the top and bear pronounced protrusions below the rim (Figure 1.5n) (Porter and McClellan 1998: 29). Occurring less frequently are bowls which stand on three tubular feet.

The so-called 'champagne' vessels, distinguished by their long stems and wide flaring bases, continue in abundance at several northern Euphrates tomb assemblages in Phase 4 (Figure 1.6f). Approximately 100 such vessels were uncovered in the monumental Tomb 302 at Jerablus Tahtani (Peltenburg in press a). They were also found in the Hypogeum at Tell Ahmar, where they featured a variety of stem lengths (Thureau-Dangin and Dunand 1936: pl. 23, 5–14). Besides these pedestalled bowls, globular-shaped, short-necked jars also appear on high stemmed bases of varying lengths in the Ahmar Hypogeum assemblage. They attest to the variability of ceremonial vessels associated with the funerary rites of this impressive tomb.

Many varieties of jars are present in the Phase 4 Euphrates repertoire. The most common are medium-sized jars with long necks and ring bases. Their rims have either double or multiple grooves (Figure 1.6a–b). Many of these jars are quite thin-walled, smooth and highly fired, such that they almost warrant classification as Euphrates Fine Wares. None of these jars, however, feature corrugations, painted bands or spiral burnishing (Porter 1999: 313).

The most distinctive jars in Phase 4 have narrow-necks, wide, globular bodies and two loop handles, set high on the shoulders (Figure 1.6c). These

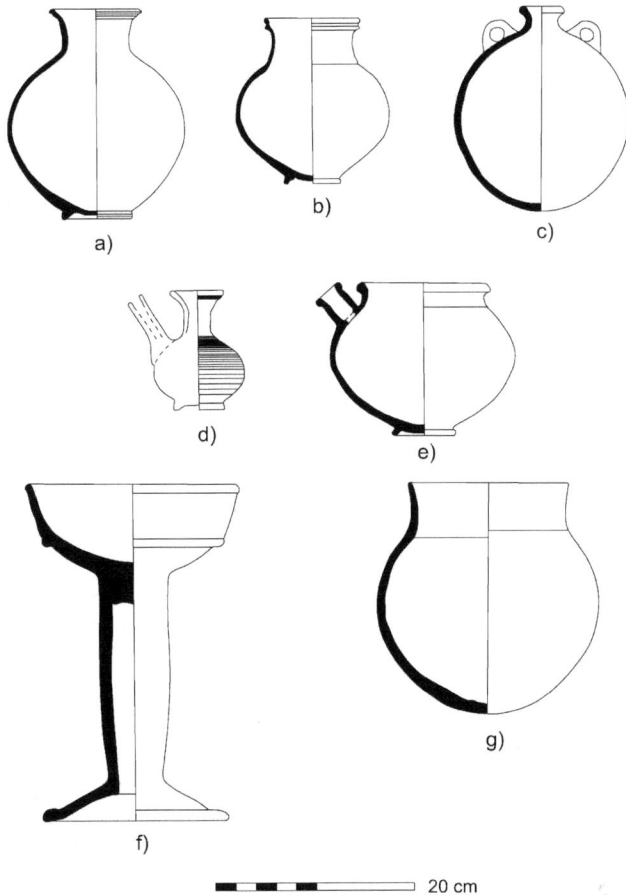

Figure 1.6 Phase 4 plain simple ware (a–f), and cooking pot (g).

jars are attested at several Euphrates sites, including Tell Banat, where they are reported to be a common component of one of the Area D kiln assemblages. Perhaps this was one of the places where they were being manufactured (Porter and McClellan 1998: 30).

Several types of spouted vessels appear in Phase 4. Medium-sized jars with single spouts extending from the shoulder probably represent a continuation of the spouted jars first appearing in Phase 3. In Phase 4, however, these jars are distinguished by low ring bases (Figure 1.6e). Another type of spouted vessel has a very narrow neck and a long, sometimes slightly bent spout (Figure 1.6d). There are also vessels with spouts that are shaped like the heads of animals. The zoomorphic jars from Tell Ahmar's Hypogeum are especially well known, although a fragment of a zoomorphic spout has also been found at Jerablus Tahtani (Peltenburg *et al.* 1995: Figure 27:1).

19

Cooking pots, made by hand and usually taking the form of jars with triangular lugs protruding from externally thickened rims, continue to be manufactured in Phase 4. The exterior walls and rims of several of these cooking pots are burnished. Another cooking pot type attested at a few Euphrates sites has a rounded body, straight neck and simple tapering rim (Figure 1.6g). Although these vessels have a wide distribution in the Euphrates, being found as far north as Jerablus Tahtani and as far south as Selenkahiye, they appear less frequently than the distinctive triangular-lugged pots.

Phase 5 (2300–2100 BC)[5, 6]

Although this is the newest phase that has been properly identified, it represents a significant time in the Euphrates Valley. Some sites had already ceased to be occupied during this period (for example, Jerablus Tahtani, Tell Banat). Tell es-Sweyhat was long regarded as an unusual case since it was a large, densely occupied city during this late stage of the third millennium. Present evidence now shows that Tell es-Sweyhat was one of many northern Euphrates sites inhabited during this phase. Halawa Tell A continued to thrive in this period, as did Tell Habuba Kabira, Tell Hadidi and Tell Amarna. The small settlement at Tell Kabir was clearly inhabited, although the nature of its occupation remains elusive. The settlement at Selenkahiye existed, although there are signs of decline in its last settlement, reflected by the occupation of fewer houses and cursory repairs to houses and fortifications that had been previously destroyed by fire. The most recent Syrian-German excavations at Emar, which have uncovered a good sequence of late third millennium domestic architecture and Phase 5 pottery, have confirmed that this site was also occupied (Finkbeiner 2002: 130–9; 2003: 65–90).

The combined evidence suggests that while one or a series of events may have contributed to the end of some settlements, others continued to hold on, and some were even able to grow and flourish during this period. We will discuss reasons for the persistence of settlement in the Euphrates region during this time and into the subsequent Phase 6 in our final chapter.

Because the pottery of Phase 5 is still in the early stages of being properly understood, only a few observations and accompanying illustrations are presented here. Overall, the phase is defined by strong ceramic continuity from the earlier Phase 4, although a few new forms appear. Some of the older wares decline in frequency quite dramatically. The most noticeable decline is that of the Euphrates Fine Ware, whose highly-fired, thin-walled red banded and spiral burnished vessels disappear altogether during this period. They are replaced by assemblages almost exclusively made up of Plain Simple Wares.

Some of the older Plain Simple vessel forms still appear during this time. The 'Hama goblet' exhibits both plain and corrugated walls and the same range of tapered or beaded rims as in Phase 4 (Figure 1.7a, c). A new type of cup, however, seems to have evolved out of these goblets. Although its rims

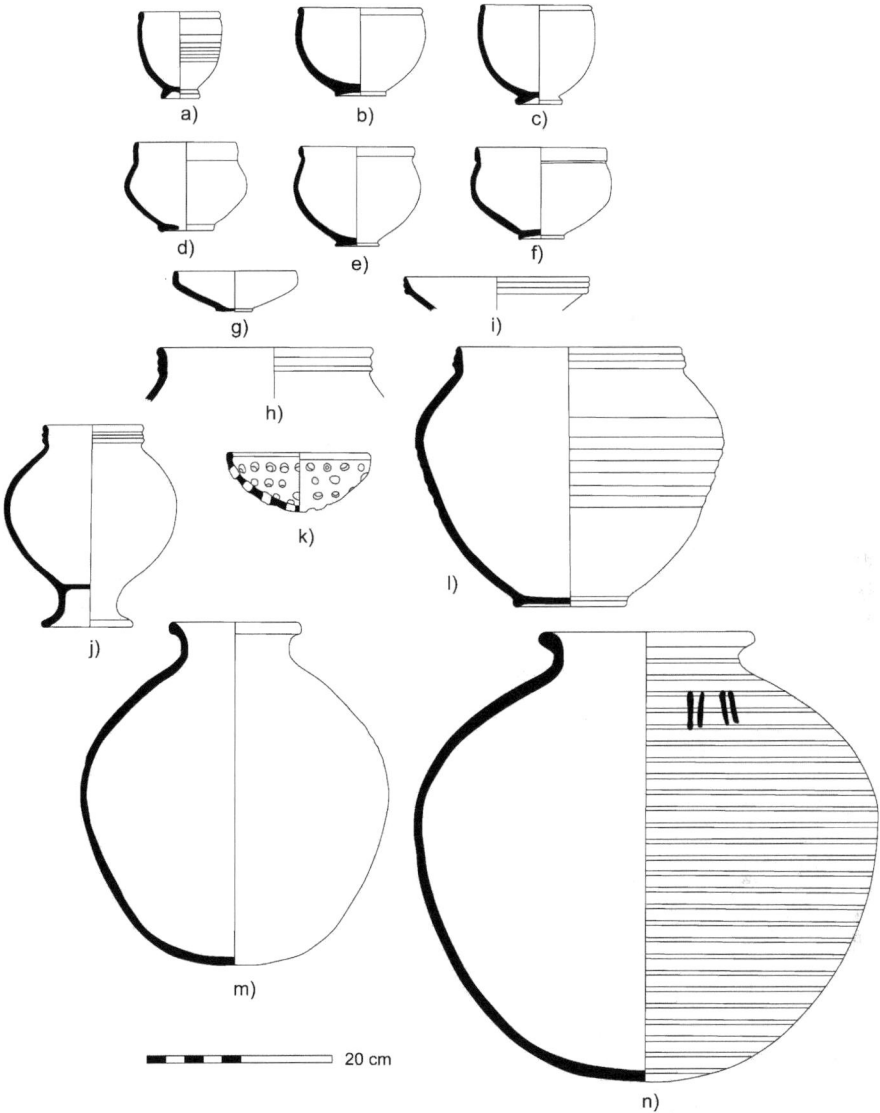

Figure 1.7 Phase 5 pottery.

and ring bases are identical to the goblets, it is less barrel-shaped than the goblets and has a wider body (Figure 1.7b).

Another new type appearing in Phase 5 is the collared-rim cup or goblet (Figure 1.7d–e). This is perhaps the most diagnostic vessel shape of Phase 5 since it is rarely encountered in earlier phases and is found throughout the Euphrates region. The distinctive collared rim of the vessel usually appears

21

on a cup form whose walls are rounded and wide. Some of these vessels are particularly wide, such that it may be more appropriate to call them collared-rim bowls rather than cups (Figure 1.7f).

Several bowl types continue from the earlier Phase 4. Bowls with externally thickened rims, for example, are still present, as are bowls with in-turned rims with slight protrusions below the rims. Perhaps evolving out of these latter forms are bowls whose rims are now more vertical than in-turned, and which frequently feature multiple grooves (Figure 1.7g, i).

A distinctive medium-sized jar has a wide, rounded body. It is neckless, with a vertical rim that is frequently grooved. While this jar is usually characterized by a simple ring base, there are also instances in which it is set on a high pedestal base (Figure 1.7j).

Another diagnostic form are jars characterized by multiple-grooved rims that rise vertically above a very short neck (Figure 1.7h, l). These jars make their first appearance in Phase 5, but they continue into Phase 6, where they become even more frequent. For the most part, these jars have wide, globular bodies. Many may be akin to the jars just mentioned since they are usually neckless, although many have wider bodies and rim diameters.

Phase 5 is defined especially by the appearance of many restricted necked storage jars. These jars take on many forms, although the most diagnostic are noticeably wide-bellied and have slightly convex bases (fig 1.7m). Such large jars have no precursors in the earlier phases of the Early Bronze, but they continue into Phase 6 and the subsequent Middle Bronze Age, albeit with different rim forms. During Phase 5, these jars are usually characterized by thickened, everted rims. Many of these Phase 5 jars are also distinguished by incised potter's marks which usually occur on their shoulders. One wonders if these marks have anything to do with the storage function of the jars, possibly identifying the owner of the goods stored within, or the destination of the jar.

Aside from potters' marks, most large jars are undecorated. The exception are those with parallel bands of cream-coloured reserve slip decoration covering much of the exterior surface of their bodies and necks (Figure 1.7n). This form of decoration is especially prevalent at Tell es-Sweyhat, where it has been observed on many large jars found in the buildings on the main mound as well as the extensively occupied late third millennium lower town. The presence of this slipped decoration on large jars from Wreide and Emar, however, confirms that this is not a local development (Orthmann and Rova 1991: IIC:4; Finkbeiner 2002: Abb. 14:a).

A few other distinctive vessel forms characterize Phase 5 of the northern Euphrates Valley. These include small colander or strainer-type bowls, distinguished by numerous holes pierced through their bodies (Figure 1.7k). These bowls have a variety of rims, although simple tapered and beaded rims appear to be the most frequent.

Last, the phase witnessed the increased frequency of decorated vessels with applied and incised animals and human figures. One interesting example comes from Room 7 of the Area IV 'warehouse' on the main mound at Tell es-Sweyhat. This particular spouted pot features two strange beasts facing towards a bird. The beasts' heads have been applied in relief, while the rest of their bodies as well as the central bird have been incised into the clay wall of the vessel (Holland 1976: 59). A similarly decorated pot with spout was found at the site of Munbaqa, this also featuring a centrally incised bird flanked by two animals, identified in this example as lions (Machule *et al.* 1986: Abb. 15). Although these are the only two vessels which are complete or nearly complete, the discovery of several fragments of applied and incised animals and people from other sites such as Halawa Tell A indicates that these vessels were fairly common during this time period (Hempelmann 2001). The vessels' frequency in the temple precinct and its vicinity at Halawa Tell A may indicate that they had some association with religious activities (Hempelmann 2001: 158–9; see also Chapter 7).

Phase 6 (2100–1900 BC)[7]

Phase 6 represents the last period during which Early Bronze Age cultural features appear in the Syrian Euphrates Valley. It also marks the beginning of the Middle Bronze Age, defined by several new cultural elements. Many have preferred to call this period 'transitional', thus acknowledging the blend of both old and new features.

Phase 6 is still elusive archaeologically. It seems that at the end of Phase 5, many settlements were abandoned or experienced dramatic decreases in population and settlement size. Environmental degradation or some kind of socio-political collapse may have taken place that precipitated this decline in settlement, although we cannot precisely define the nature of the upheavals. Whatever the reasons for its settlements' decline, the northern Euphrates Valley of Syria was not abandoned altogether. Architectural and artifactual remains at several sites indicate that occupation continued without a significant break during this phase, and that local populations continued to support themselves, albeit on a less intensive scale, with the resources of the fields and pastures of their hinterland.

The pottery of Phase 6 is very transitional in nature (Figure 1.8). The pottery possesses several morphological analogies to forms prevalent in the earlier Phase 5 repertoire in the Syrian Euphrates, while at the same time, it has new features which compare favourably with the succeeding Middle Bronze Age ceramic assemblages of this region. Given the repertoire's strong cultural connections in both directions, it is actually difficult to pinpoint a vessel type that distinguishes this phase in particular.

Small cups that appear in Phase 6 appear to represent a development from the earlier collared-rim cups of Phase 5. They have the same general body shape of the earlier cups but the rim has become less vertical and collared,

Figure 1.8 Phase 6 pottery from Tell Kabir.

and is either lightly ridged (Figure 1.9a), or takes the form of a simple everted rim that tapers at the tip (Figure 1.9b). This latter form, in turn, will continue to occur well into the subsequent Middle Bronze Age, becoming a prominent feature of many MB Euphrates assemblages.

Bowls of Phase 6 take several forms. On the one hand there is the continued prevalence of bowls with vertical or grooved rims (Figure 1.9c), as had been seen in the earlier Phase 5. On the other hand, one now begins to see the increased frequency of bowls with carinations on the body or near a strongly everted rim (Figure 1.9f, h). These are features that will become quite prevalent in subsequent MB assemblages in the Euphrates region, as well as at Ebla to the west. It is also during Phase 6 that one sees an early appearance of out-turned bowl rims that are almost flat on the top and ribbed. None are illustrated here, but they have been reported at Tell Hadidi in its transitional phase (MBI: Dornemann 1992: Figure 20: 20), and more recently in Phase 6 at Tell es-Sweyhat, in its very latest EB assemblage.

Of restricted necked jars, Phase 6 features large, wide-bellied jars with everted rims of the same type that had appeared in Phase 5 (Figure 1.9i). Several of these jars, however, feature flanged rims, a very distinctive feature that becomes the hallmark of large storage jars in the succeeding Middle Bronze Age (Figure 1.9j). Once again, the transitional nature of Phase 6 is very apparent among these vessel forms.

Still other jars persist into Phase 6. Large wide-bodied jars with vertical grooved rims are still abundant (Figure 1.9d, g). According to counts made

24

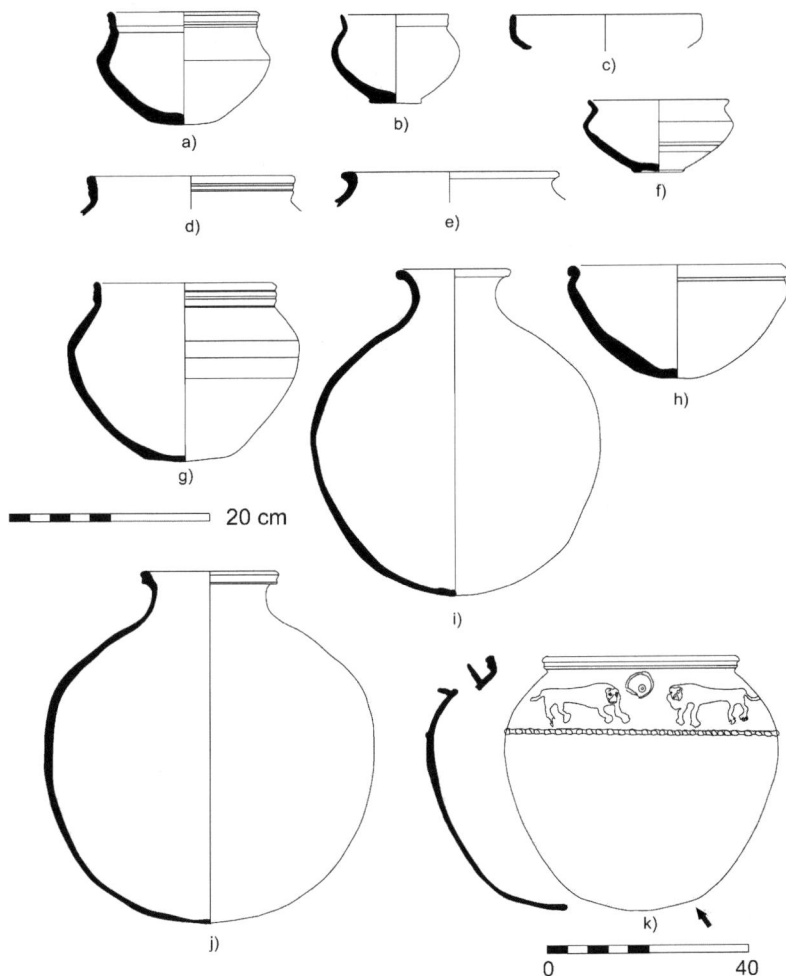

Figure 1.9 Phase 6 pottery.

of these jar types at both Tell Kabir and at Tell es-Sweyhat, these jar types actually increase in frequency during this transitional phase. They have also been reported in subsequent Middle Bronze Age levels, although by this time they have begun to dwindle in number.

One interesting large, wide-bodied jar found at Tell Kabir has a grooved rim of a type prevalent in the transitional period, while additionally featuring a spout and a motif of incised and applied lions (Figure 1.9k). This jar is clearly derived from the decorated spouted pots of Phase 5.

As a final comment, we note that the handmade triangular lugged cooking vessels of the earlier phases of the EB have disappeared. They are replaced by cooking pots with ovoid bodies and thickened, out-turned rims, these bearing strong affinities to Middle Bronze Age cooking pots in terms of their clay fabric constituents and production technology (Figure 1.9e) (Dornemann 1992: 80; Figure 4:10; Cooper 1998: 274). It is striking that such a common utilitarian vessel should have experienced such a significant change during this time. No doubt it reflects the extent to which dramatic cultural transformations were being felt at all levels of society during this unsettled, changeable time period.

2

ENVIRONMENT AND
SUBSISTENCE

Without question, the environment of the Syrian Euphrates region played an important part in moulding the character of human settlement during the third millennium BC. Although we cannot deny the impact that human agency had in shaping the distinctive and remarkable ways in which events unfolded during this significant period of antiquity, the environment, to no small degree, set the stage for these events and developments. It encouraged or limited some human actions and choices, while stimulating responses to other challenges. During the third millennium BC, in our view, the environment provided much of the incentive for human groups both to move beyond simple small-scale pastoral-agrarian livelihoods and to adopt increasingly complex economic enterprises and exchanges as well as distinctive social-cultural traditions and ideologies. The environment contributed greatly not only to the growth and success of urban life in the Euphrates region, but also to the unique character that urban settlements acquired over the course of their long development.

The northern Euphrates Valley was essentially a marginal environment, in which low amounts of rainfall per year made dry farming in this region a very risky undertaking. This climate has characterized the region for at least the past 5,000 years. At the same time, however, the natural environment of the river valley and its environs made up in several ways for this shortfall in precipitation. The alluvial flood plains provided other natural resources in abundance. The vast grassy upland plateaus, extending away from either side of the valley, provided the potential for flourishing pastoral activities and they abounded in wild game. Trading opportunities afforded by the Euphrates River itself opened up the region to long-distance contacts. Such commercial relations were responsible for the procurement of surplus goods as well as foreign influences and cultural exchanges. In short, the Syrian Euphrates region provided a challenging environment, but once its potential was realized, ample opportunities presented themselves for human groups to enjoy economic prosperity and a certain degree of socio-political stability. As we shall see, such groups seemed particularly attuned to the positive potential of the Euphrates environment, as attested by the numbers of EB settlements established within the river valley and strategically positioned so as to take advantage of favourable economic opportunities. Overall, people's ability to harness the advantages of the environment not only enabled their settlements to grow and flourish but also gave them a degree of resilience and flexibility, enabling them to endure for many centuries.

PHYSICAL ENVIRONMENT

The natural landscape of the Euphrates River Valley of northern Syria, extending for approximately 100 km from the modern Turkish-Syrian border in the north to the region below the ancient city of Emar in the south, presents a sharp contrast to the dry, deserted land that surrounds it. Through the lonely expanse of the treeless, undulating steppe land of the northern Syrian plateau, the Euphrates River cuts a deep trough, creating a fertile valley of alluvial plains and terraces on either side of its banks. Human groups were attracted to this river valley in antiquity because of the variety of plant and animal life that they could exploit for food, clothing and shelter. In addition, the navigable waterways of the Euphrates River provided an effective means of communication, enabling economic and cultural links between the inhabitants of this otherwise isolated region and people of other populated, cosmopolitan regions of Mesopotamia, Anatolia and the Levant.

The Euphrates River begins its long journey in the highlands of eastern Turkey, where its headwaters are fed by rainfall and melting mountain snow. After a steep descent through Anatolia, the Euphrates enters Syria just below the ancient city of Carchemish. As it flows through northern Syria, the river's meandering channel is contained within an alluvial plain that is as wide as 10 km in some places, while in other areas, it flows through long, narrow gorges featuring flood plains no wider than 500 m, surrounded on both sides by precipitous limestone bluffs that rise up over 100 m (Serrat and Bergadà 1999: 239–40). Where the river valley is wider and the channel is less deeply entrenched, minor streams break off and rejoin the main channel between lengths of 3 and 6 km (Wilkinson 2004: 20). The river may also occasionally break through its meanders, causing a shift in the course of the channel altogether. In such cases, ancient settlements that were once situated near the river's edge have either been completely erased by river erosion or obscured by sedimentation (Wilkinson 2004: 34). In other cases, sites are now situated on the edges of relict channels which lie at a considerable distance to the present river course (Besançon and Sanlaville 1985: 11).

While the modern dams constructed along the Euphrates have largely regulated its flow, the amount of water carried by the river in the past would have varied tremendously according to the seasons of the year. The river was at its lowest in the dry months of August, September and October, but melting snow and winter rains in the Anatolian highlands caused the river to reach its highest levels in the April and May (Wilkinson 2004: 21). This annual flooding would have inundated many of the fields of the adjacent flood plain. Unfortunately, unlike other river regimes of the world, where flooding coincides with the agricultural growing season, and fresh water and alluvial soil are welcomed as much needed nourishment for crops, the Euphrates flooded at precisely the wrong time of the year, just when cereal crops were beginning to ripen and large volumes of water were no longer required for their growth. Such poor timing clearly made winter-spring farming on the flood plain a high-risk venture (Danti 1997: 92). Consequently, most crops were grown on the gently sloping river terraces elevated several metres above the flood plain, safely beyond the limits of the annual inundation.

Flood plain

Due to the risk of flooding, the banks immediately adjacent to the Euphrates would also have been unsuitable for human habitation, although recent field surveys and satellite imagery have confirmed that some ancient settlements exist in this precarious environment. These sites are perched on older sections of the alluvium, where accumulations of river silt as well as aggrading wadi fans from the higher terraces to the east and west have raised the terrain a few metres above the current level of the flood plain (Wilkinson 2004: 22). These small rises of land would have offered some measure of protection for the settlements, at least during years of normal flooding.

During the third millennium BC, the sites of Jerablus Tahtani, Tell Kabir and Tell Jouweif were among the settlements that existed in the flood plain on such relict channels (Peltenburg et al. 1995: 4; Porter 1995b: 125; Wilkinson 2004: 22). It is possible that the sites' proximity to the river allowed them to take advantage of economic opportunities afforded by commercial traffic along the river. Alternatively, the strategic location of these sites at key crossing points over the river may have enabled them to control overland caravan traffic arriving from points to the east and west. Tell Jouweif's position along one such overland crossing point is attested by its location directly opposite the large, contemporaneous third millennium centre of Tell Hadidi on the west bank of the river (Wilkinson 2004: 186). Aerial photographs have also identified ancient roadways radiating out from Tell Jouweif. These roads head either in the direction of Tell es-Sweyhat to the east, or they go to the southeast in the direction of the upland plateau. From there, the road continued past a series of wells that would have provided overland caravans with vital drinking stops on their journey to the Balikh River and beyond (Wilkinson 2004: 186).

Besides favourable trading opportunities, other advantages of the Euphrates flood plain were its natural resources. Riparian forests of poplar, willow and tamarisk trees provided valuable construction materials and wood fuel (Miller

1997b: 124). Animals such as fish, fowl and fallow deer were hunted for food in this lush riverine environment (Weber 1997: 141). It may also be possible that small plots of summer crops, namely legumes, were flood-water farmed along the river banks, just as beans were cultivated in this area in the recent past (Wilkinson 2004: 173).

Years of exceptional inundations could have had disastrous effects for settlements in the flood plain, as confirmed by geomorphological investigations conducted around the site of Jerablus Tahtani. Here, a series of abnormally high flood events towards the end of the third millennium BC not only devastated agricultural fields around the site but were probably responsible for the total abandonment of the settlement and the dislocation of its people (Peltenburg 1999a: 103).

Terraces

On either side of the river, a series of terraces gently slopes down towards the flood plain. These are the dry remnants of the large and oldest channels of the river, formed during the mid-to-late Pleistocene Era (Danti 2000: 23). Composed of chalky white limestone bedrock superimposed by a layer of brown limestone, river gravels and silty soil, the terraces now stand several metres above the level of the alluvial plain (Wilkinson 2004: 19). Since they are safely above potentially destructive flooding events, they are favourable places to practise dry farming.

Where the meanders of the most ancient river channels have shifted dramatically, terraces take the form of broad plains often extending for several kilometres before reaching the bluffs of the upland plateaus. The terrace upon which the site of Tell es-Sweyhat is situated is one such plain. This large crescentic embayment, which is about 7 km east–west, and 10 km north–south, would have offered extensive agricultural and grazing opportunities. Moreover, it would have supported a number of both small and large settlements in antiquity, as it does today. In other areas of the Euphrates Valley, river terraces are merely narrow strips running alongside the flood plain, the steep uplands rising immediately behind them. While agricultural activities would have been constrained by this kind of topography, settlements' proximity both to the alluvial plain and the higher steppe lands would have enabled them to exploit a variety of alternative resources within only a short distance.

Seasonal watercourses, or *wadi*s, carrying water runoff from the upland plateau during the winter rainy seasons, cut deep paths through the terraces as they make their way to the lower elevations in the river valley (Wilkinson 2004: 24, 31). As these *wadi*s not only carry water but fresh silt, the cultivation of crops would have been especially successful along their banks, or in basins nearby where increased moisture was retained in the soil. Occasionally, basins where water was collected from these *wadi*s may have served as drinking holes for animals, thus also increasing the suitability of pastoral activities in these areas.

Because of deforestation and the low amount of annual rainfall, the terraces of the Euphrates River Valley around the site of Tell es-Sweyhat were virtually treeless by the late third millennium with the exception of a few remnant stands of oak forest. The trees' presence is indicated by the small amounts of oak charcoal found in paleobotanical collections (Miller 1997a: 101). In addition, the Tell es-Sweyhat faunal assemblage has yielded a small number of bones of red deer and aurochs, animals that favoured open oak woodlands (Weber 1997: 141). Travelling further to the north in the direction of the Turkish border, the moister climate would have encouraged the growth of greater amounts of woodland vegetation on the terraces. Although there is scant evidence from the paleobotanical record thus far, it is probable that occasional stands of oak forest existed in the terrace zone of the river valley directly to the south of Carchemish and extended down as far as the site of Tell Ahmar.

Uplands

The uplands rise beyond the flood plain and terraces. Their edges are strongly scarped, rising in steep banks as much as 100 m above the level of the river valley (Zettler 1997a: 2). On the western side of the Euphrates, the upland plateau extends in the direction of western Syria, while on the river's eastern side, the uplands comprise what is known as the *Jezireh*, a vast undulting upland steppe that extends all the way across northern Syria into northern Iraq, where it reaches the Tigris River (Wilkinson 1994: 484).

The vegetation of the upland plateau consists of grasses and wild and weedy plants. While most areas are unsuitable for agricultural cultivation, this open steppe land is ideal grazing land for sheep and goats, and pastoralist activities would have flourished in this area in antiquity. Although few ancient encampments of pastoral nomadic groups have been identified in the archaeological record owing to the ephemeral nature of much of their remains, we can postulate that in the third millennium the region abounded in such groups, moving their flocks across this broad region in their quest for favourable grazing land and available sources of water.

The uplands are generally unsuitable for agricultural activities, although an interesting observation made by Michael Danti suggests that some upland areas may have been cultivated in the third millennium. While investigating the subsistence economy of the inhabitants of the Sweyhat embayment, Danti noted that the settlement itself receives between 200–250 mm of rainfall per year, just barely enough to practise successful dry-farming. To the east of the river valley, however, a downward slope in the 250 mm isoyhet may have provided some upland regions with greater amounts of rainfall per year (Danti 1997: Figure 5.1; 2000: 266). This higher rainfall provided a potential for agriculture, particularly in areas adjacent to the highland plateau to the east which are additionally fed by large amounts of runoff and water-born silts brought down by branching *wadi* systems (Danti 1997: 85). It is possible that settlements and fields located along the *wadi* systems utilized the concentration of runoff for the cultivation of crops. Today this area is a patchwork of dry-farming and pump-irrigated fields, although we know that prior to the nineteenth and early twentieth centuries, before the resettlement of modern upland villages and the introduction of mechanized agriculture and pump irrigation, this region was important for its wells for watering flocks of sheep and goats (Danti 1997: 85, 87–8).

Surveys conducted by Danti in this upland region between the Euphrates and the Balikh Rivers, approximately 10–30 km to the east of the Sweyhat embayment, found traces of ancient settled occupation (Danti 2000: 272). In one area where a wadi had been diverted into a low-lying region to form a small lake, a third millennium site called Tell Jedi was identified. The site was occupied during the late Early Bronze Age (Phases 4–5), when Tell es-Sweyhat and other settlements of the Euphrates and Balikh basins were experiencing peak periods of urbanization (Danti 2000: 276). This site's presence thus points to the utilization of these agriculturally productive areas of runoff even as early as the third millennium. Settlements such as Tell Jedi may have served as satellite communities for the burgeoning urban centres of the Euphrates River valley, supplying their increasing populations with necessary surpluses of agricultural and pastoral goods (Danti 1997: 92).

SUBSISTENCE

Several forms of subsistence were possible for the inhabitants of the Syrian Euphrates region, given the region's physical environment, vegetation, and climate. These methods of subsistence were practised at varying levels of intensity during different periods of the third millennium and according to local levels of rainfall, topographical characteristics and the availability of natural resources. Because the region has a marginal environment in which annual rainfall levels are low, a combination of dry farming, pastoralism, hunting and commercial exchanges would have been the most effective way of sustaining the region's population and offsetting losses that would have been incurred if only one or two of these economies were practised on their own.

Agriculture

Much of our understanding of the dry-farming regime of the Euphrates River Valley derives from T.J. Wilkinson's in-depth investigation of the agricultural economy around the Tell es-Sweyhat embayment area (Wilkinson

1976; 1994; 2004). Wilkinson's study combined geomorphological investigations with site survey and the mapping of off-site sherd scatters and linear hollows. His principal objectives were to ascertain the periods during which settlements were occupied in the Sweyhat embayment in antiquity, and to clarify ancient agricultural practices and the agricultural potential of this area (Danti 2000: 7). While Wilkinson's study of agriculture focussed on only one area of the Syrian Euphrates, his findings can generally be applied to most of the Euphrates region considered in this study. Only a slight adjustment is needed for the area to the north as one approaches the site of Carchemish at the Turkish-Syrian border. Here, increased rainfall would have made dry-farming of cereal grains more feasible and successful. Moreover, increased moisture would have permitted the cultivation of other types of plants besides the hearty, drought-resilient barley crops predominantly grown in the Sweyhat embayment and in other areas of the river valley to the south.

Wilkinson has effectively shown that dry-farming, while possible in this region, becomes increasingly precarious as one travels further to the south. This is because the region receives the minimum amount of annual rainfall in which dry-farming can be successfully practised. The site of Tell es-Sweyhat falls close to that limit, experiencing a mean annual rainfall of around 250 mm (Zettler 1997a: 2; Wilkinson 2004: 41). The other significant observation about the rainfall is that it fluctuates tremendously from one year to the next. It is, therefore, far from regular and reliable. In some years generous amounts of well-timed rainfall can result in a successful crop; in other years crop failures occur because precipitation levels have fallen well below the annual mean amount. By applying modern levels of rainfall in northern Syria over a 30-year period to the third millennium BC, and accounting for inter-annual variability, Wilkinson calculated that crop failure would have occurred in the area around Tell es-Sweyhat once every five years if the inhabitants had not taken additional measures to ensure the success of their crop through the incorporation of a yearly fallow system or manuring (Wilkinson 1994: 499–500). This statistic clearly underlines the marginal nature of the region and the necessity of incorporating strategies in the agricultural economy to offset losses resulting from insufficient rainfall.

To the north, in the direction of the Turkish-Syrian border, higher rainfall levels would have permitted more reliable crop production and the successful growth of a wider variety of plant species. The Euphrates region below Carchemish received between 300–400 mm of precipitation per year, judging by maps and tables that illustrate key rainfall isohyets (Wilkinson 1994: Figure 1; Miller 1997b: Figure 7.2). In contrast, the potential for crop failure would have increased dramatically as one travelled south along the river. Around the site of Selenkahiye, mean annual precipitation was about 200 mm (Van Loon 2001: 16.589). At Meskene/Emar, at the southern limit of the area considered here, crop failures may have occurred as often as every two years given that annual rainfall levels frequently fall below 200 mm (Wilkinson 2004: 44).

Since there are ways of counteracting the deleterious effect of inadequate rain, it is somewhat erroneous to assume a one-to-one correspondence between annual rainfall levels and successful dry-farming. Wilkinson comments on strategies employed by landowning farmers today, who are able to absorb some of the risk of crop failure by extending their fields over large distances, and can even enjoy profits in wet years (Wilkinson 2004: 41). Local topographic conditions may also have contributed to the success with which crops were grown. The exploitation of flat terrain, where less rainfall is lost to runoff and soil moisture is higher than in areas of undulating land, may have resulted in greater crop yields. Crops planted near water runoff from *wadi*s, which represent areas of enhanced moisture concentration and richer soil, may also have had advantages (Wilkinson 2004: 30).

Other land use strategies can offset some of the negative effects of a marginal environment. One common practice is fallowing, in which land is left uncultivated in alternate cropping years. Rain that falls onto the uncropped land is retained in the soil until the next cropping year rather than being consumed by crop growth (Wilkinson 2004: 47–8). Wilkinson has effectively shown that while dry-farming alone often produces crop failures in the region around Tell es-Sweyhat, the application of fallowing, allowing uncropped fields to retain their moisture, effectively reduces shortfalls, such that virtually no crop failures occur. While this practice is less productive agriculturally, it is certainly sustainable and resilient (Wilkinson 2004: 48–9).

Another way in which to enhance crop growth is to apply fertilizer, namely manure, on the land. Phosphorus and nitrogen contents of manure are favourable for plant growth. In addition, by increasing the growth of the plant canopy, the resultant shade can increase the amount of water moisture retained in the soil. Uses of manuring practices in many dry-farming zones in the world today have been largely successful, although in years of extreme drought, manuring may 'heat' the soil so much that it causes young plants to die off (Wilkinson 2004: 50).

Interestingly, it has been possible to infer extensive manuring practices in the fields around ancient settlements in the Syrian Euphrates by observing the extent to which low-density scatters of worn potsherds occur within or on top of the existing topsoil. It is unlikely that these sherds represent places of sedentary occupation given their even distribution across the land as well as their abraded character. Rather, these sherds are the result of spreading fields with refuse, principally manure, in order to fertilize the soil and thus increase plant production (Wilkinson 1994: 491–2). Much of this fertilizer would have been collected from refuse dumps within the settlement, in places like animal byres, streets and kilns. These types of dumps were also places where broken or old pots were thrown along with kiln slag, stone quern fragments, lithic debitage and fragments of figurines. Although the fertilizer which had been spread over the ancient fields has long since disappeared, these durable pieces of rubbish have remained in the plow topsoil over several millennia (Wilkinson 1994: 492; Wilkinson 2004: 72).

While many ancient tells are distinguished by observable scatters of sherds and other small artifact fragments, only a few Near Eastern sites' scatters have been systematically studied. Careful observations of scatter densities and the distance which sherds extend from the site may yield valuable information about the nature and intensity of land use. Wilkinson's survey of the sherd scatter found around Tell es-Sweyhat is one such study (Wilkinson 1994: 491–2; 2003: 117–18). By measuring the sherd scatter zone around the site he concluded that the fields within a 3–4 km radius from the site had been manured and cultivated. Moreover, the fact that the majority of diagnostic sherds were dated to the late third millennium (Phase 5) indicated that manuring practices did not take place until quite late in the history of this settlement's occupation, when Sweyhat had reached its largest size and population density (Wilkinson 2004: 68).

Wilkinson's significant finding suggests that the settlement at Sweyhat, which was now somewhere around 40 ha in area, and may have supported more than 100 people per ha, would have needed to cultivate all available land in the vicinity of the settlement in order to sustain its present levels of consumption. The decision was made to manure the fields, which would have increased crop productivity. In this period of maximum urbanization, however, there may also have been a temptation to cultivate annually, thus violating fallowing strategies in favour of annual cropping (Wilkinson 2004: 175).

Unfortunately, in this semi-arid region, the long-term effects of such intensive agricultural practices were likely quite disastrous, particularly if the population exceeded over 100 people per ha (Wilkinson 2004: 175). Fields would no longer be able to retain their moisture, resulting in crop failures during the drier years. The breakdown of this system may have been exacerbated further by the demands for supplemental feeding in the form of crop residues and barley required by the increasingly growing numbers of sheep and goats, whose steppeland pastures may have been dwindling as a result of overgrazing and the onset of soil erosion (Danti 2000: 65; Wilkinson 2004: 174). Overall, Wilkinson's prediction that the region around Sweyhat could not have sustained such levels of agricultural intensity for very long without ruinous outcomes may match up with the archaeological record from Tell es-Sweyhat. The data show that shortly after the site had reached its maximum urban extent, it suffered some kind of collapse, resulting in settlement contraction, the disuse of large-scale public buildings and fortifications, and the dwindling of its population.

Zones of agricultural activity

The greatest cultivation of crops took place on the river terraces, around the major settlements. These terraces provided sufficient soil cover for crops, and their elevation above the flood plain prevented fields from being accidentally inundated.

Given the abundance of water carried by the Euphrates and its proximity to agricultural fields, one might assume that the river was harnessed for irrigation. This is unlikely, however, since the river channel is deeply entrenched, and water would have been difficult to convey up to the level of the fields (Danti 2000: 23). It must also be remembered that because water was most needed when the level of the river was low, it would have been necessary to haul the water up over a vertical distance of several metres. Such an undertaking, which may only have been possible with more sophisticated hydraulic engineering such as animal-driven and water-driven scoop wheels, may not have come into existence until Roman times (Van Loon 2001: 16.590). Irrigation was also problematical on account of the fact that the Euphrates River exhibits high, poorly timed floods that would have been difficult to control. Moreover, it frequently breaks through its meanders or shifts its course (Besançon and Sanlaville 1985: 11; Danti 2000: 23; Wilkinson 2004: 38). While it is possible that advances in irrigation technology and the employment of canals enabled some settlements, like Emar, to be irrigated as early as the Late Bronze Age (Wilkinson 2004: 38), there is no physical nor paleobotanical evidence to indicate that such irrigation strategies were utilized as early as the third millennium (Miller 1997a: 100).

Types of crops

Archaeobotanical remains collected during excavations at the site of Tell es-Sweyhat have provided rich information, not only about the nature of the environment during the third millennium, but also the types of plants that were exploited for human and animal consumption during that time (Miller 1997a). Studies from other sites, namely Jerablus Tahtani, Qara Quzaq and Selenkahiye, have also provided useful data concerning the ancient environment and subsistence economy (Matilla Séiquer and Rivera Núñez 1994; Peltenburg et al. 1995; 1996; Rivera Núñez et al. 1999; Van Loon 2001: Chapter 16).

The first archaeobotanical samples collected by the Tell es-Sweyhat team between 1973 and 1975 revealed the presence, in late third millennium storage contexts, of pure crop remains, principally in the form of two-row barley, grass pea and a small jar of wild caper buds (van Zeist and Bakker-Heeres 1985: 308–10). Further plant remains were collected when excavations were extended across the site under Richard Zettler, beginning in 1989. These collections were extensively studied and summarized by

Naomi Miller (Miller 1997a). Miller not only endeavoured to identify the types of plants represented by the carbonized seeds but also considered how these plant remains arrived at the site and the types of contexts in which they were found. She concluded that much of the charred remains, collected from installations such as hearths, ovens and pits, derived from dung fuel. This finding is based on the high percentage of wild and weedy plant remains among the archaeobotanical remains, probably consumed by Sweyhat's sheep and goats (Miller 1997a: 95–6). This finding certainly underlines the strong pastoral component of the subsistence economy of the people of Tell es-Sweyhat, who were not only growing crops but also grazing large flocks of sheep and goats in the steppe lands beyond the limits of the cultivated zone.

Besides the preponderance of wild and weedy steppe plants, Miller concluded that two-row barley was the principal crop grown in the embayment plateau around Tell es-Sweyhat. Given that two-row barley is more drought resistant than the six-row type, it is more likely to have been grown successfully in Sweyhat's marginal environment (Miller 1997a: 96). Barley was not only consumed by humans but likely used as supplemental fodder for animals. This assumption is supported by the charred remains of dung fuel, containing not only quantities of wild and weedy plant seeds but also barley, charred straw and chaff (Miller 1997a: 102–3; Danti 2000: 265). Barley may have been especially important in the winter, when snow cover and depleted pastures in the steppe may have required this supplemental form of feed (Miller 1997b: 128).

Wheat is far less evident in the archaeobotanical remains. Since wheat tends to have a higher water requirement than barley, and since Sweyhat's environs are only marginal for rainfall agriculture, it is likely that wheat was, at most, a minor crop (Miller 1997a: 97). Since wheat has been found in far greater abundances in third millennium collections from Kurban Höyük and Hacinebi in Anatolia to the north, it is likely that as one travelled above Tell es-Sweyhat towards Carchemish, wheat crops would have steadily increased in abundance (Miller 1997b: 127–8). Confirmation of this trend is provided by the archaeobotanical remains from Jerablus Tahtani, just south of Carchemish, which reveal that although two-row barley was the most common cereal grain, wheat, in the form of emmer and einkorn was present in some quantities (Peltenburg *et al.* 1995: 25; 1996: 20).

Pulses in the form of lentils and peas were found in small amounts in the same trashy deposits as the other seeds at Tell es-Sweyhat (Miller 1997a: 97). No doubt these were grown as crops, although it is difficult to know the extent to which they were cultivated. Their low quantities in the settlement debris may simply be due to the fact that they were not used as animal fodder and thus had not become incorporated in dung fuel (Miller 1997a: 97). Quantities of *Lathyrus* or grass pea were also recovered at Tell es-Sweyhat. Since this legume was found in storage vessels in Room 6 of the 'Burned

Building' in Area IV at that site, it is likely that it was used for human food. It could have been ground for use in breads, although it did not constitute a principal plant food since it is toxic in large quantities, with a tendency to cause paralysis (Wilkinson 2004: 167–8).

Archaeobotanical remains of grapes are exceedingly rare at the sites of Tell es-Sweyhat and Selenkahiye (Miller 1997a: 97). Nonetheless they seem to have been a common component of the plant samples collected to the north at Jerablus Tahtani, owing to the moister climate (Peltenburg *et al.* 1995: 25; 1996: 20). Figs, olives, pistachios, almonds or prunes may also have been grown in the region around Jerablus Tahtani, although their presence has not yet been confirmed. They are certainly common in paleobotanical samples retrieved from Kurban Höyük further to the north (Algaze *et al.* 2001: 63). Linseed/flax has been identified at Jerablus Tahtani, whereas only two wild seeds have been recovered at Sweyhat (Peltenburg *et al.* 1996: 20; Miller 1997a: 98). Linseed is absent from the southern site of Selenkahiye altogether (Van Loon 2001: 16.586).

Pastoralism

One of the noteworthy features of the northern Euphrates Valley of Syria during the third millennium was the prevalence of pastoralism. Although agriculture produced vital crops to sustain both people and animals, animal husbandry was another essential component of the Early Bronze Age subsistence economy. Recent research has especially underscored pastoralism's importance to the sustenance and prosperity of the Euphrates region, as well as its connection to people's way of life, their ideologies and social organization (Danti 2000; Porter 2002a; Fleming 2004). These studies have demonstrated that a true understanding of the urban society and culture of this region cannot be accurately gauged without considering the important and pervasive role of pastoralism (Danti 2000: 12).

Domestic sheep and goats were the animals principally involved in pastoralist activities (Figure 2.1). Where analyses of the faunal assemblages of third millennium Syrian Euphrates sites have been carried out, the results consistently show that sheep and goats were the most common of all identified animal specifies. Thus, 75 per cent of the animal bones collected from the site of Tell es-Sweyhat were identified as sheep or goat (Weber 1997: 135). At the sites of Halawa Tell A and B, sheep and goat constituted between 30–52 per cent of the total animals (Orthmann 1989: 117). Most of the animal bones identified at Selenkahiye also belonged to sheep and goat (Van Loon 2001: 15.574).

Sheep and goats, providing products in the form of meat and milk, would have afforded a diverse and nutritious supplement to the inhabitants' diet of cereal grains and legumes (Danti 2000: 63). They were also economically advantageous in that they produced wool and hair. The fleece of sheep was

Figure 2.1 Sheep, Tell es-Sweyhat.

used to make clothing, while goats, contributing coarse hair, were used for the manufacture of carpets and tents (Danti 2000: 63). Upon the animals' death, large quantities of horn and bone could also have been used for the manufacture of various implements (Danti 2000: 64). Products like sheep's wool and goat's hair may have been particularly advantageous for export. Unlike meat and milk products, which perished after only a short period of time, wool was durable and could have been easily transported over long distances. The incentive to maintain large herds in the Euphrates region may have been prompted by the economic advantages of exporting wool, since it provided an important means of acquiring foreign goods through trade (Danti 2000: 64). The production of wool may also have intensified during periods when the Euphrates region of Syria was under the economic domination of foreign powers such as Mari and Ebla. It is likely that bulk wool and textiles were the principal commodities given as tribute to these polities (Danti 2000: 307).

Pastoralism was carried out successfully in the Syrian Euphrates region because the upland steppe, which provided wide tracts of grazing land, was only a short distance from the settled towns and agricultural fields of the river terraces. During the early months of spring, when the uplands had grown a new grass cover, sheep and goats were led out to the steppe pastures to graze (Danti and Zettler 1998: 213). Consequently, over the course of the arid summer, when pasture land and water dwindled in the uplands, grazing would have shifted to areas closer to the Euphrates River, where in-field

39

fodder had become available after the last harvest, or in fields that had experienced crop failures. Last, during the wet months of winter, when both in-field fodder and upland steppe pastures were unavailable, herds were kept close to the settled zone and provisioned with supplementary feed in the form of stored barley (Danti and Zettler 1998: 213). This annual cycle of grazing largely concurs with modern pastoral strategies practised in Syria today (Wilkinson 2004: 53). It is also supported by the archaeobotanical remains from Tell es-Sweyhat, where pastoralism constituted an important part of the third millennium subsistence economy. As we have already reported, much of the carbonized plant remains, which derive from sheep and goat dung, contained a wide variety of steppic plants, these having been consumed by herds while they grazed in the uplands. In addition, the carbonized remains contained large amounts of barley, the result of supplementary feed during the months of the year when steppe resources were depleted.

Still other evidence might be summoned to support the intensity of pastoralism in the Euphrates region, even during the early part of the third millennium. Some of this information derives from Hajji Ibrahim, a site located in the Tell es-Sweyhat embayment, about 500 metres beyond the southeast corner of Sweyhat's outer town wall, on the edge of a *wadi* (Danti 1997: 89–90). Hajji Ibrahim was a very small site that was principally occupied in the first centuries of the third millennium BC (Phases 1–2). In its best-preserved phase (phase B), excavations exposed rectangular mud brick structures which surrounded a single central building and courtyard. Because these structures had no ground-level entry, and their walls and floors had been heavily coated with mud and lime plaster, they were interpreted as silos or storerooms (Danti 1997: 91). Paleobotanical remains recovered from the central building nearby indicate that barley was processed here (Danti 1997: 91).

Based on the available evidence, Tell Hajji Ibrahim is interpreted as a grain storage and processing centre (Danti 1997: 91). Nevertheless, it is probably erroneous to reconstruct this site as a grain storage facility for the inhabitants of Sweyhat, given that the site was no more than 5–6 ha in this early EB phase and probably would not have required crop surpluses to feed its inhabitants. It is more likely that this facility functioned as a feeding station for transhumant pastoralists who moved in a yearly cycle from the river embayment to the uplands to support their herds of sheep and goats. They owned agricultural territories in the embayment along the *wadi*s, where they grew crops, namely barley. This grain would have been processed and stored at Tell Hajji Ibrahum as supplemental fodder, and used to feed the flocks when steppe plants became unavailable in the uplands during the winter (Danti and Zettler 1998: 223). Wool and hides, products that may have been used in interregional exchange, may also have been stored at these sites (Danti 2000: 304).

We have already reported that some upland areas may have supported small-scale agriculture, especially in areas of *wadi* runoff and slightly higher levels of rainfall. It is difficult to envision that the crops produced by these pockets of cultivable land supplied major riverine centres with grain surpluses given their distance from those settlements. On the other hand, one can easily reconstruct such upland areas as permanent stations for the production and storage of conserved feed for the region's flocks, their wells serving as places for watering livestock (Danti 1997: 92). Overall, the effects of extending grazing areas further into the uplands and establishing a network of feeding and watering stations beyond day-long forays from the river (over 15 km) greatly augmented pastoral production within the region (Danti 1997: 92). Moreover, these distant sites would have helped to distribute evenly animals on rangeland, thereby preventing overgrazing and soil erosion (Danti 2000: 67; Wilkinson 2004: 53).

Hunting

In addition to pastoralism, the hunting of wild animals was also part of the subsistence economy of many third millennium Euphrates sites. The best single source about hunting derives from the analyses of animal bones collected from third millennium occupation levels at Tell es-Sweyhat but other sites' collections have also been useful (Clason and Buitenhuis 1978; Orthmann 1989: 113–52; Weber 1997). These studies indicate that several varieties of deer were hunted, as well as gazelle and aurochs (Clason and Buitenhuis 1978: 80; Weber 1997: 135–6). Equid bones also constituted a substantial portion of the faunal collections. During the third millennium, the Euphrates region would have supported equids in the form of the domestic ass, the wild half-ass (*Equus hemionus*), or a sub-species known as the Syrian onager (*Equus hemionus hemippus*) (Weber 1997: 137–8). Morphological and metric studies of these latter bones do seem to indicate that the majority of equid bones were of the wild variety, thus indicating active hunting practices.

Wild animals, which included mainly equids, gazelle and deer, constituted about 11 per cent of the animals consumed by the inhabitants of Tell es-Sweyhat (Weber 1997: 141). Since onager and gazelle would have been animals that flourished in the steppe, their presence in the faunal record confirms that hunting, alongside pastoralism, was practised in the upland plateau behind the Sweyhat embayment. On the other hand, the presence in the assemblages of fallow deer, which would have roamed the riparian forests of the flood plain, confirms that hunting also took place near the Euphrates River. Finally, red deer and aurochs, which are comfortable in open woodland, were probably hunted in the remnant stands of oak forest that existed on the river terraces beyond the flood plain (Weber 1997: 141).

It is significant that at Tell es-Sweyhat, the percentage of wild animal bones, particularly equids, reached a maximum when Sweyhat's population was at its highest at the end of the third millennium (Phase 5) (Weber 1997: 141). This would seem to indicate that in times of maximum population, the varying ecological niches of the surrounding hinterland centre were exploited to their greatest extent. One should note, however, that this pattern, in which high numbers of wild animals were hunted, alters as one travels further to the north along the Euphrates into wetter regions. As the region of the Turkish-Syrian border is approached, it would seem that the number of wild animals decreases while the number of domesticated animals, such as pigs and cattle, increases. Nonetheless, sheep and goats are still found in large numbers, and their presence testifies to the prevalence of pastoralism in these more northerly areas (Peltenburg *et al.* 1995: 24; Weber 1997: 142).

Other economic opportunities

While past studies have focussed on the agricultural regime of the northern Euphrates Valley, and more recently on the significant role of pastoralism and hunting, our overall understanding of the region's economy is not complete without acknowledging the importance and sustained role of riverine commerce during the third millennium.

The archaeological record confirms that the Euphrates had long been a principal avenue of trade and cultural exchange. It attained a true importance, however, during the Late Uruk period at the end of the fourth millennium, when settlements with an unmistakable southern Mesopotamian material culture appear along the banks of the Euphrates River as far north as Anatolia. The majority of these settlements were likely inhabited by southern Mesopotamian colonists and merchants, who situated themselves in this distant region in order to acquire raw materials such as silver and copper from the mines of the Taurus Mountains, or timber from coniferous forests of the Taurus and Amanus Mountains (Akkermans and Schwartz 2003: 203). In both cases, the Euphrates River would have provided such traders with a direct line of access to these raw materials. That the importance of the river continued into the third millennium is deduced from textual sources like those from the western Syrian city of Ebla. This city's foreign relations and commerce were facilitated by the Euphrates River, which led to important Mesopotamian cities in the southeast such as Mari and Kish, and provided the means by which precious goods such as lapis lazuli were conveyed to Ebla in exchange for other materials such as wool, oil, wine, and grain (Astour 1995: 1406). Even towards the end of the third millennium, the Euphrates River continued to be used as an active route of commerce. Mesopotamian rulers such as Gudea of Lagash, for example, are known from textual sources to have obtained cedar and boxwood from the Amanus Mountains, which were cut into logs and formed into rafts that were floated down the Euphrates River to the south, along with other imported goods such as metal and stone (Astour 1995: 1408; Edzard 1997: Gudea E3.1.1.7.StB).

Exotic and precious materials, discovered at several Syrian Euphrates sites considered in this study, also attest to the importance of Euphrates River as an avenue of trade. The copper ore that was used to fashion the weapons, tools and pins which have been found in EB tombs at the sites of Carchemish, Jerablus Tahtani, Tell Ahmar, and Qara Quzaq, for example, was obtained from the Ergani-Maden mines of eastern Turkey. Similarly, the silver used to produce various torques, pendants, bracelets, finger rings and other adornments found in tombs at Jerablus Tahtani and Selenkahiye must also have come from mines in Anatolia. Without question, the Euphrates River would have provided the fastest and most effective means by which these metals were conveyed to these Early Bronze Age communities.

Local evidence also attests to riverine traffic from the south. The discovery of a stone cuneiform weight at Tell es-Sweyhat, inscribed with the cuneiform script of the Ur III period of southern Mesopotamia surely demonstrates contact with the south (Holland 1975). We might also add the presence of several cylinder seals and impressions at sites such as Selenkahiye and Jerablus Tahtani, whose designs emulate southern Mesopotamian styles or are themselves clear imports from the south (Van Loon 2001: 12.496; McCarthy in press). The Euphrates River would have been the most likely avenue by which these items were conveyed to the region.

Not all cultural interaction and trade, however, were conducted along the north–south trajectory of the Euphrates River. There were also important routes running from east to west, along which goods were conveyed between northern Iraq and the cities and trade emporiums of the west, as far as the Mediterranean coast. Algaze has postulated that most east–west communications took place further north, at the ford in the Samsat-Lidar region and in the Zeugma-Birecik area of Anatolia, where the Euphrates finally breaks out of its steep constraining canyon (Algaze 1999: 536–7). Such crossing points served to connect the Syrian plains west of the river and the northern Mesopotamian plains east of it (Algaze 1999: 537). Algaze's northern fords, however, must not have commanded all east–west traffic, judging by evidence from the Syrian Euphrates region to the south. In particular, it would seem that some EB settlements were located at key crossing points along the Euphrates River. Tell Ahmar, which was well known to have been at a major crossing point in later periods (Copeland and Moore 1985: 69), stands on the left bank of the river directly opposite the mouth of the Sajur River, flowing from the west from the direction of Aleppo. Archaeological surveys conducted in the Sajur River Valley testify to the frequency of EB settlements along its banks, and support its importance as a major thoroughfare in the third millennium (Copeland and Moore 1985: 176). Similarly, Tell Amarna is conveniently located on the right bank of the Euphrates flood plain, at the point where the west–east Nahr Amarna (first a *wadi* and then a stream), debouches onto the flood plain. This stream also supported several EB settlements (Copeland and Moore 1985: 71; Peltenburg *et al.*

1995: Figure 1). In both cases, therefore, key Early Bronze Age sites were sited along the river's edge at places that gave access to further routes to the west, surely underlining their role in east–west commercial traffic.

Wilkinson's intensive investigations of the Tell es-Sweyhat embayment have also produced evidence for east–west roadways and important crossing points along the river. As we have already reported, one such crossing point may have existed at Tell Jouweif on the left bank, which is directly opposite Tell Hadidi. Judging by linear hollows, which mark the remnants of ancient roadways, a second crossing point may have existed a few kilometres to the north, connecting Tell Hadidi on one side of the river to Tell Ali al-Haj (SS 17) on the other (Wilkinson 2004: 139, Figure 7.5). In both cases, the growth and success of Tell Hadidi and Tell es-Sweyhat, the principal cities on either side of the river at this point, can be attributed not only to the abundant agricultural and pastoral resources which they exacted from their broad hinterlands, but also their role as key control-points along an important east–west commercial route (Wilkinson 2004: 185).

DISCUSSION

This chapter has outlined some of the most salient features of the natural environment of the northern Euphrates Valley of Syria. It has described the principal constituents of the physical landscape of the region, which include the river channel and flood plain, the ancient river terraces and the upland steppes that rise beyond the valley to the east and west. Although this landscape and its accompanying climate limited the degree to which intensive dry-farming practices could be carried out, they made other types of economies possible. We have described, for example, the importance of pastoralism, which no doubt formed a major part of every settlement's economy during the third millennium. Hunting also appears to have been practised, judging by the quantities of wild animal bones found in the faunal collections of third millennium sites. Last, trade that took place both along the Euphrates as well as along overland routes which traversed the river at key crossing points, must have been influential to the success with which settlements were able to grow and flourish during this period.

The range of potentially exploitable resources in this region stands in marked contrast to other regions of the Near East, where such varied economic opportunities were not as widely and easily available. With such limitations, many ancient economic systems tended to place emphasis on one or two subsistence strategies to support their populations. Under the right conditions, these forms of economic specialization could frequently have extremely favourable results, resulting in flourishing settlements and growing populations. On the other hand, such systems lacked the flexibility which those with more variable economic strategies possessed, and as a consequence they were more vulnerable to stresses such as environmental degradation and political instability. We shall return to this issue of flexible versus rigid economies in Chapter 10 when we discuss the collapse of complex societies at the end of the third millennium BC. For now, we wish to stress that the variability of the subsistence strategies available to Euphrates communities not only enabled them to establish themselves successfully in this unusual, marginal region for the better part of the third millennium but also provided them with the means to grow into vibrant urban communities that persisted over several centuries.

Beside the different resources and subsistence strategies available in this unique Euphrates environment, we should like to point out another interesting development that this variable economy may have engendered. On the one hand, trade and cultural exchanges afforded by boat traffic along the Euphrates River exposed this region to many outside influences. We can expect that foreign contacts, especially those with southern Mesopotamia – which during the third millennium was experiencing full-blown urbanism and the dramatic rise of states and empires – would have left some impression upon the inhabitants of the northern Euphrates region. It is true that no Euphrates settlement grew to the same size and stature as any southern Mesopotamian city, nor can we identify any entity that emulated the configuration and hierarchical structure of a Mesopotamian city-state. Nonetheless, the growth of elite power and wealth, as manifested by richly accommodated tombs and monumental secular architecture at a number of Euphrates sites, may have been induced or amplified through contact and influence from the south, where elites played a dominant role in the organization and administration of the cities which they inhabited. We may also wish to attribute elite growth to the region's contact with the rich and powerful city of Ebla to the west, whose economic empire expanded to include most or all of the Syrian Euphrates region during the twenty-fourth century BC. Many of the new urban material cultural features that developed in settlements during this particular time, in addition to the increased prominence of social-economic inequalities, may have been strongly influenced by the hierarchical, urbane character of this pre-eminent Syrian city.

On the other hand, the continued prominence of rural life in the Euphrates region of Syria was assured by the region's strong engagement in pastoralism. This way of life, which developed out in the open range lands far beyond the confines of river valleys and settled communities, had at its core a kin-based tribal structure that favoured collective, cooperative social-economic relationships and heterarchical political systems. Pastoralism, and the mode of life that it embraced, therefore, contrasted sharply to the settled, urban behaviour encouraged by contacts with other parts of Greater Mesopotamia. It is difficult to imagine how such opposing modes of economy and seemingly incompatible ways of life could have co-existed within one region, and yet in the case of the northern Euphrates Valley, they do seem to operate in concert. While we cannot begin to understand all of the myriad and complex ways in which rural versus urban elements intermingled and overlapped with one another in this land, we can recognize the products of this unique inter-play, manifested in distinctive forms of art and architecture at various Euphrates EB settlements, and the unique traditions and ideologies reflected by such material cultural remains.

3

SETTLEMENT AND SOCIO-
POLITICAL STRUCTURE

Many ancient villages, towns and cities were established in the Euphrates River Valley in antiquity, having been supported by the economic opportunities available by the river itself, the valley in which it is situated, and the uplands beyond. The third millennium BC appears to have been an especially prolific period for settlement in the river valley, if we judge by the number of ancient mounds bearing evidence for occupation during some or all phases of the Early Bronze Age. Almost every few kilometres along the river brings into view another small or large mound that was settled during this period. Nor is settlement restricted to this stretch of the river as its runs through northern Syria. As one travels north of Carchemish into Turkey, a continuous string of third millennium settlements appears for a considerable distance up the river. Guillermo Algaze's survey of this region of the Turkish Euphrates as well as subsequent excavations at a number of key settlements prior to the completion of the Birecik and Carchemish Dams, further attests to the frequency of third millennium occupation in the region, and the complexity and uniqueness of some of the communities established there (Algaze et al. 1994; Kepinski-Lecomte and Ergeç 2000; Marro et al. 2000; Ökse 2002).

Settlement location

Based on archaeological reports of surveys as well as excavations in the Syrian Euphrates region, a map has been devised which locates the majority of third millennium sites within this region (Figure 3.1). For the most part, places of ancient human habitation take the form of mounds of earth (tells) (Figure 3.2), rising conspicuously above the level of the surrounding river flood plain or terrace and often littered on the surface with artifacts such as potsherds, fragments of grinding stones and chipped stone, as well as the remnants of ancient stone or mud brick structures. The map also includes the location of third millennium cemeteries, whose presence is attested by shafts or pits cut into the limestone conglomerate, a few still containing human remains and accompanying grave goods, especially pottery.

47

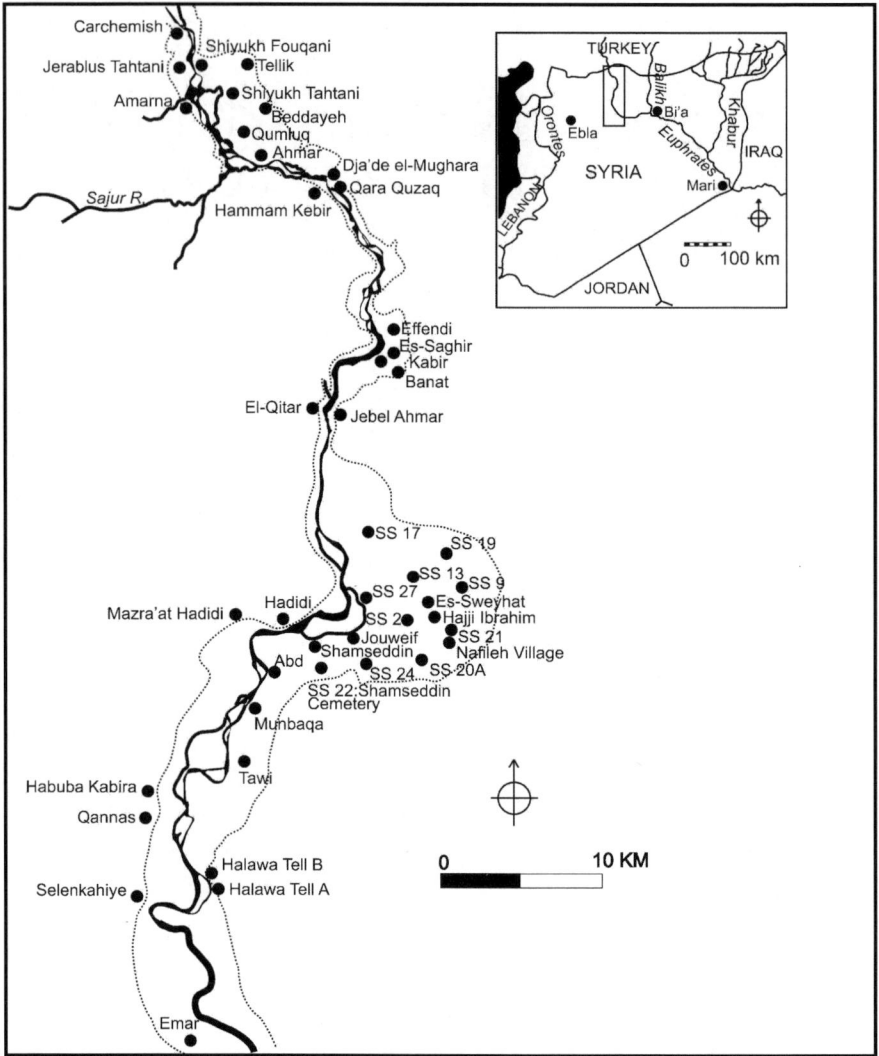

Figure 3.1 Northern Euphrates River Valley of Syria, showing location of EB settlements (dotted line indicates edge of river valley).

Accompanying the map is Table 3.1, which provides a list of the third millennium Syrian Euphrates settlements and cemeteries, along with the EB phases during which their occupation has been confirmed. Like the map, the data used to formulate this table are derived from a multitude of survey and excavation reports generated over the last century. Although extensive, this information is still incomplete. Many sites have never been sufficiently explored due to lack of time and resources.

Figure 3.2 Tell es-Sweyhat (low mound in distance).

Table 3.1 EB Euphrates settlements, phases during which they were occupied, and size estimates

Settlement Name	Phases 1–2	Phase 3	Phase 4	Phase 5	Settlement Size (in ha)
Carchemish	x	x	x	x	0.5–44.0
Shiyukh Fouqani	x		x		1.8[a]
Tellik			x		0.65[b]
Jerablus Tahtani	x	x	x		1.5[c]
Amarna			x	x	3–5.0[d]
Shiyukh Tahtani	x	x	x	x	1.2[e]
Beddayeh	x	x	x	x (?)	10–13.0[f]
Qumluq			x (?)		?[g]
Ahmar	x	x	x	x	2.0[h]
Hammam Kebir		x	x		2.8[i]
Dja'de el-Mughara		x			–[j]
Qara Quzaq	x	x	x	x	0.8[k]
Effendi		x (?)	x (?)		?[l]
Banat (+Bazey)	x (?)	x	x		30.0+[m]
es-Saghir		x (?)	x		1.5[n]
Kabir	x (?)	x (?)	x	x	2.3[o]
el-Qitar			x		1.9[p]
Jebel Ahmar			x (?)		?[q]
es-Sweyhat	x	x	x	x	5–6 (Ph.1–2), 10–15 (Ph. 4) 40 (Ph. 5)[r]
SS2	x				0.33[s]

49

Settlement Name	Phases 1–2	Phase 3	Phase 4	Phase 5	Settlement Size (in ha)
SS3 = Hajji Ibrahim	x		x		0.25[t]
SS5 = Nafileh Village		x	x	x	0.49[u]
SS8 = Jouweif			x	x	1.7[v]
SS9	x				0.5[w]
SS13	x				0.2[x]
SS14	x	x (?)			0.05[y]
SS17			x (?)		?[z]
SS19 = Khirbet Abour al-Hazu 2	x				0.2[aa]
SS20A = Othman	x	x	x	x	0.4–1.8[bb]
SS21	x				0.6[cc]
SS22 = Shamseddin Southern Site and Cemeteries	x	x	x	x	0.5[dd]
SS24				x	0.2[ee]
SS27				x	0.4[ff]
Hadidi	x	x	x	x	56.0[gg]
Mazra'at Hadidi	x				1.0[hh]
Shamseddin Central				x	2.06[ii]
al-'Abd		x	x	x	4.0[jj]
Munbaqa	x	x	x	x	1.7[kk]
Djerniye		x			–
Tawi Cemetery		x	x		–[ll]
Habuba Kabira	x	x	x	x	1–3.0[mm]
Qannas			x	x	1.0[nn]
Halawa B	x				1.4[oo]
Halawa A		x	x	x	15.75[pp]
Selenkahiye			x	x	12–14.0[qq]
Wreide			x	x	–
Emar			x	x	37.0?[rr]

a   Bachelot gives the dimensions of the main mound at Shiyukh Fouqani as 150 m × 120 m (=1.8 ha) (Bachelot 1999: 143). This is the size that is listed by Bunnens (in press).

b   Bunnens (in press) gives an estimate of 0.65 ha for Tell Tellik based on the map provided in Copeland and Moore 1985: 86, Figure 2. Since the site was occupied for many periods after the Early Bronze Age (Copeland and Moore 1985: 68), however, it is possible that Tellik was smaller during the third millennium.

c   Bunnens' (in press) estimate of 0.9 ha for the EB occupation of Jerablus Tahtani is based on the map in Peltenburg et al. 1995: Figure 3. Peltenburg et al. 1995: 4 gives the total dimensions of the site as 180 m × 220 m (=3.96 ha), which is significantly larger, although in a later report, the actual area that is enclosed by the EB fortification walls is given as only 300 m² (Peltenburg et al. 1996: 8). Peltenburg's most recent minimum estimate of the site, comprising occupation both within and outside of the walls is 1.5 ha (pers. comm.).

d   Amarna's size is calculated to be 3 ha based on the map provided in Tunca 1992: 40 (Bunnens in press). Moore's dimensions for the site are 250 m × 200 m (= 5 ha), which is somewhat larger (Copeland and Moore 1985: 53).

e   The site of Shiyukh Tahtani measures 6 ha in total, consisting of a main mound and a lower town, which surrounds the tell on three sides. To date Early Bronze occupation has only been recovered from trenches along the edge of the main mound (Areas B, C and D). The lower town seems to have been a late expansion, probably dating to the Roman and Byzantine periods (Falsone 1999: 137). The EB settlement, therefore, is about the area of the tell, which is 100 m × 120 m, or about 1.2 ha in area (Falsone 1998: 25).

f   Bunnens' estimate of 10 ha (in press) is lower than the dimensions of Beddayeh provided by Moore, which are given as 360 m in diameter (= 13 ha) (Copeland and Moore 1985: 54).

g   Qumluq's dimensions are given as 250 m × 200 m (= 5 ha) by Moore, along with a 160 m circular mound at one end (Copeland and Moore 1985: 54). At present, we are completely uncertain as to the extent of EB occupation at this tell, although pottery collected from this site by Woolley does confirm habitation from this period (or a cemetery) (Sconzo in press a).

h   EB settlement was restricted to the area of the high mound, whose dimensions have been calculated from a map of Tell Ahmar (Bunnens 1990: 8). Bunnens (in press) gives an estimate of 2 ha.

i   Bunnens' (in press) 2.8 ha estimate for Hammam Kebir is based on the dimensions provided by Moore: 300 m × 95 m (= 2.85 ha) (Copeland and Moore 1985: 48).

j   Thus far, the only EB discovery at the predominantly PPNB site of Dja'de el-Mughara has been an isolated tomb (Coqueugniot *et al.* 1998). The nature of EB occupation at this site remains ill-defined.

k   The dimensions of Qara Quzaq are reported by Moore as 160 × 100 m (= 1.6 ha) (Copeland and Moore 1985: 55). Valdés Pereiro (1999) reports, however, that the maximum diameter of the site is 150 m (2.25 ha). Bunnens' (in press) own conservative estimation of the EB site as 0.8 ha takes into consideration the site's expansion during the later Roman and Byzantine times.

l   No dimensions are provided for the site of Tell Effendi.

m   Thomas McClellan's estimate of 30 ha for the site of Tell Banat may not take into account the area of EB occupation that has recently been found on Jebel Bazey (McClellan 1999: 413, 417).

n   Anne Porter gives the size of Tell es-Saghir as 1.5 ha (Porter 1995a: 1).

o   Anne Porter gives the size of Tell Kabir as 2.3 ha (Porter 1995a: 1).

p   Based on the map published in Culican and McClellan 1983–84: Figure 1, Bunnens has provided an estimate of 1.9 ha for the size of el-Qitar during the EB (Bunnens in press). It should be noted that no EB structures or pottery have yet been excavated at the site of el-Qitar, although McClellan and Porter, in their survey report, do confirm that EBIV pottery (Phases 4–5) has been found there (McClellan and Porter in press). In addition, a shaft tomb of EBIVA date (Phase 4), located to the north of el-Qitar on the road to the village of Yusef Pasha, was cleared and investigated (Sagona 1986: 107).

q   There are no dimensions for Jebel Ahmar, a site located on a small conical mountain opposite el-Qitar.

r   It is estimated that during Tell es-Sweyhat's earliest third millennium occupation was no more than 5–6 ha (Danti and Zettler 1998: 219), but then expanded to 10–15 ha by the third quarter of the third millennium (Danti and Zettler 1998: 219). Its largest extent, which included the area south of the outer wall, made Tell es-Sweyhat about 40 ha in size in the late third millennium BC (Zettler 1997b: 51).

s   SS 2's dimensions are 55 m × 60 m (= 0.33 ha) (Reichel 2004: 199).

t   SS 3's dimensions are 50 m × 50 m (= 0.25 ha) (Danti 1997: 91).

u   SS 5's dimensions are 70 m × 70 m (= 0.49 ha) (Reichel 2004: 200).

v   SS 8's dimensions are 180 m × 120 m (=2.16 ha) (Reichel 2004: 202), although Wilkinson's estimate of 1.7 ha for the EB occupation may be more accurate given this site's subsequent occupation in later periods (Wilkinson 2004: 175).

w   SS 9 is described as two mounds, each 50 m × 50 m in diameter (= 0.5 m total) (Reichel 2004: 202).

x   SS 13 is described as having a 30–50 m diameter (Reichel 2004: 204).

y   SS 14 is described as a small site located on the spur of a limestone escarpment overlooking Nafileh. It may have been nothing more than a watchpost, 20 m × 20 m (Reichel 2004: 204–5). Wilkinson estimates its size as 0.05 ha (Wilkinson 2004: 175).

z   The presence of EB occupation at SS 17 (Tell Ali al-Haj) is still uncertain given the equivocal date of the remains found there (Reichel 2004: 207). It is described as a medium-sized tell of 200 m diameter (4 ha), its large size probably due to later Bronze and Iron occupation (Reichel 2004: 207).

aa   SS 19 is described as a number of very small mounds with an intervening space of 70 m × 80 m (Reichel 2004: 208). Wilkinson estimates the size of this site as 0.2 ha (Wilkinson 2004: 175).

bb   SS 20A's dimensions are given as 150 m × 150 m (= 2.25 ha) (Reichel 2004: 209), although Wilkinson estimates 0.4 ha for the site's earliest EB levels and 1.8 ha for its later EB occupation (Wilkinson 2004: 175).

cc   SS 21's dimensions are given as 100 m × 100 m (= 1 ha) (Reichel 2004: 210), although Wilkinson estimates that its early EB occupation was only 0.6 ha (Wilkinson 2004: 175).

dd   SS 22 consists of a low mound that was surrounded by several other areas where EB pottery was found, many of these indicating the location of EB cemeteries (see Meyer 1991). The dimensions of the tell are given as 190 m × 90 m (1.7 ha) (Reichel 2004: 210–11), although Wilkinson prefers a far more conservative estimate of 0.5 ha for the EB occupation on this mound (Wilkinson 2004: 175).

ee SS 24 is described as a small flat site. Wilkinson estimates that it was about 0.2 ha in area (Wilkinson 2004: 175).

ff SS 27's dimensions are given as 100 m × 50 m (= 0.5 ha), although Wilkinson gives a slightly lower estimate of 0.4 ha for the site's late EB occupation (Wilkinson 2004: 175).

gg Dornemann calculates the size of Hadidi as 135 acres (or about 55 ha) at its largest extent (Dornemann 1985: 50). He also reports that the earliest EB settlement covered the entire tell, as it did in the later EB (1985: 50). McClellan's estimate of 56 ha for the maximum size of Hadidi, which essentially concurs with the figure above, derives from an unpublished excavation report (McClellan 1999: 413, and n. 4).

hh Mazra'at Hadidi's dimensions are 200 m × 50 m (1 ha) (Reichel 2004: 232).

ii The site of Shamseddin Central Tell is estimated to be 140 m × 140 m (= 2.06 ha) (Reichel 2004: 249).

jj The site of Tell al-'Abd, which is perched on a limestone cliff overlooking the left bank of the Euphrates, is 210 m × 220 m in area (= 4.6 ha) (Bounni 1979: 49), although it was probably somewhat smaller in size if we only factor in the settlement that existed within the EB fortification walls (= 4 ha).

kk According to Peter Werner, the Early Bronze Age settlement at Munbaqa was limited to the area of the 'Kuppe' and covered an area of about 170 m × 100 m (1.7 ha) (Werner 1998: 38).

ll Tawi is predominantly the place of Early Bronze Age cemeteries. The date of settlement at Tell Djefle, the tell that is located nearby, is still uncertain, although it could have some EB occupation (Kamp-schulte and Orthmann 1984: 5; Reichel 2004: 240–1).

mm J.-C. Heusch calculates that the settlement at Tell Habuba Kabira would have covered about 3 ha, although only 1 ha is enclosed by the city walls, which for a long time constituted the main area of EB settlement (Heusch 1980: 161).

nn The site of Tell Qannas is said to cover an area of about 1 ha (Reichel 2004: 242).

oo Orthmann calculates the size of Halawa Tell B as about 140 m × 100 m (= 1.4 ha) (Orthmann 1989: 8).

pp Orthmann calculates the size of Halawa Tell A as about 450 m × 350 m (= 15.75 ha) (Orthmann 1989: 10).

qq The site of Selenkahiye was originally measured to be about 600 m × 250 m in area (= 15 ha) (Meijer 1980: 117). In the final report, however, the walled area is estimated to have encompassed about 520 m × 200 m (= 10.4 ha) (Van Loon 2001: 3.25). It is also reported that to the west, additional remains of houses represent habitation outside of the town wall some time during the late Early Bronze Age. These remains were found as much as 220 m to the west of the settlement's outer defences (Van Loon 2001: 3.94). If we factor in this area of habitation, then the size of Selenkahiye may have been another 2–5 ha in area, bringing its total to about 12–15 ha. McClellan's own estimate of 15–20 ha for Selenkahiye may be too generous (McClellan 1999: 413).

rr Emar's EB occupation is estimated to be 37 ha by Weiss, although this size has not yet been confirmed (Weiss 1983: Figure 11).

In Figure 3.1, one can note the high number of EB settlements reported in the left bank embayment around the site of Tell es-Sweyhat. Although the length and breadth of this curving plain no doubt encouraged the growth of settlement in antiquity, we must also attribute the inordinate number of sites identified in this region to the intensive, systematic surveys that have been conducted there by a number of archaeological teams over the past few decades. It is possible that other areas of the Syrian Euphrates were equally heavily settled, but that many of their sites, especially those smaller than 1 ha in area, have not yet been positively identified on the ground because of less comprehensive survey strategies.

As we might expect, the majority of third millennium settlements are located on the fluvial terraces, where their proximity to the river allowed them to exploit riparian resources, while their elevation protected them from seasonal flooding and more exceptional fluvial intrusions. As we have already reported, only a few EB sites have been positively located directly on the flood plain. They were founded on slightly elevated beds of gravel and silt, this alluvial terrain offering some level of protection against seasonal flooding.

In a few cases, third millennium settlements were perched significantly high above the level of the flood plain. The site of Selenkahiye is located on an elongated ridge that is 20 m above the course of the river to which it runs parallel. In addition, a depression that runs alongside the site to the west is 10 m lower than the top of the ridge (Van Loon 2001: 2.14). Rather than seeing the threat of flooding as the reason for Selenkahiye's lofty location, we might regard its position on top of a high ridge as a defensive measure, protecting its inhabitants against attacks and raids. The fact that this site is also characterized by thick city walls, towers and a sloping rampart further underlines defensive concerns of this nature. Halawa Tell A, located slightly to the north of Selenkahiye on the river's opposite bank is also situated on a high terrace. Its eastern side slopes steeply down to the river's edge, while its northern end is protected by a deeply cut *wadi* (Orthmann 1981: 3, Taf. 21). No doubt, this location was also chosen for its natural defensibility. The settlements at el-Qitar and Jebel Ahmar, located on opposing sides of the river where it runs through a narrow gorge, are situated on what can realistically be described as small mountains. The mountain upon which el-Qitar is located rises 76 m above the Euphrates River plain, and is rugged and even insurmountable in places. Clearly such a location would have offered the inhabitants of the settlement excellent natural protection (Culican and McClellan 1983–84: 31). This factor, coupled with man-made constructions such as towers, walls, and a glacis, which we know were built at the site in later periods, would have made el-Qitar a formidable and intimidating fortress (Culican and McClellan 1983–84: 39).

The natural topography of the terraces and ridges alongside the Euphrates Valley, while offering defensive advantages, clearly constrained the growth of some settlements. The ridge upon which Tell Halawa B was situated is small and would not have permitted the physical expansion of this early third millennium settlement beyond a certain size. It is perhaps for this reason that around the middle of the third millennium occupation was moved to Tell Halawa A, located on a broader ridge directly to the south of Tell B (Orthmann 1981: Taf. 21). This new locale would have supported the growing population and settlement, although on account of the steep slopes that characterize the ridge on all sides, Halawa A too would have eventually been unable to support further settlement expansion.

In contrast to the high, relatively narrow ridges upon which Selenkahiye and Halawa A and B are situated, Tell Hadidi and Tell es-Sweyhat are located on broad, level plains. It is also striking that both Tell Hadidi and Tell es-Sweyhat are among the only sites of the Syrian Euphrates characterized by high acropolis mounds and extensive lower towns. While there could be political and economic factors associated with this type of settlement configuration (see below and Chapter 4), we might also attribute this layout to the wide areas upon which structures of the lower towns of these sites could expand.

One should not overlook settlements located at greater distances from the river's edge. Such sites have been found in areas where the older river terraces are especially wide. Tell Tellik and Tell Beddayeh, for example, are both located at the eastern limit of a wide plain on the left bank of the Euphrates as it flows south of Carchemish (Copeland and Moore 1985: 54). Furthermore, although Beddayeh is several kilometres from the main course of the Euphrates River, there are two springs in the vicinity of the tell (Copeland and Moore 1985: 68). Tell Banat, perhaps one of the most well known sites in the Euphrates Valley on account of the spectacular discoveries made there, is located almost 3 km to the east of the current channel of the Euphrates River (McClellan and Porter in press). Finally, the ancient settlement at Tell es-Sweyhat, which stands in the centre of a large plain formed by a broad crescent-shaped embayment, would also have been 3 km from the river in antiquity (Zettler 1997a: 2). The presence of these three sites at considerable distances from the flood plain indicates that settlements were supported by other resources besides those from the river and its flood plain. It might be tempting to postulate, given the position of several of these sites almost at the edge of the upland plateau, that these settlements were strategically located to exploit and/or control resources deriving from the upland steppe country, namely pastoral products and hunted animals.

Settlement size

Although we are fairly well informed about which Euphrates sites were occupied during the Early Bronze Age, and have even ascertained during which phase of the EB they were settled, it has been difficult to ascertain each site's overall size during this period. Frequently, subsequent centuries of occupation have all but obscured the remnants of EB habitation since later buildings have been built directly over the settlement's earliest constructions. At the site of Emar, excavations have successfully penetrated into the earlier phases of EB occupation and have confirmed habitation during this time (Finkbeiner 2002, 2003), but later buildings erected over this settlement phase, especially during the Late Bronze Age, have made firm statements about the nature and extent of the EB occupation well nigh impossible. Similar problems plague our understanding of the layout and size of the EB settlement of Carchemish, which experienced a massive expansion and transformation during the later Iron Age, when the site became the centre of an important Neo-Hittite dynasty (Hawkins 1976–80).

Although archaeological surveys have successfully identified ancient habitation on the visible, artificially elevated mounds or tells, their techniques have often failed to detect the extent to which occupation spread to the surrounding unmounded areas. The recognition of such occupation requires careful prospection of surrounding areas through the mapping of sherd scatters and the recording of other features such as the remnants of building walls, door sockets, supports, kilns and pavements. When such intensive surveys are conducted, the results may significantly alter one's original estimation of the extent of ancient occupation. A case in point is the EB site of Tell Taya in northern Iraq. Although the mounded area of Tell Taya includes a 1 ha high tell and an 8 ha outer town, low-density occupation attested by foundation walls and artifact scatters extending over areas of 70–160 ha around Taya increases its settlement-size several-fold (Reade 1968: 239; 1971: pl. 24; Wilkinson 1994: 485). In the region under investigation here, a detailed prospection was made of the unmounded area beyond the limits of the outer enclosure wall at Tell es-Sweyhat. Late EB occupation in the form of artifact scatters and fragmentary wall footings to the south of the Lower City's southern wall added another 10–15 ha to the whole site (Wilkinson 1994: 487). Unfortunately, because most surveys conducted on and around ancient sites in the Euphrates Valley have not been carried out as intensively as at Sweyhat, other settlement-size estimates can only be considered tentative at best.

Table 3.1 also gives the estimated size of sites occupied during the Early Bronze Age. The data presented here derive from size approximations provided in both survey and excavation reports. In a few exceptional cases, site sizes during individual phases of the Early Bronze Age have been determined, as in the case of Tell es-Sweyhat. The fact that Sweyhat grew from a 5–6 ha town in the earliest phases of the EB (Phases 1–2), to a city of over 40 ha in the Late EB (Phase 5), testifies to the dramatic growth that settlements could experience during this period of the third millennium (Danti and Zettler 1998: 213). This example should caution us against drawing too many conclusions about settlements and their importance until we have more precise size estimates for the specific phases in which they were occupied.

Unfortunately, the greatest uncertainties with regard to settlement size lie with Carchemish, at the extreme northern end of this regional study, and Emar, at the southern limit. This lack of data regarding size is especially disappointing given that textual sources from the third millennium, principally the cuneiform archives from Ebla, make specific mention of both of these sites (Edzard 1981; Archi 1990; Lacambre and Tunca 1999; Meyer 1996: 155–70). As was reported above, the extent of EB occupation at Emar has been difficult to determine due to the large size of the settlement and the monumentality of its structures in later periods, these having been built directly over the EB town. We have provided Harvey Weiss' estimation of 37 ha for the Early Bronze Age size of Emar, although we acknowledge that it is highly conjectural (Weiss 1983: Figure 11).

In the case of Carchemish, since that site has never been properly surveyed, reliance must be put on the results of the early twentieth-century British investigations of the site. These excavations concentrated on the magnificent Neo-Hittite remains of the first millennium BC, and only penetrated into earlier levels in small sondages (Woolley 1921; Woolley and Barnett 1952; Algaze *et al.* 1994: 5). From these investigations, we know that Early Bronze Age levels were exposed on Carchemish's acropolis mound (Woolley and Barnett 1952: 214–26; Algaze *et al.* 1994: 12). On this basis, Guy Bunnens proposes a size estimate of 4 ha, arguing that EB occupation did not extend beyond the Acropolis (Bunnens in press). He additionally argues that the small size of Carchemish is consistent with the data derived from the Ebla archives, in which it would appear that Carchemish was under the political control of Ebla. Last, since the settlement was not actually mentioned frequently in the Ebla tablets, it may not have been particularly important or large during this period (Bunnens in press).

In contrast to Bunnens' modest estimate, Thomas McClellan proposes a size of 42 ha for Carchemish, which is a measurement of the Inner Town and acropolis according to the map produced by Leonard Woolley in his 1921 report (Woolley 1921: pl. 3; McClellan 1999: 413 and n. 2). McClellan's inclusion of the Inner Town is no doubt based on references in the reports to various Phases 3–4 Metallic Wares that were found in various points within the Inner City (Woolley 1921: 48; Algaze *et al.* 1994: 15). One can also report here that during an archaeological survey of Tıladir Tepe, a site directly across the river from Carchemish, G. Algaze and his team found late EB/Early MB sherds littered across the surface, indicating that this settlement covered an area of some 12 ha (Algaze *et al.* 1994: 15). If Tıladir Tepe is to be regarded as a suburb of Carchemish, then one could expect Carchemish itself to have been no less in size during this period.

Algaze's own estimate for the size of Carchemish's Inner Town is given as 44.5 ha, which would seem to include the dimensions of the acropolis as well. Nevertheless, he is cautious to provide only a minimum estimate of 0.5 ha for the duration of occupation at Carchemish during the EB (Algaze *et al.* 1994: 61). In the end, the evidence does not yet present a firm conclusion as to the size of Carchemish during the EB, and as a result, we have left the figure ranging widely between 0.5 and 44 ha.

Whatever sizes we accept for Carchemish and Emar during the Early Bronze Age, the table (Table 3.1) shows us that the majority of settlements in the northern Euphrates Valley were quite small, usually under 5 ha. None of these settlements attained the size of cities found in other parts of the Near East during the third millennium. They contrast especially to the massive urban sites of the Mesopotamian plains of southern Iraq. The centre of Uruk, for example, grew as large as 400 ha during the early part of the Early Bronze Age and may have supported between 40,000 and 80,000 people (Wilkinson 1994: 503). Northern Euphrates sites also did not attain the sizes of settlements in other parts of Upper Mesopotamia, such in the *Jezireh* of northern Iraq and northeastern Syria. Tell Taya and Tell Leilan, for example, grew as large as 90–160 ha in area (Wilkinson 1994: Table 2).

Tony Wilkinson has cogently pointed out that differences in site sizes in these regions are directly related to the productive capacity of the territories surrounding the settlements and the amount of food surplus and other essential products that these hinterlands could generate in order to support the settlements' populations (Wilkinson 1994). Further, sources of available labour to harvest and process food surpluses, and the limited distance across which bulk food products can be transported, also dictated the carrying capacity of cities and their overall size. Considering these factors, we may see why the environmental and geographical conditions of southern Mesopotamia made it an exceptionally favourable region for urban growth. The existence of an irrigation system permitted higher and more dependable crop yields, thus enabling towns to increase above normal limits. Moreover, the use of boats would have facilitated the ease with which bulk food items could be transported, thus 'nullifying the frictional effect of distance' (Wilkinson 1994: 503). Moving into the Upper Mesopotamian *Jezireh*, we find large tracts of cultivable land and rainfall that were sufficient in most years to support a healthy regime of dry-farming, thus permitting the growth of large settlements (Wilkinson 1994: 485). But unlike the cities of southern Mesopotamia, these Early Bronze Age settlements did not exceed a ceiling of 100 ha, probably due to the constraints of available labour and the day-return access threshold of some 15 km radius from the core towns to the furthest 'feeder' dependent towns and villages that supported the centres (Wilkinson 1994: 483, 505).

In contrast to both southern Mesopotamia and parts of the *Jezireh* of Upper Mesopotamia, the Euphrates River Valley was a marginally productive region. Dry farming was frequently precarious in this region, owing to insufficient rainfall. Many of the sites considered in this study are located below areas receiving a mean-annual precipitation of 250 mm, which is the lower limit in which dry-farming can be practised successfully (Danti 2000: 4). Furthermore, available areas for dry-farming were limited because of the region's topography, in which only land relatively close to the flood plain of the Euphrates could support reasonably productive agricultural regimes. It is likely, therefore, that environmental factors, which constrained agricultural productivity in the Euphrates region, may explain in part the relatively small size of cities in this region compared to those found in other parts of the Tigris-Euphrates Basin.

While it is true that none of the Syrian Euphrates sites grew to sizes attained in other parts of Mespotamia, neither is it true that they were all diminutive. Tell Hadidi had already reached a size of 56 ha early on in the Early Bronze Age. Tell Banat, during its fluorescence in the mid-to-late third millennium (Phases 3–4), grew to 30 ha, while in the late third millennium,

Tell es-Sweyhat attained a size that exceeded 40 ha (Phase 5). Sweyhat's urban extent is especially significant given that its largest size was attained when other settlements in the Euphrates Valley and beyond had been abandoned. Moreover, the site grew in excess of that predicted by models of agricultural sustainability (Wilkinson 1994), forcing us to look for other factors that might explain its success. Last, it is significant to note that many Euphrates EB settlements attained substantially larger sizes than urban centres in Palestine and Jordan from the same time period (Joffe 1993: 73–82; Philip 2001: 181).

We can summon still other features of Euphrates EB settlements that underscore their noteworthy urban-like character. Subsequent chapters of this study will present settlement evidence in the form of monumental temples, large-scale secular structures, craft specialization, planned domestic neighbourhoods and extensive fortification systems, of all these reflecting rather surprisingly high degrees of complexity. The appropriation of wealth, attested also by the monumentality of some Euphrates graves as well as the frequency of exotic, valuable objects that accompanied these interments will also underline the urban character of these sites. In sum, it is difficult to dismiss all northern Euphrates sites as simple, small-scale communities of food producers that paled in comparison to the more developed and sophisticated 'urban' communities of other parts of Mesopotamia. A variety of factors can be proposed to explain the relatively complex composition of Early Bronze Euphrates sites, and the relatively large size that some of these sites attained. At this point, it suffices to state that site size alone cannot be used to gauge accurately the importance, range of functions or degree of urban complexity of the settlements of this region. A settlement's constituent features must also be considered. Moreover, the types of socio-political interactions and economic exchanges these communities engaged in both within and outside of the region need also to be carefully scrutinized.

Settlement hierarchies

Settlement hierarchies occur when sites expand in size to a point where the food requirements of the city exceeds that of the food producing capabilities of the city's environs. As a consequence, that city begins to exact tribute from rural communities beyond its immediate landscape. These communities produce the required surpluses to support the populations and institutions at the centre (Wilkinson 1994: 484; Matthews 2003: 110). Through this phenomenon, towns and villages of the rural hinterland become dependencies of the city, being tied to that centre by obligation, by force or by economic factors (Wilkinson 1994: 484). We see this kind of development clearly at Uruk in southern Mesopotamia, which during the late fourth millennium and early third millennium expanded to such a size that it dominated a large area which included many smaller towns, villages and hamlets. These smaller settlements became Uruk's tributaries (Pollock 2001: 195).

Settlement hierarchies may also be present in the *Jezireh* of Upper Mesopotamia. During the Early Bronze Age one sees the development of a 'ranked' or 'three-tiered' settlement hierarchy dominated by the site of Tell al-Hawa. This settlement attained a size of 66 ha, while at a distance of 9–12 km from this centre were secondary sites ranging from 10–19 ha. Below these towns were small satellite villages with areas of 1–5 ha (Wilkinson and Tucker 1995: 81). This settlement configuration reflects the fact that, as a prime centre, Tell al-Hawa overshadowed in size the settlements in its neighbourhood, transforming these smaller secondary and tertiary sites into tributaries.

In contrast to the pattern found in the northern *Jezireh* and Southern Mesopotamia, Wilkinson observes that settlements in the northern Euphrates Valley tend to be less distinctly ranked, possibly because of the topographically fragmented terrain. In this region, riverine terraces enclosed by limestone hills restricted the area of land that could be put under cultivation (Wilkinson 1994: 489). But even while no hierarchies of the order of southern Mesopotamia or the region around Tell al-Hawa occur in this region, it would appear that large settlements could occasionally grow to overshadow other sites in their neighbourhoods. At the third millennium settlement of Titris Höyük in southeastern Turkey, for example, it would appear that a few outlying settlements were drawn into the Titris system, supporting that centre through the generation of surplus production (Algaze 1999: 548; Algaze *et al.* 2001: 56–7).

Can any such settlement hierarchies be detected in the Euphrates Valley of northern Syria? It has been observed that as the settlement at Tell es-Sweyhat began to grow in size around Phase 4 in the mid-third millennium, other smaller sites in Sweyhat's embayment continued to be occupied or new sites were founded (SS 5, 8, 17, 20A) (Wilkinson 2004: 138, Figure 7.5; Danti 2000: 263). By the time of Tell es-Sweyhat's largest expansion in Phase 5, the same sites continued to be occupied and new settlements were founded on or near the flood plain (SS 24, 27) (Danti 2000: 264). Certainly, none of these attained Tell es-Sweyhat's large size of 40 ha. Although their precise relationship with Sweyhat remains largely unexplored, it is plausible that these villages were drawn into Sweyhat's system as it expanded, supporting the core site with whatever surplus and services they were capable of generating.

Similar settlement configurations might be postulated further north along the left bank of the Euphrates River, particularly where the flood plain has broadened to form wide, relatively fertile embayments. On the left bank south of Carchemish, the plain widens to nearly 6–7 km wide at its greatest extent. This area not only supported the settlement of Beddayeh, located along the eastern limit of this plain, but also Tell Tellik to the north, and the sites of Shiyukh Fouqani, Shiyukh Tahtani, and Tell Ahmar alongside the main course of the Euphrates or one of its subsidiary channels. Tell Qumluq, which is located about 5.5 km northwest of Tell Ahmar on the edge of a terrace overlooking the flood plain to the west, may also have been occupied during this period (Copeland and Moore 1985: 54). One can note that Beddayeh, in its position furthest from the river's edge, attained the largest size in this region, growing to some 10–13 ha in the late third millennium BC. In contrast, the other sites do not appear to have been larger than 2 ha at any period in the Early Bronze Age.

Further down the river towards the southern end of the Tishreen Dam Basin, another wide plain supported several Early Bronze Age settlements. Besides the prominent settlement at Tell Banat, which was located about 3 km inland from the Euphrates, other smaller settlements were known to have been occupied during the same time period. These included Tell Effendi, located at the north end of the alluvial plain, and Jebel Ahmar, at the region's southern limit. Clustered around the site of Tell Banat itself were the sites of Tell Kabir and Tell es-Saghir. Tell Banat was the largest site in this region, attaining a size of around 30 ha during the period of its maximum expansion in the mid-to-late third millennium (Phases 3–4). Of the other sites in its neighbourhood, the largest was probably Tell Kabir, which grew to no more than 2.3 ha.

Can we suggest that some sort of settlement hierarchy existed in these Euphrates embayments, in which the smaller settlements became dependencies of the larger towns, and provided produce and labour to those centres, receiving administrative and ceremonial services, protection and redistributed goods in return? It is tempting to accept this proposition, given the location of the 'core' towns towards the back of the fertile plains (Beddayeh, Banat), and thus in advantageous positions to exploit and control both the produce of the agricultural fields of the Euphrates plain as well as the pastoral resources of the surrounding upland steppes. At the same time, smaller sites poised along the river would have provided the centres with dry-farmed or flood-water irrigated produce of their immediate vicinity as well as imported goods deriving from commercial exchanges along the river.

On the other hand, a true settlement hierarchy of the type observed in other parts of Mesopotamia is not particularly supportable for the Euphrates River Valley if we factor in other observable aspects of the settlements under investigation. As has already been noted, the small size of many of the river's Early Bronze Age communities masks an underlying complexity that one might not expect of small settlements that are simply viewed as small-scale dependencies of larger central places. Turning more closely to the evidence from the regions discussed above, for example, one may note that while Tell Ahmar is a relatively small settlement (2 ha) in comparison to the much larger site of Beddayeh (10–13 ha), it has yielded a late Early Bronze tomb of monumental proportions and highly valued tomb objects, suggesting a high degree of wealth and access to resources on the part of the individuals who were interred within the tomb. At Tell Kabir, excavations have revealed a monumental temple *in antis* of a type well known at other sites in the Euphrates River Valley and beyond, but unaccounted for at Tell Banat, the large settlement in whose shadow it stands. In light of the nature of this evidence, it seems fallacious to reconstruct a truly ranked settlement hierarchy in these Euphrates locales. Rather, we might view settlements within these systems as possessing complementary or specialized functions, possibly serving the larger communities in some respects but at the same time maintaining high degrees of autonomy and authority. We might additionally envision that depending on various economic, ideological or military conditions and concerns, these communities had close connections with settlements even outside of their local systems. Thus, rather than a neat system of discrete, hierarchical 'city-states', we should probably reconstruct a more heterarchical web of settlements whose variable and overlapping functions and activities linked them to a variety of settlements of different sizes and geographic locations (McClellan 1999: 416).

Socio-political structure

The distinctive heterarchical character of the northern Euphrates region and the unusual way in which third millennium settlements were configured may be attributed in part to the persistent tribally-structured composition of the region's inhabitants, defined by loosely organized confederacies of both agrarian and pastoral nomadic kin-groups. Their membership often transcended the boundaries of individual centres or specific places of residence. Furthermore, their political relationships included the dissemination of power and decision-making across the community rather than being solely concentrated in the hands of a few elite individuals. It is possible that the region's pronounced subsistence strategy of long-range herding sheep and goats encouraged this tradition of collective power, since it is 'the tendency of pastoralists to manage access to grazing land at the collective level, for whole communities' (Fleming 2004: 218).

The type of political organization posited here agrees well with the model formulated by Richard Blanton and his colleagues, who observe that the political systems of some complex societies are not entirely and rigidly hierarchical in their structure. Rather, Blanton *et al.* see two principal types of power strategies coexisting within one larger system. One of these is 'exclusionary' in that it centres on individual leadership and the monopolistic control of sources of power, while the other 'corporate' political strategy is more group-oriented, with power being shared across different groups and sectors of society (Blanton *et al.* 1996: 2; Fleming 2004: 177). Within this system, there is a constant tension between the two political actions, one striving to concentrate power in the hands of one individual or a single authoritative group or class within the society, while the other attempts to offset the attainment of absolute power by maintaining an emphasis on collective political authority (Blanton *et al.* 1996: 2; Porter 2002b: 167; Fleming 2004: 180).

While Blanton and his colleagues used their model to elucidate better patterns of political action in ancient Mesoamerican civilization (Blanton *et al.* 1996), its application to other complex societies around the world, including the ancient Near East, is highly tenable. Most recently, this so-called 'dual-processual' model has been applied by Daniel Fleming to the political world of the Mari Archives of ancient Syria during the Middle Bronze Age of the early second millennium BC (Fleming 2004). Through his consideration of the textual sources of this period, Fleming cogently observes that although Syrian cities and states were controlled by leaders or kings who ruled from well-demarcated urban centres and who expressed their status and sovereignty by building palaces and other impressive monumental structures and fortifications, a collective decision-making tradition continued to exist throughout this period as well. There is, for example, frequent mention in the textual sources of this period of the presence of 'elders', whose collective authority was distinct from that of a king (Fleming 2004: 190–1). Such assemblies of 'elders' are known to have taken part in negotiations with outsiders and engaged in diplomacy. They also acted as witnesses in legal affairs, and played important roles in religious rituals (Fleming 2004: 191–2). The authority of the elders appears to have varied widely during this period from place to place. In some cities, these individuals acted as representatives of their king, while in other instances, the elders served as an official body that decided town affairs in the absence of a local individual chief or king (Fleming 2004: 195–200). Whatever the case, abundant references to these collective assemblies or town councils in the textual sources suggest that a 'corporate' political strategy, much like that described by Blanton and his colleagues, was prevalent during this period of ancient Syrian kingdoms and existed alongside more 'exclusionary' forms of political authority.

The presence in the letter of the Mari Archives of a collective decision making group called the *tahtamum* stands out as a particularly significant form of assembly of elders since it is known especially from Tuttul and Emar, two cities situated along the Euphrates River of Syria at the southeastern end of the region considered in this work (Durand 1989: 27–44; Fleming 2004: 212–16). Fleming suggests that the towns' distance from the shadow of major kingdoms may have allowed this distinctly collective political tradition to thrive with relatively little interference from outside powers (Fleming 2004: 213). Besides the fact that the *tahtamum* has its origins in the Early Bronze Age as attested by the term's occurrence at third millennium Ebla (Fleming 2004: 214), both Tuttul and Emar were known to have been prominent Early Bronze Age towns, suggesting that this institution of elders may well be rooted in this earlier period (Fleming 2004: 214). In light of this evidence, it is highly plausible that neighbouring third millennium Euphrates cities, such as the ones under examination here, also shared the same collective political traditions.

As we shall see in forthcoming chapters, there is considerable archaeological evidence testifying to the presence of corporate power traditions at a number of Euphrates sites. One can attribute, for example, the distinctive dispersed layout of some cities' important buildings, the somewhat eclectic design of fortifications and the non-centralized nature of craft production to this type of socio-political structure. On the other hand, elite residences and wealthy tombs attest to the presence of 'exclusionary' forms of power. It is interesting that these opposing systems can be present at one settlement while absent at another nearby. Alternatively, they can operate contemporaneously within the same settlement. These patterns serve all the more to underline the highly variable socio-political character of northern Euphrates Valley settlements, and the distinctive local traditions of their populations.

Economic or political control from elsewhere?

Foreign powers or states may have exerted their political or economic authority over the northern Euphrates region at one time or another during the course of the third millennium. Yet how, if at all, did their exercise of power affect the size, composition, socio-political structure and configuration of settlements in the Euphrates region?

One of the most widely known regional powers to have existed in Syria during the Early Bronze Age was the kingdom of Ebla, located in western Syria. Our information about this great centre comes from the thousands of inscribed clay tablets found in the archive rooms of Royal Palace G on the main mound at Ebla. The palace was destroyed in a massive conflagration when the city was conquered by the Akkadian king Sargon or his grandson Naram-Sin sometime during the latter part of the twenty-fourth century BC (Akkermans and Schwartz 2003: 244).

The cuneiform tablets from the Ebla archives span about 50 years during the reigns of the three successive Eblaite kings of the twenty-fourth century. From these tablets we learn that the city of Ebla had gained control over several smaller kingdoms and land through military actions and political alliances (Zettler 1997a: 1). Through its expansion, it came into contact with several other major political powers including Mari, an ancient city located on the Euphrates River near the modern border between Syria and Iraq.

Both Ebla and Mari had interests in the northern Euphrates Valley, and fought against one another in a series of wars for political and economic control over this region. Valuable information about this rivalry comes from a letter written by Enna-Dagan, king of Mari, to an unnamed individual at Ebla, in which he describes political and military events taking place during this period of inter-state warfare (Edzard 1981; Meyer 1996: 155–70). The events described in the letter appear to have taken place during the reigns of three Eblaite rulers, who probably lived some time in the early part of the twenty-fourth century. It would seem that for a period of time, the kingdom of Mari had gained considerable territory, having campaigned successfully into Upper Mesopotamia, where it took control over parts of the Khabur Plains, and conquered towns and cities along the Euphrates River as far north as southern Turkey. At this time, Ebla was obliged to pay tribute to Mari (Astour 1992: 39). The political successes of Mari were reversed, however, during the period of the king Irkab-Damu, who was able to re-assert Ebla's power, consequently taking for itself many of the cities and towns that had previously fallen to Mari (Astour 1992: 39–40).

Through Ebla texts such as Enna-Dagan's letter, we gain precious information about the Euphrates River Valley. We learn the names of several important towns and cities that were taken in Mari's military campaigns, among them, Emar, Ebal, Gasur, Ra'aq, Burman, and Carchemish (Astour 1992: 32; Bonechi 1998: 227–8; Bunnens in press). The exact location of Emar and Carchemish on the Euphrates is secure thanks to later inscriptions and archaeological evidence. Of the remaining cities, their appearance in other Ebla texts, often in close association with Emar and Carchemish, strongly suggest that they too should be located in the Euphrates River Valley. Astour places many of these sites in the Tabqa region above the site of Emar, on the left bank (Astour 1992: 34). While their precise location is still uncertain, some scholars have suggested that the city of Burman should be equated with the site of Tell es-Sweyhat (Astour 1992: 35 n. 213; Meyer 1996: 170; Zettler 1997a: 9), while Gasur could be represented by the third millennium settlement at Halawa Tell A (Meyer 1996: 169).

While Ebla had control over the northern Euphrates Valley of Syria after its victory over Mari, it is difficult to understand the exact nature of this control. On the one hand, Ebla texts often describe the Euphrates cities as having been ruled by an 'en'. This term generally refers to a king at the city of Ebla, an individual in whom political, economic and religious powers were concentrated. The Ebla texts tell us, for example, that Burman was the seat of an 'en' and we even know the name of that ruler (En'ar-Halam) and his queen (Zimini-barku) (Danti 2000: 83). Gasur is also reported as having had an 'en', although after Ebla regained this kingdom it was dismantled and thereafter may not have been ruled by such an individual (Astour 1992: 45). The city of Emar was the most noteworthy, having been ruled by a queen (*ma-lik-tum*) whose name was Tiša-Lim who herself may have been from the ruling family at Ebla.

On the other hand, there are several other places for which no mention of an 'en' is given at all. The city of Carchemish, for example, was not distinguished by this kind of authority, although we learn that it was governed by an 'ugula' or overseer. Guy Bunnens argues on the basis of this evidence that Carchemish was only a settlement of minor importance during the period of the Ebla archives, and thus should not be considered of the rank and power of other Euphrates kingdoms (Bunnens in press).

One must remain somewhat cautious, however, of how such terms for individuals or officials are interpreted, especially when they are applied to the Euphrates Valley. All the available historical information derives from Ebla itself, and its administrative documents were largely composed and inscribed by Ebla officials and scribes. These individuals may have had a different perspective on the political and economic organization of a distant region like the Euphrates Valley than what actually existed in that area. Thus, individuals referred to as 'en's in that region may have had different responsibilities and degrees of authority from those of the great kings at Ebla. Moreover, it is important to remember that the political structure of each polity within the Euphrates Valley was itself highly variable. Some cities were defined by rulers of considerable status and power, while in others absolute power was constrained or offset by more collective decision making groups or assemblies. As we have already discussed, later textual sources from Mari, which describe the highly divergent responsibilities of the assembly known as the *tahtamum* from city to city, provide excellent documentation of the fluctuating nature of political power in this region. Thus, while terms such as 'en' and 'ugula' in Ebla tablets may seem to be describing individuals with well-defined, well-understood roles and responsibilities, in reality these individuals performed highly divergent functions according to the local political traditions of the settlements in which they exercised authority.

Whichever way we reconstruct the political organization of the Euphrates Valley, the relationship between this region and its Ebla overlord likely consisted of client kingdoms who, although swearing allegiance to the Ebla king, at the same time, maintained a high degree of local autonomy. Obligations to the king of Ebla would have included the payment of a fixed amount of tribute in the form of various goods such as metals, livestock, cloths and other crafted goods. When requested, teams of corvée workers may also have been sent to Ebla (Astour 1992: 40, 45, 51–2). Nonetheless, matters concerning the administration of local communities and the methods by which tribute was to be extracted were probably left entirely up to local authorities to organize and execute.

Archaeologically, there is slim evidence testifying to Ebla's supremacy over the Euphrates region. The twenty-fourth century, corresponding to Phase 4 in our Euphrates sequence, does not witness a radical re-organization or re-configuration of settlements. Sites previously occupied in Phase 3 continue to be inhabited during Phase 4. There is no appreciable increase or diminishment in site size during this period. Although it has already been observed that Euphrates Valley sites never attained a large size during the Early Bronze Age, one cannot easily attribute this situation to a regional power such as Ebla, which in its pre-eminent position in Syria constrained other settlements from growing and becoming potential rivals. Euphrates settlements had been small long before Ebla's rise to power, and most would not grow larger after its demise. As was discussed earlier, other factors such as the marginal environment of the region, which impeded the productive capacity of most communities, as well as the river valley's topography, in which only a limited amount of cultivable land was available, are more likely to have affected the size of settlements than the territorial ambitions of a large regional power.

There is little physical evidence from within Euphrates sites that attest to Ebla's position as an overlord. Artifacts associated with an Eblaite administrative system, such as inscribed tablets, Eblaite cylinder seals, and other objects, such as measures and weights, are conspicuously absent. It is also difficult to identify any large building from which a governor or overseer of Ebla might have ruled. The large warehouse, kitchen building and public reception hall on the main mound at Tell es-Sweyhat might be the best candidate for such a governor's 'palace', but this complex does not appear until Phase 5 of the Euphrates Early Bronze Age sequence, well after Ebla's demise.

One noteworthy development might prove to be linked to the power of Ebla. During Phase 4 in the Euphrates Valley, several new settlements were founded, most of them consisting of small villages and towns. These settlements' appearance probably reflects a concurrent intensification of the subsistence economy during this period, in which more land was put under cultivation and pastoral production increased. It is possible that this intensified economy was linked to the demands made from regional centres such as Mari and Ebla, whose requested tribute would have consisted of goods primarily in the form of agricultural produce, goat's hair and sheep's wool. The consolidation of additional key control points and crossing places along the river (e.g. el-Qitar, Jebel Ahmar and Tell Jouweif), might also be linked to this system of tribute supply, serving to regulate and ensure an efficient flow of surplus goods to Ebla. Thus, even though direct evidence attesting to the economic and political power of Ebla is invisible in the Euphrates Valley, this more indirect evidence, in the form of land intensification and improved transport links, could well highlight that city-state's important presence in the Syrian Euphrates.

These foreign demands hardly had the effect of crippling the communities of the Euphrates region. On the contrary, concurrent with the increase in the number of settlements in Phase 4, one sees considerable urban development at several settlements, reflected by the increase in grandiose works such as monumental temples, shaft and chamber tombs with rich burial offerings, burial tumuli, and substantial fortifications. It would seem that the region's contact with foreign powers such as Mari and Ebla served only to augment its urban character, encouraging the growth in complexity of its internal socio-economic structures, and opening it up to cultural influences and economic relationships from the outside.

DISCUSSION

This brief overview has shown that human settlements were abundant during the third millennium in the northern Syrian Euphrates Valley. Ancient sites have been identified along the entire course of the Euphrates River under investigation here, and their occupation ranges from the earliest phases of the third millennium up to its closing centuries. It would appear that settlement reached its peak frequency during Phase 4 in the third quarter of the millennium. As we will elaborate further in forthcoming chapters, it is also during this period that most settlements exhibit their strongest urban character, characterized by monumental works, planned domestic housing, institutionalized religion, developed funerary traditions as well as the activities of craft specialists. Even though this period witnessed military interventions and economic pressures from regional powers such as Ebla and Mari, it was a time of relative abundance, when human groups had successfully harnessed the resources of their environment and consolidated their local socio-political structures so as to enjoy considerable prosperity.

At the same time, the landscape and climate of the Euphrates region constrained the sizes and urban scale of such settlements. The narrow and segmented landscape of the river valley, and its climate of limited rainfall, meant that settlements could only expand to a certain size before running out of physical space in which to grow, and before exhausting their local resources. In this way, Euphrates settlements differed considerably from those in other parts of Greater Mesopotamia. Thus, even the site of Tell Hadidi, attaining a grand size of 56 ha during the Early Bronze Age, is still only half of the size of some cities that developed in the wide, well-watered Khabur Plains of northeastern Syria and northern Iraq during the same time period, and but a fraction of the massive Early Dynastic cities that developed in the southern Mesopotamian alluvial plain.

But what Euphrates settlements lack in terms of size, they make up for by their interesting and distinctive urban character, which sets them apart from contemporary cities elsewhere. We might even argue that the same factors that limited settlement growth were also responsible for these unique qualities. Thus, the fragmented landscape and the narrowness of the river valley that prevented settlements from growing beyond a certain point also prevented any one settlement from developing to such a size and stature that it could dominate other settlements beyond its own small neighbourhood. As a result, the Euphrates Valley of Syria does not witness the formation of any type of political configuration that approaches the level of a regional state, controlled by one pre-eminent city that politically or economically dominated all other settlements. Even within the smaller, river embayments of the Euphrates, we have shown that settlement hierarchies were relatively undeveloped, such that even small sites possessed a degree of autonomy, wealth and urban character, these features incompatible with their total subordination to a larger settlement. Again, we might attribute this distinct-ive settlement configuration to the composition of the riverine environment. Its variable landscape and the diverging, local economic opportunities it provided meant that settlements could grow relatively independent of one another, each developing its own economy, socio-political structure and ideo-logical traditions, and thus each in turn cultivating its own distinctive form of urban life. To the best of our knowledge, this very interesting and unique settlement phenomenon finds no precise parallels elsewhere in the ancient Near East.

4

DEFENCE OF EARLY BRONZE AGE CITIES

Defensive systems were an extremely common feature of cities in the Syrian Euphrates region during the third millennium. They testify to the ever-present threat of hostilities which characterized the region during this time. This threat of danger seems to have been especially present towards the end of the Early Bronze age, when nearly all sites bore some evidence of strong, defensive structures. Given their proximity to vast tracts of empty steppe land rising behind the narrow strip of river valley, the settlements were probably perennially vulnerable to pillaging and attacks by desert marauders. It is also possible that with the growth of cities in the Early Bronze Age and their accompanying wealth and territorial expansion, hostilities developed between neighbouring polities in competition over available natural resources, pasturages and agricultural land. Such competition may have been further exacerbated by climatic fluctuations or environmental degradation (Weiss *et al.* 1993; Algaze *et al.* 2001: 69–70; Wilkinson 2003: 104–5).

That some military aggression emanated from cities and states beyond the Syrian Euphrates is known from ancient cuneiform sources. These outline the territorial aspirations of the kings of Ebla and Mari during the twenty-fourth century BC, both of whom were known to campaign into the northern Euphrates (Edzard 1981; Astour 1992: 26–40; Meyer 1996: 155–70). The indomitable armies of the Akkadian kings Sargon and Naram-Sin also forayed into the north, passing through the Euphrates en route to their capture and destruction of Ebla and Armānum, two powerful cities to the northwest (Frayne 1993: E2.1.1.11, E4.1.4.26). Reports of such military campaigns, in which cities and fortresses are described as being defeated and turned into 'tells and ruins', indicates that siege tactics were the most common form of warfare, at least during the period in which these sources were composed (Burke 2004: 50–1). In view of the presence of these foreign aggressors and their numerable victories, it is understandable that many settlements would have spent considerable time, energy and resources protecting themselves against the predations of these formidable forces.

Early Bronze Euphrates fortifications ordinarily took the form of thick walls of stone and mud brick encircling the principal part of the settlement, usually located on high ground. In at least one case a second wall was known to have enclosed a lower town where additional housing, food-producing installations and craft workshops were situated. Fortification walls frequently featured buttresses, towers, fortified gates, sloping ramparts, glacis and fosses. Such defensive elements provided protection against enemy attacks, in which hazardous missiles such as arrows, sling stones and javelins were directed against the besieged inhabitants. High fortification walls would have deterred enemy attackers from scaling the defences with ladders, while thick walls would have made breaching, tunnelling or undermining a costly and labourious undertaking (Burke 2004: 72–3). Thick, steeply sloping ramparts constructed against the outer face of the city walls protected these walls from erosion (Parr 1968: 43). They also deterred the use of the battering ram, a highly effective weapon used to prize away pieces of city walls in order to breach or undermine them (Burke 2004: 78–80). Large ramparts may also have lengthened the distance between the defenders and the attackers, making enemy arrows and sling stones fall short of their targets (Tubb 1985: 193–6). Ditches or fosses carved in bedrock at the base of a rampart would have prevented any siege engine or battering ram from being brought directly up against the fortifications (Burke 2004: 77). Enemy sappers, in their efforts to tunnel through the city defences, would have been compelled to dig through bedrock, all the while being exposed to the deadly arrow-firing defenders on the walls above the ramparts (Stager 1991; Burke 2004: 24).

Besides the threat of enemy aggression, these thick walls also possibly served to protect some settlements from natural forces, namely flooding, which may have been quite hazardous and destructive during seasons of exceptionally high river inundations. Settlements located in or just above the level of the Euphrates flood plain were particularly vulnerable to this type of natural calamity, and their inhabitants may have constructed thick perimeter walls as a defence against encroaching waters. That such flooding did occur in antiquity has been documented through geomorphological investigations conducted at the site of Jerablus Tahtani. These studies show that excessively high Euphrates flooding took place towards the end of the Early Bronze Age, possibly having negative effects not only on the settlement itself, but also on its immediate agricultural environs (Peltenburg 1999a: 103).

Not only were defensive works typical of large settlements, such as Tell es-Sweyhat and Tell Banat, they constituted essential elements of even the smallest settlements, such as Jerablus Tahtani and Tell al-ʿAbd, neither of which were more than a few hectares in area during periods of their largest settlement extent. Such measures taken to fortify strongly even the smallest settlements testify to the importance of the sites in spite of their diminutive size. In addition to serving simply as places of residence, these sites no doubt acted as repositories, where valuable raw and finished goods and agricultural produce could be stored and safeguarded. Important personnel serving the communities in religious or secular administrative capacities were also lodged and protected within these strong encircling walls.

Chronology and overall configuration of city fortifications

The beginnings of Early Bronze Age defensive systems can be traced back to the earliest EB levels at the site of Tell Habuba Kabira (levels 2 and 3), which date to the first centuries of the third millennium BC (Phases 1–2) (Figure 5.5a). Excavations along the southeastern side of the site have revealed a series of mud brick buildings which were built side by side, and whose back walls formed a solid line along the eastern side of the site facing the Euphrates River (Heusch 1980: 161). Overall, these buildings would have given the exterior facade of the settlement a strong, defensive appearance (Heusch 1980: 163). In the earliest levels of occupation at the site of Tell B at Halawa, another early EB site (Phases 1–2), a thick mud brick wall, reinforced several times over the course of its lifetime through the addition of parallel courses along its interior and buttresses on the exterior, seems to have enclosed several of the early habitations of the settlement (Figure 5.1) (Orthmann 1989: 87–8). The presence of these substantial works at both Tell Habuba Kabira and Halawa Tell B indicates that even during this early period of urban development in the Euphrates Valley, there existed some form of organized labour and pooling of resources on the part of the settlements' inhabitants to construct such lines of defence. This evidence also shows a preoccupation with the protection of the settlements' population and assets, possibly prompted by the threat of attacks from the outside.

Besides the early evidence for defensive works at Tell Habuba Kabira and Halawa B, excavations in the area of the central mound at Tell es-Sweyhat have exposed a high mud brick structure dating from the early to middle part of the third millennium (Phase 3). Built of solid mud brick, it had been enlarged a number of times over its long history (Figure 4.1) (Danti and Zettler 2002: 40). The core section, built in segments, was at least 5.5 m high, and appears to have been an irregular rectangle whose northern face was at least 10 m in length. Its face was stepped back, or battered, and covered with a heavy red plaster (Danti and Zettler 2002: 40–1). The latest enlargement of the structure was on the western side. Taking the form of a rounded face, it was constructed of red and grey bricks set on and against stone footings (Figure 5.7). Some of the stone courses of this foundation were quite substantial, comprising several rows of large boulders (Figure 4.2). Overall these massive stones gave the structure an impressive, monumental appearance on this side (Armstrong and Zettler 1997: 18).

Figure 4.1 Section through mud brick core of citadel structure, Tell es-Sweyhat.

Figure 4.2 Large boulders of rounded bastion of citadel structure, Tell es-Sweyhat.

A 1 metre-wide wall, perhaps part of a tower, projected from the front of the western face (Danti and Zettler 2002: 41). Excavations have further revealed at the northern end a stairway leading to the top of the platform, while on top, a vaulted corridor led to the east (Danti and Zettler 2002: 41).

Originally there was speculation that this massive construction at Tell es-Sweyhat might have had a religious function, possibly serving as a massive cult platform or *bamah*, or a support for an as-yet-undiscovered temple (Danti and Zettler 2002: 42). Further probes in and around this structure, however, have confirmed that this was a massive citadel wall. It would have both raised the settlement several metres above its original height, and supported structures within it. Future excavations on the summit of this citadel may eventually help to determine the nature and significance of the buildings it enclosed. Whatever the case, this mud brick structure was a massive building project. Considerable planning, resources and labour must have been required for the successful completion and maintenance of this formidable, imposing fortification during an early phase of the site's urban development.

Solid defensive walls continued to be built throughout the remainder of the Early Bronze Age, serving to encircle and enclose principal areas of occupation. The back walls of interior structures were occasionally used to form segments of the wall, although it was more common for interior houses and other buildings to have been constructed separately from the city wall. By the middle of the Early Bronze Age (Phase 3), substantial city walls have become a characteristic feature of a number of sites along the length of the Euphrates River, including Jerablus Tahtani, Tell Banat, Tell al-ʿAbd, Tell Habuba Kabira, and Munbaqa. The late Early Bronze Age (Phases 4–5) witnessed some of the most sophisticated and imposing defensive wall systems of the third millennium, attested at sites such as Tell es-Sweyhat, Tell Qannas, Halawa Tell A (Figure 4.3), Habuba Kabira (Figure 5.5d–f) and Selenkahiye.

While the norm was for a single city wall to encircle most or all of a settlement, at least one Euphrates site boasted two lines of defences. At Tell es-Sweyhat, during the period of its fluorescence in the Late Early Bronze Age (Phase 5), the central high mound was encircled by a 2.5 metre-wide brick wall (Figure 4.4). Along its western side rose a 7 metre-wide tower (Holland 1977: 37). Caches of clay sling bullets and a willow leaf-shaped arrowhead found in rooms immediately inside the city wall and tower confirm the defensive function of these features (Holland 1976: 49, 1977: 37). At the same time, excavations, aerial photographs and geomagnetic mapping confirm that Tell es-Sweyhat's outer or lower town, which had grown around all four sides of the acropolis mound, was also encircled by a wall or series of walls of varying construction (Armstrong and Zettler 1997: 48–51; Peregrine *et al.* 1997: 78–9; see also below). Although this double fortification configuration has been verified only at Tell es-Sweyhat, it is also possible

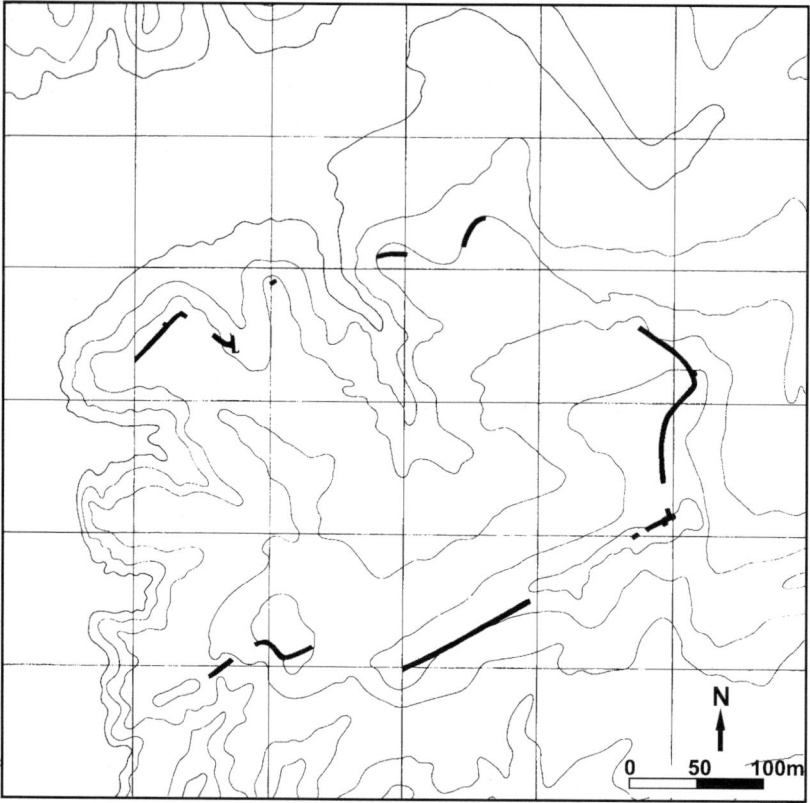

Figure 4.3 Line of city wall around EB settlement at Halawa Tell A.

that the large site of Tell Hadidi, directly across the river, also featured two lines of defence. The high tell was probably fortified in the Early Bronze Age, as evidenced by fragmentary remains of a wall that was subsequently damaged or removed by later Bronze Age defensive systems (Dornemann 1979: 116). The lower town, which comprised an extensive area of domestic neighbour-hoods and burials by the end of the Early Bronze Age, may also have been encircled by a city wall, although no investigations of this defensive system have been undertaken to date (Dornemann 1979: 116).

Citadel cities

The configuration of a double line of defence on the acropolis and lower town seems closely connected to the function and nature of the structures enclosed by these fortifications. A. Leo Oppenheim was the first to describe what he dubbed 'citadel cities', in which the palace of the ruler, as well as

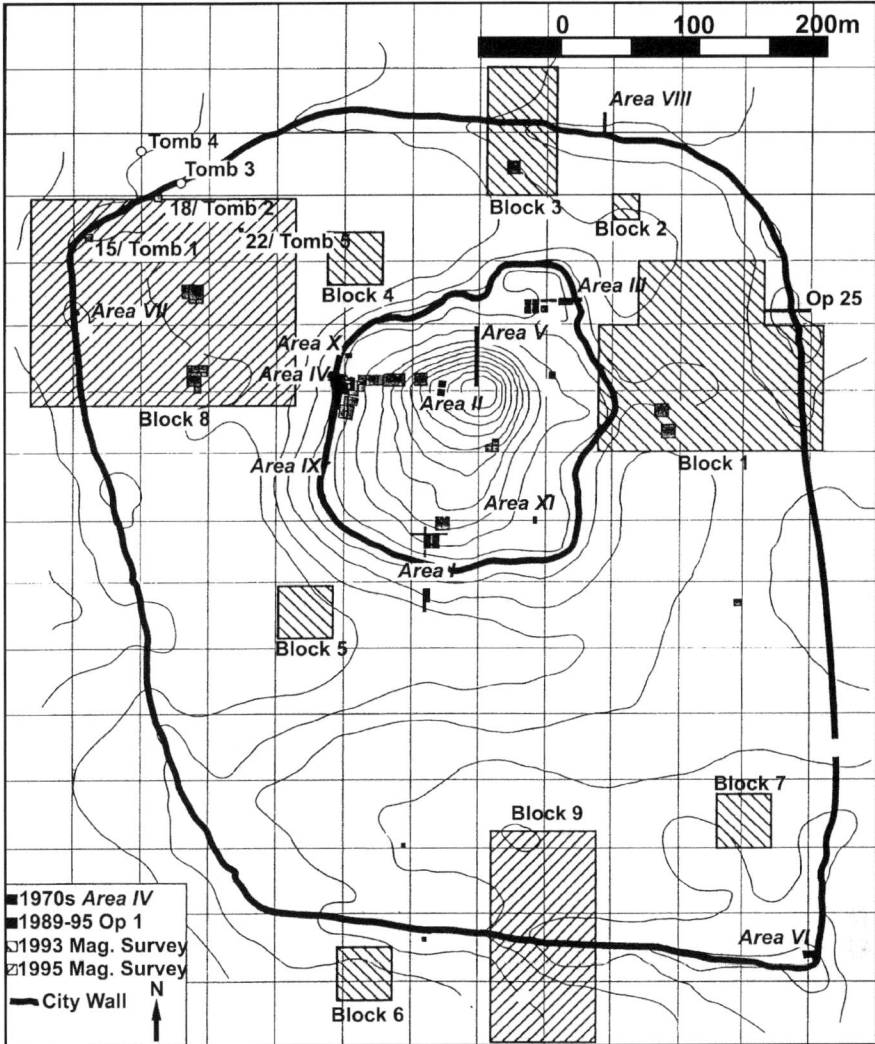

Figure 4.4 Tell es-Sweyhat, showing excavated squares and inner and outer city walls.

the treasury, military headquarters and temples, occupied a high central position in the city. These structures were encircled by a defensive wall, while the citizenry were settled outside them and were protected, as a rule, by a second line of walls (Oppenheim 1964: 130; Zettler 1997a: 7). 'Citadel cities' were seen as particularly diagnostic of the urban landscape of Upper Mesopotamia, Syria, Anatolia and Palestine (Oppenheim 1964: 130; Zettler *et al.* 1996: 19).

75

Archaeological investigations of several third millennium sites such as Tell Taya in northern Iraq and Tell Leilan in northeastern Syria have shown that northern Mesopotamian cities are quite consistent with Oppenheim's description of 'citadel cities'. Both these sites are distinguished by high, central mounds and densely occupied lower towns (Zettler 1997a: 7). The so-called *Kranzhügel*, or 'wreath-mounds', of the relatively dry regions to the east of the Euphrates, between the Balikh and Khabur Rivers, may also be included as a distinctive form of 'citadel cities'. Tell Chuera and Tell Beydar are excellent examples of the curiously circular *Kranzhügel*, both of which featured fortified upper towns containing palaces and temples, and surrounding lower towns which were enclosed by circular mud brick defensive walls (Novák 1995: 173–82; Akkermans and Schwartz 2003: 256–9; Suleiman 2003: 303). Finally, ancient textual sources from Ebla present a similar picture of a city dominated in the centre by a high acropolis where the palace and its royal dependencies were located, while the lower city comprised residential neighbourhoods of more modest structures (Zettler 1997a: 7).

In the Euphrates Valley of Syria, Tell es-Sweyhat is surely a 'citadel city', with its central high mound comprising a principal reception hall and associated warehouses, kitchens and workrooms, all circumvallated by a thick fortification wall, while the bulk of the population settled in a fortified lower town. As we have already noted, Tell Hadidi may have had a similar configuration. It is possible that Tell Habuba Kabira was also of this type in the late third millennium, when important elite buildings appear to have been given pride of place within the central walled high place of this settlement. It is unfortunate that the nature and extent of this site's 'lower town', which extended down the slopes beyond the fortified centre, have only been cursorily investigated and described (Heusch 1980: 172).

These examples of 'citadel cities' highlight a situation in which a city's power and authority were concentrated on a central high place, strongly safeguarded and demarcated from the remainder of the settlement by fortification walls. While such 'citadel cities' are present, however, they are not representative of all settlements of the Euphrates Valley of northern Syria. Many settlements appear to have been enclosed within single defensive walls only, the temples and other elite buildings sharing the same interior space as domestic housing and production installations. At Halawa Tell A, for example, excavations have revealed that the interior of the heavily fortified settlement was characterized by both domestic neighbourhoods and a long-roomed temple. While the temple was demarcated from secular architecture by a temenos wall, this wall had no defensive function, and the temple complex as a whole did not tower over the rest of the settlement. The site of Tell Banat was almost certainly enclosed by a large wall during its existence in the Early Bronze Age. But excavations on the highest, western ridge of the mound have unearthed a series of pottery kilns and potters' workshops, not elite temples and palaces (McClellan 1999: 417). The elite architecture uncovered at Tell Banat is located in Area C, several metres lower than the high western ridge (McClellan 1999: 417). The settlement at Selenkahiye, circumvallated by a strong defensive system of walls and a rampart, was primarily characterized by areas of domestic housing, particularly in the central sector of the site. It is possible that an elite building of some importance for the community occupied the elevated area to the south where the modern cemetery exists, although this area has not been explored (Van Loon 2001: 3.95). Even so, this locale is not significantly higher than other parts of the settlement, nor is it particularly central.

It may be important to note that even true 'citadel city' configurations such as at Tell es-Sweyhat did not develop until quite late in the Early Bronze Age. Tell es-Sweyhat was settled more or less continuously throughout the third millennium BC, but it did not grow to include a central high tell and expansive fortified lower town until the very last centuries of the third millennium in Phase 5, when it experienced a dramatic increase in population. Before this time, all settlement would have been restricted to the citadel in the central mound area, where there may have been little architectural or spatial distinction between common and elite architecture.

A similar development appears to characterize Tell Habuba Kabira, another settlement with a long occupation history spanning much of the third millennium BC. While the mound appears to have been reconstructed with elaborate fortifications and possibly elite buildings in the latest phases of the Early Bronze Age (Phases 4–5), for much of the earlier third millennium, settlement inside the city walls appears to have featured simple domestic installations and household complexes. There is no evidence that any additional settlement existed outside of this area in the earliest periods, nor did a second line of defences exist.

In sum, true 'citadel cities' do not appear to be distinguishing features of the Euphrates Valley of Syria until late in the third millennium BC, but even at this period they do not characterize every urban settlement. The reasons for this varied pattern are unclear. We suggest that as well as geographical-spatial considerations, physically constraining or limiting the ways in which settlement features, including defensive systems, were laid out, perhaps certain social and political tendencies within the communities influenced their configurations. The presence of 'citadel cities' presupposes the existence of a strongly hierarchical system of control and authority, in which an elite power in the community presided over the settlement in most economic, political and religious affairs, and upon which all inhabitants of the city were dependent. Yet, for the Euphrates Valley of Syria, we argue that during much of the third millennium BC, the continued existence of decentralizing tendencies within the social and political fabric of the Euphrates communities may have offset or hindered the growth of such systems of centralized authority and power. Such tendencies could explain the absence in many Early Bronze Age settlements of clearly distinguishable central zones of elite structures, demarcated by citadel walls and dominating the community of citizens that surrounded them.

City walls: materials and thicknesses

While some of the earliest examples of city walls appear to have been built solely from mud brick,[1] city walls constructed from the mid-to-late third millennium usually consisted of heavy stone foundations with super-structures of mud brick.[2] Foundation trenches for the stone bases of these walls have not been discerned. Rather, courses of stone were laid out over the site's natural contours, often directly on top of virgin soil (Orthmann 1981: 10; 1989: 13; Finkbeiner 1995: 56). On occasion, wall foundations were set on prepared surfaces of pebbles and gravel, as in the case of the city wall of Selenkahiye (Van Loon 2001: 3.51 and 3.86), or on a thick layer of clay, as at Tell es-Sweyhat (Zettler 1997b: 49, 53).

City walls were of varying thicknesses, ranging from one metre to 10 metres. Although none of the mud brick city walls from the Syrian Euphrates have been preserved to their original heights, it is possible that many of these walls stood quite high. Aaron Burke, in his magisterial study of ancient Near Eastern fortifications, summons evidence from archaeo-logical, textual, and modern sources in order to ascertain the original heights of ancient mud brick defensive walls from the Middle Bronze Age in the Levant (Burke 2004: 117–19). His estimate of 10 m (Burke 2004: 315) as the average height seems a reasonable figure to apply to most EB Euphrates defences as well, especially noting that the majority of their foundations were over 3 m in thickness, an ample base for a high mud brick wall.

Site size appears to have no correlation whatsoever to the thickness or the height of defensive walls. Thus, Tell al-ʿAbd, a site estimated to have been no more than 4 ha during the middle phase of the Early Bronze Age (Phase 3), boasted the widest city walls, measuring up to 10 m in places (Finkbeiner 1994: 116; 1997: 100). In contrast, the nearly 16 ha settlement at Halawa Tell A had a city wall that did not exceed 3.6 m (Orthmann 1981: 9). Wall-size might be more accurately related to the natural defensibility of the settlement. Thus, in the case of Halawa Tell A, the settlement was located on a high terrace, well-protected on its sides by steep wadis and the river valley itself. These topographically favourable conditions, together with Halawa's other defensive features, including towers, buttresses and a rampart, may have made a wider city wall unnecessary. In contrast, Tell al-ʿAbd, located on a relatively low terrace near the edge of the flood plain, had no natural features to aid in its defence. A thick wall, with the addition of a formidable sloping rampart, was the kind of human initiative required to fortify this vulnerable settlement.

City walls clearly grew larger and stronger over the course of the third millennium. Thus, whereas Tell al-ʿAbd's first city wall, founded around the beginning of Phase 3, was only 2.5 m in width, it was succeeded by a second phase of fortifications which comprised a wall thickness of up to 10 m (Finkbeiner 1997: 100). The settlement at Tell Habuba Kabira went from possessing a city wall which in Phase 3 was less than 2.5 m in width (level 6: Heusch 1980: 166), to a wall that in Phases 4–5 had nearly doubled in size (level 15: Heusch 1980: 174). Halawa Tell A experienced similar reinforcements in its second major phase in Phase 5 of the EB (Orthmann 1981: 9). In one sector of the city at Selenkahiye, where the sequence of city walls is particularly clear, one may observe progressive re-buildings and enlargements of the city wall, from its original width of about 2.50 m (Van Loon 2001: 3.51) to its final phase, late in the EB, when the wall measured about 3.6 m in thickness (Van Loon 2001: 3.53). These successive reinforcements and enlargements to the city wall suggest that the threat of danger in the region had not subsided over time, but increased in the last centuries of the third millennium. It is interesting that a similar trend has now been observed in the Upper Euphrates basin of southeastern Anatolia. At the site of Titriş Höyük, for example, the fortification system that encircled most of the settlement was re-built and strengthened in the late EB (Algaze et al. 2001: 33–4). One wonders if all of the Northern Euphrates Basin may have been confronted by similar sources of warfare and instability, and if so, what the source of these troubles may have been.

Casemate walls

Casemate walls, which are composed of two parallel walls with compartmentalized spaces in between, are well-known from later periods of antiquity, especially from the Levant (Herzog 1997: 320). Their origins, however, seem to hearken back to the early third millennium elsewhere in the Near East. In the Euphrates Valley, a casemate system has been reported at the early EB site of Halawa Tell B, where a long mud brick wall along the northern slope of the tell featured buttresses, cross-walls, and 1.5 × 1.5 m square chambers found full of settlement debris (Orthmann 1989: 88). The Halawa excavators suggest that this 'casemate' system of filled spaces in the wall may have served to relieve the pressure caused by the massive quantity of surrounding brickwork, producing overall a stable and enduring defensive system (Orthmann 1989: 88). Alternatively, the system would have served to economize on construction costs by decreasing the amount of prepared material and labour (Herzog 1997: 320). Another site possessing a mud brick casemate wall is Munbaqa, dating to the mid-to-late third millennium BC (Phases 4–5) (Figure 4.5). This wall, which encircled the hilltop or 'Kuppe' where the Early Bronze Age settlement was located, was distinguished by small 1.2 metre-wide interior compartments, principally

Figure 4.5 Eastern casemate wall on the 'Kuppe' at Munbaqa.

along the eastern side (Eichler *et al.* 1984: 73; Machule *et al.* 1986: 81–3). These spaces had mostly been filled with broken mud bricks, although in one instance, a large storage jar had been sunk into the space (Room 9: Eichler *et al.* 1984: 73). Given this evidence, we can suppose that during periods of potential attacks from the outside, efforts were made to fill in the casemate spaces, thus creating a solid and effective line of defence, but during periods of comparable safety, this casemate system was used as an area for storage and additional habitation space (Burke 2004: 122).

The outer town of Tell es-Sweyhat may also have been equipped, at least in part, with a casemate wall. In Operation 15, sited along the northwestern side of the lower town, excavations have revealed a thick wall oriented northeast by southwest, and a wall running perpendicular to it on the interior, southeastern side (Zettler 1997b: Figure 3.12). This was posited to be part of a casemate outer fortification wall, although the evidence here is still equivocal and further investigations will be required to clarify the situation (Zettler 1997b: 49).

Buttresses and towers

In addition to the stone and brick courses of the city's enclosure wall, accompanying defensive works often existed. Towers were frequently erected, these either built at intervals along stretches of the city wall, or at especially

80

vulnerable or strategic positions in the city's defences. Towers have been reported at Jerablus Tahtani along the fort's eastern side in Area I, one of which was situated immediately south of the postern entrance of the fort annex (Peltenburg *et al.* 2000: 56). Another tower-like structure was reported on the fort's northern side (in Area IV), attached to the wall's exterior (Peltenburg *et al.* 1996: 8). Last, it is reported that two towers flanked the southern entrance at the base of the settlement by the river. Lack of time and erosion prevented a further investigation of the area around these towers, but it may be possible that these features were part of a second, lower circuit wall (Peltenburg *et al.* 2000: 71).

Tower-like projections have been reported at the northern end of the gateway through the city wall on the northern side of Tell al-ʿAbd's circuit wall (Finkbeiner 1995: 57–8). In levels 5 and 6 at Tell Habuba Kabira, the southeastern corner of the outer wall was fitted with a solid rectangular structure, possibly the base of a tower (Heusch 1980: 164–5). Such a tower would have been an appropriate defensive structure to guard one of the principal entrances to the inner city of the tell, which was situated directly to the west. At Selenkahiye, a gateway through the city wall on the western side of the settlement was flanked by two square towers that projected into the interior of the settlement (Van Loon 2001: 3.89).

At Halawa Tell A the city wall was fortified at fairly regular intervals with a series of projecting buttresses. Such a buttress is reported in Quadrant U1a, for example, where it takes the form of a projection in the wall, producing a 2.5 metre-wide wall at this location (Figure 4.6). There is another buttress in Area X.6d, preserved as a row of stones to the north of the city wall (Orthmann 1981: 10). A larger buttress is seen in Quadrant PII (Orthmann 1989: 16 and Beilage 2). In at least two of these cases, the buttresses were added to the city wall in the later phase 3b (Orthmann 1981: 10; 1989: 13), suggesting additional efforts to support and strengthen the town defences.

Like buttresses, towers appear to have been later additions at Halawa Tell A, associated with the later EB phase of settlement there (Orthmann 1989: 13, 16). The base of a tower was found along the site's eastern side, where the city wall makes a turn to the north at a corner on the top of a high crest (Quadrant P). The tower was built at the corner, projecting to the east and south (Orthmann 1989: 12, 16; Beilage 2). Only the solid stone foundations of this tower have been preserved, although it could well have featured a mud brick superstructure that stood quite high (Orthmann 1989: 16). Another, similar construction was found further to the north along the eastern side (in U.1c–2c), where the wall takes an abrupt turn, this time to the northwest (Figure 4.6). The tower itself was built just to the northwest of that corner, and projected outward about 6 m (Orthmann 1989: 13; Beilage 1).

At Selenkahiye, there are several places at the northern end where the city wall extended further than the regular course of the wall, and these may

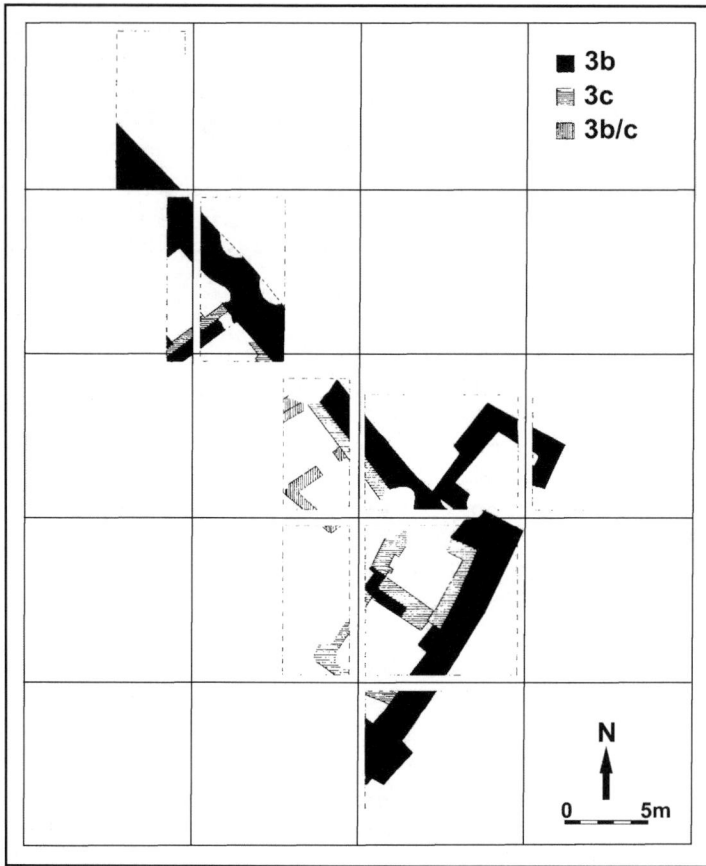

Figure 4.6 City wall, with projecting buttress, and corner tower (Quadrants U and T), Halawa Tell A.

possibly be interpreted as small buttress-like jumps in the wall (Van Loon 2001: 3.87). The kind of inset-offset effect that such buttresses produced is not too unlike that found in the latest fortification wall at Tell Habuba Kabira, which, in addition to featuring a large tower that juts out in the north, comprises a similar set of buttresses (Figure 5.5f) (Heusch 1980: 174–5).

The most prominent tower-base at Selenkahiye was located protruding from the town wall along the west part of the settlement (Figure 5.13). It was founded on large stones and measured about 5 × 5 m. This construction is generally thought to have been added fairly late in Selenkahiye's sequence of occupation, and thus represents one further example of efforts made at this site through time to strengthen and enlarge the settlement's defensive capabilities (Van Loon 2001: 3.89; Figure 3.18).

As a final example of an impressive tower-base, we may turn again to the inner fortification wall at Tell es-Sweyhat, which encircled a group of important public buildings on the central, high mound during the last phase of occupation at the site late in the third millennium BC (Phase 5). Excavations have revealed there a 7 metre-wide mud brick tower base, projecting out from the exterior western side of the citadel wall (Figure 6.4). This tower had been badly damaged either by attack or subsequent erosion (Holland 1977: 37). The fact that a cache of 35 complete and over 60 fragments of clay sling bullets were found in rooms immediately inside the citadel wall at this point underline the feature's defensive function (Holland 1977: 37).

Ramparts and glacis

Accompanying many city walls in the Euphrates Valley of Syria are ramparts, which are characterized by thick, sloping layers of gravel, or packed clay and earth, usually thrown up against the exterior face of the wall and sometimes adding elevation to it, in an effort to impede the advance of an enemy approaching the city walls (Mazar 1995: 1527–8; Herzog 1997: 320; Burke 2004: 96). Most of these ramparts are also accompanied by glacis, which refer to the surface treatment of the slope of the rampart. Such glacis, which were made from a variety of materials including gypsum plaster, crushed limestone, pebbles or packed clay, made the surface of the rampart impervious to rain and thus resistant to erosion (Burke 2004: 96). Originally believed to be Hyksos inventions of the second millennium BC, many earlier third millennium examples of ramparts and glacis have now been confirmed in Anatolia, Syria and Palestine (Parr 1968: 36–42; Burke 2004: 166–8).

In the northern Euphrates Valley of Syria, traces of such EB constructions have been reported at the site of Tell al-ʿAbd, where they were completed in conjunction with the enlargement of the city wall during the settlement's second phase in Phase 3 of the EB. The rampart is particularly well preserved in the northern end of the settlement, where it consisted of a sloping layer of packed clay built upon stone foundations and resting up against the mudbrick superstructure of the second phase of the city wall. The brickwork of the city wall receded in layers in order to accommodate this sloping revetment (Finkbeiner 1995: 56; Abb. 4; 1997: 100).

An impressive rampart has been found at the site of Jerablus Tahtani, attributed to the site's occupation in the mid-to-late third millennium BC (Phase 4). This artificial bank had been thrown up against the exterior of the city wall in the second phase of the city's defences. Not only did this bank dramatically change the outer appearance of the fort, internal arrangements were also affected, the most significant change being that much of the earliest phase of fort occupation was filled in, resulting in a new occupation level raised substantially above the level of the surrounding plain (Peltenburg *et al.* 1996: 8).

Where the bank or rampart is clearest in cross-section it can be discerned as a sloping fill consisting of bricky deposits and charcoal-flecked lenses which were covered with a thick layer of imported, crushed limestone. It was constructed in ascending horizontal courses, and sealed with a white-plastered smooth glacis surface laid at a slope of 25–30 degrees (Peltenburg *et al.* 1996: 8; Peltenburg 1999a: 101). In some places this white plaster cover was 10 cm in thickness (Peltenburg *et al.* 1996: 8–9). The excavators remark that the addition of this massive rampart and accompanying glacis would have altered the appearance of the site from one surrounded by a free-standing wall to a gleaming edifice artificially raised to an impressive height beside the river (Peltenburg 1999a: 101). One wonders if the addition of this rampart construction served more than a defensive function. Not only might it have provided additional protection against river erosion, but it may have served to give Jerablus a more imposing character, possibly imitating the monumental platforms that have recently been encountered at Tell es-Sweyhat and Tell Banat.

At Selenkahiye, in late EB strata (Phases 4–5), it is reported that a glacis of small pebbles sloped down to the north and covered a retaining wall built in front of the city wall (Van Loon 2001: 3.86). Further traces of a pebble glacis were discovered along the western outer face of the city wall. The glacis here appears to have filled a kind of fosse or gully about 5 m to the west of the outer wall face, suggesting the existence of an earlier pre-rampart defensive work at the base of the site (Van Loon 2001: 3.89).

Like Selenkahiye, the defensive rampart at Halawa Tell A was probably constructed some time in the Late EB (Phase 5). The sloping construction appears in conjunction with the earliest phase of the city wall, but becomes a much more imposing defensive feature in the subsequent phase. The first construction was actually only a glacis, since it consisted of a surface created by smoothed plaster and gravel, coating the outer surface of the slope of the natural hill for some 25–30 m (Orthmann 1989: 18, 37). Then, in the subsequent phase, this construction was thickened substantially with earth and packed clay, thereby transforming it into a formidable rampart over the slope of the hill (Figure 4.7). In places at the top of the rampart, just in front of the city wall, a stamped and levelled strip of clay and small stones, 2 to 5 m in width, formed a kind of walkway beside the city wall (Orthmann 1989: 15, 17). This 'walkway' was divided from the descending rampart by a narrow mud brick revetment wall constructed 2 to 5 m in front of the city wall itself. Such constructions are easily visible in Quadrant P (Orthmann 1989: 17, Beilage 2), and in front of the city wall in the area of Q.1e and Q.0d (Orthmann 1989: 37, Beilage 8).

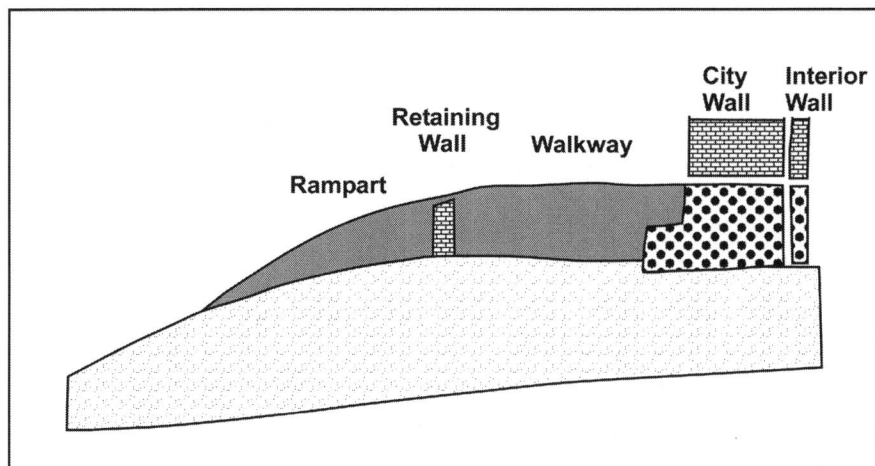

Figure 4.7 Schematic section of rampart, retaining wall and walkway against city wall, Halawa Tell A.

Fortifications of varying components

The site of Tell es-Sweyhat poses a special problem vis-à-vis city fortifications, since it appears to be composed of a number of highly varied defensive features. To date, investigations by archaeological excavations and geomagnetic prospection have failed to detect any consistency as to the layout and construction of these features from sector to sector. In one operation in the eastern lower town (Op. 25), the outer fortification consisted of an earthern rampart, approximately 18.50 m in width, that had been faced on the outside with a sloping stone revetment. On the inside, the rampart was supported by a 1.15 m mud brick wall set on stone foundations (Zettler 1997b: 49; Figures 3.13–14). It is uncertain if such a construction originally carried a higher embankment or wall on top. In any event, this type of rampart is unique to the Euphrates Valley of Syria thus far, although this construction has been compared to defensive systems at the EB sites of Titris Höyük, to the north in southeastern Anatolia, and Tell Mozan to the east (Buccellati and Kelly-Buccellati 1988: 58–9, 61–4; Algaze *et al.* 1995: 21–2; Zettler 1997b: 49).

In another area in the northwestern side of the outer town of Tell es-Sweyhat, excavations revealed fortifications of quite a different character (Op. 15). Here was found a wall, some 1.80 m in width, that consisted of courses of mud brick set over stone foundations (Zettler 1997b: 49). Running perpendicular and bonded to this wide wall on the interior was a somewhat narrower wall, dividing this interior space into two spaces, possibly rooms. As was reported earlier, this arrangement is suggestive of a casemate wall construction (Zettler 1997b: 49). The results of the geomagnetic mapping in the northwestern corner, however, have revealed a different configuration consisting of not one but two parallel runs of the outer wall. This double line was also detected along the northern stretch of the outer town (Zettler *et al.* 1996: 33). Last, a double line in the northwestern corner of the outer settlement was picked up on lower level aerial photographs (Zettler 1997b: 49; Peregrine *et al.* 1997: Figure 4.2). This double line could perhaps represent two fortification walls, one perhaps later than the other. Alternatively, it is possible that these linear features represent rampart revetments similar to those uncovered in Op. 25 on the eastern side (Peregrine *et al.* 1997: 77). In sum, the outer town fortifications at Tell es-Sweyhat present a rather diverse set of features that appear to vary from one city sector to another. Future investigations will no doubt shed further light on this unique set of constructions.

The town defences at Selenkahiye display considerable variation in planning and execution. The excavators of Selenkahiye have observed that the city wall was not consistently built. Several changes in direction, for example, were noted along the city wall's northern length. Along the western edge of the tell, the wall seems to take a 'curious, squiggly course' (Van Loon 2001: 3.103). All along the wall one sees changes in the dimensions of the wall. There is no regular or predictable placement of buttresses and towers, and a great number of variations in the numbers of reconstructions and enlargements have been observed.

Taken together, the evidence from Selenkahiye suggests perhaps that while city authorities may have generally indicated where the wall was to be built, the actual construction and refurbishment of that wall was left to individual quarters, or blocks, of the settlement. Accordingly, this assumption could mean that while a central authority may have existed at Selenkahiye, it was limited in power (Van Loon 2001: 110). One wonders if the town fortifications at Tell es-Sweyhat, also exhibiting considerable variability from one area to the next, can be explained in the same way.

DISCUSSION

Archaeological evidence clearly indicates the presence of well built, solid fortification systems along the length of the northern Euphrates Valley of Syria. Their appearance at the majority of settlements occupied during the Early Bronze Age indicates the necessity for safeguarding the cities' inhabitants and their possessions during a period that was probably marked by inter-city rivalries or the threat of attacks and raids by outside groups. Towards the end of the Early Bronze Age, when city defences grew particularly formidable, the presence of insecurity and the threat of attacks must have been quite pronounced, calling for the most secure of defensive systems. The fact that most EB settlements were destroyed, abandoned or experienced a dramatic decline in population and settlement size shortly after this period clearly testifies to the upheavals that must have shaken the region at this time.

While protection against attacks and raids was clearly the primary motivation for the construction of fortifications, it is also important to emphasize the psychological impact that such lines of defence may have had. Leo Oppenheim astutely observed that Mesopotamian city walls, by virtue of their large size and the quality of their construction, underlined the impressive urban character of the cities they encircled (Oppenheim 1964: 129). These walls served as potent symbols of the wealth, sophistication and strength of the populations whom they protected, setting them apart from the unsettled, less 'civilized' populations and regions that existed beyond.

We may imagine the dramatic impact that such works would have had upon outsiders, particularly in the case of EB settlements of the Euphrates, which are characterized not only by simple encircling walls, but also formidable towers, buttresses, ramparts and smooth, gleaming glacis. Moreover, the fact that even some of the smallest Euphrates' settlements were distinguished by such monumental constructions demonstrates membership within this urban landscape regardless of their size. Part of the reason for this is that many of these settlements gained their livelihood from participation in the brisk trade conducted either along the river or overland. Thus even the smallest commercial storage facility, tariff outpost or crossing station along the river would have needed to keep up appearances of stability and security, afforded by these impressive fortifications, if it wished to maintain its participation within this important, profitable exchange network.

Even from an early phase of the Early Bronze Age, a coordinated effort on behalf of the community must have existed in order to summon the necessary resources, planning and labour to construct and maintain these defensive works. While the fortifications imply a sophisticated level of organization within the settlement, it is still difficult to define the exact nature of this effort. As we have pointed out, double fortification systems, or 'citadel cities' are present in the region. Their configuration may be the result of the presence of a centralized political authority, in which all efforts of the city, including its defence, were planned and supervised by a few powerful individuals who ruled the city from its acropolis. We have also shown, however, that cities do not all reflect such a hierarchical system of political authority, as indicated by the absence of a distinguishable fortified acropolis at many sites. Centres of power and authority seem to be spread throughout the community, and were enclosed by a single fortification wall. Moreover, the city walls themselves, which show differences in alignment, construction techniques, and even variable defensive systems from one sector to another, suggest that not all city construction projects fell under the direction and execution of a single authority. On the contrary, some efforts may have been left to individual community groups, or city neighbourhoods, to coordinate and complete. This evidence may betray a more heterarchical form of political control at some cities, where authority was dispersed among several groups spread out across the urban community. To be sure, this argument is conjectural, but as we shall see, it appears to find support in other aspects of the Euphrates' archaeological record.

5

HOUSING AND HOUSEHOLDS

Clusters of roofed structures, courtyards and streets, representing the remains of domestic neighbourhoods, have been brought to light at several Euphrates' sites. The common folk of Early Bronze Age settlements resided in these places, and daily activities, such as food preparation, eating, sleeping, and small-scale craft activities, were carried out there. Fortunately, enough domestic spaces have been excavated to make some general observations about the social and economic character of the individuals who inhabited them and the ways in which their status and livelihood changed over time. We will also comment on how the houses reflect the growing and distinctive, urban character of the Euphrates region of this period.

Early-to-Middle EB housing (Phases 1–3)

Halawa Tell B

Some of the earliest manifestations of Early Bronze Age houses in the northern Euphrates Valley of Syria were discovered at Halawa Tell B (Figure 5.1). Dated to the earliest centuries of the third millennium BC (Phases 1–2), the structures of Period I, level 3 were found inside a thick brick enclosure wall set on virgin soil. At least six individual mud brick structures were identified within this walled space. They either abutted one another or were free-standing, separated by narrow streets or alleyways. Each house seems to have been originally conceived as a single room enclosed on four sides by thick mud brick walls. The interior of the house was accessed by a narrow doorway in one of the sides. A flat roof, likely consisting of several horizontally placed wooden beams, may have been additionally supported by internal wooden posts positioned either in the centre of the room, or along one or more of its sides (Orthmann 1989: 89; Pfälzner 2001: 127). Internal or external mud brick buttresses also helped to support the house's superstructure and roof. That the interior space of these structures was the locus of domestic activities is suggested by the installations and artifacts found within them. Hearths and ovens point to the cooking of food, benches against the walls appear to

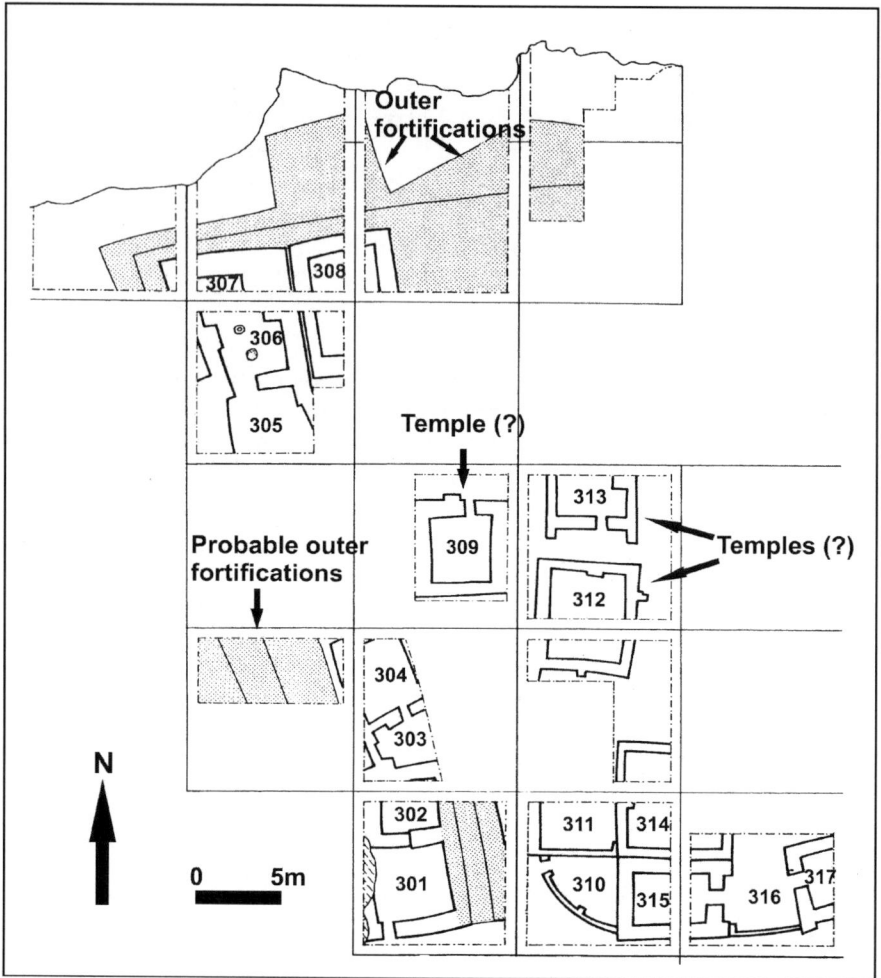

Figure 5.1 Early EB settlement at Halawa Tell B.

be working platforms, and vessels set into the floors undoubtedly served as storage receptacles.

We have evidence too of more complex households. Evidently some of the single-roomed houses expanded over the course of time through the addition of rooms and the enlargement of interior space. Of particular note is the household in the southern area of the settlement (Rooms 310–11, 314–17). This building consisted of several rooms and courtyards connected together to form a large complex, although in its original conception, it probably comprised several separate single-roomed houses similar to those discovered to the north (Pfälzner 2001: 356). A street or open space, for example, may have existed between two of the rooms (315 and 317), making these originally two free-standing, single-roomed houses. The two units were later amalgamated into one complex with the addition of a narrow wall along the southern side, forming a courtyard space between them (Room 316) (Orthmann 1989: 90; Pfälzner 2001: 356). Another wall was built to enclose a courtyard space (Room 310) between two other rooms in the southwestern part of the complex.

Of all of the rooms within the household complex, the central square room (Room 314) appears to have been the most important, given its large size, neat, square plan, and fine, white plastered interior that featured wall paintings with geometrical motifs (Orthmann 1989: 91).

Noteworthy are the artifacts discovered in the southwestern courtyard of the household complex, which included a stone mould of a straight axe and a large quantity of bone tools, among them awls and needles (see Figure 8.2) (Orthmann 1989: 91, Abb. 70). Such artifacts point to the presence of craft activities within the house, including metalworking. The additional discovery in Room 314 of a long bronze axe-head may be connected with this activity (Orthmann 1989: 91, Abb. 69:9; Pfälzner 2001: 357). It may be that specialization in metalworking, which probably augmented the household's economic livelihood, accounts for the house's spatial expansion.

While some of the houses at Halawa Tell B grew in size, others retained their single-roomed ground plan for the duration of their occupation. Free-standing, single-roomed houses, for example, dominated the central area of excavation on the tell (Rooms 309, 312, 313). Since the central area was unfortunately much disturbed by later building operations and erosion, little of the structures' interior repertoires has survived. One view of these buildings is that they functioned as houses where a variety of domestic activities took place (Pfälzner 2001: 356). On the other hand, it is tempting to posit a sacred character given the buildings' position in the centre of the settlement and their location directly under the cult platform and temple of the subsequent Period II settlement. Distinctive architectural features often characteristic of EB sacred buildings elsewhere further support a religious character. Two *antae*-like projections on the southern exterior of Room 313, for example, are reminiscent of other third millennium long-roomed temple *in antis* shrines found in northern Syria such as at Tell Chuera and Halawa Tell A (Moortgat 1960: Abb. 9; Moortgat 1962: Plan II; Orthmann 1989: Beilage 10). Exterior pilasters on the central-most Room 312 may be regarded as precursors to the more elaborate arrangement of buttresses and recesses of the succeeding temple that was built almost directly over that building (Orthmann 1989: Beilage 13). It is noteworthy too that at the end of its use, Room 312 was emptied of its contents and filled with mud brick (Orthmann 1989: 89), a practice known to have been carried out at other religious structures in northern Mesopotamia when they were being 'de-commissioned' (Schwartz 2000: 171).

The presence of wall paintings on the interior white plastered walls of both Rooms 312 and 313 may also point to the buildings' religious character. Particularly suggestive is the subject matter of the wall painting found on the southern wall of Room 312, which portrays a central, large face with eyes, nose and mouth (Figure 5.2). The face is framed by two red and black concentric circles and an intervening zigzag line. Rectangular forms filled with geometric motifs project from the top, bottom and sides of the face. They neatly divide the outside space into four separate quadrants, each of which contains representations of what appear to be people, animals, plant and mythological creatures (Orthmann 1989: 102). Pictured in the top right-hand corner is the representation of a creature with a human and bird-like body. Also noteworthy are the bird-headed figures in the lower right corner, at least one of which is characterized by long wavy hair in a style somewhat reminiscent of earlier painted designs found on pottery vessels from southern Mesopotamia (Orthmann 1989: 102). While it is difficult to be certain of the meaning of the painting, it is very possible that a religious scene is being portrayed. One interpretation is that the scene represents the worship of a cult image (Akkermans and Schwartz 2003: 227). This suggestion is supported by the observation, that with the exception of two frontally depicted figures at the top, all the other figures turn towards the central face. They either hold their hands up towards the face as if they are worshipping it, or else they raise up objects of uncertain identity (Dunham 1993: 134).

Interestingly, a parallel to this painting takes the form of a fragmentary painted limestone stele, found out of context at Halawa B, but stratigraphically

Figure 5.2 Wall painting from Room 312, Halawa Tell B.

belonging to the same phase as the wall painting from Room 312 (Orthmann 1989: Abb. 67). The stele may also represent a cult image. It too shows a painted image of a large, round face. The eyes, eyebrows and line for a nose are represented, while a thick dark border encircles the whole face and short straight lines radiate out from it, possibly to indicate hair (Orthmann 1989: 102; Dunham 1993: 135). The combined evidence of these representations seems to suggest facial aspects of a deity.

Wall paintings are found at Halawa Tell B in other locations. As mentioned above, fragments of wall paintings were found in the large square plastered room of the southern house (Room 314: Orthmann 1989: 91). Other wall painting fragments were found in a structure to the west (Room 304: Orthmann 1989: 89).

An intriguing wall painting was found in the principal living room of a four-roomed house located to the south of the main temple platform in level 1, a subsequent early EB phase at Halawa B (Figure 5.3). Depicted in the centre of this painting is what has been interpreted as the representation of a sacred tree with several branches emanating from it, while to the right, two curving lines are identified as boats with people on board (Orthmann 1981: 42; Dunham 1993: 135). The identification of the central image as a kind of sacred tree, however, should perhaps be modified by the observation that two circles separated by a thick tapering stalk rise up on top of what has been taken as a tree trunk. These circles are remarkably akin to the large circular eyes separated by thick tapering necks rising above the shoulders seen on standing anthropomorphic figures in a wall painting from an EB building at Tell Munbaqa (Figure 5.4). Furthermore, the outstretched branches of the

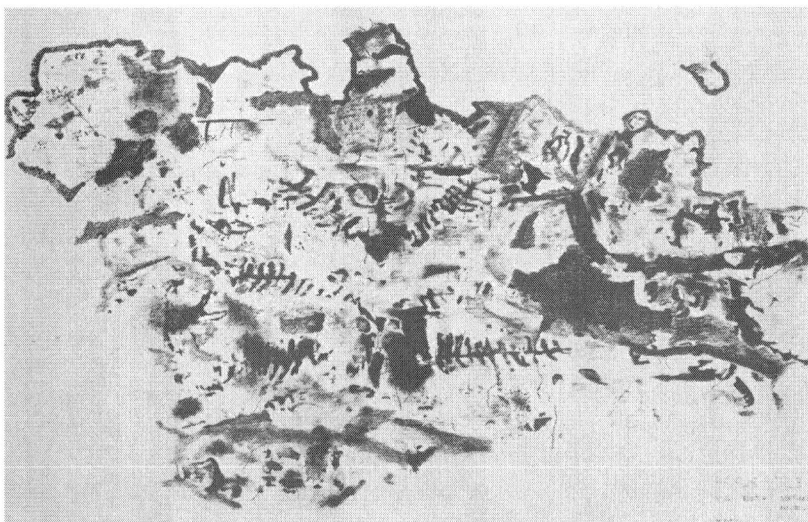

Figure 5.3 Wall painting from room (101) in house, Halawa Tell B.

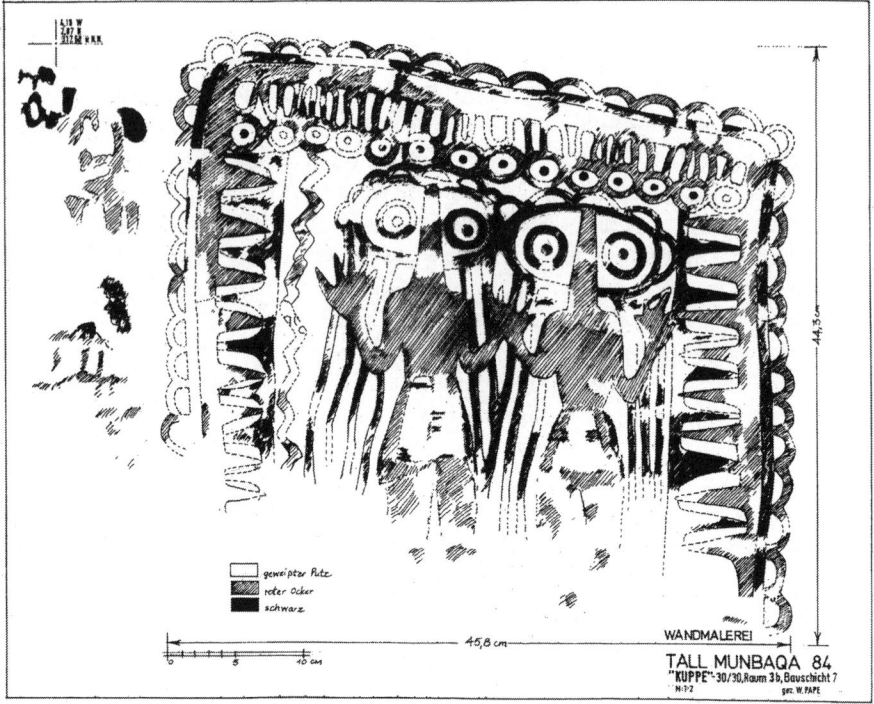

Figure 5.4 Wall painting in Room 3b in structure on 'Kuppe' at Munbaqa.

'tree' in the Halawa painting are similar to the tree branches that are clearly being held in the hands (and possibly feet?) of a worshipper in the top left-hand corner of the wall painting from Room 313 at Halawa B, described above. It seems possible, therefore, based on these parallels, that the central representation in house from level 1 at Halawa Tell B is that of a large-eyed anthropomorphic figure holding tree branches. Its identity as a cult image is in no way discredited by this new interpretation.

Whatever the meaning of the wall paintings at Halawa Tell B, the presence of wall paintings in the single-roomed free-standing structures of Room 312 and 313 at Halawa B do not necessarily secure the buildings' identification as cult shrines. While some of their other architectural features and their location may suggest a sacred character, their single-roomed ground plans and internal painted decoration parallel those of other household structures at the site. These buildings, therefore, may have been sacred or profane. We must bear in mind that in this early phase of settlement in the EB clear distinctions between religious and non-religious space probably did not exist.

Tell Habuba Kabira

Other early house plans have been reported from the oldest EB levels at the site of Tell Habuba Kabira (Phases 1–2), probably occurring only shortly after the decline or collapse of the nearby Late Uruk community. Where excavations have been able to penetrate into these early layers along the southeastern side of the tell, they have exposed at least two building complexes in level 3 (Figure 5.5a). The so-called 'Southern Complex' can be judged to be a single house since its interior space of four rooms (1–4) is connected via doorways, and the house is separated from the suite of rooms immediately to the north by double walls. Nonetheless, it is likely that this house plan represents an adaptation and modification of what had originally been two smaller houses. This is suggested by the remnant of the double wall that exists between rooms 1 and 3 on the east, and the unusual, somewhat oblique nature of the middle section of wall separating the two rooms, which is likely to be a later construction (Pfälzner 2001: 368). The original design here was probably two separate houses, positioned side by side along the southeastern corner of the settlement. Each household was characterized by a single square-planned room with internal pilasters, which in size and plan would have resembled well the single-roomed houses encountered in the early levels at Halawa Tell B. Subsequently the houses were expanded, first with the addition of rooms to the west, and then with a connecting passageway set between the two, transforming the formerly-separate buildings into a single, larger household (Pfälzner 2001: 369).

The fire that destroyed the 'Southern Complex' brought down the roof and sealed much of the house's artifactual inventory. The rooms' functions have been posited on the basis of this *in situ* material, although even with such information, reconstructions are varied. The function of the small square southwestern room (Room 2) has been especially disputed. On the one hand, the presence of a row of four shallow clay basins has been taken to indicate pottery production activities. It is argued that the basins were vats for levigating clay with water (Heinrich *et al.* 1971: 12; Strommenger 1980: 76; Akkermans and Schwartz 2003: 228). The discovery of both worked stone discs in the room, possibly the remnants of turntables for potters' wheels (Heusch 1980: 164), and 'finished' vessels standing nearby further supports the room's function as a potter's workshop. The lack of clay lumps, pottery wasters and unfired pottery, in addition to the enclosed nature of this room, however, argues against such an interpretation (Pfälzner 2001: 161). An alternative and more reasonable function for this room was that of storage and preparation of food. Some of the worked stone fragments may have been the remains of milling stones. The mud brick platform against the south wall could represent a milling platform (Strommenger 1980: Abb. 73; Pfälzner 2001: 145). As for the shallow clay 'vats', these may be more correctly interpreted as stands for pottery vessels, serving especially

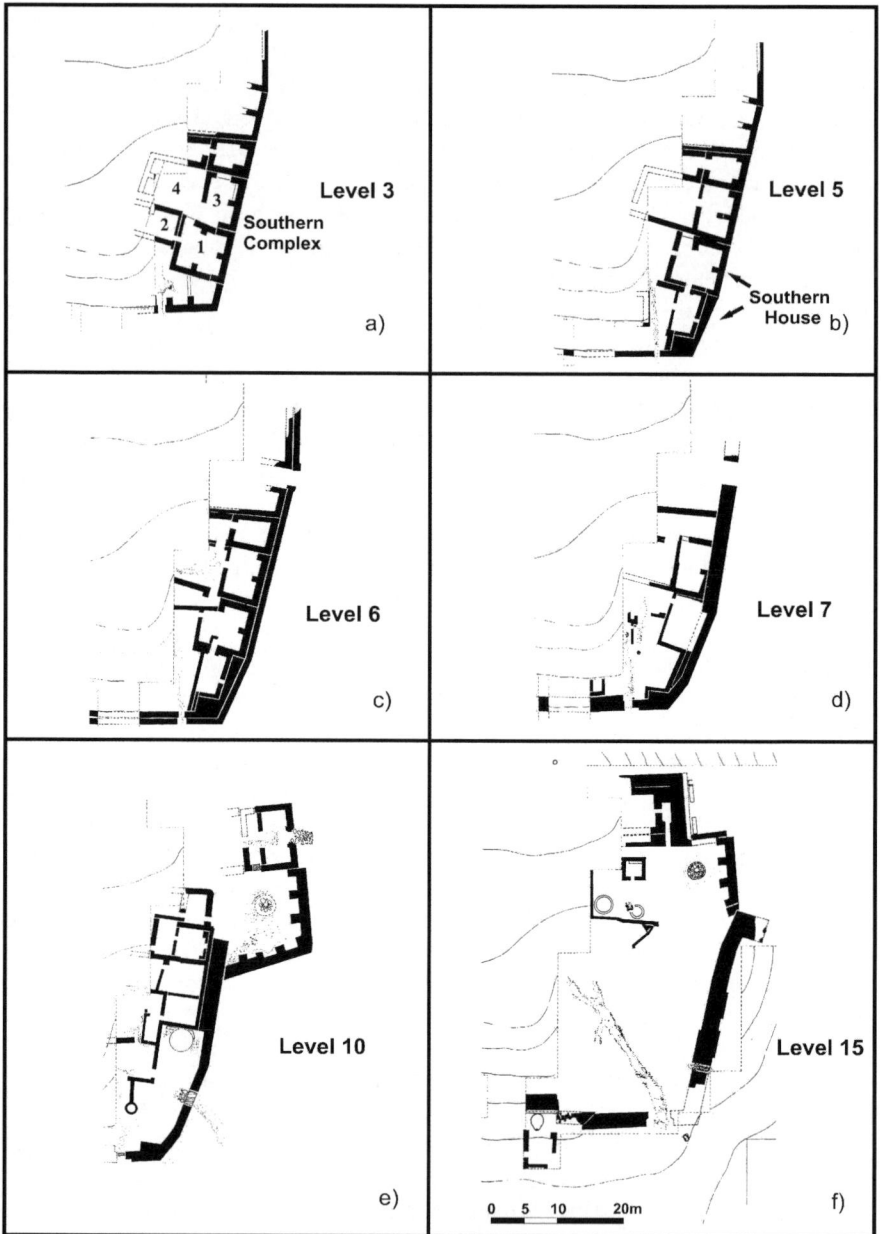

Figure 5.5 Houses at Tell Habuba Kabira.

to provide stability for vessels with rounded bases (Pfälzner 2001: 161–2). These installations and the quantity of ceramic vessels found within the room, suggest that storage, probably of foodstuffs, was concentrated here (Pfälzner 2001: 369).

Clay platforms, benches, and vessel stands, in addition to fireplaces and storage vessels in other rooms of the 'Southern Complex', indicate that, for the most part, activities within this household were domestic in nature, related to the storage, preparation and consumption of food at the household level (Strommenger 1976: 7, Abb 2; Heusch 1980: 163; Pfälzner 2001: 369).

Shiyukh Fouqani

At Tell Shiyukh Fouqani, six houses, dated to Phases 1–2 on the basis of associated ceramic vessels, were unearthed in Area D on the western slope of the high tell (Figure 5.6). Like the earliest structures at Halawa Tell B and Habuba Kabira, these houses consisted, for the most part, of rectilinear, single-roomed buildings of mud brick. The houses were positioned on either side of a long street that ran from north to south. The huge quantity of ashy refuse that had accumulated in the street over time probably attests to the food preparation activities that were carried out on in these buildings. Evidence of storage vessels, hearths, ovens and grinding stones within the houses further support their domestic character (Bachelot 1999: 144).

Building 3 was larger than the other buildings, comprising two rooms separated by a kind of entrance corridor. The larger of the two rooms featured a niche between two buttresses on its eastern wall. These features, and the fact that the walls and floors were well plastered could indicate that this was the locale of cultic activities (Bachelot 1999: 145). It may be equally appropriate, however, to envision that both ritual and secular activities were

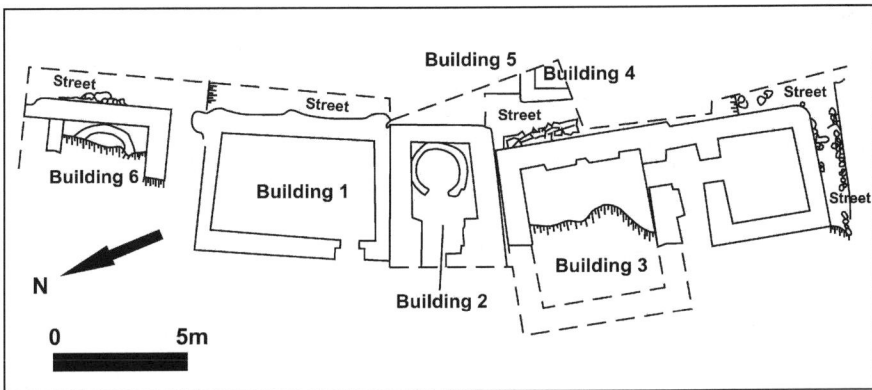

Figure 5.6 Buildings 1–6, Shiyukh Fouqani.

carried out in the same space in this house, much like the central building and southern house at Halawa Tell B. The fact that a crucible fragment was also found in the room is noteworthy, and points to metallurgical activities connected with this household (Bachelot 1999: 145).

Tell es-Sweyhat

An altogether different arrangement of domestic architecture was encountered at Tell es-Sweyhat, setting it apart from the simple house complexes observed thus far. The structures were found on the western side of the high mound in Operation 1, and they date to Phases 1–2 of the early third millennium BC, when Tell es-Sweyhat was still a fairly small settlement (Armstrong and Zettler 1997:13–14, Figure 2.4; Danti and Zettler 1998: 219). Besides the remnants of two rectangular buildings, each made of mud bricks set on low stone footings and featuring plastered interior walls, a 'pit house' was uncovered (Figure 5.7). This distinctive oval building had been built into a pit that had been cut into virgin soil, thus producing a semi-subterranean construction, measuring c.4.5 m × 6.5 m (Armstrong and Zettler 1997: 14). The wall of the pit house was built of mud bricks set on a low stone footing. Both its interior and exterior walls had been heavily plastered, probably to keep the building warm and watertight (Armstrong and Zettler 1997: 14, 17). While the superstructure was not preserved, it is conceivable that the top would have been made of branches and brush supported by interior posts and beams, much like pastoral pit houses of recent times. Pottery was found inside the pit house, in particular a number of jars with fitted lids that may have been used for storage, as well as a model chariot wheel, chipped stone, bones and shell (Armstrong and Zettler 1997: 16).

While the pit house differs in plan from other early third millennium Euphrates houses, its presence in this region is not altogether unusual. Ethnographic research has shown that similar semi-subterranean buildings were used by semi-sedentary tribal populations in the Euphrates Valley and elsewhere in Syria even up to the relatively recent past (Armstrong and

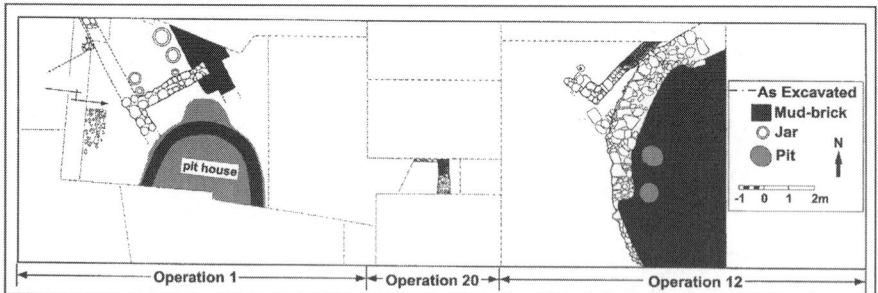

Figure 5.7 Pit house and bastion, Operations 1, 20 and 12, Tell es-Sweyhat.

Zettler 1997: 16). The presence of a pit house from the Early Bronze Age at Tell es-Sweyhat, therefore, might indicate that a semi-sedentary or trans-humant population existed at this settlement in antiquity. Moreover, the pit house's location directly next to contemporary solid rectangular houses points to a co-existing population of both sedentary and non-sedentary elements (Danti and Zettler 1998: 219). This reconstruction concurs very well with the posited subsistence economy of the Early Bronze Age communities in the Euphrates Valley gathered from other sources, which shows that a mixture of both sedentary farming and transhumant pastoralism prevailed in this region (see Chapter 2).

Tell al-ʿAbd

Well-preserved evidence for domestic housing during Phase 3 comes from the site of Tell al-ʿAbd. In the central part of the settlement just inside the city wall as it runs along the eastern side of the tell, the remains of several houses forming a small residential quarter were found (Finkbeiner 1995: 63; 1997: 100). These houses were preceded by earlier structures whose remnants have only been cursorily investigated.

The houses of Tell al-ʿAbd are similar to those from Tell Halawa B in that they consist primarily of square, single-roomed spaces, where a variety of domestic activities would have been carried out (Figure 5.8). Their domestic function is confirmed by the number of storage and cooking installations found within them. Several such houses exist, abutting one another or separated from one another by a narrow, gravel-lined lane. While most of the houses appear with one room only, the centrally located House A consisted of a nearly square principal room (Room 1), to which an anteroom (Room 2) and a small courtyard bordering on a street to the south, had been added. The walls and floors of the principal room had been thickly and repeatedly coated with white limestone plaster. Even so, the domestic function of this room is indicated by the benches that were set into the corners of the room, the presence of a small fireplace, and a jar that was sunk into the floor near the doorway to the antechamber. The antechamber itself featured additional domestic installations, as did the courtyard to the south, where vessels sunk into the ground were either used for storage or served as circular ovens (Finkbeiner 1995: 65).

Mid-to-Late EB housing (Phases 3–5)

Tell Habuba Kabira

As time progressed through the Early Bronze Age, Euphrates' domestic architecture underwent significant changes. In level 5 at Tell Habuba Kabira, the house that had earlier expanded into one large household was once again

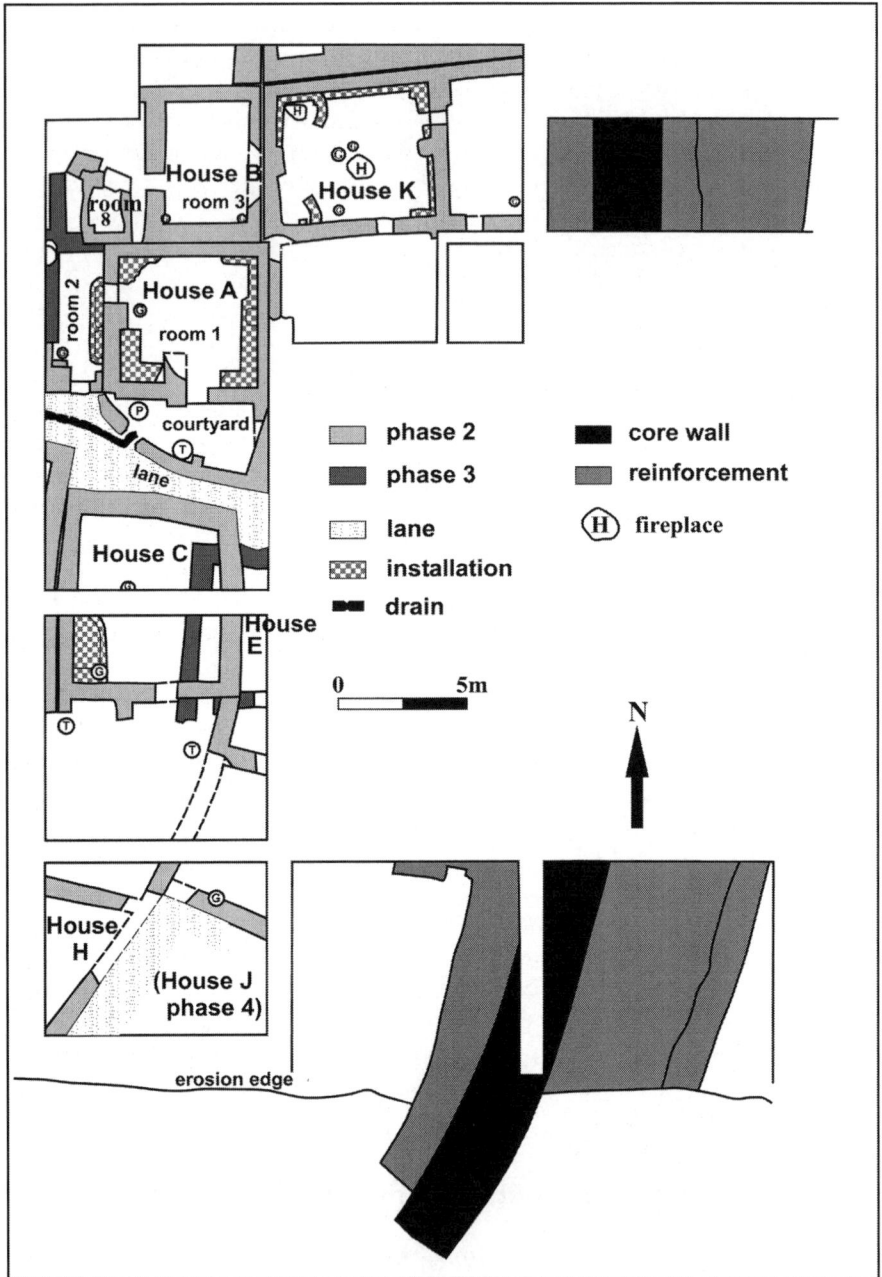

Figure 5.8 Area III houses and outer fortification wall, Tell al-ʿAbd.

sub-divided into two separate units. In the southern house, the principal square room was now attached to a new long room to the south (Figure 5.5b). Noteworthy in this southern room is evidence for the manufacture of jewellery, which consisted of limestone, alabaster and shell beads and amulets. Attested are the flint and obsidian tools used to make such items, as well as the adornments themselves, which appear in both their half-finished and finished state (Heusch 1980: 164). Further changes occurred in the subsequent Habuba level 6, when the house to the north experienced a significant expansion (Figure 5.5c), and then in level 7 (Figure 5.5d), when all rooms were reconstructed according to a new design which no longer featured thick buttressed walls or a central wooden support, this having been the architectural norm until this time in the EB (Heusch 1980: 169; Pfälzner 2001: 370). The overall spatial layout of the southern house at Tell Habuba Kabira remained unchanged, however, and the manufacture of jewellery continued, indicating that the house continued to be occupied by members of the same household (Pfälzner 2001: 370). It should also be noted that in addition to craft activities in this building, fire installations and vessels sunken into the ground suggest that other domestic activities such as cooking and storage continued. The evidence indicates, therefore, that we are still dealing here with a small household, not a craft workshop (Pfälzner 2001: 370).

In level 10 at Tell Habuba Kabira, the entire aspect of the settlement on the tell altered significantly as it reached its greatest areal extent (Figure 5.5e). In addition to the introduction of a new building technique in which mud brick walls were now set over proper foundations of stone, the southeastern area of the tell was significantly altered by the construction of a large double-entryway gate and a large fortified terrace with a well (Heusch 1980: 168–70). The earlier southern house with jewellery manufactory was now converted into an open courtyard that featured a large circular working platform, while to the north were a series of rooms belonging possibly to a very large house whose overall plan could not be discerned. The entire area of the upper tell may now have been converted into an area of public architecture and monumental constructions, in connection with the new seat of a local administrator (Strommenger 1980: 69). Domestic housing of commonfolk appears now to have been relegated to the slopes outside of the tell's fortification walls (Heusch 1980: 172).

Halawa Tell A

At the site of Halawa, settlement shifted from Tell B to Tell A during the second half of the third millennium BC. In level 3, which corresponds mostly to the mid-to-late Early Bronze Age (Phases 4–5), houses differed greatly from their predecessors at Halawa Tell B. Unlike the single-roomed structures of the earlier settlement, all houses at Halawa Tell A were conceived from the beginning as multi-roomed buildings. Owing to the broad

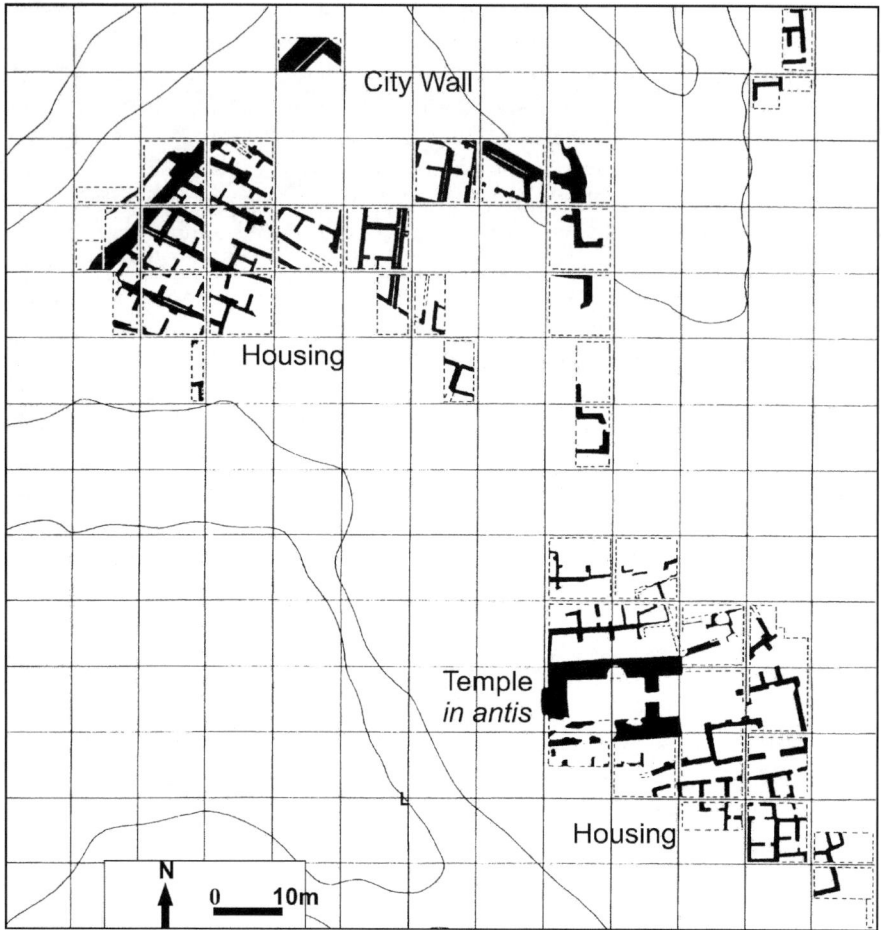

Figure 5.9 EB settlement, level 3, Halawa Tell A.

areas where third millennium settlement has been exposed at Halawa A, one can distinguish the plans and artifactual repertoire of at least 20 houses on the tell (Figure 5.9) (Orthmann 1989: 39). Houses were found along the western side just inside the city wall, along the northern edge inside the city wall, and both to the south and north of the temple *in antis* (Orthmann 1989: Beilage 8–10). The houses were arranged side by side in blocks, and aligned on either side of streets that ran the length and breadth of the settlement.

The houses at Halawa Tell A, all of which were constructed of mud brick above stone foundations, adopted a fairly standardized rectangular ground plan. In its basic form, this plan consisted of a large open courtyard at the front of the complex, followed in the centre by one or two rooms that

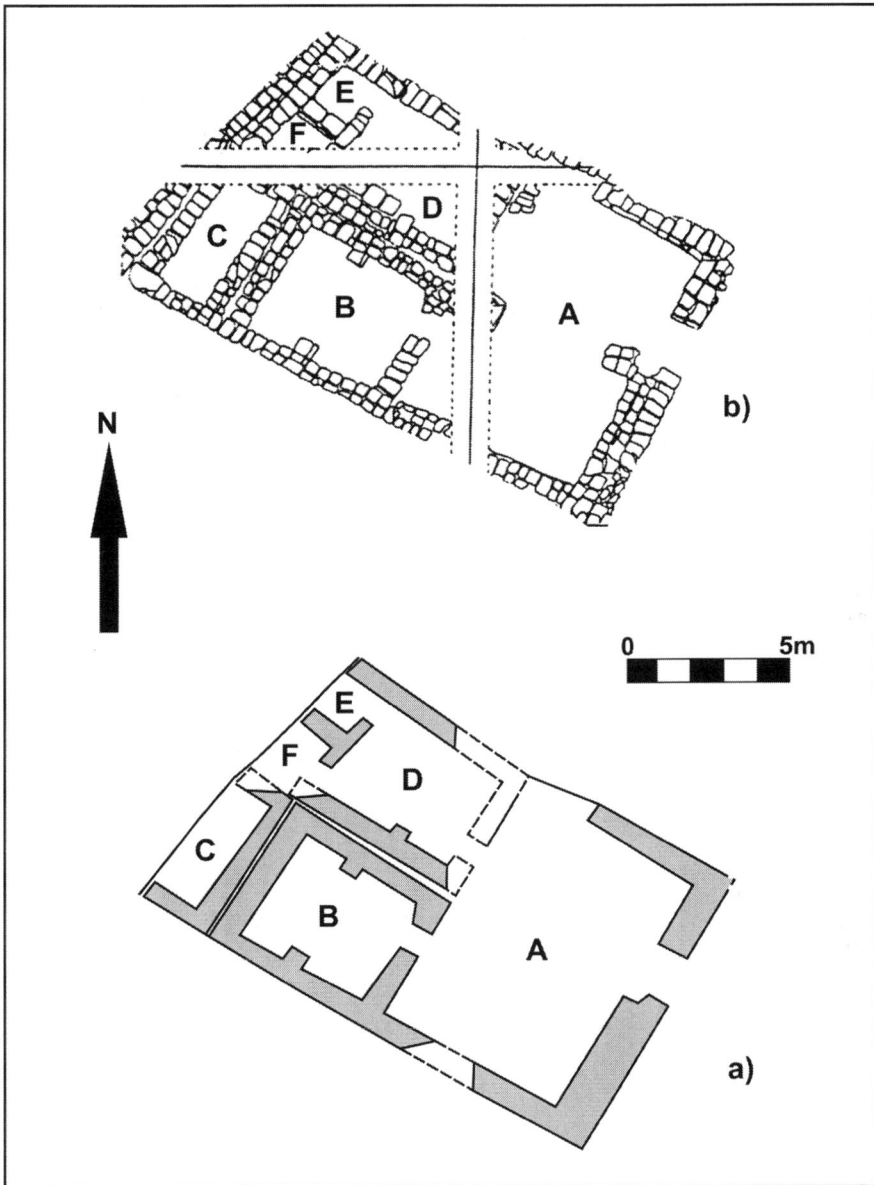

Figure 5.10 House 1, Halawa Tell A: original plan (a), and later phase (b).

represented the heart of the household, while in the back were one or more smaller rooms that served as storage spaces. This house plan can be clearly observed along the western side of the tell in Quadrant Q, directly inside the fortification wall. The best preserved, central-most house in this area is distinguished by an entrance at the front that gives access to a large court-yard (House 1) (Figure 5.10 Room A). This open space would have been used for a number of work activities and storage, attested by the ground stone tools, circular fire installations, bitumen-lined basins, benches serving as working platforms, and large vessels found within it (Orthmann 1989: 42–3, Abb. 21).

Behind the courtyard were two similar square rooms (B and D) separated from one another by a double wall, each carefully plastered. One or both may have served as central 'reception rooms' of the household, where sleeping and eating took place, although food processing seems also to have been carried out here from time to time (Pfälzner 2001: 349). These rooms were also distinguished by rectangular niches that were set into the long walls (Orthmann 1989: Abb. 20). Since the surrounding plaster on the walls was covered with smoke blackening, it is conceivable that such niches served as the place for lamps (Orthmann 1989: 41). Alternatively, the niches may have been places for cultic paraphernalia, as suggested by the discovery of a stone figurine, possibly an ancestor figure, in a niche in a reception room of a house south of the *Antentempel* (House 3–35: Meyer and Pruss 1994: 210). The three remaining rooms at the back part of the house (C, E–F) served as spaces for storage. Their function is confirmed by the discovery of large quantities of storage vessel fragments. In the southern-most room of House 1, 32 large ceramic jars were resting *in situ* among the burned brick and carbonized wood of the fire that destroyed the house at the end of its lifetime (Orthmann 1989: 41; Abb. 18–19).

Peter Pfälzner, in his study of houses and households in Northern Mesopotamia, provides some illuminating observations about change in the domestic structures at Halawa Tell A (Pfälzner 2001: 349–50). He notes that while the houses may originally have been laid out according to the same standard-ized plan, in many cases modifications and additions over the course of time changed their appearance and internal layout considerably. The house dir-ectly to the northeast of House 1 in Quadrant Q illustrates such changes (House 2–3). In its original conception this house was of roughly equal dimensions to those of House 1 (Figure 5.11b). It was designed with a front courtyard and at least three rooms in behind. Over the course of its lifetime, however, it was subdivided into two separate households (Figure 5.11a). Each house was now roughly half of the original ground plan and as a result, possessed significantly narrower internal spaces (Pfälzner 2001: 349; Taf. 71). A similar house division can be observed in Quadrant Q–5e, just inside the northern fortification wall (Pfälzner 2001: 350–1). The house directly to the southeast of House 1 illustrates another form of change (House 4). An entrance vestibule that gave access to the street to the south appears to have been added on to the front of the house, while the once large, open courtyard was subdivided into smaller units, possibly to accommodate different types of household activities (Pfälzner 2001: 350; Taf. 72).

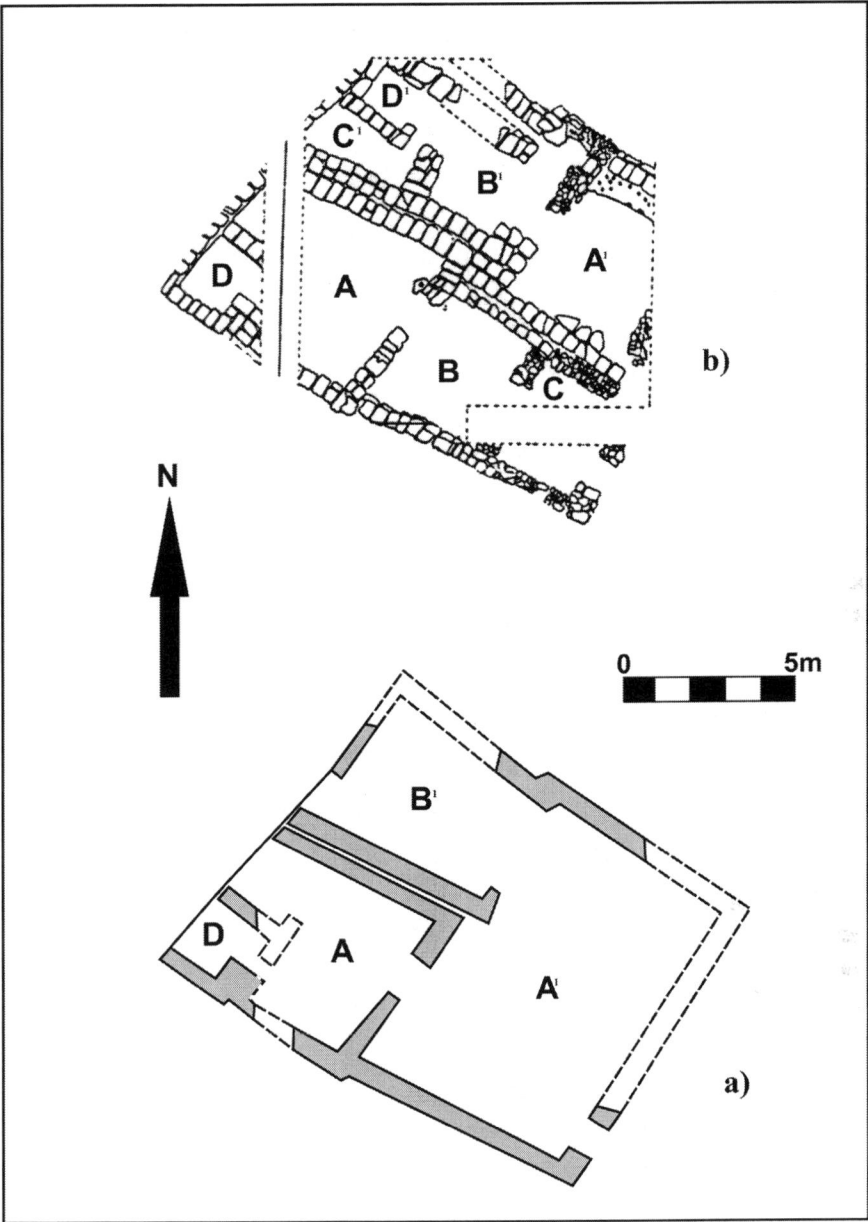

Figure 5.11 House 2–3, Halawa Tell A: original, single house-plan (a), and subsequent sub-division into two smaller houses (b).

Similarly-sized architectural units tend to occur in groups or blocks at Halawa Tell A. Each of the houses to the south of the temple *in antis*, for example, has a uniform width of about 7.5m. This width contrasts to the 9 metre-wide houses from the western side of the settlement. The block of houses to the south of the street below the north fortification wall are each characterized by 6 metre-wide structures (Pfälzner 2001: 354). Despite these variances in dimensions, however, the houses appear to share in common the basic room organization of courtyards, central living rooms and storage spaces at the back, as described above.

Observations concerning the layout and internal organization of the excavated households permit some interesting statements about the organization and administration of the EB settlement at Halawa Tell A. The presence of a standardized room arrangement throughout the different neighbourhoods of the settlement, regardless of their overall dimensions, is significant, as is the arrangement of houses into blocks of uniform width along well-defined, straight streets. We may also add to this the observation that unlike other third millennium sites, where houses have a uniform width at the front but vary in breadth towards the back, most of the houses at Halawa Tell A exhibit the same width along their entire length (Pfälzner 2001: 354). Considered together, these architectural features indicate that a high degree of planning went into the layout and construction of the houses, probably in order to make the best use of available space and to provide easy and effective communication between architectural units within this fortified urban settlement. Such planning may perhaps have entailed some form of coordinated effort on the part of the town's inhabitants for the programme of preparation and development, as well as the organization of the labour and resources necessary to carry this extensive housing project through to its completion.

Tell Hadidi

Urban planning is evident also at the site of Tell Hadidi, where excavations in Area C on the lower tell have brought to light many structures which almost certainly comprise blocks of late EB houses (Phases 4–5) as well as what could have served as a small neighbourhood shrine (Dornemann 1979: 117). Although specific details about the layout, size and internal accommodations of these houses are still forthcoming, it is reported that the buildings were arranged for more than 48 m along one side of a street (Dornemann 1979: 116). The presence of a such a long thoroughfare through the settlement is more likely the result of careful planning in conjunction with the laying out of well aligned city blocks, than the product of organic growth, which would have produced a more haphazard, irregular configuration (Van de Mieroop 1997: 84).

Selenkahiye

Information about housing is plentiful at Selenkahiye, a site situated on the right bank of the Euphrates, only a few km downstream from Halawa on the opposite bank. Like Halawa Tell A, Selenkahiye was settled during the latter half of the third millennium BC (Phases 4–5). Also like the former site, it contained a densely occupied area of domestic housing, arranged in blocks along lengthy pebble-paved streets.

Vernacular architecture was exposed wherever excavations were conducted, indicating that domestic occupation was widespread at this settlement. The majority of houses were found in the central part of the tell where the largest excavation exposure existed (Figure 5.12) (Excavation B: Van Loon 2001: 3.50–3.83). In this area, houses were arranged on either side of two long streets, called Sunset Boulevard and Main Street by the excavators. Domestic architecture was additionally encountered in the southern area of the tell, both to the north and south of a modern bulldozer trench that had been cut for irrigation (Excavation A: Van Loon 2001: 3.31–3.50), and at the northern end of the settlement, inside the northwestern corner of the city wall (Excavation C: Van Loon 2001: 3.83–3.86). The remains of houses found outside of the city wall to the west attest to some extramural occupation (Van Loon 2001: 3.94). This occupation, which represents the expansion of the settlement to its largest extent, probably occurred somewhat late in the Early Bronze Age sequence.

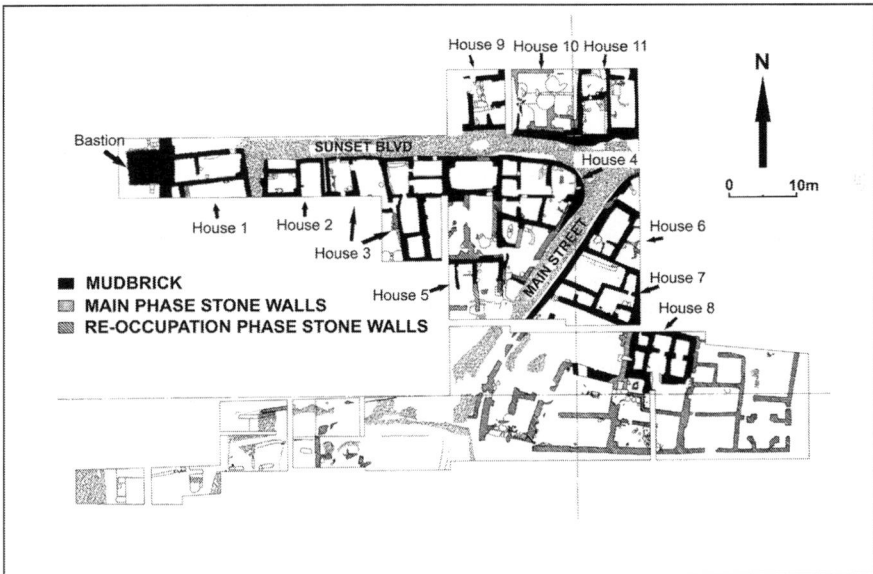

Figure 5.12 Housing in Central Town Area, Selenkahiye.

From the very beginning, the settlement of Selenkahiye served as a place of residence. This is implied by the discovery of houses that were founded directly on virgin soil. Such houses even seem to have been constructed before the settlement was fortified with a city wall. In some of the western squares of the central area B, for example, early house structures founded on virgin soil were subsequently filled in with ash and mud, and strewn with pebbles in preparation for the foundations of the first town wall (Van Loon 2001: 3.51). Furthermore, evidence from House 1 in this central area, in the form of the slightly oblique orientation of its wall in relation to the town wall, suggests that there may have been forerunners of this house in a period when the town wall did not yet exist, or at the very least, when a wall existed in some other place (Figure 5.13) (Van Loon 2001: 3.62).

Subsequent to the installation of Selenkahiye's city wall, houses were frequently affected by refurbishings and repairs to the fortifications. When the western city wall's mud brick superstructure was widened in an effort to strengthen it, for example, rooms in a house in the western central area (in square Q26) were partially filled in with bricks and narrowed (Van Loon 2001: 3.58). A similar in-filling of rooms also took place in the northwestern corner, when the city wall was reinforced in this sector (Van Loon 2001: 3.85). That such measures were undertaken despite considerable compromises to individual houses underline the importance attached to maintaining the city's fortifications. Defence clearly continued to be a central concern to the inhabitants of this region, especially towards the end of the third millennium (see also Chapter 4).

One of the biggest challenges at Selenkahiye has been to correlate local phases of houses with the sequence of fortifications and other structures in an

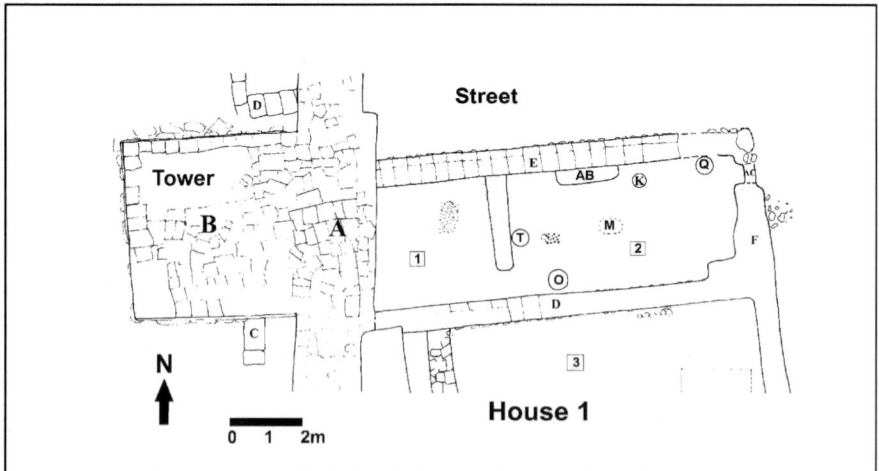

Figure 5.13 House 1 and Tower, Selenkahiye.

effort to produce a coherent settlement history with a site-wide sequence of occupation phases. This has proved difficult given the lack of stratigraphic connections between the main areas of excavation. The lack of a clear correspondence among the local architectural phases is also confounded by the fact that each area is quite unique in terms of the methods of construction employed, the building materials used and the duration of its structures. In any event, it is fair to say that all of the houses at Selenkahiye experienced a wide variety of changes over the course of the last three or four centuries of the third millennium BC. These took the form of renovations, expansions, contractions, and in some cases, complete re-buildings. Nonetheless, throughout this history, the buildings appeared to have remained primarily domestic in function, performing a variety of functions and activities related to the requirements of relatively simple households.

The houses of Selenkahiye were constructed of mud brick of varying colours and consistency. Stone foundations were used only occasionally, such as, for example, in places where the underlying ground was subject to subsidence. They were used also to block doorways, and to shore up walls that had deteriorated or were sagging (Van Loon 2001: 3.27). Since most rooms were relatively small and house walls were fairly narrow, it is generally assumed that the houses possessed only one storey although there may be a few exceptions with the larger houses. Sleeping may have taken place on the roof of the houses or in the open air in one of the courtyards (Van Loon 2001: 3.28). In one house (House 4), however, an elevated brick platform in a small room (Room 4), could be evidence of an interior sleeping place (Van Loon 2001: 3.67). Generally it is assumed that most roofed areas were flat. They were constructed of wooden beams that were set horizontally over the tops of the walls, covered with reeds or mats, and waterproofed with mud (Van Loon 2001: 3.28).

The houses at Selenkahiye seem to have been planned and laid out rather loosely within the settlement. Their internal arrangements varied greatly. There is no uniformity, for example, in the number of rooms they possessed. While some houses appear to have had only two or three rooms (e.g. Houses 9 and 12), other houses could possess at least seven rooms of varying sizes and functions (e.g. Houses 4 and 7). The lack of uniformity in house size, shape and room arrangement at Selenkahiye differs rather sharply from the situation at Halawa Tell A, where houses exhibit similar architectural configurations. It is uncertain why the architectural features of these two sites should differ so greatly, given their contemporaneity and geographical proximity. In any event, their differences underline the variability in individual occupational histories of settlements in the third millennium BC, an observation that manifests itself in other aspects of the archaeological record from this region as well.

Many houses at Selenkahiye were fitted with outdoor courtyards. These were frequently the first spaces of the houses to be accessed from the streets.

The fact that the rooms were pebbled facilitated the proper drainage of rain-water. Upon entering either House 3 or House 4 from the street, for example, one would have found oneself in a court that was all or mostly paved with gravel (Van Loon 2001: 3.65).

At least one room of each house accommodated one or more ovens. It is suggested that the majority of such rooms were outdoor spaces. The majority of ovens would have been used for cooking food for household consumption. Other artifacts and installations associated with food preparation have also been found, often in the same rooms as the ovens. These installations take the form of bitumen or clay plastered surfaces set into the floors, which have been interpreted as kneading places (found in Houses 1, 2, 6, 9, 11, and Room 24 in square Q26). A number of grinding stones and mortars were also found in many of the houses (Houses 4 and 8) further testifying to the preparation of food. In one case, an andiron, or portable hearth, distinguished by three protruding knobs on the inside of its walls, was found in House 12 (Van Loon 2001: 3.78).

Besides food preparation, storage facilities have been uncovered. These took the form of plastered pits or bins (House 1, House in W42/43), or jars that had been sunken into the ground (House 3, House in W42/43), and in at least one case, a jar was found with a lid still covering its opening (House 13). Mangers or troughs have also been reported in a few of the houses (House 3). Last, there are instances in which curving constructions made of clay or stone have been found on the floors of some rooms of houses. These features may be the remnants of grain silos with domed roofs (Houses 4 and 7, V22 reoccupation phase; Van Loon 2001: 3.79).

The most intriguing find was made in a house in the northwestern corner of the city (Square T 06, Room 9), where some 82 vessels were found scattered about a small room. It is suggested that many of these vessels had been stored on shelves. It was additionally observed that charred grains of barley were found in and among the vessels, along with a white powdery layer, suggesting the loose storage of foodstuffs in this room (Van Loon 2001: 3.86).

Wall niches have been reported in a few houses at Selenkahiye. They are particularly evident in Room 10 of a house found in the northwestern corner of the city in square T 05, where three simple, small niches with curving walls were found in the walls of the room. As was suggested for those found at Halawa Tell A, the niches may not have been intended for storage, but rather for the placement of oil lamps, stone figurines or other small items (Pfälzner 2001: 160).

Some unusual installations have been reported in several houses at Selen-kahiye, whose function remain uncertain. In House 2, a basin-like feature with a mud brick partition was found in the northwestern corner of one of the rooms. As it was paved with the sherds of a large jar that sloped up against the room walls, it may have served to contain a liquid of some type, or perhaps as a platform for a porous jar (Figure 5.14) (Van Loon 2001: 3.64).

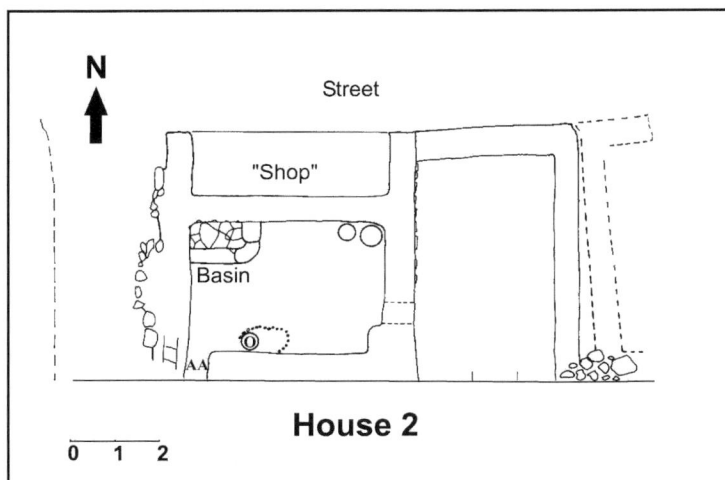

Figure 5.14 House 2, Selenkahiye.

Flagstones occupying much of the floor area in Room 9 of House 4 may also relate to a household activity that involved the use of water, although the precise function of such an installation is obscure (Van Loon 2001: 3.68).

While the majority of buildings served as habitations for households of families, the houses were by no means solely domestic in function. Other activities beyond simple food preparation and storage for the household's consumption were carried out in some of these homes, as evidenced by certain unusual installations that have been found, particularly in the houses north of Sunset Boulevard. In House 9, for example (Figure 5.15), Room 3 contained two ovens in a corner with a working platform, while near the centre of the room a square plastered bin was situated next to the remains of an oven wall, indicating that this may have been the kitchen courtyard (Van Loon 2001: 3.74). Room 1, on the other hand, contained an unusual construction. It consisted of a plastered recess in the western wall that was flanked by two benches with arm rests, behind which were vent holes (Van Loon 2001: 3.76). The function of this installation is far from certain, but to be sure, no other house featured such a construction. The special function of this installation indicates that unique activities took place within House 9.

House 11 also featured some unusual constructions (Figure 5.15). One of its rooms, room 1, had been equipped with two ovens. One of the ovens (AL) was different in that there was a partition separating the interior into two parallel chambers. The other oven (AX) was cut off at the corner, and had a flue for letting in air. This flue ended against a stone in the adjacent wall, from which an air shaft would have gone up vertically. It is interesting also

111

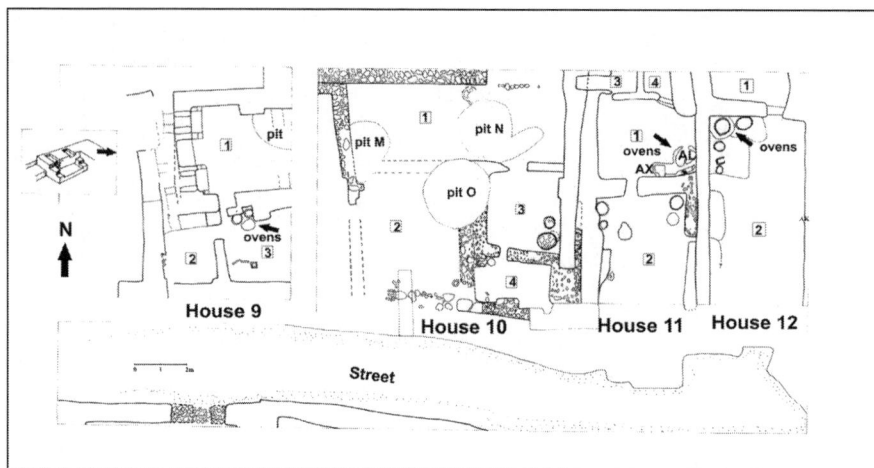

Figure 5.15 Houses 9–12, Selenkahiye.

that a terra-cotta 'lid' was found inside this oven, serving to shut the flue (Van Loon 2001: 3.77). The unusual nature of these ovens may indicate that some kind of industrial activity was carried out here, rather than simple household pursuits. The excavators suggest that the function of the flued oven was a smelting oven, although that interpretation remains highly conjectural (Van Loon 2001: 3.100). Finally, one can note that in addition to the two ovens in Room 1, an additional three ovens were found in the adjoining Room 2. This house, therefore, possesses the largest number of ovens. It may have served as a bakery, with the two small back rooms serving as places for the storage of flour. The extra oven with the flue might have been added as a specialized installation for side-line activities (Van Loon 2001: 3.101).

Another unusual house was House 2 (Figure 5.14). In addition to having a room with ovens, a working surface and an unusual basin with a surface of potsherds, all described above, the house possessed a shop-like rectangular space that was open to the street to the north (Van Loon 2001: 3.64). Although no opening was found between this 'shop' room and the room with the basin in behind, it may be that there was a connection between the two constructions. If the basin was accessible through a window, it may have functioned as the placement for a porous jar, holding a cold drink that would be served in the shop (Van Loon 2001: 3.99).

House 1 may have served as a guardroom, given its location right against the western city wall, precisely at a point where a large stone bastion jutted out from the city wall. It is suggested that as the roof of House 1 was probably flush with the parapet of the town wall, it would have given access to it (Figure 5.13) (Van Loon 2001: 3.99 n. 61).

112

When its constituent rooms are all considered together, House 8 stands out as a rather exceptional house. This house had six rooms, regularly laid out. They were contained within relatively thick walls, indicating perhaps that the building had two storeys. It is rather strange that no ovens or hearths were found in the house, nor rooms that could be construed as court-yards or animal pens, suggesting that the owner was not engaged in any agricultural activities (Van Loon 2001: 3.100). In addition to these rather uncommon characteristics, the house produced an interesting inventory of artifacts that consisted of metates and a mortar, pots of various forms, a strainer, and a human figurine. Also curious was a find of a small bowl that contained two statue eyes and fragments of ostrich egg shells. These items may have been buried in the house debris by the owner after the house had been burned, to be recovered in safer times (Van Loon 2001: 3.73). Other interesting items in the house included a marble mace head, two haematite weights, two ivory pins, and a bronze spearhead. Altogether, the wealth of objects and the absence of evidence related to agricultural activities suggested to the excavators that the owner was a merchant (Van Loon 2001: 3.100).

Near the southern end of the settlement at Selenkahiye, the excavators unearthed a large structure which they called the Southern Mansion. The large size of this Southern Mansion, its internal arrangements and special contents indicate that this was an important building within the settlement, possibly the residence of an elite official of the city. A description of the Southern Mansion will be given in the chapter relating to large-scale secular buildings (Chapter 6).

Tell es-Sweyhat

One last third millennium settlement to be discussed here in reference to housing is Tell es-Sweyhat. By the late EB in Phase 5, the city consisted of both a fortified, high mound in the centre of the settlement, and a surround-ing lower town, also enclosed by a city wall. Sectors of both the upper and lower towns have yielded evidence for domestic structures, although their overall exposure and preservation varies from area to area. Concerning the high or main mound, Tom Holland exposed several phases of EB housing in Area II (Holland 1976: 39–48). This was a narrow sounding, however, and very little information about the size and internal arrangement of the houses could be discerned. The same goes for Area III, located on the lower north-eastern terrace of the main tell. Here it is reported that private dwellings consisting of mud brick superstructures set over stone foundations were found, along with a good assemblage of late third millennium ceramic cups and cooking pots, figurines, model chariot wheels and bronze pins (Holland 1976: 48–9). Nonetheless, information about the size and internal arrange-ments of such domestic structures is still forthcoming. Area IV on the main mound has certainly yielded the most noteworthy architecture at Tell es-Sweyhat, which in the late third millennium consisted of a large warehouse, a kitchen building where food was prepared on a grand scale, and a central reception building. Because of the elite character of these buildings, they will be discussed in Chapter 6.

Investigations of the lower town have generated additional data concerning domestic housing at Tell es-Sweyhat. Geomagnetic mapping conducted over fairly broad areas of the lower town in the 1990s, under the supervision of Peter Peregrine, provided useful information about the arrangement of vernacular architecture (Zettler *et al.* 1996; Peregrine *et al.* 1997). Particularly noteworthy are the magnetic data collected from Block 1, an area surveyed to the east of the high mound. Several room blocks spread across the entire area of Block 1 were revealed in this sector, which encompasses nearly 1.5 ha (Peregrine *et al.* 1997: App. 4.1:d). A gate in the eastern lower town wall was also identified through this prospection. A long street was shown to have extended from it to the west in the direction of the high mound, while other streets branched off from it (Peregrine *et al.* 1997: 78). One way to interpret this combined data is to infer the existence of dense quarters of domestic housing, arranged in blocks on either side of a series of streets that bisected the lower town, and which provided communication with the city gates and the 'citadel' on the high mound.

Excavations in a number of operations in Block 1 have confirmed the presence of housing in this sector. In Operation 16, traces of a stone founded building, probably part of a house, were unearthed in two occupation phases associated with the third quarter of the third millennium BC (Phase 4) (Zettler 1997b: 47). Several rooms were found next to an open space or courtyard, which was characterized by a bench and a hearth (Zettler 1997b: 46–7; Figure 3.9). Unfortunately, further information about this house proved difficult to obtain because of the limited area that was excavated. Moreover, the original layout and function of the domestic spaces appears to have been radically altered in the succeeding phase of occupation, dated to the latest EB phase (Phase 5), when several large kilns were installed and the whole area seems to have been converted into an industrial zone characterized by pyrotechnic activities, notably the firing of pottery (Zettler 1997b: 47).

In other areas of the Lower Town, housing was encountered, although knowledge of the domestic arrangements of these structures is largely fragmentary due to heavy damage by later pits and ploughing (Zettler 1997b: 43). In Operation 9 in the northwestern sector of the lower town, the main phases of domestic occupation date to the late third millennium BC (Phase 5). The remains of at least three buildings were identified in this operation in association with outdoor activity areas. Sunken storage jars and bins, plastered and stone-paved floors and grinding stones characterized these areas, as did plastered basins and associated drains that were possibly used in connection with the processing of grapes or the tanning of hides (Holland 1993–94: 279; Zettler 1997b: 45–6). A stone-lined water conduit, running through the area from southwest to northeast between the buildings, was also exposed. It is conceivable that the conduit served to channel water from a nearby well (Zettler 1997b: 45). Although drinking water was probably obtained directly from the wells, the conduits provided water for other purposes or permitted waste water to be flushed away (Zettler 1997b: 45).

One of the most extensive exposures in the lower town at Tell es-Sweyhat was Operation 4, located in the western sector of the city. A large, fairly well preserved building dating to the end of the third millennium BC (Phase 5) was revealed here (Figure 5.16). The building possessed at least eight interior

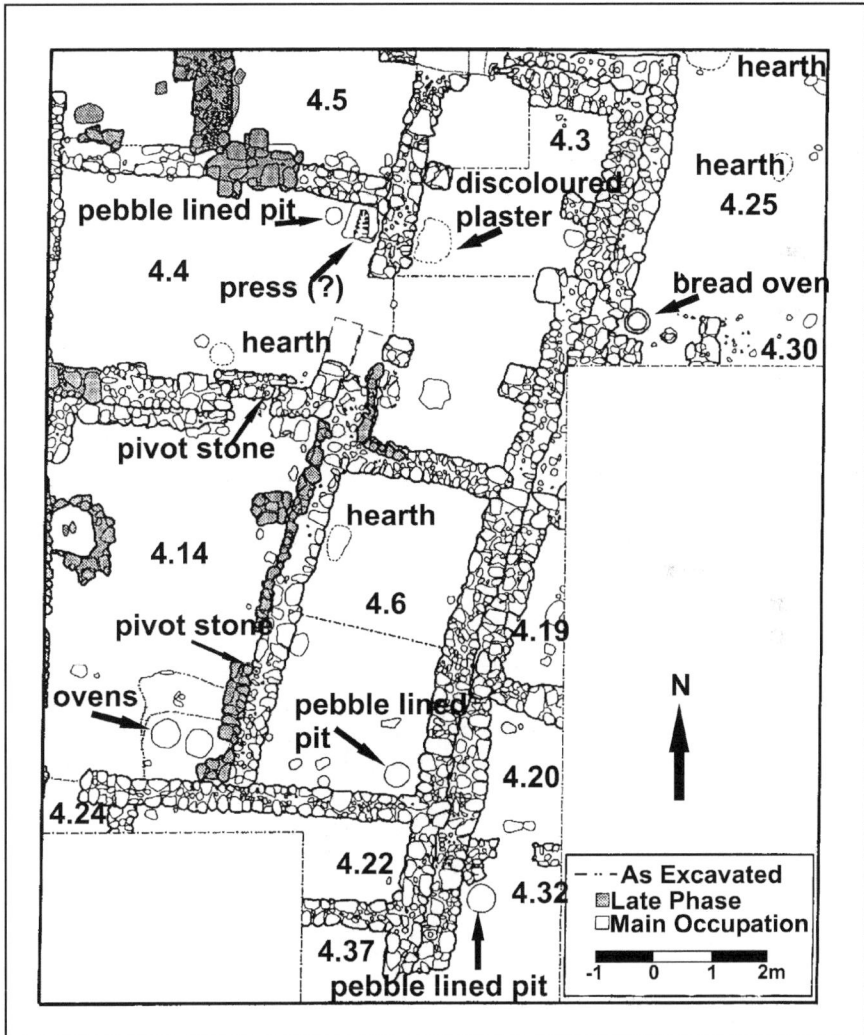

Figure 5.16 House in Op. 4, lower town, Tell es-Sweyhat.

rooms as well as several additional rooms abutting the building to the south-east (Zettler 1997b: 39–43; figs. 3.5–3.6). With a floor space that exceeded 110 m^2, this is a large building indeed (Zettler 1997b: 43). Nonetheless, since its internal features suggest that it was a place of domestic activities, we are fairly confident in identifying this structure as a house.

One room of the house was interpreted as a courtyard due to its large area (Room 4.14: 7 m × 4.5 m). Its floor was paved with pebbles, and its south-eastern corner was distinguished by two circular plastered pits with traces of burning inside. These are likely cooking pits or ovens (Zettler 1997b: 42). Thus, like the courtyards reported at Selenkahiye and Halawa Tell A, this space also appears to have been the locus of food processing within the house.

Other types of installations were encountered in other rooms of the house. A hearth and circular storage pit were found in a room to the east of the courtyard. In the room to the north of the courtyard was found a large limestone block with a truncated oblong depression and narrow channel, pos-sibly the remains of some kind of press, while a circular clay and pebble lined pit was found in the floor next to it (Zettler 1997b: 40, 43). Room 4.3 to the east was particularly unique, as three piers abutted its southeastern wall. Such piers, which would have been used to buttress the walls, may also have provided support for a second story. The presence of two storeys is not well attested in settlements in the Euphrates Valley from this period, although terra-cotta house models from the nearby site of Ali al-Haj (SS 17), and also the site of Assur in northern Mesopotamia confirm that such houses existed (Andrae 1922: 36–8; Masuda 1983: 153–60; Zettler 1997b: 41). In the same room were found two baked clay disks with central perforations on the floor which have been spindle whorls, possibly attesting to the activity of spinning in this locale. Last, directly outside of the house to the northeast were found the remains of hearths and one circular beehive-shaped oven. Further cooking activities, possibly the baking of bread, may have been carried out here (Zettler 1997b: 43).

The large building found in Operation 4, therefore, appears to have served as a house comprising a full array of domestic installations and associated household artifacts. The house may also have been the locus of specialized activities, possibly related to cloth-making, evidenced by the spindle whorls, and grape processing, as attested by a 'press'. While somewhat uncommon, such small-scale activities are not absent elsewhere in domestic contexts in the Euphrates Valley and should not be construed as overly unusual. Nonetheless, it remains uncertain whether such side-line activities have any relationship to the size of the house. Moreover, it is uncertain whether these activities represent a small-scale 'cottage industry' for local use, or if they contributed to a larger site-wide industry that was connected with external trade (Holland 1993–94: 279).

Household terra-cotta figurines

In addition to the usual assemblage of objects associated with household activities such as food processing, storage and eating, it is also common to find terra-cotta artifacts in third millennium Euphrates houses. Some of these objects may be reflective of the household residents' belief in the supernatural and practice of sympathetic magic.

The terra-cotta objects in question consist mainly of baked clay anthropomorphic figurines and animal representations. To a lesser extent, baked clay components of miniature four-wheeled wagons and two-wheeled chariots have also been recovered from household contexts. The miniature vehicles' function is still largely uncertain. It may be noteworthy, however, that unlike human and animal figurines, terra-cotta wheeled vehicles also appear in EB tomb contexts, suggesting that they may have served a somewhat different function from the figurines.[1]

Considerable speculation has revolved around the meaning and purpose of the figurines, especially the anthropomorphic beings. Meaningful conclusions about their function and significance, however, can only be formulated after several different factors are considered together. These include the visual properties of the figurines, breakage patterns, provenance, and the objects' association with other artifacts and architectural features.

Terra-cotta figurines have been reported from a number of EB Euphrates sites.[2] The majority of the figurines appear to date to contexts that are from the mid-to-late third millennium BC. Together, the stylistic characteristics of the figurines of the northern Euphrates River Valley form a corpus that is distinct from other cultural zones of Syria. The precise cultural boundaries of this horizon of figurines have yet to be precisely determined, although it would appear that they extend down as far as Tell Bi'a to the southeast, and to Tell Chuera in the east (Liebowitz 1988: 26; Meyer and Pruss 1994: 53–4). To the north, the border could extend well up the Euphrates into Anatolia, where many sites with EB occupation have now been reported. At present, the greatest concentration of figurines are found within the northern Syrian Euphrates sites whose EB urban occupations constitute the focus of this work.

Although the figurines' exact find spots are rarely provided in the archaeological reports, they do appear to have derived from household contexts or places where common folk carried out daily activities. Figurines were found in and among the house ruins and debris of rooms, courtyards and streets adjacent to houses. At Selenkahiye, several figurines were deliberately laid down in spaces under niches, doorsills, ovens and walls, before these new constructions were built over them (Van Loon 1979: 100, 102; 2001: 6.343). Elsewhere, figurines are reported as having come from trash deposits which are physically separate from domestic structures. The fact that these deposits are characterized by quantities of ash and refuse in the form of carbonized grain and broken utilitarian pottery, however, suggests that they represent the by-products of activities associated with ordinary domestic contexts.

Halawa Tell A and Selenkahiye, two late EB sites with the widest exposure of domestic structures, yielded the greatest number of terra-cotta figurines. A distribution map of the EB city of Halawa A, which highlights the location of anthropomorphic figurines is especially telling because of the heavy concentration of such objects in domestic houses (Meyer and Pruss 1994: Karte 7). While some figurines have indeed been unearthed in the zone of the long-roomed temple *in antis*, they are far fewer than in the residential quarters of the site. It is also significant that only two specimens were found within the temple building itself, while the remainder were found in smaller associated buildings and the open courtyard within the enclosed sacred enclosure. These latter spaces may have been places where common folk were admitted, while the sacred space of the temple itself provided access only to priests and cult functionaries. Whatever the situation, there is not a strong correlation between anthropomorphic figurines and institutionalized religion, at least at Halawa Tell A.

Animal figurines include the representations of equids, bulls, sheep, goats, and birds. There are also occasional examples of animal and rider figurines, in which crudely rendered human figures sit side-saddle on equids that are usually identifiable as donkeys (Liebowitz 1988: 18). The fact that animal figurines have roughly the same household distribution as anthropomorphic figurines, and that the majority were found broken suggests a similar function to the latter. One noteworthy exception to the concentration of animal figurines in households is the discovery of over 70 parts of animal figurines in area D at Tell Banat (Figure 8.10) (Porter and McClellan 1998: 24, Figure 21). It has been conjectured that this was the locale of a large pottery manufactory, owing to the number of workshop spaces, kilns and waster deposits associated with the forming and firing of ceramic vessels (Porter and McClellan 1998: 18–24). The location of many of the animal figurines in kiln dumps may indicate that they too were being produced in this area, possibly for a wide number of consumers (Porter and McClellan 1998: 24).

Anthropomorphic figurines are both of females and males. We will not repeat here the detailed classification of these figurines, based on visual traits, which has been carefully undertaken by others (Badre 1980; Liebowitz 1988; Meyer and Pruss 1994). Only some of the objects' general characteristics are described. The majority of figurines are pillar-shaped standing figures with splaying, slightly concave, circular or oval bases (Liebowitz 1988: 4). The bases of most of the figurines suggest standing figures in long garments, rather than bare legs (Figure 5.17 left) (Van Loon 2001: 6.341). While the faces of the figurines usually have prominent noses, there is a notable absence of mouths and chins (Liebowitz 1988: 4). Details of dress are normally restricted to necklaces, which are characterized by one or more applied strips of clay around the neck, often incised or scored (Figure 5.18). Only occasionally does

Figure 5.17 Female (left) and male (right) terra-cotta figurines, Halawa Tell A.

Figure 5.18 Female figurine head, Tell Hadidi.

one find additional details on the body such as incised lines to indicate a hairy chest, or crude renderings of a belt and dagger (Liebowitz 1988: 4).

Differences in the gender of the figurines are based on the different ways in which the head and upper limbs have been rendered, and not on the presence of genitalia and beards, which are only occasionally rendered. Female breasts are also only occasionally featured on female figurines (Figure 5.17 left). Generally, figurines whose hands are placed on their chests and who wear elaborate hairstyles are identified as females. Their hairstyles are characterized by tresses that are composed of strips of clay applied to each side of the face and sometimes incised, a crown-like fringe across the forehead, pin curls and/or a thick ponytail or bun at the back of the head. Females may also have hair that is piled high on top of the head (Figure 5.19). Figurines with arm stumps that are extended in front of them are identified as male. Conical headdresses are also identified with male representations (Figure 5.17 right).

While the eyes and nose are usually modelled, the mouth is rarely ever represented on the faces of figurines. It is also noteworthy that the remainder of the body, with its long pillar-like base hardly reflects the natural contours of the human form (Petty 2004: 194–5). Concerning these characteristics, Alice Petty has drawn attention to the fact that in ancient Mesopotamia, the mouth is associated with the enlivenment of an anthropomorphic image. Thus the omission of the mouth, along with the other non-naturalistic characteristics, implies that the objects could never be enlivened, and 'that they were explicitly intended to be understood as products of the artisan's hand' (Petty 2004: 197). In this way, then, it is probably more appropriate to regard the objects as suggestive or symbolic of a character or concept rather than as actual representations of such things (Petty 2004: 197).

Another important observation about the figurines is that the overwhelming majority of them were found broken. Although some figurines may

Figure 5.19 Female figurine head, Tell Hadidi.

have been broken post-depositionally, many seem to have been deliberately broken during their use. The patterns of breakage can vary, although it was very common for figurines to have been broken at the neck. Alternatively, many figurines were broken at the level of or below the waist.

How can one interpret these figurines? The suggestion that they are representations of deities or other cult figures seems unlikely for a number of reasons. These figurines do not have analogies with any representations of deities that have been found in purely religious contexts at the settlements, which is what one might expect if these were regarded as cheap or miniature household versions of cult objects or worshipper statues (Meyer and Pruss 1994: 56). Further, as we reported earlier, these figurines are not found prolifically in temple contexts. Finally, enthographic studies that have been conducted around the world have shown that because of their potency, cult figures are usually carefully disposed of at the end of their use; they are unlikely to be found in ordinary garbage (Voigt 1991: 36). While some carefully buried figurines at Selenkahiye may fit this pattern, one still needs to explain the overwhelming majority of figurines, which were found broken and disposed, it seems, in regular household trash.

A more persuasive suggestion is that the figurines represent vehicles of magic. Cross-culturally, such objects tend to include a wide range of activities and behaviours which can range from pious burials in sub-floor contexts, disposal in trash or placement underneath other features. Moreover, it is not uncommon for vehicles of magic to be deliberately broken (Petty 2004: 198). Perhaps magical potency is thought to be released from the figurines as they are broken, or else the act of breaking them brings about some desired effect, such as the termination of an illness, or the expulsion of a malevolent ghost. In many cases, once the object has been used and has been drained of its magical power, it can be tossed aside. Last, it is worth reporting that vehicles of magic need not stand directly for the human, animal or the thing that they represent in terra-cotta (Voigt 1991: 36). The figures may be symbolic of some concept or idea. The representation of a wild bull, for example, does not have to symbolize the life of the bull or even the concept of the fertility of the herds. The wild bull could be a symbol of male virility among humans. Whatever the exact symbolism of these magical objects, their frequency in domestic contexts probably indicates their utilization by common folk, and their connection to concerns about personal or kin-group activities and interactions taking place within the cities' households.

DISCUSSION

In this chapter, we have presented in full the evidence for ancient domestic architecture, and as well as some of the artifacts and decoration found within such contexts, pointing out specific features of importance. Thus, for the different sites, we have discussed patterns relating to the physical layout, function and transformation of domestic space as well as the behaviour of the occupants of this space over time. In the pages to follow, we will summarize the evidence for urban planning in Euphrates settlements of the Early Bronze Age. We will also describe changes that occurred in households in these settlements. Of particular importance in this regard will be the strong relationship between the nature of housing and the urban character of the settlements of this period.

Urban planning

In Phases 1–2 of the EB, domestic houses were relatively small and simply laid out. Nearly all the early EB houses from Halawa Tell B, Tell Habuba Kabira and Shiyukh Fouqani, for example, were single-roomed households, sharing similar mud brick construction techniques and internal arrangements. These structures apparently provided living quarters for individual nuclear families. While some domestic activities took place within the houses, limited space probably led to many activities being carried out in exterior open areas, possibly in communally shared spaces within the settlements.

In spite of the simplicity of these houses, indications of urban planning are already evident. Some of the houses at the northern end of the settlement at Halawa Tell B, for example, appear to have been well aligned within the massive city wall. The houses at Shiyukh Fouqani were laid out on either side of a straight street. At Tell Habuba Kabira, the neat alignment of the exterior eastern walls of the houses produced a solid, defensive line, thereby enhancing the protection and security of the settlement as a whole. While these examples indicate some form of community organization and pooling of labour, a super-ordinate elite authority was probably not responsible for their successful undertaking and completion. Most of the town planning manifested in these small early EB settlements could easily have been carried out by inhabitants who coordinated their plans and cooperated in their neighbourhoods' foundations and construction.

By the latter half of the third millennium (Phases 4–5), urban planning had become quite apparent. Sites such as Halawa Tell A, Tell Hadidi, Tell es-Sweyhat and Selenkahiye were characterized by long streets, some intersecting at right angles, and well-aligned city blocks of domestic houses. Such urban configurations suggest intensive planning to increase the efficiency of communication and transport within what were becoming increasingly large and densely inhabited city sectors. At the settlement of Halawa Tell A, there is even evidence that houses were built of roughly the same dimensions from front to back, and that they were characterized by the same standardized room arrangements. This level of architectural regularity suggests centralized planning and the mobilization of labour beyond the level of the household, although precisely what form such centralized organization took is difficult to reconstruct.

Patterns of recurring, standardized houses occur elsewhere. At the third millennium site of Titris Höyük in northeastern Anatolia, for example, two basic household modules with standardized internal arrangements have been reported in the Outer Town (Matney and Algaze 1995: 40–1). Groups of standardized house sizes and similar internal room arrangements have likewise been reported within various sectors of the EB settlement at Tell Chuera to the east (Pfälzner 2001: 348). Common also were orderly alignments of similarly-sized houses along streets. These houses were organized into city blocks. Such configurations have likewise been reported at Titris Höyük, Tell Chuera, as well as Tell Taya in northern Iraq (Matney and Algaze 1995: 49; Orthmann *et al.* 1986; Plan II; Reade 1973: pls. 60–1). We should not see these patterns as indicative of a single overarching authority imposing its conventions of architectural standardization and town planning upon all settlements of northern Mesopotamia. Rather, such patterns appear to be the result of a general trend towards urbanization that most areas of northern Mesopotamia began to experience around the middle of the third millennium BC. In this milieu of urban development, in which cultural exchange between settlements was a natural product of frequent trade contacts, political alliances and other forms of communication, shared information about town planning and the internal organization of space would have circulated, especially among growing, similarly-structured cities.

Household expansions

Even during the earliest phases of EB occupation, simple single-roomed houses were occasionally transformed into larger households. At Halawa Tell B, houses were expanded by the addition of enclosed areas and courtyards. Similarly, at Tell Habuba Kabira, the so-called 'Southern Complex' represents an adaptation and modification of what had originally been two smaller houses. This pattern of expansion continues into the middle of the Early Bronze Age. At Tell al-ʿAbd, it was observed that various additions in the form of anterooms and courtyards had been added to the principal rooms of houses.

During the mid-to-late EB (Phases 4–5), almost all Euphrates houses were planned from the beginning as multi-roomed buildings. Most houses were characterized by large courtyard spaces that were furnished with fire installations and other equipment related to food preparation. Other rooms of the house served as spaces for sleeping, eating, entertaining, additional food processing and storage.

What causes may there have been for the late EB interior expansion of household space? It is possible that households were growing in family size. It is difficult to summon specific evidence for this supposition, but we may safely assume that as families increased in size, their needs of greater space and defined space emerged.

There is considerable evidence of household space now being used for specific activities. The internal division of domestic space into a number of smaller units reflects the various activities taking place in the household. Functionally discrete spaces appear where these activities could be performed to their maximum efficiency. In early periods of the Early Bronze Age, various household activities, such as food preparation, sleeping and eating, occurred in the same internal space. In later periods these activities were given distinct spaces, separated from one another by walls, benches, alcoves and other partitioning constructions.

Along with this development, inhabited space came also to be divided into sacred and profane areas. In the earliest phases of the EB the appearance of architectural features and wall paintings connected with religious practices existed in what appeared to be rooms of simple domestic structures. Sacred and profane spheres of behaviour at this time were not clearly demarcated. With time, however, a distinction between the two developed. By the end of the EB, the separation of sacred and profane is most clearly manifested in the appearance of several visibly recognizable temples at Euphrates settlements. These religious complexes were neatly segregated from the other non-religious sectors of the urban community by temenos walls and gate-houses.

Another example of the growing complexity of the household is the increasing privatization of space (Akkermans and Schwartz 2003: 269). The appearance of enclosed courtyard spaces observed by the mid-third millennium BC in almost every Euphrates household is probably related to this development. Activities, previously carried out within open communal spaces in a settlement, were now undertaken in enclosed spaces within individual households (Akkermans and Schwartz 2003: 269). Another feature of these households consists of household storage spaces of increased size and number. At Halawa Tell A and Selenkahiye, storage rooms positioned at the rear of the house were found still full of ceramic jars resting *in situ* amid charred grains of barley.

Changes to the household can be ascribed to the growing complexity of urban life and the economic inequalities that accompanied such a development. At this time, the means of acquiring economic prosperity grew through trade, the acquisition of agricultural land and the intensification of farming and pastoral pursuits. Concurrent with these activities, there probably developed a preoccupation with personal gain and, by extension, personal possessions. The household, comprising individuals bound by kinship ties emerged as the most important unit of social and economic organization in this region. The household served for the safeguarding and stockpiling of resources. Thus we have evidence for additions to and expansions of interior household activity and storage space. In contrast, evidence that reflects efforts on the part of the urban communities to pool commodities and to hold such resources in communal ownership are absent.

In some instances, economic successes of individual households resulted in the expansion of house size and complexity well beyond that of other houses in the city. It would seem that this development began to occur quite early in the EB, as evidenced at Halawa Tell B, where several smaller houses were subsumed into one extraordinarily large house at the southern end of the settlement. In later periods, Selenkahiye's House 8 was unusually large and distinctive, as was the large 'manor' found in Operation 4 in the lower town of Tell es-Sweyhat.

In some cases, certain economic activities appear to have a correlation with the size and wealth of these houses. Thus, for example, the expansion of the household at the southern end of Halawa Tell B might have been tied to its metal-working activities. At Tell Habuba Kabira, the presence of a jewellery manufactory in one household may have been related both to its size and also the long duration of this household, which persisted through several phases of occupation within the city. Within the large house at Tell es-Sweyhat, artifacts and installations point to activities such as textile production and olive or wine making. House 8 at Selenkahiye may have been engaged in long-distance trading activities.

As a last remark, we would like to suggest that there was a connection between the increasing complexity of the household – in terms of its size, the number of activities performed within it, and the variety of economic ventures it engaged in – and the growing frequency and complexity with which we find manifestations of sympathetic magic. Such phenomena are most visibly expressed in the form of anthropomorphic terra-cotta figures and animal figurines, and possibly also miniature wheeled vehicles. These figurines, which likely served as vehicles of magic, display considerable stylistic variation, breakage patterns and methods of burial and disposal. Their variety underlines the multiplicity of ways in which they must have functioned in the realm of the supernatural, serving to expel, entreat, destroy, create or cajole any number of spirits, ghosts, sensations, impulses and passions within the physical space of the household, including within the individuals themselves who inhabited these spaces. The variety of concerns expressed by these figurines surely corresponds with the growing complexity of urban life experienced by people in the Euphrates communities, who would have faced on a daily basis a complicated and entangled array of economic and social partnerships, rivalries, opportunities and new challenges within the urban communities developing around them.

6

LARGE-SCALE SECULAR
BUILDINGS

Large-scale buildings are among the more conspicuous architectural features of third millennium Euphrates sites. These buildings are physically grander and usually have a more complex arrangement of rooms than typical domestic structures. In this chapter, we will deal with large-scale buildings where secular, as opposed to religious, activities were carried out. One is likely to find material remains attesting to the acquisition and possession of wealth in these structures, as well as the performance of complex or frequent economic activities. In contrast, remains attesting to sacred, ceremonial activities are rare.

It is probable that large-scale secular buildings served as the residences or headquarters of an elite group of citizens, or at the very least, some corporate body of city inhabitants who possessed a measure of influence or authority within the city. We have avoided using the term 'public' to refer to these structures since some buildings may have been restricted or closed off to the majority of the inhabitants of the settlements in which they existed. At the same time, we cannot reject altogether the possibility that some important economic and political activities of the city were organized through these centres. In this sense, therefore, some of these buildings may have had a 'public' function since they served in some capacity to administer to the wider urban community.

Although the term 'large-scale' was chosen to designate the greater size of these structures in relation to common urban houses, we have refrained from using the term 'palace' to denote most of these third millennium structures. It may be true that these buildings have a character of monumentality and comprise several features that one may also find at other buildings of third millennium Syria whose identification as palaces has gone unchallenged. On the other hand, none of the excavated Euphrates structures are of an overall size that is comparable to other palatial structures from Syria during the third millennium. None of these Euphrates' large-scale buildings, for example, approach the dimensions of Palace G at Ebla, which comprised a vast and rambling interconnected complex of courtyards, archive rooms, reception halls, private apartments and storage wings (Dolce 1988; Akkermans and Schwartz 2003: 235). The excavated area covered by rooms of the Ebla palace already amounts to more than 2,400 m², and it is likely that this royal complex extended across the entire summit of the acropolis (Matthiae 1997: 181). Similarly, the third millennium palace complex at Mari to the southeast far exceeds in size and monumentality all of the north Syrian Euphrates buildings excavated thus far. Dating between 2500–2300 BC, the palace's complex of rooms, courtyards and an impressive columned throne room, could well exceed 6,000 m² once all of its ground plan has been revealed (Margueron 1982: 94–5; Figure 52; 1990a: Figure 2). At this size, Mari's massive palatial complex might have been almost three times the size of Building 6 at Tell Banat, which at approximately 2,500 m², appears to be the grandest large-scale secular building in the northern Euphrates region known at this time (Porter 2002b: 157).

Besides its large size, the term 'palace' inevitably brings to mind the presence, especially in the ancient Near East, of a ruling class or ruling house, characterized principally by a king who exercised absolute power over a subordinate population. While the presence of this kind of royal authority may be an appropriate way of describing the exercise of power in other third millennium cities in Mesopotamia, we are not certain that it is correct to speak of the Syrian Euphrates urban society in terms of hierarchical, monarchical systems of class distinction (Porter 2002b: 167). An urban elite was certainly present in Euphrates Early Bronze Age societies, particularly towards the late third millennium, when large-scale structures became especially prominent. It remains uncertain, however, whether or not we should assign a superordinate status to these cities' elites, and to characterize them as wielding extensive control over the social, economic and political institutions of the urban communities which they dominated, as in the manner of kings. We have already suggested that power need not always be concentrated in the hands of a small, exclusive group of aristocratic individuals. The responsibilities of the organization and maintenance of the city and control over its resources could just as easily have been dispersed among many individuals or groups from divergent lineages and socio-economic backgrounds. Furthermore, rather than envisioning only one type of power structure that uniformly characterized all third millennium settlements in the region, it is possible that the nature of power varied widely from one city to the next. It is important to recognize the individual, distinctive character of each Euphrates settlement, and the unique way in which each settlement developed and transformed over the course of several centuries of urban life.

Large-scale secular structures may have existed at several of the Syrian Euphrates sites, although archaeological excavations have enabled only a few buildings to be positively identified as such. Thus, the remains of a large structure with wide walls, designated as Building A, was found near one of the principal city gates at Tell al-ʿAbd, although its precise function remains undetermined (Finkbeiner 1995: 58–9; 1997: 98–100). Some large-scale buildings may have been positioned on the summit of the small but defensively impressive mound of Jerablus Tahtani, although that area remains largely unexplored. At Tell Habuba Kabira, excavations along the southwestern slope of the mound have revealed in a late third millennium level (Phase 5) a monumental terrace and gate-house that may have served a larger structure or complex higher on the mound. Unfortunately that complex has also not been recovered (Strommenger 1980: 72).

Buildings 6 and 7 at Tell Banat

Although we are uncertain about the existence and function of some sites' large-scale buildings, we are relatively well informed about two large buildings at the site of Tell Banat, which existed during the peak of the site's pre-eminence, roughly between 2600–2300 BC (Phases 3–4) (Figure 6.1). It is unfortunate that the modern village, which is located directly over the ancient mound, has prevented excavations from uncovering the entire ground plans of these extraordinary edifices, although sufficient investigations have been undertaken to get some sense of their size and grandeur. These structures clearly had a special function, although curiously they were not located in an exceptionally visible or elevated place at the site. On the contrary, the buildings were sited in a low, flat area, several metres lower than the western ridge, where the potter's quarter was located (McClellan 1999: 417).

As we will outline in greater detail in Chapter 9, Tell Banat appears to have functioned primarily as a mortuary centre, where a variety of tombs and tumuli were erected, and where elaborate funerary festivals and cultic activities served to commemorate the dead and to strengthen the bonds of kinship and community among the living. Given the overwhelming mortuary character of Banat, it seems likely that these large-scale buildings served in some association with the funerary traditions observed at the site. That the buildings were located only a few metres away from several tombs further supports their funerary association. It may be additionally significant that the walls of the earlier Building 7 were set directly into a clean gravel filling that entirely covered an earlier monumental mortuary tumulus (Mortuary Mound II) (McClellan 1999: 418–19; Porter 2002a: 16).

Although it is not common to find large-scale residences connected to funerary structures in southern Mesopotamia during the third millennium, this association is not out of place in Syria. At Ebla, a royal tomb was discovered under the floor of one of the rooms of the EB Palace G (Akkermans and Schwartz 2003: 238). Similarly, a large above-ground mausoleum at Tell Bi'a may have been connected to an elite ruler's palace nearby (McClellan 1999: 419; Strommenger 1997: 113). Elaborate multi-chambered corbelled tombs were also found under the floors of the impressive late third millennium *shakkanaku* palace at Mari (Margueron 1990b). In light of this evidence, it is possible that some of the funerary structures located in proximity to

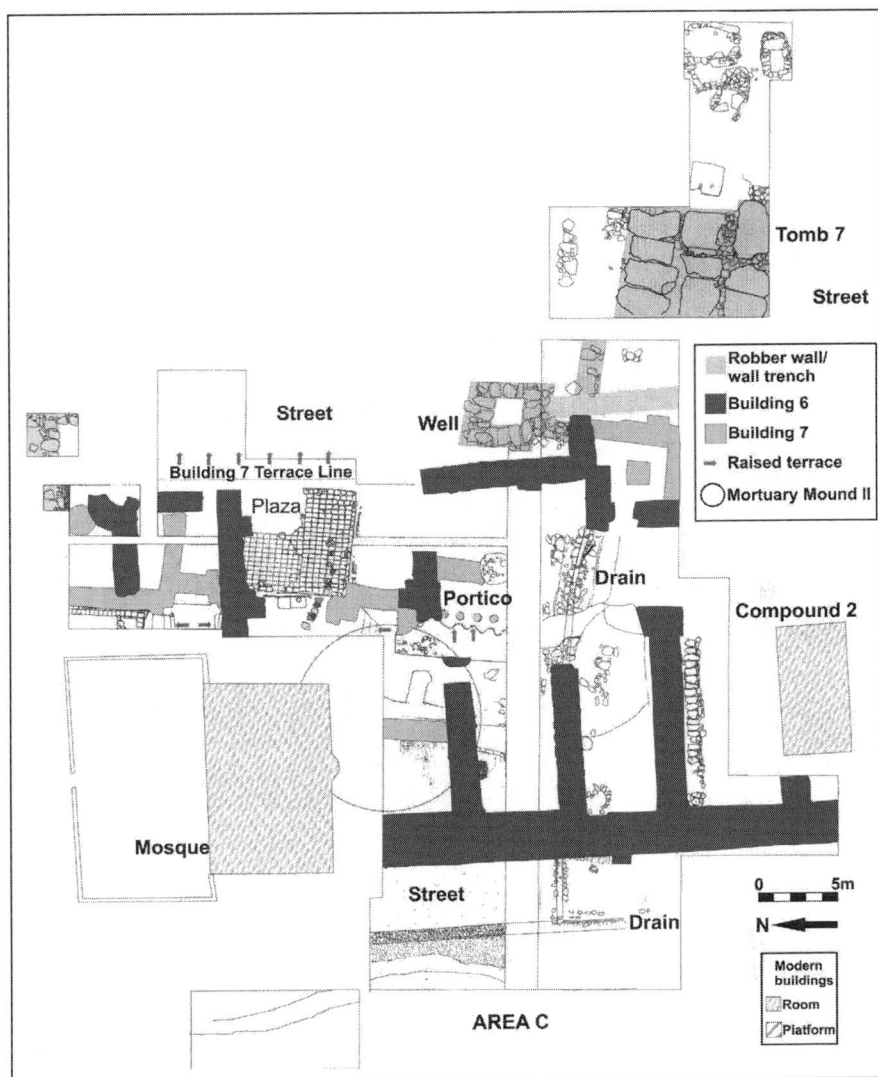

Figure 6.1 Buildings 6 and 7, Tell Banat.

Buildings 6 and 7 belonged to or were in some way connected to the individuals who had resided in these structures, and that such individuals commanded some degree of power or influence within the settlement at Banat. The impressively constructed and richly equipped Tomb 7 is an especially likely candidate to be linked to Buildings 6 and 7, given that it is precisely contemporary with these structures and located only a few metres away (Porter 2002b: 158).

129

Of the two structures, Building 7 is the earlier, having been occupied during Phase 3 (2600–2450 BC), while Building 6, which was built directly over Building 7, dates to Phase 4 (2450–2300 BC) (Porter 2002b: 158, 161). Only a small portion of the earlier Building 7 was brought to light, although enough was recovered to ascertain that this had been a well built, elegant structure (Porter and McClellan 1998: 26; McClellan 1999: 419). Building 7 was multi-chambered, comprising rooms, interconnecting hallways and courtyards spread out over at least three terraces. The remains of column bases over one metre in diameter were found some 20–25 m to the east of the principally exposed section of the building, suggesting that this was a structure of considerable size and monumentality (McClellan 1999: 419). In the best preserved portion of Building 7 the remains of two square rooms, 7 × 7 m in area, were found paved entirely with baked clay tiles set in bitumen mortar (Porter and McClellan 1998: 25–6). This tiled installation gave the rooms a fine, finished appearance, reflecting the care and expense involved in the construction of the building. Ascending and descending staircases between rooms negotiated the terraces upon which the building was erected. To the south, four column bases were found, forming the portico of a room, while in the far south, the building comprised a rectangular room with a central newel.

Building 7 was replaced by Building 6, which was a much more extensive, solid and imposing structure. The walls of this edifice were constructed of heavy stone boulders, often several metres in thickness. The western wall of Building 6, about 3 m in thickness, was traced for about 25 m to the south. From this wall, four lateral walls extended eastward forming narrow rooms, possibly storerooms (McClellan 1999: 419). Three more rooms were recovered further to the north, the walls of one of which was buttressed along its southern side (Porter and McClellan 1998: 29). The baked tile surface of one of the square rooms of Building 7 continued to be used in Building 6, serving as a kind of central axis around which the other rooms revolved (Porter 2002b: 161). Overall, the thick stone walls gave Building 6 a more restricted, sequestered character than the earlier Building 7. The excavators wonder if this development reflects an increasingly segmented, stratified society at Banat in the later period, during which the inhabitants or users of this building made greater efforts to set themselves apart from the rest of the community (Porter 2002a: 27).

Selenkahiye's Southern Mansion

The largest and most unique building recovered at the site of Selenkahiye was named the Southern Mansion, owing to its large size and the grandeur of its construction (Figure 6.2). The building is located near the southern end of the settlement and appears to have been in use in the second half of the third millennium BC (Phases 4–5), around the same time that a dense cluster

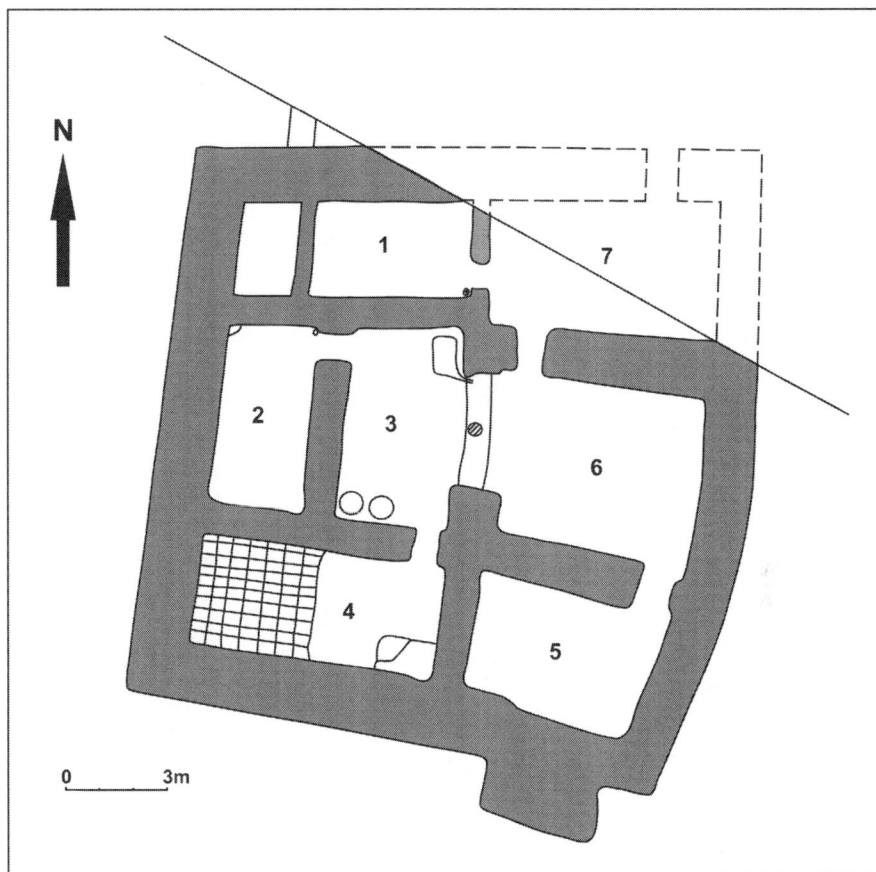

Figure 6.2 Southern Mansion, Selenkahiye (local phase 7).

of houses occupied the central area of the settlement and the city fortifications enclosed the site. The Southern Mansion experienced at least two major destructions, the first causing a collapse of brickwork in several of the rooms, while the second consisted of a major conflagration, leaving traces of heavy burning everywhere and filling the rooms with burnt debris (Van Loon 2001: 3.38–3.41). Within this debris, the skeleton of a child was found, probably a victim of the disaster, while another male victim was found lying prone with his head shielded by his raised arm. His toggle and an adze were found nearby (Van Loon 2001: 3.41). After this violent event, the Southern Mansion was occupied once more, although evidence in the form of blocked doorways and the construction of several ovens suggests a functional shift from an important spacious house to the cramped quarters of several families (Van Loon 2001: 41). For the purposes of our discussion here, we will restrict our discussion of the Southern Mansion to the period before its final 're-occupation' phase.

The layout of the Southern Mansion was quite regular, and all of the walls of the house were bonded, showing that the building had been conceived and constructed as a whole (Van Loon 2001: 3.35). The foundations were made of large unhewn blocks of stone, topped by courses of bricks. The walls averaged 80 cm in thickness, which is wide enough to support a second story. The outer walls were especially wide, measuring about 1.20 m (Van Loon 2001: 3.35).

The entrance to the Southern Mansion was probably located in the north-eastern corner in Room 7, although it was not recoverable due to damage by erosion and a bulldozer cut. The interior of the house comprised several rectangular or square rooms, the most unusual of which was the centrally located Room 3. The eastern entrance of this room had a raised mud brick threshold upon which was found a drum-shaped white limestone column base. This base supported a poplar column, whose burned traces were clearly recognizable (Van Loon 2001: 3.37). To date, no other columned arrangement like this has been recovered from third millennium contexts in northern Mesopotamia. Its closest parallel comes from a much later date in the seventeenth century BC, in level VII of Yarim-Lim's Palace at Alalakh. Here a room with a columned entrance has also been recovered. Perhaps the Selenkahiye Southern Mansion represents one of the earliest examples of this distinctive feature of elite north Syrian architecture (Van Loon 2001: 3.96).

It is likely that the western side of the Southern Mansion had two storeys. In addition to the thickness of the walls, the western rooms contained more destruction debris than the eastern rooms. Moreover, bitumen-coated fragments of beams and reeds were found in one of the rooms, suggesting that some kind of waterproof installation like an indoor basin or reservoir existed somewhere on the second floor (Van Loon 2001: 3.39 n.8). Room 3 itself may not have had a second storey, although its ceiling could have been raised to a higher level. In the reconstructed drawing of the Southern Mansion, the high walls of Room 3 are shown with open spaces flanking a second column above the lower one (Figure 6.3) (Van Loon 2001: 3.96).

It is possible that in the second phase of occupation of the Southern Mansion, the southwestern corner was converted into a tower. Given the mansion's location in the southern extremity of the settlement, this defensive feature would not have been unusual. Evidence for this tower takes the form of a filling of large mud bricks that were laid in mortar in the western half of Room 4. A platform in the southeastern corner may have served as a support for wooden stairs leading to the upper part of the tower (Van Loon 2001: 3.40–3.41).

Artifacts from several rooms of the Southern Mansion testify to the building's importance before its second destruction. Many unbaked clay sealed jar stoppers, some carrying the imprints of strings that had secured the covers of

Figure 6.3 Reconstruction of Southern Mansion.

jars or other containers, as well as two cylinder seals, were recovered from at least three of the rooms (Van Loon 2001: 3.35–36, 3.40, 12.495). The centrally located Room 3 yielded the largest number of seal impressions, each seal design occurring one or more times on a total of 77 clay lumps (Van Loon 2001: 12.495). Deliveries to the mansion were probably received and opened in Room 3. These items clearly attest to the administrative or economic activities of the occupants of this building.

A broken pedestal and feet of a worshipper statue, found near the doorway leading from Room 6 to Room 7, and a statue fragment with fringed clothing nearby, suggest that some cultic activities were carried out in the house before it was destroyed by fire and plundered (Van Loon 2001: 3.41). Perhaps the Southern Mansion possessed a kind of 'house-chapel', similar to that found in House XXXVIII at Khafajeh in Mesopotamia (Delougaz *et al.*

1967: pl. 10; Van Loon 2001: 3.97). Whatever the case, it would be erroneous to assume that the entire building had a cultic function given the lack of podia, the presence of several ovens and storage containers in some of its rooms, and the defensive tower in the southwestern corner (Van Loon 2001: 3.97).

In layout and contents, the Southern Mansion has no parallels with any of the other houses at Selenkahiye. The central room with column was clearly an important room in the structure, serving as a point of access to all of the other rooms, and playing a key role in the administrative activities of the building's occupants (Van Loon 2001: 3.95). The Southern Mansion is also the largest building at Selenkahiye. In light of these attributes, it is likely that the structure served as the residence and administrative quarters of an wealthy, elite household.

Tell es-Sweyhat's high mound: Area IV 'warehouse'

The most coherent plan of a large-scale secular building at Tell es-Sweyhat comes from Area IV, located on the lower northwest terrace of the central high mound. The building comprised several rooms that had been built against the wide, inner fortification wall of the settlement, while its eastern side was bordered by a long pebble-paved street that ran parallel to the town wall (Holland 1993–94: 278). The building eventually came to be dubbed the 'Burned Building' owing to the massive conflagration that destroyed it sometime around 2100 BC (Figure 6.4). After this fire, traces of further late

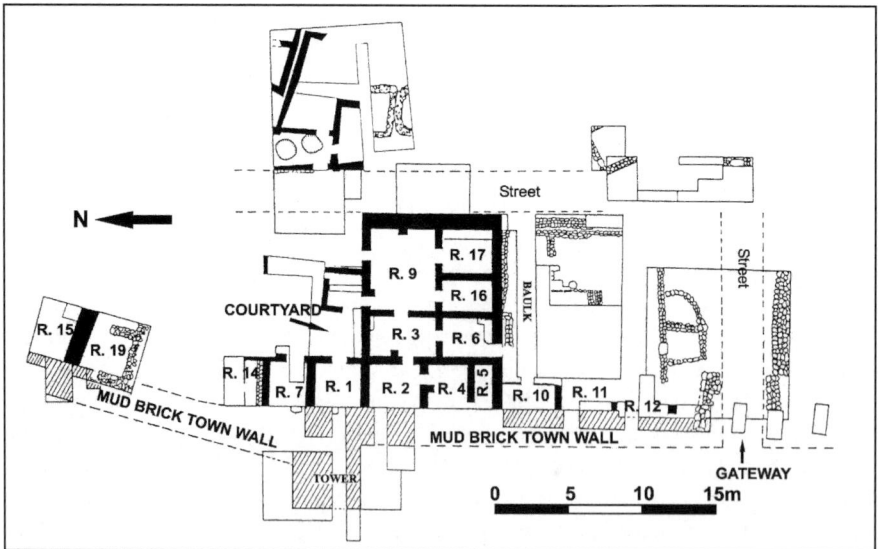

Figure 6.4 Area IV 'Burned Building' complex, Tell es-Sweyhat.

third or early second millennium occupation were recovered in and among the rooms of the burned complex as well as further to the east in Area IVZ, in Operations 1, 20 and 12 to the north, and in Operation 8 to the south (Holland 1977: 42–3; Holland 1993–94: 280; Armstrong and Zettler 1997: 27–30). The evidence provided by this later occupation, however, represents a somewhat impoverished phase of settlement on the tell, when the overall size of the settlement had diminished and the architecture was more ephemeral. In light of this development, our discussion here will focus only on the architecture and artifacts of the Area IV building prior to its destruction by fire. This building's occupation would have coincided with Sweyhat's fluorescence, when the city had reached its greatest size and defensive strength (Phase 5).

The innermost rooms of the Area IV complex (Rooms 14, 7, 1, 2, 4, 5, 10–13) were built directly against the inner face of the citadel's fortification wall, and appear to have served primarily for the storage of materials. This storage function was particularly apparent in Room 4 of the complex, where many pottery vessels were found crowded together on the floor (Holland 1976: 57), and in the adjacent Room 5, where heavy burning had preserved large quantities of carbonized seeds, suggesting the function of this room as a grain storage bin (Holland 1976: 59; Van Zeist and Bakker-Heeres 1985). In Room 3, a crucible and associated metal tools attesting to metal working were found among several pottery vessels. Discovered nearby also was an inscribed cuneiform weight, which points to economic transactions within the complex, possibly in connection with the production of metal (Pfälzner 2001: 367). On paleographical grounds the inscribed weight can be dated to the Ur III period (c. 2113–2006 BC) (Holland 1975). Radiocarbon dates taken on samples of charcoal and carbonized grain from the building's original floor have also confirmed a late third millennium date, specifically some time shortly after 2150 BC (Armstrong and Zettler 1997: 25–6).

An abundance of human and animal figures were recovered from several of the rooms of the Area IV building (Rooms 1, 3, 4, 6, 8, 9) (Holland 1976: 55, 57, 59, 61, Figure 15; Holland 1977: 41, Figure 11). One of the horse figurines is especially noteworthy in that it features a well-modelled and applied forelock, mane and sexual organs (Figure 8.10 top left). A hole bored through the muzzle indicates the place for a ring emplacement to hold reins. If this is a representation of a domestic horse, it is, along with the figurines from Tell Banat, among the earliest examples discovered in the Near East (Holland 1993–94: 283, Abb. 111; Porter and McClellan 1998: 24, Figure 21: 2 and 4).

The Area IV building yielded a rich assortment of other artifacts besides terra-cotta figurines. Stone mortars, pestles and other grinding stones, often in association with work platforms and benches were found within the complex, attesting to food processing activities (Rooms 6, 8 and 12: Holland 1976: 55; Holland 1977: 39–41). Several bronze implements consisting of hasps, pins, a collar, a silver fitting of some sort, and a very fine silver bracelet were also found (Holland 1976: Figure 15: 32–4, 36, 38–9, 41). The quantity of metalwork is considerably greater than that found elsewhere at the site, underlining the richness of this building. Several unique vessels, possibly functioning as a special serving container or for use in ritual activities, were also noteworthy finds (Holland 1976: 55, 57, 61). A finely decorated alabaster bowl was included among these vessels (Holland 1976: Figure 15: 52), along with two decorated, spouted ceramic cauldrons (Holland 1976: Figure 7; Holland 1993–94: 279). Finally, a large quantity of storage vessels was found inside the complex. Many of these jars are distinctive, either being incised with potter's marks or being of a somewhat uncommon form.[1] Several specimens of a single-handled, flat-based 'Vounous-Type' storage jar, for example, are included among this corpus of pottery. Although they are presently uncommon at other sites in the Euphrates Valley they have good parallels with jars found as far away as Gaza in southern Palestine (Holland 1976: 57; Holland 1993–94: 282, Abb. 109). Holland's suggestion that these vessels are reflective of long-distance trade, and that the site of Sweyhat was a key transshipment point along a route for goods travelling from east to west, emphasizes the Area IV building's participation in such distant exchanges, especially since these unique vessels have not been found elsewhere at the site (Holland 1993–94: 282).

Tell es-Sweyhat's high mound: 'kitchen building'

Besides the Area IV building complex, information about the nature of occupation on the main mound has also been provided by investigations in Operations 1, 20 and 12 directly to the east (Figure 6.5). While these soundings penetrated into earlier Early Bronze Age levels, this operation's Phase 4 is of special interest as it can be stratigraphically linked with the Area IV complex to the west and thus also dated to the end of the third millennium BC (Euphrates sequence Phase 5).

Phase 4 of Operations 1 and 20 was principally characterized by several

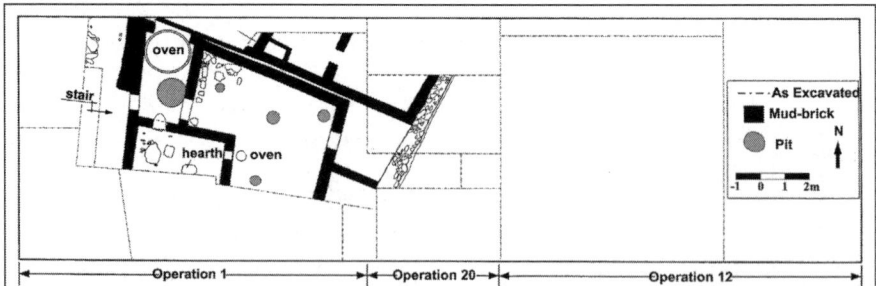

Figure 6.5 Kitchen building, Operations 1, 20 and 12, Tell es-Sweyhat.

rooms of a rather large building that was bordered on the north by a set of rooms belonging to one or two buildings, and to the west by a street or alleyway (Armstrong and Zettler 1997: figs. 2.8–2.9). This street separated the building from the Area IV building complex to the west. Locus 1.13, a rectangular room that was entered directly from the street, was equipped with a large circular oven, 2.2 m in diameter, which occupied all of the northern end of the room. The oven, which was originally domed and probably had a flue at the top or back, was probably used for cooking rather than industrial purposes. Although its interior walls had been reddened by fire, it otherwise showed no signs of high heat (Armstrong and Zettler 1997: 21).

Another room, Locus 1.15, was found to the south of the oven-room. It contained a hearth and fire pit in addition to large slabs of stone which presumably served as work installations (Armstrong and Zettler 1997: 23). Accessed from both of the front rooms of the complex was an L-shaped courtyard, Locus 1.16, characterized by several re-floorings. It contained a large number of fixed features, including cylindrical pits, one of which contained several grinding stones and mortars (Armstrong and Zettler 1997: Figure 2.15). Other installations, namely a beehive-shaped oven, a platform of large stones and an L-shaped stone work bench with several stone slabs lying on the floor in front of it, indicate that food preparation activities such as the grinding of grain and cooking took place here (Armstrong and Zettler 1997: 24). At the back of the building, two more rooms were encountered, connected to one another by an archway. One of the rooms may also originally have contained an oven, judging by the quantity of heavy black ash that had accumulated there (Armstrong and Zettler 1997: 25).

Given the number of work surfaces and cooking installations, it is reasonable to suggest that large-scale food preparation was the principal function of this building. Hence, its designation as the 'kitchen building' seems appropriate (Armstrong and Zettler 1997: 25). Thus, while the Area IV building complex served as a kind of warehouse, where grain, liquid, traded goods and household equipment were stored, the kitchen building was the place where food was prepared and cooked. The fact that the kitchen building possessed numerous installations and associated artifacts implies that food was prepared here on a rather grand scale. It is thus possible that this kitchen complex and its neighbouring Area IV building represented components of a large-scale residence.

Tell es-Sweyhat's high mound: 'reception building'

Excavations in 2000 and 2001 at Tell es-Sweyhat have provided the most conclusive evidence for the important, elite character of the high mound area during the end of the third millennium. Investigations near the summit of the mound revealed part of a large building with wide mud brick walls set on stone footings, which were buttressed on the outside and thickly plastered with white gypsum (Danti and Zettler 2002: 39). One of the excavated rooms, which featured a wide plastered doorway with a stepped stone threshold and a low mud brick bench lining the interior walls, had been burned in antiquity. This was attested by the quantity of charred roof beams found on the floor, these overlying several smashed ceramic vessels. As these jars parallel vessels found in the Area IV complex and 'kitchen building', the contemporaneity of these buildings is quite secure (Danti and Zettler 2002: 39).

The most intriguing features of the building on Sweyhat's summit were its wall paintings, which were found in a deep recess between two buttresses on the exterior of the building (Danti and Zettler 2002: 39). The paintings had been executed in black, yellow and red paint on gypsum plaster. Although they were extremely fragmentary, it was possible to make out the representation of a man with distorted head and raised arms, standing next to a woman with prominent hips and hands clasped at her waist (Danti and Zettler 2002: 40). This painted scene is quite reminiscent of the wall paintings from other EB Euphrates sites such as Tell Halawa B and Tell Munbaqa, where human figures with upraised arms were also represented. The wall paintings are probably also comparable to fragments of painted scenes that were found in an earlier phase at Tell es-Sweyhat itself, uncovered in the early 1990s on the south side of the high mound. There, in Operation 5, excavations revealed a portion of a massive mud brick wall that featured wall paintings on its plastered, buttressed, western face (Holland 1993–94: 279). Fragments belonging to at least two painted wall scenes included geometric borders, tree branches and stylized human figures with 'Medusa'-like hair styles, also comparable to the figures represented at Tell Halawa B and Munbaqa (Holland 1993–94: 280–1). The depiction of a cow standing on a mountain side with a suckling calf, and a painted geometric pattern on its side, was also found on a large plaster fragment (Holland 1993–94: 281, Abb. 107). It was postulated that these paintings belonged to a very large public building, possibly a temple, which dated to the middle part of the third millennium BC (Holland 1993–94: 279).

The presence of wall paintings from two phases of Early Bronze Age occupation at Tell Sweyhat spanning the second part of the third millennium BC, and their presence in an early phase at Tell Halawa B shows that such wall paintings remained popular in the Euphrates Valley for an extremely long period of time, spanning much of the third millennium. It is striking that the subject matter of the paintings also seems to have remained remarkably static over this long period, demonstrating a continuity in beliefs, ideology, or at the very least, aesthetic preferences over many centuries.

While the precise function of the large, late third millennium building with wall paintings at Tell es-Sweyhat cannot be positively ascertained, its position near the centre of the high mound, its size, monumentality and wall decorations suggest that it had an important function in the settlement. This building may have served in some connection to a high official of the city. If we regard this building as part of a residence of such an elite individual, perhaps the Area IV 'warehouse' and the 'kitchen building', which are located on terraces further down the western slope of the high mound, were attached complexes that served this elite household. Such a reconstruction accords quite well with what we know about the palatial complex at Ebla from the twenty-fourth century. Here, a series of structures, including a 'southern storehouse', where food for immediate needs of the extensive royal establishment was stored, was attached to the royal Palace G (Dolce 1988).

An alternative possible function for the excavated building on the summit is that it served as a gathering place for the elders of the city. This public reception function is perhaps supported by the mud brick benches which lined the walls of the building (Danti and Zettler 2002: 39–40). This reconstruction also accords with third millennium inscriptions from Syria, which make reference to elders who either stood independently or alongside the king as the highest authority of the city (Danti and Zettler 2002: 40; Fleming 2004:190–200; Chapter 3 above).

DISCUSSION

From the investigations of large-scale structures from Tell Banat, Selenkahiye and Tell es-Sweyhat, we can offer some conclusions about the role and significance of these structures in Early Bronze Age urban society.

The size and monumental features of the buildings underline the fact that the individuals who were responsible for the construction and maintenance of these buildings had access to considerable wealth and resources. Materials such as stone for the massive walls and column bases of Building 6 at Banat, and the copious amounts of bitumen, a valuable imported substance used to coat the baked tiled floors of Building 7, reflect access to large amounts of raw materials and the mobilization of labour to assemble these materials and to transform them into impressive monumental structures. At Selenkahiye, the wide walls of the Southern Mansion, which possibly supported two stories, and the large size of the building in comparison with all other excavated structures at the site emphasize its wealth and prominence. At Tell es-Sweyhat, the large size and the functional discreteness of the warehouse and kitchen building suggest the presence of a complex, well organized household or institution which required large amounts of food, metals and other supplies, as well as the economic means to acquire these goods. The discovery of an inscribed weight at Sweyhat, along with the profusion of cylinder sealings at Selenkahiye, also fit appropriately with these contexts, testifying to the frequent and complex economic activities that were undertaken in these large-scale complexes. In all, the evidence reflects the elite status of the occupants of these buildings, whose status, authority and wealth exceeded that of the other inhabitants of the local communities in which they were situated.

Observable variations in the layout and context of these large-scale structures, however, underline their distinct function and varying significance within the settlements in which they were located. We have already reported that Buildings 6 and 7 at Banat were located in close proximity to several burials and funerary monuments, indicating their connection to the mortuary activities of this site. This relationship is further confirmed by the observation that some of the same raw materials (i.e. bitumen) that were used in the construction of both Buildings 6 and 7, were also used in the monumental Tomb 7 nearby. Because of the quality and amount of the materials used for these complexes, the high level of technical skill reflected in their construction as well as their large size, it is fair to say that these monumental constructions belonged to one and the same elite group.

At the same time, none of this evidence from Tell Banat permits us to assume that these elite individuals wielded autocratic authority or control over the mortuary centre in which they were prominently present in both life and death. As we have reported, Buildings 6 and 7, while monumental, were not located on high ground or on an acropolis where they would have dominated the site. On the contrary, the buildings were located in a hollow behind a high ridge where pottery production took place (Porter 2002b: 167). Moreover, the absence of artifacts within these structures that point to large-scale economic or administrative activities cannot confirm that this elite group had any socio-economic or political control over the rest of the Banat community. Finally, the overall character of Tell Banat as adduced principally by its funerary remains, where tendencies of incorporation and corporate collectivity strongly offset divisions based on social status and exclusionary power, indicates that if elite groups did exist at this site, their authority was never allowed to attain excessive levels of control and subordination (Porter 2002b: 167).

The ground plan and setting of the Southern Mansion at Selenkahiye is completely different from that of Buildings 6 and 7 at Tell Banat. Here no obvious connections to mortuary activities can be discerned, suggesting that the occupants of the Southern Mansion had an altogether different set of concerns and activities. As attested by the building's large size, its singular ground plan and especially the frequency of its economic transactions, we submit this is the residence of an elite household, whose wealth was generated by activities relating to the trade and exchange of various commodities both within and beyond the confines of the city. On the other hand, none of the data recovered from the Southern Mansion justify attaching superordinate status and authority to the building's occupants. While they may have been wealthy, the elites of the Mansion did not necessarily supervise or control the economic, social or political activities of the city as a whole. The fact that the Southern Mansion is located at one end of the settlement at an elevation comparable to other settlement structures, where it is neither literally or figuratively at the centre or apex of this community, further abrogates its role as a pre-eminent power at Selenkahiye.

If we consider all of the excavated buildings on the main mound at Tell es-Sweyhat together as part of a unified complex, then we have here the most likely candidate for a palace, with its warehouse of food stores and metal supplies, its kitchen facilities for preparing food for a large household, and its prominently-located reception hall. This eloquent testimony to elite status within Sweyhat's late third millennium city almost certainly reflects the owners' abilities to extract considerable resources from the surrounding community and countryside, and their ability to mobilize and sustain labour for the construction and maintenance of this grand complex. As will be outlined in greater detail in a later chapter on craft production, the concentration of metals and metalworking on the main mound reflects the control over the production and distribution of metal, a material that has frequent connections with elite status and kingship elsewhere in Syria (Philip 1995: 152). As powerful and wealthy as the elite individuals who inhabited this elevated space may have been, however, there is no compelling evidence to indicate that their power entailed highly centralized control over the surrounding city and hinterland in which they were prominently situated.

Unlike at Ebla, where the palace received the bulk of the city's resources principally in the form of grain and wool, and where most of the city's residents were palace dependents who were paid in kind for their labour and other services, this type of highly centralized and bureaucratized royal establishment is absent at Sweyhat. Furthermore, none of the material remains from outside of the main acropolis mound at Sweyhat demonstrated any strong links to the central complex. The diversity of house structures, the variability of outer city defences, and the presence of independently operated production facilities suggest that many aspects of this city fell well outside the controlling forces of the acropolis complex. In sum, while an elite group almost certainly existed in late third millennium Sweyhat, and while they managed to assume a high degree of wealth and power that enabled them to mobilize and organize a considerable amount of the city's resources, it seems unlikely that their power within the city was all-controlling or all-pervasive.

Overall, our examination of large-scale secular architecture has served to further highlight the distinctive character of each individual Euphrates site. Through the specific layout and contents of these buildings we are sometimes provided with a deeper glimpse into the varying functions and foci of the communities in which they existed. Even further, these buildings serve to illustrate the varying nature of authority itself. While it is fair to say that elite groups did exist, differences in the buildings' plans, layout and association with other structures as well as the artifacts associated with these buildings suggest that elite wealth and power fluctuated greatly from one site to another. Thus while the Southern Mansion at Selenkahiye was impressive in contrast to other buildings in the settlement, it did not have the scale and complexity of the complex on the summit of the main mound at Tell es-Sweyhat, with its large storerooms, kitchen buildings and reception hall, all enclosed within a citadel wall. Such evidence would suggest that while elite groups and their associated structures played a prominent role in socio-economic and political activities at some sites, and may have had a degree of wealth or control over some facets of urban society, still other sites had a tradition in which an exclusionary or centralizing authority was far more limited. Almost certainly, these differences are largely attributable to the individual histories, traditions and successes of the individual Euphrates urban communities and the unique way in which they autonomously grew and flourished over the course of the Early Bronze Age.

There are some Euphrates settlements where such large-scale secular struc-tures have not been encountered at all. While some sites are obviously in need of further archaeological investigations, sufficient excavation work has allowed one to confirm the presence or absence of such buildings. Thus, the site of Halawa Tell A, which has been extensively investigated, has failed to yield any large-scale secular building. Perhaps pronounced social, political or economic inequalities did not even exist at this site. Alternatively, the pres-ence of a monumental temple at Halawa may indicate that a powerful group was present at the site, but that it was largely religious in character, compris-ing cult authorities who directed the ritualistic and spiritual life of the community. Perhaps no secular elite group existed at Halawa. This inter-pretation of the Halawa A evidence would underline all the more the varying and singular nature of the exercise of power in the Euphrates region, even among urban communities which were contemporaneous and located in close geographical proximity to one another.

7

COMMUNAL PLACES OF WORSHIP

Religious worship was a regular and recurring activity among the inhabitants of the Syrian Euphrates judging by the recovery at several settlements of buildings of a sacred character. Large and solid structures, carefully segregated from the rest of the urban communities, served as places where sacred rites and cult festivals dedicated to the gods were celebrated. These religious structures had a long history that reached back even to the earliest phases of third millennium occupation in the region. Some of these early sacred complexes reveal a striking degree of monumentality and organization, reflecting the presence of well established religious traditions and institutionalized offices of religious leadership.

Although some of the architectural features and associated equipment and furnishings of the Syrian places of worship appear to have been inspired or influenced by religious art and architecture from other regions of the Near East, notably southern Mesopotamia, the overall character of these Syrian temples is distinctive, reflecting the unique religious traditions of the northern Euphrates Valley during the third millennium. Even among individual sites, singular expressions of devotion and ritual activities can be discerned in the material cultural remains, setting urban communities apart even from their nearest neighbours.

Phases 1–2 temple complexes

Halawa Tell B

The religious complex at the site of Halawa Tell B stands out as an impressive example of sacred architecture in the Euphrates Valley during Phases 1–2 of the Early Bronze Age. It also provides robust evidence for the presence of a well-established religious institution that dates just after the settlement's initial occupation. Concerning this initial settlement at Halawa B, its religious character remains equivocal. In this phase (Period I, level 3), at least three free-standing, single-roomed mud brick buildings stood in the central part of the settlement (Rooms 309, 312 and 313) (Figure 5.1). The buildings' sacred character is suggested by a number of distinctive features that included pilasters and *antae*-like projections on the exterior walls and the buildings' north–south or east–west axes, which differed from the obliquely-angled houses built against the fortification walls (Orthmann 1989: 91). The buildings were also located directly under the massive brick platform and temple of the subsequent phase of occupation at the site (Period II), when the central area of the settlement was transformed into a religious complex of monumental proportions. While these features suggest a religious character, the structures' similarity in form and dimensions to other single-roomed domestic buildings that were constructed and inhabited during this phase of occupation at Halawa suggests that they were simple houses. Given these somewhat conflicting data, it is impossible at this time to reach a firm conclusion as to the sacred or profane character of these central buildings in the earliest phase.

While the earliest architecture at Tell Halawa B is elusive, the next highest occupation phase (Period II, level 2) comprises structures that are unambiguously sacred in nature given their large scale, elevated position and architectural embellishments, which compare with sacred buildings from elsewhere in Greater Mesopotamia. The phase is distinguished in particular by the construction of a 1 metre-high mud brick platform in the centre of the settlement. This terrace was built directly over the earlier Room 312 of Period I, whose interior space had been emptied entirely of its contents and filled with bricks (Orthmann 1989: 89). The walls of a mud brick building, designated Building II, were constructed above this platform surface.

Building II was an impressive structure (Figure 7.1). Although it consisted only of a single room with an area of 12 m × 10 m, its eastern and western facades were adorned with niches and buttresses. These embellishments gave the exterior of the building an elaborate appearance that can be compared to the niched and buttressed exterior walls of sacred structures from southern Mesopotamia from around the same time period. The principal entrance to Building II was located in the centre of the buttressed eastern side, this being characterized also by two side-*antae* that ended in inwardly-projecting pilasters, forming a shallow porch. The porch was approached by two steps which led up from the base of the temple platform and an open courtyard beyond (Orthmann 1989: 92).

Inside the sanctuary, a white plastered podium was set against the northern wall. A rectangular black discoloration found in the white plaster above this feature may represent the remains of an object made of some organic material that originally stood there, possibly a cult statue (Orthmann 1989: 92). The inside walls of the sanctuary were lined with very low and narrow white plastered benches.

A small room, also standing on the brick platform, was built against the western face of Building II. This room was characterized by a deep niche in the back wall. In the southeastern corner a small fireplace was found, but no

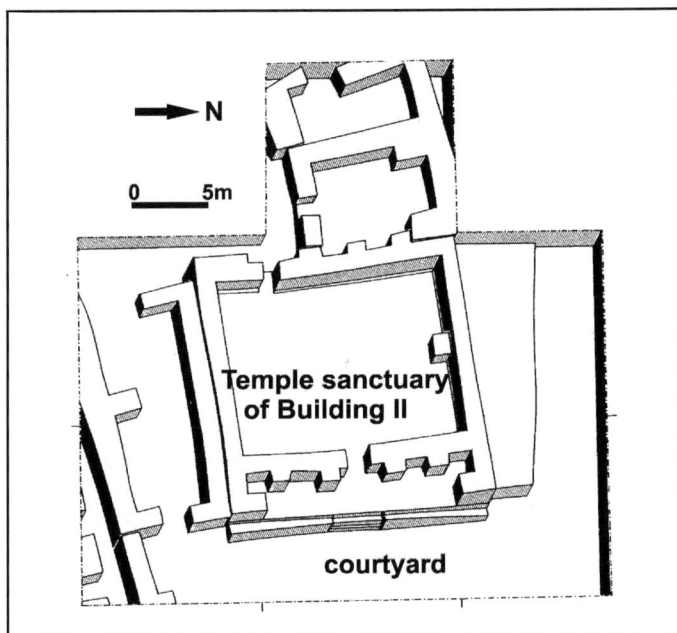

Figure 7.1 Building II of temple complex (Period II, level 2), Halawa Tell B.

other artifacts or installations were recovered from this room (Orthmann 1989: 93).

The approach to the temple platform and surrounding precinct in the northwest was through a long, narrow room (112) that served as a kind of gatehouse that gave access to a stone staircase that led up to the temple platform on the northern side (Orthmann 1989: 94, Abb. 61). On the opposite side of the temple platform and extending a considerable distance to the east, a long mud brick wall featured inwardly-projecting buttresses at fairly regular intervals. This wall served as a temenos enclosure, separating the temple precinct from secular structures located across a street directly to the south (Rooms 101–5) (Orthmann 1989: 94). One could enter into the complex only through a passageway at the eastern end of the precinct, which in turn was flanked by a series of small rooms on one side (Rooms 203–4), and a larger building on the other. This latter building was characterized by a single, slightly elevated, white plastered broad room and external buttressed and niched facade. Because of its similar proportions and embellishments to Building II, this building was also thought to be a place of worship, and accordingly designated 'Small Temple 2' (Orthmann 1989: 95–6).

Several changes were made to the temple precinct at Halawa B in its latest major architectural phase (Period II, level 1) (Orthmann 1989: Beilage 14–16). The most significant change concerned the central temple platform, which was raised to a higher level by the construction of additional layers of brick (Orthmann 1989: 97). In subsequent sub-phases of this level, much of the area to the south and east was also elevated, forming a series of stepped terraces around the main temple which was now designated Building I (Figure 7.2) (Orthmann 1989: 97–101). This arrangement of monumental terraces and a grand temple standing above all can be regarded as a somewhat scaled-down version of the stepped temple ziggurats of southern Mesopotamia.

The main sanctuary, Building I, was built directly over Building II. While it retained its buttressed walls, the entrance to the cult room was moved to the southern side, and flanked immediately to the left and right by two projecting antae. Ramps, which approached from the east and west and led up to the new elevated temple platform, further enhanced the grand appearance of the temple. During this period, the room that had been west of the main cella was no longer in existence, having been filled in and covered over by the new platform (Orthmann 1989: 98).

In the latest level, part of a curving temenos wall was traced along the northern side of the complex. This wall was embellished with internal buttresses that formed a counterpart to the temenos wall on the south side (Orthmann 1989: 98). Several new rooms were constructed within this enclosed precinct to the east of the main temple platform, including a small square room with projecting antae that was designated 'Small Temple 1'.

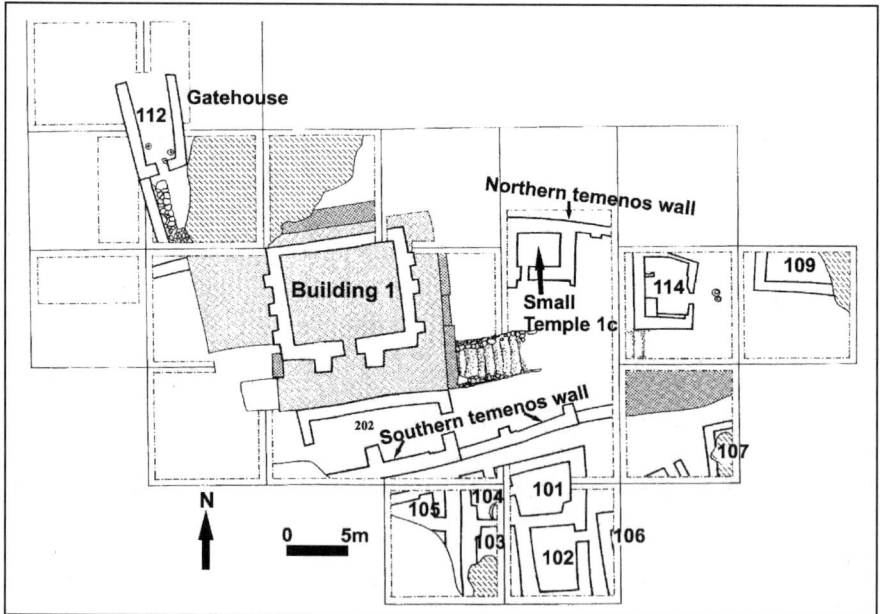

Figure 7.2 Temple complex (Period II, level 1), Halawa Tell B.

146

This temple was further elaborated by the addition of a second room in a later phase of level 1, and elevated to a higher terrace (Orthmann 1989: 98–101). A series of other small buildings to the east were also present in the sacred precinct, although their functions are not entirely clear. To the northwest of Building I, the gatehouse was retained and continued to serve as the principal entrance to the temple precinct.

In all, the religious precinct at Tell Halawa B is an impressive example of sacred space from the early part of the Early Bronze Age in the Syrian Euphrates Valley. Its presence indicates that only shortly after Halawa's initial phase of settlement, a religious establishment had emerged with plentiful resources, control over labour, and planning abilities to lay out and lavishly accommodate a monumental religious complex that in its central, elevated location, would have dominated the settlement and played an important role in the religious activities of the inhabitants that it served.

Qara Quzaq

We know now that Tell Halawa B did not stand alone in its possession of monumental religious architecture. Recent excavations at the site of Qara Quzaq have also brought to light the remains of substantial structures and installations that were associated with religious activities. Their somewhat different character, however, indicates that Qara Quzaq's religious traditions followed a different trajectory than those at Halawa, despite the two sites' geographical proximity.

Some of the earliest evidence for sacred architecture at Qara Quzaq derives from the second phase of Level V, which has been dated to Phases 1–2, or around the second quarter of the third millennium BC (Olávarri and Valdés Pereiro 2001: 14). Like the temple complex at Tell Halawa B, this religious complex was located on a high terrace in the central part of the tell. The remains of a long, thick wall running from east to west marked the southern limits of the religious precinct and served to segregate the sacred complex from the secular space of the settlement, much like the temenos wall at Halawa Tell B (Olávarri and Valdés Pereiro 2001: 25–6). A long, stone-lined canal was installed across the high terrace upon which the sacred precinct stood, serving to drain excess rain water from this area (Olávarri and Valdés Pereiro 2001: 16–17).

The central and most important structure of the precinct was Temple L.247 (Figure 7.3). Although only fragmentarily preserved, we know that this temple was elevated above all surrounding structures by a solid, square, 2.3 metre-high brick platform upon which it stood. The 1 metre-thick walls of the temple itself were made of red bricks, as was the floor. These bricks had been laid over a thick layer of clean compact earth, forming a pure and solid base befitting a structure of sacred character (Olávarri and Valdés Pereiro 2001: 19).

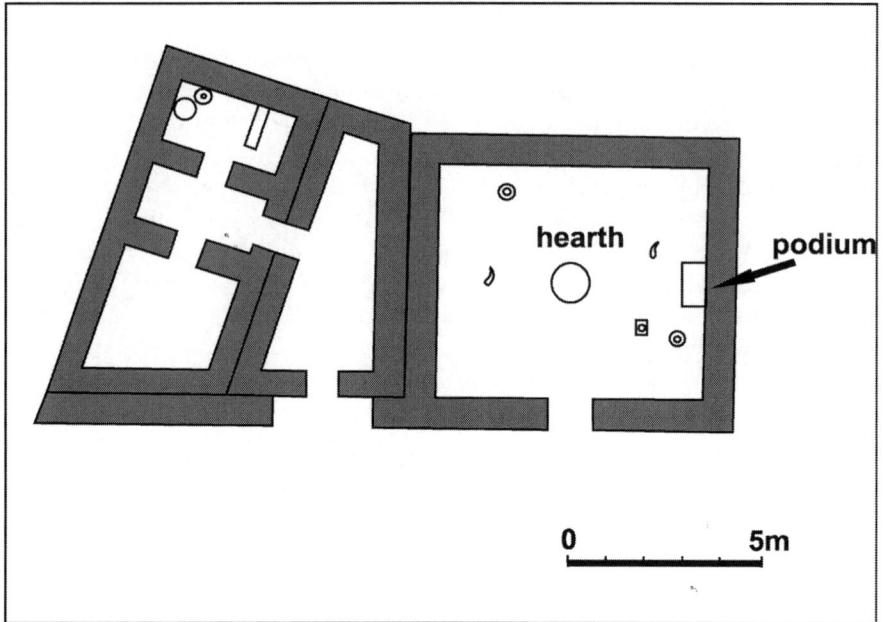

Figure 7.3 Temple L.247, Qara Quzaq (local level V).

The temple was about 8.2 m × 8.4 m in area, and was oriented along a north–south axis. It contained one interior room, whose floors and walls had been carefully covered with a layer of thick white limestone plaster. One entered the temple through a doorway on the broader, southern side and then turned right to face a podium that was set against the eastern wall. Presumably offerings were placed on the podium, or else it supported a statue of the god (Olávarri and Valdés Pereiro 2001: 18). There was a slightly sunken hearth in the centre of the room, beside which were found two large horns of an aurochs and two fragments of a truncated cylinder carved out of limestone. No doubt these objects constituted the remains of the cult furniture of the temple (Olávarri and Valdés Pereiro 2001: 18).

Several rooms to the west of the temple would have served functions related to religious activities. Included among these was a room of trapezoidal plan (L.300.20) which gave access to three other smaller rooms to the west (L.100.2, L.300.19 and L.300.12). Painted frescoes decorated the interior walls of this vestibule. Only fragmentary pieces of these paintings were recovered in the rubble of the collapse, but one can make out geometric and floral motifs. Of the three rooms to the west, the one at the north contained a hearth, jug and bread oven, possibly suggesting it functioned as a kitchen. The excavators have tentatively interpreted these rooms to the west of the temple as the residence of the priest in charge of the temple (Olávarri and Valdés Pereiro 2001: 24).

The distinctive character of the sacred precinct of level V-2 at Qara Quzaq is highlighted especially by the next buildings, which are somewhat peculiar. One of the structures, L.12, is an above-ground, red brick building. Located to the west of temple L.247 and directly north of the temenos wall, L.12 contained two chambers, L.12E and L.12W, each of which contained the partially cremated remains of an individual and a rich assortment of accompanying funerary offerings that included ceramic vessels, metal pins, weapons and jewellery (Figure 9.8) (Olávarri 1995b: 16–17). The building had no windows, and after the burials had been deposited, its single doorway was walled up (Olávarri 1995b: 15–16). Additional details of this funerary structure are provided in the next chapter. Suffice here to say that this structure with its accompanying burials had a prominent place at the settlement of Qara Quzaq in level V-2, sharing the same central location as the temple and temple platform nearby.

Still other buildings were found near temple L.247 and enclosed by the temenos wall. They included three mud brick buildings L.400.4, and L.400.2 and L.400.3. The latter two were rectangular semi-subterranean structures possessing vaulted ceilings formed by brick arches. The interiors of both chambers were painted with white limestone plaster, and both contained small podia for receiving offerings (Olávarri and Valdés Pereiro 2001: 19–20). The funerary character of these structures is somewhat tentative since no human remains were found with the exception of an infant jar burial found inside a small stone cist tomb underneath a wall of the earliest phase of building L.400.2 (Olávarri and Valdés Pereiro 2001: 20, Figure 5c, photo VIII). Nevertheless, the lack of domestic installations and artifacts within these structures, their unusual subterranean layout and their location within the sacred precinct, near the burial chamber L.12, could indicate their association with funerary activities.

Together, the buildings found within the sacred precinct at Qara Quzaq constitute a unique set of structures. The brick chamber L.12 stands out as the most distinctive and unusual building of this complex given its funerary character and its central, visible position in the settlement next to the principal temple. While it is rare to find a clear and direct association between temple structures and burials elsewhere in the Syrian Euphrates, such a configuration has been observed at the site of Tell Chuera to the east, where a funerary deposit, consisting of a number of skeletons that were partially burned with offerings of pottery and metal weapons, was found inside a chamber of the temple designated as 'Steinbau I' at that site (Moortgat 1962: pl. V; Olávarri and Valdés Pereiro 2001: 23). Furthermore, we cannot deny that within the EB Euphrates one occasionally sees a connection between funerary rituals and religious activities, especially the cult of the ancestors, which frequently involved rituals and celebrations around the tombs of the deceased. Such ancestral cults are believed to have been a particularly strong aspect of the religious life of inhabitants at sites such as Jerablus Tahtani and Tell Banat. At these sites, prominent monuments in the form of massive stone tombs and mortuary tumuli were the focus of many ritual activities involving the worship and celebration of deceased individuals. It may be possible, therefore, to posit a similar cult at Qara Quzaq, where worship and offerings to the ancestors took place in a temple building that was located only a short distance from the places where these revered individuals were actually buried.

Phases 3–5 EB temples *in antis*

As the third millennium progressed, a simple, standardized temple plan began to appear at a number of settlements in northern Mesopotamia. The temple is commonly referred to as a long-roomed temple or a temple *in antis* on account of its long thick walls or *antae* that project outward and form a shallow porch or antecella at the front of the sanctuary. Although these temples first appeared in the Early Bronze Age in Syria, they became especially frequent in Syria and the Levant during the Middle and Late Bronze Ages, appearing at several important sites such as Ebla (Matthiae 1977: 130–2), Tell Munbaqa and Emar (Orthmann and Kühne 1974: 58–65; 77–9; Margueron 1980: Figure 11; Machule *et al.* 1991: 73–6). Their presence continued into the Iron Age, as attested by the temple at the site of Tell Tayinat in the Plain of Antioch in southern Turkey, and by one of the most celebrated sacred structures in the Near East, the Temple of Solomon in Jerusalem (Del Olmo Lete and Montero Fenollós 1998: 299).

In Syria, the temples *in antis* at Tell Chuera, an EB site located to the east of the Euphrates River valley between the Balikh and Khabur Rivers, are perhaps the most well-known. These structures have been dated between the middle and late third millennium BC (Akkermans and Schwartz 2003: 256–7). Found in several areas throughout the settlement, Chuera's temples were of a variety of sizes and monumentality, but they shared the same long-roomed plan and flanking projecting *antae* (Orthmann 1990).

Halawa Tell A

Excavations in the Syrian Euphrates have also confirmed the existence of distinctive temples *in antis*, dating to around the same time as those found at Tell Chuera (Phase 4). The one at the site of Halawa Tell A is the most well-preserved, and we are fortunate that in addition to possessing its full ground plan, we have the layout and organization of the structures that surrounded it.

The temple complex was located in the southern part of the tell (Figure 7.4). Like at Halawa Tell B, the temple and associated structures were enclosed within a temenos wall that effectively separated the precinct from other

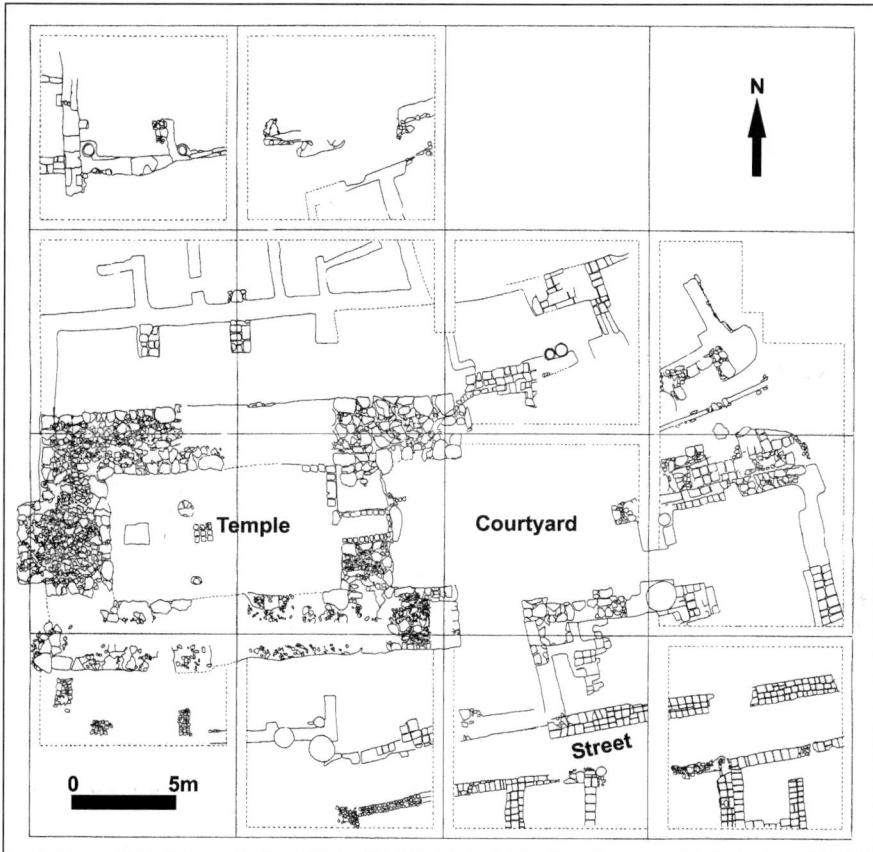

Figure 7.4 Temple *in antis*, Halawa Tell A.

structures to the north and south, the latter of which were domestic houses (Pfälzner 2001: 352–4). It is interesting that unlike the main residential areas, where houses were orientated on a northwest–southeast axis and were likely laid out in accordance with the natural topography of the hill upon which the settlement was founded, the temple complex was built on a firm east–west axis (Orthmann 1989: 63). As was observed at Halawa B, this difference in architectural orientation may have served to highlight a functional difference between this sacred complex and the other secular structures that surrounded it (Orthmann 1989: 91).

The temple precinct was entered through a kind of gatehouse that was located on the eastern side. It consisted of a narrow entrance-chamber that passed between two buttressed walls, sloping upwards to reach a large open space in front of the principal cultic structure, Building I (Orthmann 1989: 64–5).

Building I itself was planned on a large scale, with thick stone walls over 3 m in width, and extending over an area encompassing more than 20 m in length and about 13 m in width (Orthmann 1989: 65–6). As a true temple *in antis*, the structure comprised a porch which was open to the east, while to the west the porch gave access to a long, rectangular cult room (11 m × 7 m). A few notable installations were found inside the cult room, among them a mud brick podium against the middle of the rear wall underneath which was found a finely carved alabaster bowl as part of a small deposit (Figure 7.6 right top and bottom) (Orthmann 1989: Abb. 52: 1–3). The bowl was characterized by three regularly spaced lugs, and a short spout in the place of the fourth lug. It had been carefully decorated with incised patterns featuring filled triangles as well as representations of birds, walking quadrupeds, and plant-like elements (Orthmann 1989: 84).

Standing roughly in the centre of the temple was an elevated surface made of baked brick tiles, while to the north a circular sandstone base was set on the floor. In the northeastern corner of the cult room, near the bottom of the wall was a narrow bench made of mud bricks (Orthmann 1980: 66). This bench may have been a place to set votive offerings.

Among the most significant finds from within the temple were fragments of carved limestone stelae (Orthmann 1989: 66). As was the custom in other parts of Greater Mesopotamia during the third millennium, these carved stelae were mainly dedicated to the deities of the temples by prominent worshippers who participated in or sponsored various temple rituals and festivals. We may regard Halawa's most well preserved stele (Stele I), as such a dedicatory stone. It depicts a religious celebration, in which patrons of the gods, along with their family members, present themselves and offerings to the temple's deities (Figure 7.5).

The stone bears four fields of carved relief, separated from one another by raised horizontal registers (Orthmann 1989: Abb. 44). The centre of the scene is dominated by two large human figures, probably males, wearing identical long robes and facing to the left. They are holding staffs and axes, while in front of their legs are upright fenestrated axes (Orthmann 1989: 74). To the left of these two larger figures are four smaller figures, possibly women, walking to the left. Their clothing and hair are different from the two larger figures, and they are holding various items which include a child, a goat kid, and unidentifiable round objects (Orthmann 1989: 76).

Goats are represented below the register of the smaller figures. A young one feeds from its mother, while to the right two goats are reaching up to feed from branches of a tree. The lowest frieze depicts a figure who is holding a whip in one hand and the reins of an equid in the other. The animal is pulling a chariot or waggon upon which the figure is standing (Orthmann 1985: 470; 1989: 77). Alternatively, the scene may be depicting a person standing behind a plough.

Overall, this Halawa stele exemplifies well the blend of Mesopotamian and

Figure 7.5 Stele (I), found in temple *in antis*, Halawa Tell A.

local North Syrian artistic styles that prevailed in the Syrian Euphrates region during this period of the late third millennium BC. Orthmann has identified several commonalities between this object and artistic representations from southern Mesopotamia, including the styles of the long, fringed garments of the males, the hairstyles of the women, the chariot motif and the kid bearer (Orthmann 1985: 471). Furthermore, the overall layout of the stele, in which the work is divided into registers and features figures in profile, falls well within the established canon of Mesopotamian sculptural representation of the mid-to-late third millennium BC.

On the other hand, the Halawa stele bears some unusual aspects that differ from the art of southern Mesopotamia. The rather awkward position of the arms on two of the female figures as well as the way in which the left hands of the male figures stick out from the dress have been regarded as unconventional features which find no comparison among other southern Mesopotamian works (Orthmann 1985: 470). Additionally noteworthy is the fact that the kid bearer is female as opposed to male, the latter being the standard representation in southern Mesopotamia. The closest parallel to the female offering bearers is a relief from Tell Chuera, also in northern Syria, which depicts seven goddesses carrying animals or children in their arms (Moortgat and Moortgat-Correns 1976: Figure 20). There is no indication, however, that the females rendered in the Halawa stele should also be regarded as divine (Orthmann 1985: 471). Last, the driver in the lower register is a human male who swings a whip, an instrument that is rarely depicted in other late third millennium Mesopotamian representational scenes of either chariot riders or plough drivers (Orthmann 1985: 470).

While we can attribute some of these differences to the artistic abilities of the Syrian Euphrates sculptors, who demonstrate a lack of skill in rendering certain spatial relations (Orthmann 1985: 470), the remaining details may reflect divergent artistic traditions, as well as beliefs about the roles and responsibilities of gods, and men and women in the sphere of religion and sacred ritual. From these observed details we might conjecture that while north Syrian artisans were exposed to the artistic traditions of Mesopotamia and borrowed many Mesopotamian stylistic motifs, their work does not reflect a slavish artistic nor religious imitation of their southern neighbours. Rather, such motifs were part of a tradition that developed independently of the south. Their peculiarities serve to highlight the unique beliefs and cult practices of the Syrian Euphrates inhabitants, whose religion likely differed in many ways from other regions of the Near East.

Returning again to Halawa Tell A's religious architecture, Building II was found to the east of Building I, across an open courtyard. The entrance of this structure gave access to a wide room equipped with benches and a low podium. From there a wide door led to another long room to the south, at the western end of which contained a row of installations consisting of low podia and benches, and a very small room with an uncertain function in behind (Orthmann 1989: 66, Abb. 37). Perhaps we can interpret this structure as a smaller secondary shrine, much in the same way that the more diminutive, but similarly equipped buildings had been reconstructed in the earlier temple precinct at Halawa Tell B.

Besides the two shrines, the religious complex at Halawa Tell A comprised smaller, subsidiary rooms and structures which functioned as either storage facilities or places of minor cultic activities. Most of these subsidiary structures were located to the north and south of Building I. One of the rooms to the south (Room 18) was of special interest on account of the fragments of many vessels that were found within it (Figure 7.6) (Orthmann 1989: 66). Two ceramic fragments of storage jars are particularly noteworthy, having been decorated in relief and incised with representations of animals and human figures (Figure 7.6 left). On one of the fragments, the heads of two antithetically-arranged snakes are being grasped by a 'hero' standing between them, while above their backs are the paws of a quadruped (Orthmann 1989: 84, Abb. 51:3). On the second fragment, two antithetical snakes are grasped by a lion-headed bird of prey, while below is the representation of a quadruped painted with black marks (Orthmann 1989: 84, Abb. 51:1). Last, there is a terra-cotta stand, decorated in relief with the representation of two heroes (Figure 7.6 right centre). One stands between two lions, while the other stands between the hind quarters of two animals, whose backs he grasps with his hands (Orthmann 1989: 84, Abb. 52: 4–7). Overall, it is difficult to ascertain the precise meaning and significance of these vessels' unusual motifs, except to suggest that their imagery was appropriate to the cult setting with which they were associated.

In all, the structures of the religious precinct at Tell Halawa A represent an impressive complex of monumental proportions. The size of the principal temple, and the nature of the artifacts and the buildings associated with it, as well as its segregation from the rest of the settlement by an enclosure wall, clearly underline its importance and sacred character. The presence of this complex also emphasizes the continuing prominence of religious institutions in the region in the third millennium.

Tell Kabir

A large building with stone foundation was found at Tell Kabir, a small site located in the Tell Banat embayment, only about 800 m from the large mortuary centre of Tell Banat. Pottery unearthed from the temple's phases of construction and use suggest that it existed during Phase 4 (c. 2450–2300 BC) (Porter 1995b: 135).

Excavations of the Kabir temple have revealed a rectangular single-roomed building, about 22 m x 13 m in area, with large walls which were as much as 2 m thick and made of field stones often as big as 1 m^2 (Figure 7.7) (Porter 1995b: 129). Judging from the amount of bricky collapse found inside the building, the stone walls were probably topped by a superstructure of mud brick (Porter 1995b: 129). A long wall on one side of the structure projected out beyond the wall with the doorway in the southeast, forming an open porch in the front. A doorway in the eastern cross wall would have provided access from the porch to the main sanctuary room (McClellan 1999: 416). In all, this layout is highly suggestive of a temple *in antis*, similar to the one found at Tell Halawa A.

The floors of the building were first paved with mud bricks, then with packed clay, and finally with a layer of dense limestone rubble which was

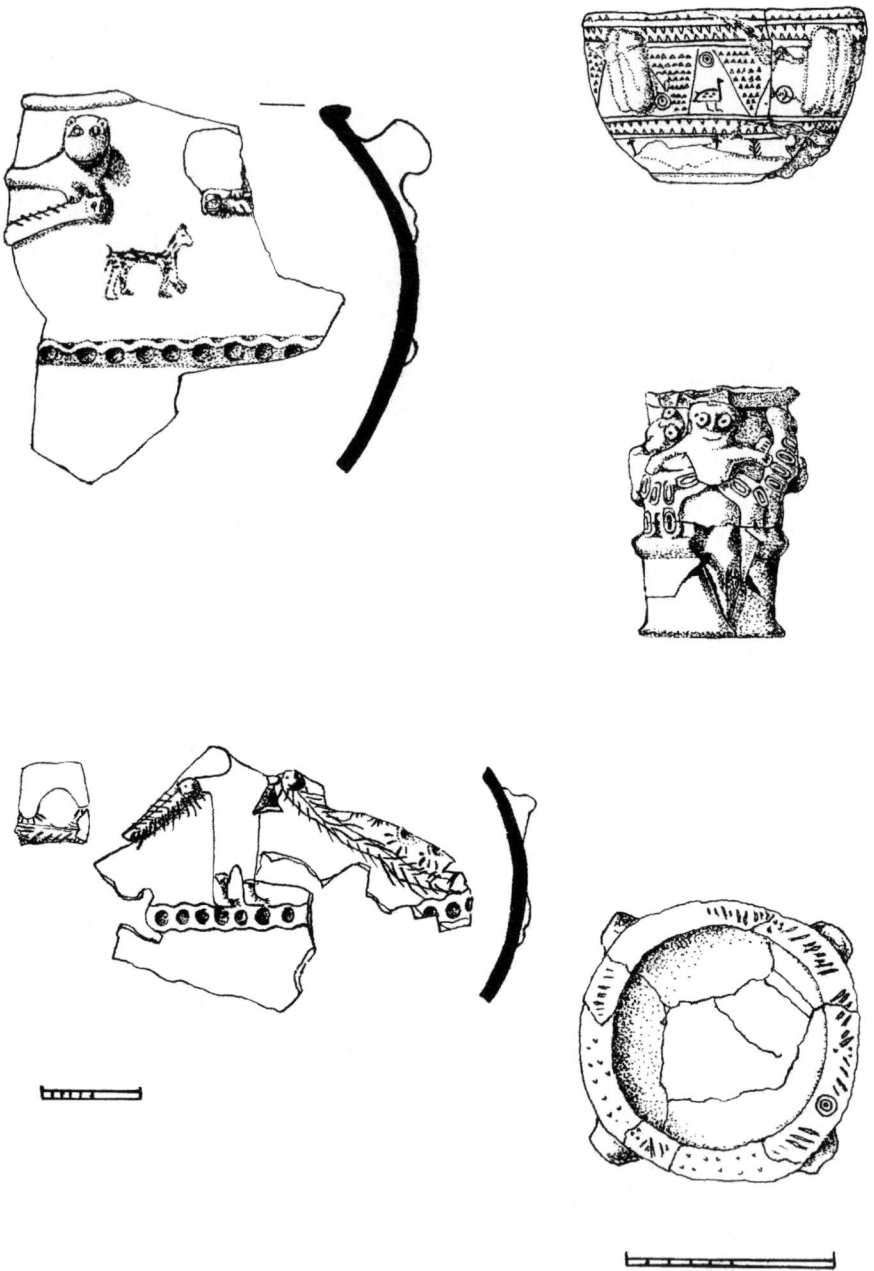

Figure 7.6 Cultic equipment from temple *in antis* complex, Halawa Tell A.

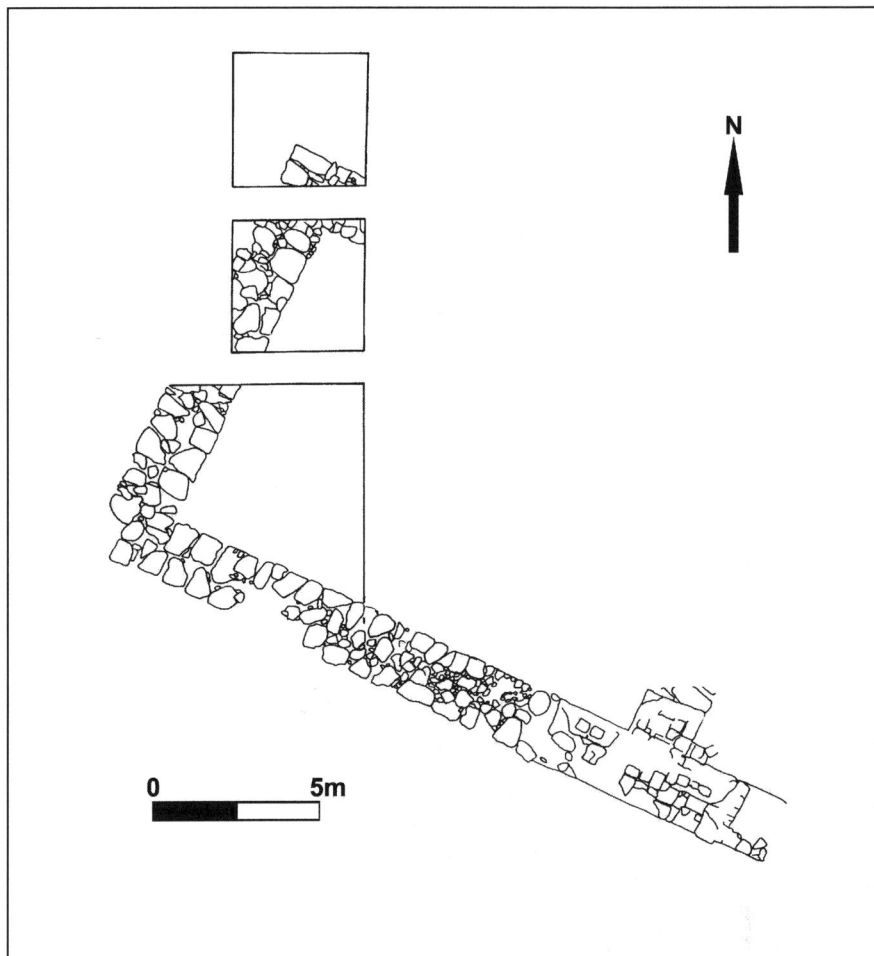

Figure 7.7 Building One temple *in antis*, Tell Kabir.

overlaid with fine lime plaster (Porter 1995b: 129–30). Over the earlier floors, several small artifacts were found, including 59 frit, stone and shell beads, a small silver earring, and fragments of lapis lazuli and ostrich shell (Porter 1995b: 129). A later floor included a fragment of a seal impression and part of a clay pipe or flute. All of the floors were otherwise devoid of occupational debris, suggesting an attempt on the part of the inhabitants to keep the interior of this building clean (Porter 1995b: 130).

The building does not appear to have been destroyed. There is no evidence for burning, nor has collapsed roofing material been found on the floor, possibly suggesting that the wood of the roof was deliberately removed when the building went out of use (Porter 1995b: 130). After a time, several large circular pits were dug over the collapsed walls of the structure. Pottery associated with these pits can be dated to the latter part of the third millennium BC, indicating that the Kabir temple went out of use well before the close of the Early Bronze Age.

Qara Quzaq

The site of Qara Quzaq provides the only other examples of Syrian Euphrates temples *in antis* positively identified thus far. The earliest structure of this type (L.23) was found in Level IV at the site, and can be dated to the middle of the third millennium (Phase 3) (Del Olmo Lete and Montero Fenollós 1998: 296). The temple, characterized by stone foundations and a mud brick superstructure, was found roughly in the centre of the settlement, overlaying the earlier sacred precinct of the preceding level V-2 (Figure 7.8). The dimensions of the building, 7 m × 5 m, are relatively modest in comparison to that of other temples *in antis*, although the overall layout of the building, which comprises a rectangular long room and small front porch resembles closely the other known examples. The building's importance is suggested by its elevated location within the settlement (Olávarri and Valdés Pereiro 2001: 27).

In the succeeding level III-2 at Qara Quzaq, a far more impressive temple *in antis* was constructed (Figure 7.9). This structure dates to Phase 4 (Valdés Pereiro 1999: 119). Although much of the structure was badly destroyed when silos were constructed directly over it in the subsequent Middle Bronze

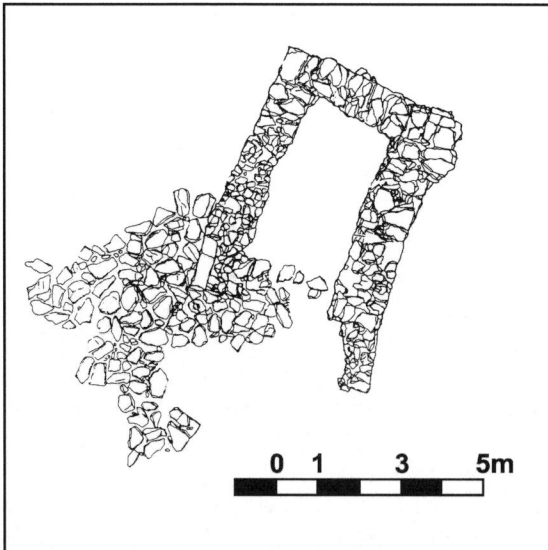

Figure 7.8 Small temple *in antis*, Qara Quzaq (local level IV).

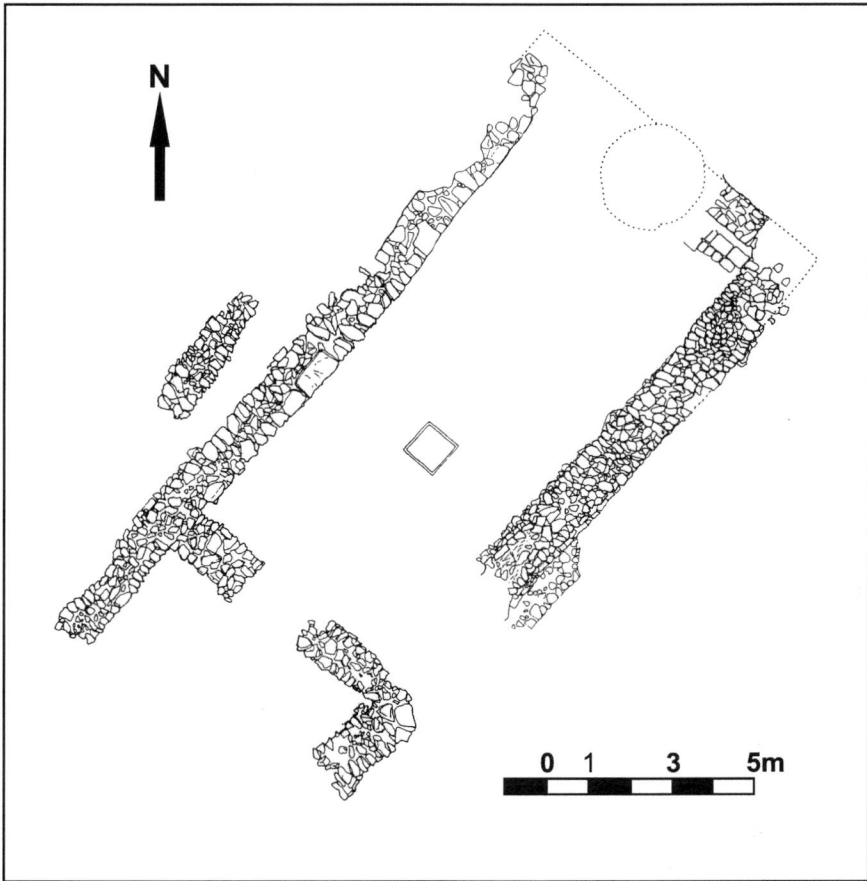

Figure 7.9 Temple *in antis*, Qara Quzaq (local level III-2).

Age, enough of its ground plan has survived to permit its classification as a true temple *in antis*.

The building (L.10) was located on a large terrace on the southern slope of the tell, facing the riverside. Rectangular in shape, the temple was 16 m in length and 7 m wide, while the thickness of its stone foundations ranged between 1–1.2 m. These stone foundations were topped by a superstructure of mud brick. At the front of the building two projecting walls or *antae* formed a vestibule or porch. A considerable amount of preparation was required for the laying-out of the structure's stone foundations, which had to be constructed at an increasingly greater depth to the south due to the downward slope in the area. Towards the east, a massive filling of stones served to elevate the area upon which the temple foundations were built (Olávarri and Valdés Pereiro 2001: 30).

159

The floor of the long-roomed cella was made of carefully laid brick and then covered over with white plaster. The walls were also white-washed. Benches, running along the entire northern and western walls, were places where votive offerings were likely placed (Olávarri and Valdés Pereiro 2001: 29). A square brick platform or podium in the centre of the cella may also have served as a place for offerings (Olávarri and Valdés Pereiro 2001: 29).

An exceptional discovery was made in the porch area of this temple. Under the floor of this room, near the western wall, the excavators recovered a storage jar containing a treasure hoard that contained 333 pieces of alabaster, mother-of-pearl, shell, bone, stone and frit objects (Valdés Pereiro 1999: 121). The majority of objects were beads, rings, pendants and animal-shaped amulets, but the hoard also contained two small alabaster vessels, cylinder seals with geometric designs, and a mother-of-pearl plaque in the form of a bull. The hoard can almost certainly be interpreted as a ritual deposit marking the founding of the temple, an act well known from other Mesopotamian temple contexts (Del Olmo Lete and Montero Fenollós 1998: 297).

Several of the objects of the deposit have parallels from third millennium contexts elsewhere. The mother-of-pearl bull, which is characterized by drilled concentric circles that decorate its body and form its eyes, compares well with mother-of-pearl bulls found at Tell Brak in a pre-Akkadian context (Oates et al. 2001: 30; 296), and at Tell ʿAtij along the Khabur River, from a burial of the Ninevite 5 period (Fortin 1990: 240).

DISCUSSION

Our available evidence demonstrates that monumental sacred architecture enjoyed a long history in Syrian Euphrates during the Early Bronze Age, extending back to the first centuries of the third millennium. Tell Halawa B's temple complex with its stepped platform, and Qara Quzaq's sacred brick buildings clearly testify to the early presence of impressive sacred works. By their central location these temples undoubtedly played an important role in the religious life of the inhabitants they served. These early places of worship, however, were defined by somewhat dissimilar elements, possibly reflecting locally divergent religious practices and beliefs. The complex at Qara Quzaq was characterized by an unusual funerary brick burial chamber and other supposed funerary buildings that were located in close proximity to the principal sanctuary. None of the remains of the terraced temple complex at Halawa, by contrast, can be positively linked to any funerary cult or activity associated with death and burial. This evidence underlines the strong degree of local character of the religious traditions of these Euphrates communities. Despite the geographical proximity of Halawa B and Qara Quzaq, these settlements' traditions, rituals and beliefs appeared to have diverged considerably from one another.

Large-scale temples continued to be conspicuous elements of Euphrates settlements into the latter part of the third millennium, although now a growing homogeneity in the overall plan of the temple emerged in the form of the long-roomed temple *in antis*. To date such temples have been identified at Tell Halawa A, Tell Kabir and Qara Quzaq. We assume that this growing standardization of religious architecture was part of a greater trend throughout northern Mesopotamia, in which many aspects of culture became shared across wide distances. This development can largely be attributed to the growth of communication and exchange networks among settlements of this region. It can also be related to the desire, especially on the part of religious and secular leaders of individual cities, to secure their inclusion within this profitable network of exchange through the emulation of neighbouring cities' material cultural accoutrements. The Syrian Euphrates was by no means excluded from this wider world, and its temples *in antis*, replicas of which can be seen outside of the region at sites like Tell Chuera to the east, reflected well this process of cultural homogenization and 'peer polity interaction' (Renfrew 1986: 7–8).

The transformation of religious architecture in the Syrian Euphrates did not also mean that local traditions were abandoned and replaced by new, standardized religious ideologies and cult practices. Quite the opposite was true. Based on the evidence that we have surveyed, it would appear, for example, that the temple *in antis* of level 4 at Qara Quzaq was founded almost directly over the sacred complex of earlier level V, thus underlining the continued sanctity of the area in which the temple was sited. It implies continuity in religious traditions despite outward changes made to the physical appearance of the sanctuary. The temple complex at Halawa Tell A likewise reflects continuity of local religious traditions. The complex was characterized by a large temple *in antis* together with a smaller subsidiary shrine, both of which were situated within a temenos enclosure. This arrangement parallels almost exactly the earlier Halawa Tell B complex, in which the principally elevated sanctuary, with its accompanying subsidiary shrine, was located within a sacred, walled enclosure. If we assume that the inhabitants of Halawa Tell A were the descendants of the people of Halawa Tell B, and that the shift in settlement from one hilltop to another immediately to the south was simply the result of relocating to a larger area in which to accommodate an increasingly larger population, we may propose that the religious establishment of this community simply changed places. The same deities continued to be worshipped in their respective sanctuaries, although the inhabitants by now had adapted their architecture to conform to the accepted norms of sacred architecture prevalent throughout northern Mesopotamia at this time. Local cult practices and religious beliefs prevailed and continued to flourish even though changes had occurred to the physical, structural spaces that provided the focus for these traditions.

We wonder if other aspects of religion, society and culture find reflection in the presence and location of temples within the Syrian Euphrates. It may be significant, for instance, that large temples were present at a number of sites of varying sizes, and not simply at the largest sites in the region. No temple *in antis* has yet been unearthed at the 30 ha site of Tell Banat, for example, although one has been located at Tell Kabir, a small 2.3 ha settlement located only 1 km away from Banat. Qara Quzaq is likewise not a significant site in terms of its size, although the evidence demonstrates that it supported a long-lived, well-established complex of sacred structures. The late third millennium settlement of Halawa Tell A, with its grand temple *in antis*, occupies an area of 15 ha, and yet at the comparably large settlement of Selenkahiye nearby, no monumental temple has been discovered thus far. When combined, the evidence provides no discernible relationship between the physical size of the site and the presence or absence of monumental temples. This interesting observation compels us to reconsider the model of a simple hierarchical settlement system for this region, in which the largest settlements acted as centres that coordinated the social, economic and religious affairs of smaller, satellite settlements in their immediate vicinity. In this model of urbanism, we should only expect to find large-scale buildings – including temples which would have governed the religious affairs of the wider 'city-state' – in the largest centres. Since the evidence from the Syrian Euphrates does not conform to this traditional type of urban hierarchical model, we must seek alternative ways of understanding how individual communities functioned within the network of settlements located in the river valley and beyond, and the special nature of their relationships to one another.

One last interesting observation about the presence of temple architecture concerns its relationship with other forms of religious expression, especially funerary traditions and their attendant mortuary rituals and ceremonies. It seems that funerary practices played an important role in the religious and social life of many Euphrates' communities, judging by the frequency with which large, visible funerary monuments in the form of above-ground tombs and mortuary tumuli are often found at these sites. Such important works will be discussed in greater detail in our chapter on burials. For the time being, we observe that none of the temples described above, with the exception of Qara Quzaq, occur at the same sites where large-scale funerary monuments have been discovered. No temple structure has been discovered at the site of Jerablus Tahtani, for example, with its impressive Tomb 302. Tell Ahmar, with its well-known Hypoegeum which may have stood within a cluster of similar tombs, has also failed to yield any central place of worship. The pattern is most cogently demonstrated at Tell Banat. This mortuary site *par excellence*, which accommodated not only monumental tombs but also massive mortuary tumuli, has not yielded a single temple, although in its immediate neighbourhood at Tell Kabir, a temple *in antis* was prominently situated.

In the absence of any textual documents that might illuminate the religious traditions of the Euphrates valley, it is hazardous to make any firm statements about the significance of this interesting spatial configuration of temples and mortuary constructions. We would like to propose as a possible explanation, however, that these two types of religious monuments reflect the existence of two separate and somewhat opposing ideological traditions among the inhabitants of the Euphrates during this period. On the one hand, temples, invariably located in built-up centres of towns and cities, have a close association with the sedentary, agriculturally-based character of the Euphrates region, this having been established fairly early in the third millennium BC, and which continued to grow and persist over many centuries. On the other hand, funerary markers and monuments of the type found in the northern Euphrates at sites such as Tell Banat may have had greater associations with the largely mobile character of many of the inhabitants of the region. Some groups were obliged to move across considerable distances in the broad steppe lands beyond the confines of the river valley in their quest for suitable grazing lands for their flocks of sheep and goats. Yet the mortuary monuments, which served as potent symbols of the tribal ancestors, provided an important focus for these pastoral nomadic groups, serving to reaffirm and strengthen their ties of kinship and social cohesion. In summary, while temples and their associated complexes may have at their roots the settled, sedentary character of many of the Euphrates' inhabitants, funerary monuments were more closely associated with the tribal, pastoral nomadic character of the population whose traditions were originally rooted in a more rural, as opposed to urban setting. The conjoining of these two contrasting elements in the Euphrates Valley over time resulted in the generation of two types of religious expression characterized by physically distinctive places of worship and divergent ritual activities and observances. Together, these ideological expressions of divine worship and ancestor veneration underscore the variegated nature of society and religion in this complex period of urban growth.

8

CRAFTS AND CRAFT
PRODUCTION

The archaeological record of the Syrian Euphrates well attests to the production of metalwork, textiles, pottery, and other crafted materials. It confirms not only regular, recurring production but also one that was sometimes organized on a scale featuring well appointed workshops and craft specialists. A full picture, however, of the nature and scale of craft production in this region during the third millennium is somewhat difficult to reconstruct owing to a number of factors. The first problem is related to issues of archaeological preservation. We are certain, for example, that some materials, such as leather, hides, wool and wood, were worked into finished products just as they were in other parts of Greater Mesopotamia (Stol 1983; Van de Mieroop 1987; Pollock 1999: 128, 138; Nichols and Weber in press), but their non-permanent, perishable composition makes it impossible to verify their presence. Facilities and tools that probably assisted in transforming these materials into finished, consumable products may also have suffered from the vicissitudes of time and nature.

A second difficulty is that facilities and materials associated with craft manufacturing activities are hard to identify correctly. Several Syrian Euphrates sites have yielded installations that may have been connected with craft activities, but they provide few unambiguous clues concerning their specific function. White limestone plastered or pebbled basins and surfaces at many third millennium north Mesopotamian sites, for example, have been variously interpreted as dye-vats for textiles, wine-processing facilities, and places for the cleaning and levigating of clay (Strommenger 1980: 71; Algaze et al. 1995: 18–19; Routledge 1998: 246). With fine-grained analyses such as micromorphological and residue investigations (e.g. W. Matthews 1995), it may soon be possible to obtain a more accurate reconstruction of some production facilities and their specific uses. For the time being, however, we can only report what has been excavated and offer suggestions concerning how the installations might have functioned within the context of known, third millennium production activities.

Most of the items manufactured in the Euphrates Valley seem to have been intended for local consumption. Some crafted materials, however, may have been traded with neighbouring cities and occasionally conveyed to consumers in other regions of northern Mesopotamia. The fact that the Euphrates River was a natural avenue of exchange, facilitating the flow of crafted goods to the north and the south, makes this likely. Ancient textual sources also allude to the presence of long-established overland routes that linked regions from the east and west of the Euphrates Valley. The considerable wealth of exotic items, especially from tomb contexts within the region, attests to the occurrence of extensive, and at times, long-lasting exchange relations with other regions outside of the Euphrates Valley. On the basis of this evidence, it seems reasonable to conclude that some goods produced in the Syrian Euphrates were conveyed outside of this region through various avenues of exchange.

In southern Mesopotamia during the third millennium, craft activities took the form of high-intensity factory-scale production. This is not the case of such activities in the northern Euphrates Valley region. But nonetheless, craft production was often regularized and well-organized, and, in some cases a high level of specialization was attained. In most instances, craft production appears to have occurred at the level of the independent household or workshop, but sometimes it seems to have been connected to prominent individuals or institutions. Some individuals of importance probably owned and operated craft production facilities, while others may have commissioned artisans to produce their goods for them, supplying the necessary raw materials or funds to buy them (Van de Mieroop 1997: 180). To date, the Euphrates archaeological evidence indicates that such prominent individuals commissioned valuable, luxury products rather than products of a common, utilitarian nature. Such production was clearly related to their desire to surround themselves with precious or sumptuous goods that illustrated their wealth, status and power. These valuable products were also frequently exchanged with neighbouring polities and elites in an effort to initiate or maintain political or economic alliances.

Past studies have often interpreted the organization of production within an ancient society in monolithic terms, suggesting for craft activities a general system that comprised uniform or affiliated modes of control, similar scales of production and corresponding rates of intensity. Such an approach to the evidence, however, fails to acknowledge that craft production, like other human activities, takes many forms. Craft organization, for example, may vary because of the different social or economic positions of the individuals involved in the process and consumption of the products. It may also vary according to the degree of specialization required for the products' manufacture, and the products' function as utilitarian or luxury goods within the society. In this study, we will attempt to demonstrate the multidimensional nature of the organization of production by investigating the different types of objects being manufactured (i.e. metal implements, pots, textiles, stone beads). We will observe where such products were manufactured and their association with other facilities and objects. The findings are significant in that they show that craft activities in the EB Euphrates Valley proceeded within a number of contexts and at varying scales of organization and intensity. These findings add to our evidence of a multiplicity of concurrent yet independent forms of human activity that strongly contributed to the complex and unique urban character of these early riverine communities.

Metals and metal working

Of all craft industries carried out in the third millennium in the Euphrates region, metal working held pride of place. Its finished products of tools, weapons and jewellery played practical as well as important symbolic roles in Early Bronze Age society. Not only were such items used for functional purposes relating to agricultural activities, warfare, protection, personal adornment and the production of other crafts but they also served to communicate within society a person's economic or social status. Textual sources from the third millennium BC city of Ebla aptly convey the social implications of possessing metalwork. These sources mention metal weapons, such as daggers, spears and axes, in the context of a gift-obligation system, connecting both internal and external elites, especially males, to the central palace economy (Archi 1985: 31; Philip 1995: 152). Through gifts of metalwork, predominantly elaborately decorated weapons, male elites could effectively display their rank, status and connections (Philip 1995: 152).

The frequent discovery of metalwork in EB graves alongside other precious items such as jewellery suggests that Euphrates inhabitants, like those of Ebla, also regarded much of their metalwork as markers of high status, power or entitlement. Other metal equipment connected with mundane, economic activities, such as agricultural and pastoral tasks, or with craft activities such as textile manufacture, is notably lacking in tomb contexts. This absence gives further evidence to the symbolic, as opposed to functional, value attached to the metal tools, weapons and items of adornment found in the burials (Pollock 1991: 180; Philip 1995: 142).

Although the exploitation of Anatolian metal can be traced back to the Aceramic Neolithic Era of the eighth millennium BC, in the fourth millennium a widespread diffusion of copper and copper alloys derived from the rich Ergani-Maden mines of the northern Tigris Basin near Diyarbakir, took place (Palmieri et al. 1993: 573). The copper reached many parts of the Near East, even as far away as the southern Levant. In this early period, it is likely that northern Euphrates sites in Anatolia, such as Arslantepe (Period VIA) and Hacinebi, derived much of their prosperity and prominence from their participation in the trade and production of such metals. Evidence for metallurgical activities has been found at these sites, even before major contacts with the Uruk world to the south (Frangipane 1998; Algaze 1999: 538–9; Özbal et al., 2000).

At the beginning of the third millennium BC, after the collapse of the Late Uruk expansion and the withdrawal of southern Mesoptomian influence, metals continued to be a conspicuous component of many northern Euphrates' assemblages. In the far northern Euphrates, at Arslantepe (Period VIB), an Early Bronze I hoard of metalwork comprising weapons such as copper spearheads, daggers and axes, along with ornaments such as pins, bracelets and hair ornaments, was found in a rich tomb from that period (Frangipane 1998). Further down the river, the region around the Early Bronze Age settlement of Carchemish produced a considerable quantity of metalwork. At Carchemish itself, several Phases 1–2 cist graves were found containing flat axes, spearheads and simple daggers along with pins with clear links to the styles represented in the hoard at Arslantepe (Woolley and Barnett 1952: pls. 59–60; Philip in press). In the burials of the Birecik Dam Cemetery about 25 km north of Carchemish, an abundance of differently styled copper pins and other ornaments, tripartite spearheads with leaf-shaped blades, 'poker' spearheards, daggers and flat axes has been recovered from many of the graves (Sertok and Ergeç 1999: 93, and figs. 9–10; Squadrone 2000). If we consider the northern Euphrates Valley of Syria itself, the most prominent collection of copper and bronze artifacts comes from a prominent brick tomb located within the enclosed religious precinct of level V-2 at the site of Qara Quzaq (Olávarri 1995b: 16–17). Its collection of copper spearheads and bronze pins finds excellent parallels to the metalwork from the other sites just mentioned (Montero 1995).

That so much superb metalwork comes principally from burial contexts emphasizes the importance of such items for indicating one's status in death. In one instance, at the site of Qara Quzaq, true tin-bronze as opposed to arsenical copper was used for the manufacture of these tomb items (Montero Fenollós 1999: 456). Since tin had to be imported from as far away as Afghanistan, its presence confirms on the one hand that even in the early third millennium, the Syrian Euphrates was participating in long-distance commercial exchanges. On the other hand, the presence of these tin-bronze items testifies to the existence of wealthy individuals who could afford such exotic and costly materials (Montero Fenollós 1999: 456). Finally, the discovery of considerable quantities of metal within tomb contexts suggests that copper and bronze were considered disposable materials, and that they were probably abundantly available.

During the middle and late part of the Early Bronze Age, burials from Euphrates River Valley sites continued to contain vast amounts of metalwork, especially in the form of copper or bronze weapons and pins, but also to a lesser extent, items in silver and gold. During this period, one sees the appearance of copper socketed axes, spearheads with hooked tangs and toggle-pins with spiral or hemispherical heads. Most of these items demonstrate considerable morphological homogeneity, and they often occur in similar combinations at different sites not only within the Euphrates Valley, but also in other parts of northern and western Syria (Philip in press). This homogeneity testifies to a well-connected and intensive trade in such materials that linked even distant communities. The growing uniformity in the metal repertoire may also be linked to the growth of locally situated elites in Syria during this time, who desired to reinforce their positions of power and wealth with appropriate status trappings, and who, in the process, increased contacts and exchanges with individuals of similar status from other urban centres (Philip in press).

The greatest collections of Phases 3–5 metalwork come from what can be considered the burials of prominent individuals. Two individuals, for example, interred in the rich stone-built 'Hypogeum' at the Euphrates site of Tell Ahmar, were accommodated with a vast number of pottery vessels. They were also left with an astonishing number of metal objects, in the form of bowls, a wide array of axes, spears and daggers, toggle pins, as well as a set of rein-rings, probably associated with a wheeled vehicle of some kind (Thureau-Dangin and Dunand 1936: 106–8, pls. 28–31). The large Tomb 302 at the site of Jerablus Tahtani seems to have been similarly furnished with a rich trove of grave goods, included among them metalwork in the form of copper shaft-hole axes, poker-butted spearheads, thin-bladed daggers (Figure 8.1), as well as a smaller array of adornments of gold and silver (Peltenburg *et al.* 1995: 10, figs. 12 and 14). At the remarkable Euphrates site of Tell Banat, tombs such as Tomb 1 have yielded a rich collection of bronzes, including tongs, daggers, adzes and pins (Porter 1995a: 8, figs. 5–7). The large stone-built Tomb 7, while yielding only a modest amount of copper and bronze items, nonetheless featured a variety of gold beads, including almost a thousand tiny circular rings cut from tubes, as well as quadruple-spiral, pumpkin-shaped and rilled beads. The burial treasure also included gold scallop shells, bell and biconical forms, mushroom-shaped pendants, long gold bars with pinched holes and a gold pendant with applied lozenge (Figure 9.13). Gold was also used as inlay in lapis lazuli bottle stoppers (McClellan and Porter 1999: 110; Aruz 2003: 185–6). It has been pointed out that many of these gold ornament styles match those found in con-temporary contexts as far away as Troy and Poliochni in Anatolia, testifying to the widespread interactions that Syrian Euphrates communities must have been engaged in during this time (Aruz 2003: 185, 271).

The shaft tombs at Tell Halawa contained metal objects, notably bronze pins, daggers, spearheads, axes, beads, earrings, arm rings, collars and handles (Orthmann 1981: Taf. 68–70). Last, at the site of Selenkahiye and its neigh-bouring cemetery of Wreide, items such as bronze daggers, axes, spearheads, and most notably pins, typically occurring as crossed pairs, accompanied several burials, sometimes along with silver adornments such as torques, pendants, diadems and earrings (Van Loon 2001: Chapters 4A–4B). In all, the middle to later part of the Early Bronze Age had by no means an impoverished metal repertoire, as these rich and plentiful tombs clearly demonstrate.

Figure 8.1 Copper alloy daggers from Tomb 302, Jerablus Tahtani.

Evidence for metal working

The discovery of artifactual remains associated with metal working at a number of Euphrates sites confirms that the manufacture of at least some of the metal artifacts found so copiously in archaeological contexts, especially burials, was undertaken on a local level. Included among this repertoire are stone moulds for casting metal implements, tools and crucibles. Although some of the contexts in which such metallurgical equipment has been found are disturbed or poorly understood, it is sometimes possible to obtain clues concerning where this important industry was carried out, and under whose auspices it was organized.

The earliest EB evidence for local metal working in the northern Euphrates Valley comes from the small site of Halawa Tell B, whose early levels of occupation can be dated to the first centuries of the third millennium BC in

Phases 1–2. Of the six structures known to have been occupied in the central walled area of the site during an early level of Halawa (level 3), the largest building (defined by Rooms 310–11, 314–17) contained an open courtyard enclosed by a curving mud brick wall in its southwestern corner (Courtyard 310). Here, along with the remnants of large jars, a stone mortar, bone utensils, and a zoomorphic vessel, excavations brought to light a limestone metal mould that would have produced a straight axe (Figure 8.2). This axe was likely an earlier version of the tanged crescentic axes seen in the Syrian Euphrates and elsewhere in the mid-to-latter part of the third millennium (Tubb 1982; Orthmann 1989: 91, Abb. 70; Philip 1989: 46). The interpretation of the courtyard as a small metal workshop is especially convincing if the limestone mortar is regarded as a type of anvil and the small fireplace in the floor near the axe mould provided a necessary source of heat (Pfälzner 2001: 226). It may additionally be significant that in another room in the same house (Room 314) a long bronze or copper axe head was found, providing further support for the manufacture of metal weapons or tools in the complex (Orthmann 1989: 91, Abb. 69; Pfälzner 2001: 357). We are interpreting this facility as a metallurgical one but we must also acknowledge that it existed within the context of a household where other domestic activities, such as the storage, preparation and cooking of food, took place (Pfälzner 2001: 356–7).

Metal working is attested in other household contexts in northern Mesopotamia during the third millennium BC. In particular, P. Pfälzner reports that at Tell Chuera and Tell Bderi, two EB sites in northeastern Syria, evidence for the manufacture of metal objects has been obtained from two houses (Pfälzner 2001: 286, 342, 357). The Tell Chuera and Tell Bderi houses were large and contained more rooms than other contemporary domestic structures from these sites, just as the house at Halawa Tell B (discussed above) was one of the largest domestic structures at the site. Such evidence indicates a possible connection between the production of metal

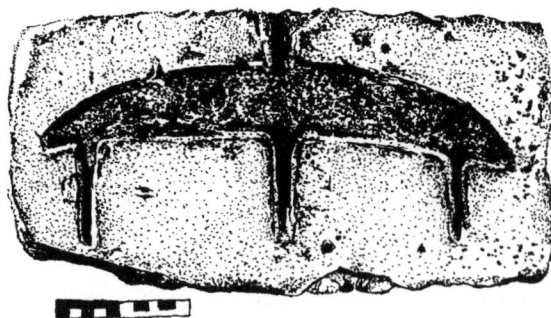

Figure 8.2 Stone metal mould for axe, Halawa Tell B.

170

implements and the economic success of the household to which it was connected.

Evidence for metal working becomes more widespread during the second half of the third millennium BC. Several stone moulds have been recovered from a number of Syrian Euphrates sites. Although their precise context is unclear, their presence implies that some form of metal working activity was carried out at these settlements. Under the tiled floor of an Iron Age building at Tell Ahmar, for example, the excavators found two stone univalve moulds in conjunction with large quantities of ash and charred wood. The typology of some objects manufactured from the moulds and their stratigraphic position suggest an early date, possibly in the second half of the third millennium BC (Thureau-Dangin and Dunand 1936: 86–8, plan C; Montero Fenollós 1999: 452). Another stone mould that was used to cast several different metal shapes was found in an isolated context at Tell Qara Quzaq in a level attributed the mid-third millennium (level IV) (Montero Fenollós 1999: 452 and Figure 1). A crucible in the form of a small ceramic bowl was also discovered in the same level at Qara Quzaq. The inner walls of this crucible had been intensely burned and contained greenish metal droplets. When analysed, these proved to be the remains of copper, iron and tin, along with other metals (Montero Fenollós 1999: 452).

Evidence for metal working is also attested at the small fortified site of Jerablus Tahtani, although, as with the examples cited above, the specific context in which this activity was carried out is uncertain. Crucibles and a dagger mould were found in an external 'courtyard' area at the northern end of the fort (Figure. 8.3) (Peltenburg et al. 2000: 61). Three other crucibles were also found in a disturbed area in the southeastern part of the fort (Area I), where a late building from the Hellenistic or Roman period intruded into the top of the corner of the earlier EB fort wall (Peltenburg et al. 1997: 5, Figure 5). Although these latter crucibles' precise date is uncertain given the disturbed context from which they came, a third millennium date seems reasonable because of their association with other third millennium pottery found in the same context (Peltenburg et al. 1997: 5). The crucibles are small, thin-walled, and hemispherical in shape, and lack pouring lips. One of them contains specks of gold embedded in a dark vitrified residue (Peltenburg et al. 1997: 5). Another crucible is distinguished by the copper alloy corrosion product that adheres to its interior (Peltenburg et al. 1997: 5). It is argued that these crucibles were used to manufacture objects from raw materials or from re-cycled items. Alternatively, they could have been used in gold assaying with lead, which would have determined the amount of base metal in the gold (Peltenburg et al. 1997: 5).

It is possible that there was an association between the metal working at Jerablus Tahtani and an elite group, whose presence at the site is testified by the ostentatious tomb Tomb 302 and the wealth of metal objects found within it. Who the owners and controllers of the metalworking facilities

Figure 8.3 Stone dagger mould, Jerablus Tahtani.

were is uncertain given the somewhat ambiguous contexts from which the moulds and crucibles came. Their identity could depend to a great extent on how the site of Jerablus Tahtani should be interpreted as a whole. Did this site fall under the control of a higher state authority, or did it function as an autonomous polity in its own right, having its own administrative infrastructure and governing elites? Once these issues have been clarified, we may be in a better position to posit the context in which metal working occurred. It may have taken place within households or workshops that were independent or partially attached to a higher local authority, or it may have been one part of an overarching productive system controlled by a higher, regional polity. Whatever the case, the current evidence for metal working at Jerablus Tahtani does not seem to point to any large-scale, intensive production at the site. Rather, the manufacture of metal implements appears to have been carried out in small working spaces of the fort's interior, within close proximity to other installations where the processing and storage of food was carried out.

The strongest evidence supporting the connection between some kind of central organization at a site and the manufacture of metal comes from the site of Tell es-Sweyhat, particularly from the western side of the main acropolis mound (Area IV). Here was found a large warehouse building ('Burned Building'), interpreted by the excavators as having served as a palace or another important public building higher up on the acropolis mound. This complex of public architecture is dated to Phase 5, in the late centuries of the third millennium, when Sweyhat reached its largest settlement size. A series of nine rooms were excavated along a 31 m stretch of an inner fortification wall in this area, one of which contained a crucible (Room 3). This crucible, coarse and heavily tempered, had a thick residue on the interior, left from the smelting of copper (Holland 1976: 51, Figure 15: 29). Along with the crucible, Room 3 also yielded a pair of bronze tongs that had been bent around a piece of metal, in addition to a flat bronze strip, which may also have been used with the tongs as a metal working implement (Holland 1976: 51, Figure 15: 37, 42). The finding of an inscribed cuneiform weight in this room may point to economic activities associated with metal working (Pfälzner 2001: 367).

Chemical analyses were performed on metal objects recovered from other rooms of the same building on the western acropolis at Tell es-Sweyhat, as well as on the copper residue of the crucible itself. Significantly, several items were found to contain the same proportions of metals – principally copper, tin, arsenic and nickel – as those of the crucible, strongly suggesting that such items were being produced from this crucible, or at the very least by one and the same smith at the site (Holland 1976: 66).

We may question whether or not actual metal-production was carried out in the room in which the crucible was found, given its location within the inner spaces of a large house-like structure, and in association with storage facilities. Alternatively, we may propose that this room served as a storage space for metal working equipment (Pfälzner 2001: 367), and that the actual production site was in some other place in the building, or in its immediate environs.

Excavations in an area at the southern end of the main mound revealed a massive mudbrick wall and associated fragments of a wall painting which are thought to be part of a very large public building, possibly a temple dated to the middle of the third millennium BC (2600–2300 BC) (Holland 1993–94: 279). Overlying this building were two pits filled with pottery in which was also found a glazed rock crystal bead containing a large concentration of copper oxide, as well as the discovery of a stone mould for either a dagger or spear (Holland and Zettler 1994: 140). Such evidence seems also to be clearly related to the copper working that was going on at this site.

Since the evidence for metal working at Sweyhat was found on the central high mound, in association with what appears to be large-scale secular architecture, it seems to have some association with a central authority or institution at the site. This contextual association possibly points to the concentration of metal manufacture in the hands of individuals of importance who occupied these buildings, perhaps a governing elite. Support for this supposition comes from further evidence. Although considerable investigations have been undertaken in the lower town at Sweyhat, and other craft installations have been discovered there, no lower town context has thus far yielded the remains of metal working facilities or equipment.

Further down the Euphrates River at Tell Habuba Kabira, evidence for the working of copper derives from level 14, also late in the Early Bronze Age sequence (Phase 5). This evidence is in the form of a cache of raw copper ingots, the tubular part of a terra-cotta bellows, copper tools and weapons, and a limestone mould from which various types of axes were cast (Strommenger 1980: 78–9). It appears in a occupational phase marked principally by a significant strengthening of the city's fortification wall. Furthermore, the area immediately inside the wall, where domestic structures were found in earlier phases, had been transformed into a large open terrace. The considerable resources and labour required for this construction may suggest the growing pre-eminence of some authority at the site who had the means to undertake this large reorganization of space on the high mound. The discovery of circular paved surfaces and other installations on the terrace (Heusch 1980: 176–5), together with the metal working items, suggests that craft activities developed in conjunction with the growth of this authority.

A similar situation to that at Tell Habuba Kabira may also have developed at the nearby Euphrates site of Tell Qannas, where metal working is indicated by the discovery of a stone mould for producing items such as daggers and knives. Such a mould was found in association with a massive deposit of ash on the eastern slopes of the tell outside of the settlement's fortified centre, where a large multi-roomed building had been located (Finet 1979: 83–6, Figure 12). As at Habuba Kabira, the evidence appears to date to the final centuries of the third millennium BC (Phase 5). The presence of a large building in the centre of the mound may also suggest a central authority at the site, to which the metalworking facilities were attached.

Metal working discussion

In light of the evidence for metal working activities up and down the length of the Syrian Euphrates Valley and through the course of the EB, we may draw a few general conclusions. First, even in the early part of the third millennium, although evidence is scanty, it would seem that metal working activities were connected to individuals or households enjoying economic success. Such a view is suggested in particular by the metal mould in the largest house at Halawa Tell B. At this point we cannot know for certain whether metal working was a factor that caused the growth of the house, or if existing prosperity enabled the household members to exploit valuable resources, including metal. Whatever the case, already in the early third millennium, this evidence from Halawa B, along with the rich cache of metal weapons in the tomb at Qara Quzaq, suggest the first signs of important individuals, who, having access to the raw materials and production facilities, could make potent symbols that would enhance their status and wealth.

174

Second, during the latter half of the third millennium, metal objects continue to be equated with the upper stratum of Euphrates urban society as attested by their frequent appearance in tombs. The production of such objects also seems to have been closely connected with individuals of high rank, suggested by the discovery of equipment such as crucibles and moulds in close association with public buildings situated on the central high mounds of Tell es-Sweyhat, Tell Habuba Kabira and Tell Qannas. None of this equipment, however, was found in what can be interpreted as massive manufactories, where the production of metals would have proceeded on an industrial scale. On the contrary, it would appear that metal working was carried out on a relatively small scale, in the same general areas where activities relating to food processing and other craft activities took place. In summary, our perspective on metal production in the Euphrates suggests that while elite individuals must have existed in the urban communities of the Syrian Euphrates with considerable access to raw and valuable materials, they never attained a superordinate level of power comparable to other elite peoples in Greater Mesopotamia at this time.

Textiles and textile manufacture

It is unfortunate that the most frequently manufactured materials in the ancient Near East, textiles woven predominantly from sheep's wool, are precisely those most poorly preserved. Unlike other durable items such as metal implements and pottery, textiles have left virtually no traces in the archaeological record, although we can presume they were used in a variety of ways including clothing, household furnishings such as carpets and wall hangings, storage and transportation containers, and shelter and protection from the elements (Bier 1995: 1567). Furthermore, the tools used in the manufacture of textiles, such as loom weights, spindles, bobbins, spools and looms, may likewise have been made of a perishable material that has left no trace in the archaeological record. It is also fair to say that many artifacts that may have been associated with the production of cloth may frequently have been passed over as meaningless trinkets or assigned another function. Such has often been the case, for example, with ancient loom weights and spindle whorls, variously interpreted as primitive counting devices, idols and amulets, and even model chariot wheels (Wattenmaker 1998: 146–7; Fortin 1999: 183).

Without doubt, wool for textiles was a major pastoral product of the inhabitants of the Euphrates Valley. As noted in the previous chapter, the raising of sheep and goats was the primary form of livestock economy in the Euphrates Valley throughout the third millennium. We can presume that while some sheep were raised for their meat and dairy products, still a good proportion of them would also have been raised for their wool, to be manufactured into clothing products, or their hair, for making items such as carpets and tents. Further analysis of the kill-off patterns among sheep and the detection of different breeds of caprines, raised specifically for wool and hair, will in the future determine the proportion which were exploited in these ways (Zeder 1998: 66).

Elsewhere in Mesopotamia and Syria, we know that sheep raising and the consequent production of sheep's wool into textiles was a major industry. While archaeological investigations in southern Mesopotamia have failed to bring to light remnants of actual textile products, ancient sites have yielded thousands of cuneiform tablets frequently mentioning the keeping of sheep for wool, and the ways in which the woollen industry operated. Textual sources from the third millennium indicate that the manufacture of textiles from wool was one of southern Mesopotamia's principal craft productions, which was carried out intensively. From several late third millennium cities of the Ur III period, from Ur itself and within the Lagash province, there was an institutionalized textile production, the sources describing massive factories that were controlled by the state or the temples. The Guabba temple, located along the southern edge of Lagash, employed 6,000 workers, mostly women and children, to manage its very large textile mill (Postgate 1992: 115). Within this place, the types and grades of cloth were carefully recorded along with their quantities and the number of days required to produce them (Waetzoldt 1972; Postgate 1992: 235).

The institutionalized production of textiles goes back to even earlier periods in southern Mesopotamia, if we judge by, for example, earlier Pre-Sargonic archives which relate how textile production was divided into a 'wool place' and a 'flax place' (Postgate 1992: 235). The archaeological record also indicates a state connection to textile production. The architectural layout and association installations of the so-called 'North Palace' at Eshununa of the Diyala Region during the Early Dynastic III and Akkadian periods may have been devoted to the weaving of cloth. This enterprise was probably related to the neighbouring Abu Temple (Postgate 1992: 115). Even as early as the Late Uruk, the presence of large textile workshops is suggested by sealings and seals depicting 'pig-tailed' women weaving in what were likely state-controlled craft institutions (Zagarell 1986: 418; McCorriston 1997: 527; Pollock 1999: 104).

Within Syria during the third millennium, considerable textual documentation concerning textile production, the trade and exchange of textiles, and livestock holdings comes from the city of Ebla, located to the west of the Euphrates River in western Syria. The state archives of Palace G at Ebla indicate the receipt of massive quantities of wool, textiles and livestock to this city. These products were recorded and then re-distributed, namely in the form of cloth, not only to subjects of the palace and city of Ebla but also to many distant centres extending from the Mediterranean coast in the west to the Tigris Valley to the east, and from Central Anatolia in the north to Palestine in the south (Matthiae 1977: 180).

At Ebla, textual sources enumerating the palace's ownership of sheep, which numbered in the thousands (Archi 1992: 27), certainly indicate the ruling authority's economic interests in the woollen industry. Such interests are further underlined by the fact that extant records show all consignments of textiles to the city were made specifically to the palace, and that it was the Ebla palace that saw to these products' redistribution. We also know from the texts that much of the manufacturing of wool into textiles was carried out under the auspices of the palace. Such activity is attested by the numerous individuals, particularly female personnel who were issued rations of wool and food in return for their spinning and weaving work (Biga 1988; Archi 1992: 25; Milano 1995: 1225).

Syrian Euphrates textile production

To reconstruct the organization of textile production in the Syrian Euphrates is a complicated task. Unlike Ebla and Mesopotamia, we do not have textual sources to help us to ascertain where and under whom production took place, nor where the bulk of manufactured items was conveyed. Clearly important to our understanding of textile production is knowledge concerning whether the products of wool and hair were destined primarily for local consumption, or if a portion of these products was saved for exchange with other communities within the river valley and beyond. Given that sheep and goats were a primary staple of the Euphrates productive economy, we can surmise that these animals and their products were part of wider exchanges in the third millennium BC. At some point in time, it is likely that pastoral products were sent as tribute to the distant centres of Ebla and Mari, which, according to textual sources, held political sway over the Syrian Euphrates and exacted tribute from the client kingdoms in this region. In spite of these wider exchanges, however, the precise form that such pastoral products took, either the animals themselves, wool and hair shorn from the animals, or textiles manufactured from these raw materials, is far from clear. One can only turn to the archaeological record for any clues about the nature of these political and economic relationships.

To date, only a few archaeological discoveries in the Syrian Euphrates have elicited any clear evidence for the manufacture of textiles and associated workshops. In Level 7 at the site of Tell Habuba Kabira around the mid-third millennium, plastered basins and work platforms were excavated in close proximity to what appear to be lumps of yellow or red colour pigments. This evidence might point to the production and dyeing of textiles (Heusch 1980: 168; Strommenger 1980: 71). Such materials and installations were found in association with the manufacture of jewellery, suggesting the presence of a multi-craft zone of activity. Nonetheless, both manufacturing activities appear to have taken place in a household context, which served as the residence for a moderately-sized family.

177

At the site of Jerablus Tahtani, in a phase after the defensive rampart was added in the late third millennium BC (Phase 4), it is reported that one room of the fort yielded as many as 42 terra-cotta bobbins suggestive of textile working (Peltenburg *et al.* 1997: 7). As at Tell Habuba Kabira, this activity appears to been carried out in areas where other domestic activities, such as cooking and food storage, took place. Such evidence implies that the production of the textiles was a household-level industry (Peltenburg 1999a: 101).

Further evidence for textile production was obtained from the site of Tell es-Sweyhat, in a large multi-roomed house in the northwestern sector of the lower town dated to the end of the third millennium BC (Phase 5). On the one hand, pierced clay disks, probably spindle whorls, were found on the floors of some rooms, indicating that such spaces may have been used for cloth-making activities (Holland and Zettler 1994: 139; Zettler 1997b: 39, 42). On the other hand, the presence of cooking hearths, a bread oven, as well as pebble-lined pits and a press, suggest a multi-functional use for this building (Zettler 1997b: 39, 42). The excavators are confident in interpreting the building not as the locale of a specialized occupation, but rather a large house (Zettler 1997b: 42).

Last, the site of Tell Banat also provides evidence testifying to the manufacture of textiles. As many as 50 circular wheels, possibly identified as spindle whorls, were recovered from contexts in and around the buildings and kiln dumps of Area D, where pottery was also being produced. The presence of such spindle whorls, along with the existence of post-holes found in many parts of the complex, which may be the remnants of looms, suggest that textile manufacture was another important craft activity carried out in this particular sector of the city (Porter and McClellan 1998: 16, 20, pl. 6d; Porter 2002b: 158).

Textile manufacture discussion

The combined evidence for the manufacturing of textiles at the Early Bronze Euphrates sites points to a different level of production from that of metal working. Unlike the former craft activity, which seems to have had a connection with an elite class, most of the evidence indicates that the spinning, weaving and dyeing of cloth took place principally in household contexts alongside other domestic activities. So far, it is only at Tell Banat that the making of textiles seems to have occurred together with other craft activities, namely pottery production, in a larger, specialized workshop. The higher frequency of craft-related tools and working surfaces as opposed to domestic artifacts does not suggest a typical household function for this area. The situation at Tell Banat, however, is unusual given its principal role as a massive mortuary centre rather than the residence of a large living community. Thus all evidence from Tell Banat, including materials relating to craft production such as textile weaving, must be considered in light of the site's special function. This site and its extraordinary facilities will be explored further in the context of our discussions of pottery production and funerary practices.

The majority of our evidence of textiles, therefore, points to household manufacture. Even if this was so, it does not mean that such products were destined merely for the individuals in whose houses manufacture took place. Textile products may have been exchanged commercially within the wider community and beyond. If exchanged in this way, they may have provided an additional means of income for households with access to the resources and specialization for such endeavours. This notion finds some support in textual evidence from the Old Assyrian city of Assur in Mesopotamia, around 2000 BC, in which textiles appear to have been largely a home-based production used to meet a commercial demand (Veenhof 1977: 114–15; Postgate 1992: 235). Alternatively, consignments of textiles may have been produced in households but destined as a form of tax and tribute paid to a higher local or regional authority.

Whatever the final destination of these products, it is fair to say that the organization of textile production did not occur within the same context and the grand scale as is attested in southern Mesopotamia and Ebla. To date, we find no evidence of large nucleated workshop areas where sheep wool and goat's hair were collected, processed, washed, spun and woven into textiles. We do not discern a connection between such activities and a higher, governing authority administering the industry. While temple complexes and a few public buildings have been identified within the Syrian Euphrates, so far none of these places has yielded any compelling evidence linking them to any kind of textile industry. Such observations are significant since they underline the altogether different systems of political and economic organization that distinguish the Euphrates riverine urban communities from other contemporaneous 'state' societies of Greater Mesopotamia.

Stone and shell jewellery and jewellery manufacture

Jewellery does not constitute a significant part of the archaeological evidence of most third millennium BC contexts, except for Early Bronze Age burials, where it occurs with considerable regularity. Jewellery is especially frequent in the larger tombs of prominent individuals and may include adornments fashioned from precious metals, such as silver and gold. In smaller, less opulent tombs, other pieces are often present in more modest quantities (e.g. Van Loon 2001: 11.487–94). These pieces usually comprise items such as beads, amulets and pendants carved from a variety of semi-precious or locally available stone, and shell.

Jewellery manufacture in the Euphrates Valley is not well attested except at the site of Habuba Kabira, where the manufacture of beads from a variety of stone materials has been reported. The evidence for jewellery working first appears in level 5 of the EB occupation (Phase 3), in the southeastern corner of the tell in a room of a house located near the outer fortification wall (Strommenger 1980: 71). Tools were found within the room, such as flint and obsidian borers and polishing stones, as well as the products themselves, consisting of both half-finished and finished beads. The raw materials for making the beads included red and white limestone, alabaster and shell (Heusch 1980: 164). This jewellery manufactory continued in existence into both levels 6 and 7, despite alterations in the layout and size of the building and the room in which it was situated (Heusch 1980: 166–8). In addition to this craft industry, other activities appear to have been carried out in the same general locale, such as cooking and storage, suggesting that this was a small household (Pfälzner 2001: 370).

We can suggest that many of these beads and amulets were locally distributed, and may eventually have ended up in burial contexts, interred with the deceased individuals who owned them. Confirming this supposition are graves to the south of Tell Habuba Kabira, which have yielded the same locally produced beads and amulets as well as copper pins and other objects (Strommenger 1980: 70).

Pottery and pottery production

Pottery constitutes the most common and abundant class of artifacts in the archaeological record of the Euphrates Valley of Syria of the third millennium BC. Since very many pieces have been found in virtually every place where excavation work and surface reconnaissance of ancient tells have been carried out, we will not attempt to describe all the contexts in which pottery has been recovered. Most types of ceramic vessels were available to the inhabitants of these settlements throughout the course of the Early Bronze Age, the pots having been used for a variety of functions relating principally to the transport, storage, serving and cooking of various solid and liquid materials in everyday life. Pottery vessels were also linked to funerary activities, placed within the tombs of deceased individuals, where they functioned as receptacles of food and drink either to be consumed by the deceased in the afterlife or to placate spirits of the underworld. Tomb vessels also represent the utensils of a mortuary feast held in honour of the deceased (Peltenburg in press a).

In contrast to common pottery, it is difficult to pinpoint vessel types that might be construed as 'elite wares' with a possible circumscribed distribution in contexts associated with individuals having access to exceptional wealth, status or power within Euphrates EB society. There are vessel types classified as fine wares because of their well-finished appearance and highly fired state. These wares, however, are accounted for in a variety of contexts that appear to cross-cut social-economic boundaries. The largest quantities of mid-to-late fine ware vessels, particularly those classified as Orange or Grey Spiral Burnished Wares or Euphrates Banded Wares, have been reported in tomb contexts. These vessels are found in a wide variety of burial types and sizes and their association with both poor and valuable grave goods prevents an unequivocal connection to an elite stratum in Euphrates society.

Recent studies of the uses and significance of pottery around the world, including the Near East, emphasize not only what the decoration and shape of pottery vessels may tell us about the people using these objects, but also what can be gleaned from understanding how the vessels were made (Schneider 1989; Blackman *et al.* 1993; Greenberg and Porat 1996; Goren 1996; Vandiver 2003; Boileau 2005). Knowledge of the various stages involved in the production of pottery vessels and the type of facilities where pottery was produced may shed valuable light on important social, economic or political systems within the ancient society. Thus, for example, the context, scale and intensity of vessel production may show the degree to which specialization was sponsored or controlled by a centralized institution or elite class (Costin 1991: 5). Similarly, the identification of the provenance of raw materials for pottery manufacture may indicate possible exchange relationships among contemporary communities and shed light on the nature and degree of economic complexity within a society during a given period of time.

Despite the recent frequent studies of pottery mentioned above, EB pottery from the Euphrates Valley of Syria has rarely been the subject of specific investigation. Our understanding of the organization of ceramic production and its connection to the overall economic, social and political dynamics of the Euphrates communities remains quite incomplete. Nevertheless, through a general scrutiny of EB vessels and the types and locations of the facilities in which they were manufactured, we hope to make some general observations about ceramic production and its place in Euphrates' urban society. Further fine-grained studies will add to our knowledge in the future.

Fine and plain simple ware production

Our first observation about EB Syrian Euphrates pottery is that both Fine and Plain Simple Ware vessels are of relatively good quality. Throughout their development in the EB, most pots were symmetrically shaped and even-walled, well fired in the kiln. Many EB Fine Ware vessels possess thin walls and relatively fine fabrics. The clays of the vessels are invariably characterized by mineral inclusions, these either occurring naturally in the clay matrices or deliberately added as temper.

Further analytical techniques are required to determine the ways and degrees to which these vessels were worked on the potter's wheel or tournette. While most vessels exhibit fairly regularly spaced concentric grooves, rilling, or striations, we now know that such markings are not necessarily the product of a fast-spinning wheel. These markings can often result from the final forming process, whereby vessels that have been hand-fashioned by coiling are then thinned and shaped on a wheel. The result is a pot whose surface features from the first step in the production sequence, namely fashioning by coiling, have been totally obliterated (Courty and Roux 1995: 18). It is significant to note that to date no third millennium wheel-thrown ceramics from northern Mesopotamia have been identified. Rather, technological analyses show that these ceramics were initially formed by coiling, then shaped on the wheel (Courty and Roux 1995: 48). Given this observation, we postulate that most Euphrates EB pots were also manufactured in this way.

Regardless of the specifics of the forming techniques, the finished vessels, by their fine appearance and consistently well-fired state, surely point to the presence of skilled potters. Even if the vessels were not wheel-thrown, the technology required to form these vessels by hand and then to shape and finish them on the wheel points to a high degree of skill that could only have been acquired from several years of training and apprenticeship (Boileau 2005: 52). Last, we observe that the uniformity of the shape, fabric and technological attributes of the pottery especially at the site level, suggests that the production of pottery was largely carried out by potters working in each individual community. We may conclude, therefore, that the majority of EB Euphrates Fine and Plain Simple Ware pots were manufactured by local specialists who were well acquainted with their craft.

Cooking pot ware production

In her study of the changing levels of EB craft production at the site of Kurban Höyük (Karababa Basin, Euphrates River Valley of Turkey), Patty Wattenmaker argues that, although most vessels at the site were manufactured by skilled potters, cooking pots remained within the domestic sphere of production and were not the work of specialists (Wattenmaker 1994: 199; 1998: 128). She observed that, since these coarse vessels were hand-made, exhibiting considerable variability in rim shape and diameter, they reflected a lower level of skilled workmanship than vessels consistently formed or finished on the wheel (Wattenmaker 1998: 131). Wattenmaker correctly proposed a distinction between the production of cooking pots and that of other vessel types, thus regarding the overall ceramic assemblage as a multi-faceted artifactual set comprising varying manufacturing techniques, potters and contexts of production. She also cogently demonstrated how shifts in the socio-political organization of the site can be chronicled through observations of the changing patterns through time of production and consumption among manufactured items (Wattenmaker 1998: 125).

Some of Wattenmaker's assumptions, however, may need to be reconsidered especially vis-à-vis cooking pots and the level of skill required for their production. Elsewhere in northern Mesopotamia it has been shown that some cooking pots, while made by hand, often share many technological and morphological characteristics, suggesting that they too may have been the product of specialist potters. In the Khabur Valley of northeastern Syria, for example, M.-C. Boileau has shown that two types of cooking pots characterize the EB assemblages of Tell ʿAtij and Tell Gudeda. Both cooking pot types were manufactured by hand, although one of the types was technologically superior and performed well over fire. Vessels of this type were uniformly tempered with crushed basalt and showed high techno-morphological homogeneity (Boileau 2005: 46). It is significant that these vessels were made of non-local raw materials, indicating that they were imported to the site. Boileau suggests that these cooking pots were the product of specialists, aware of the properties required to produce efficient utensils that would be durable and able to withstand intense sources of heat. These specialists, it appears, were so skilled that their products became highly valued and sought after by consumers in distant settlements (Boileau 2005: 54).

A general survey of Cooking Ware pots from many sites of the mid-to-late EB periods (Phases 3–5) in the Syrian Euphrates shows that they exhibit consistently similar traits. In terms of overall appearance, although the pots exhibit some metric variability, there is a remarkable uniformity in the shapes produced (Figure 8.4). Invariably the vessels comprise globular bodies, restricted necks and everted rims, with triangular lug-handles extending from the rim. The outer and the inner rim surfaces are usually horizontally burnished by hand. Although the present data are incomplete, it would appear that most cooking pots were tempered with calcite, a mineral inclusion well-known for its thermodynamic suitability (Rye 1976). All these factors suggest that EB Euphrates cooking pots, like those from the Khabur, were the product of specialist potters, possibly working from a few households, workshops or a community whose location has yet to be identified. In light of these observations, it would be difficult to draw conclusions about the changing socio-political organization of EB society based on shifting proportions of specialist versus non-specialist wares according to the method employed by Wattenmaker, since the latter wares have been shown to be largely under-represented in the EB Euphrates assemblages.

Ceramic production locales in the Syrian Euphrates

While evidence for the location of the production of pottery is sadly lacking in other parts of Syria during the Early Bronze Age, sites along the Euphrates River have yielded some remains that testify to this activity. From this evidence it is possible to make a few additional remarks, both about the nature of craft specialization within the EB communities and about the settlements' socio-political and economic complexity. The following archaeological data

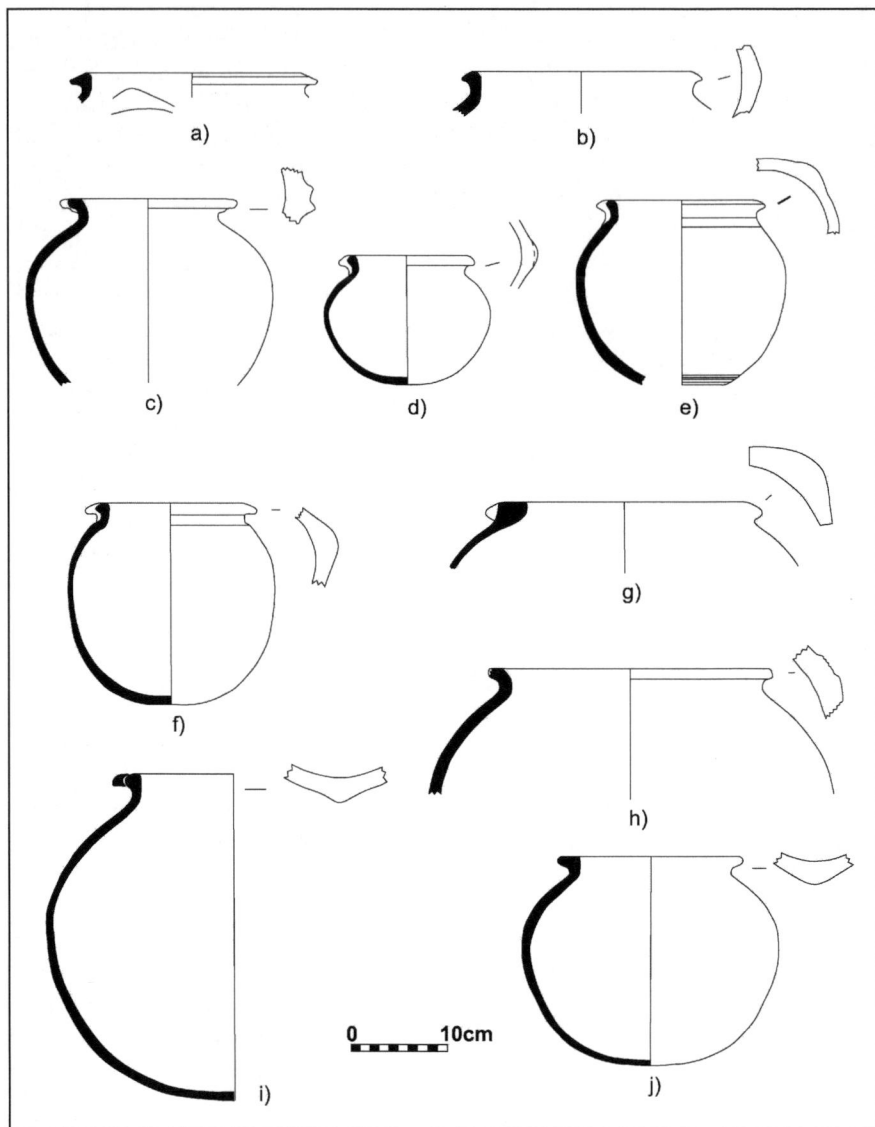

Figure 8.4 Phases 3–5 cooking pots.

derives from the sites of Tell Habuba Kabira, Halawa Tell A and Tell es-Sweyhat.

At the site of Tell Habuba Kabira, where early Early Bronze Age occupation (Phases 1–2) was exposed in the southeastern corner of the excavated tell, a small room within a house may have been the locale of pottery manufacture

(Heusch 1980: 163; Strommenger 1980: 76, Figure 73; Akkermans and Schwartz 2003: 228). Four circular basins with raised rims made of lightly fired clay were found in a slightly curved row in the floor in the northeastern section of the room. These basins were interpreted as vats where clay was washed or levigated in water (Strommenger 1980: 76). In association with these basins were pierced stone discs, argued to be parts of potters' turn-tables (Heusch 1980: 163–4). The proposed interpretation of this particular room, however, has been challenged by Peter Pfälzner. He notes that the basins are not exceptionally large and that even with their raised rims, they are too shallow to be practical for containing water. He observed that three of these four basins bear traces of burning on their interiors, hardly a by-product of an installation associated with water (Pfälzner 2001: 161). He says that the presence of many pieces of pottery in the room, including part of a vessel still lying *in situ* in one of the receptacles, suggests that such basins may have served as supports for round-bottomed pottery vessels. Thus, this room probably served for the storage, not the production, of pottery (Pfälzner 2001: 369). The additional presence of grinding stones and pestles in the room supports the assertion that food processing was also carried out in this room (Pfläzner 2001: 369). These observations suggest that it is more credible to reconstruct the room of the house as the locale of domestic food storage and preparation than that of pottery production.

An installation found in a later level of Tell Habuba Kabira dating to the late EB (level 10) is more convincingly associated with the production of pottery. During level 10, the southeastern side of the settlement was charac-terized by a double-entry gateway and fortified terrace. The installation was located on its own outside the city wall in the southeastern angle between the reconstructed fortification wall and new terrace wall to the north. It is a large two-chambered kiln, roughly square in plan with rounded corners (Figure 8.5). At the level of the baking chamber floor, the kiln was about 1.60–1.80 m in width. The lower firebox was separated from the upper baking chamber by a platform pierced with many holes (Strommenger 1980: Abb. 74–5). The stoke hole for the firebox was located on the western side of the kiln. The upper part of the baking chamber appears to have originally had a dome shape, and was probably built of branches and clay (Heusch 1980: 172). Many mis-fired, mis-shaped pottery fragments, small un-fired pieces of clay and cone-shaped objects, interpreted as supports or kiln separ-ators, were recovered from above a layer of fine gravel surrounding the kiln (Heinrich *et al.* 1973: 58). Such associated material would likely support the oven's identification as a potter's kiln.

Like the extramural location of the kiln at Tell Habuba Kabira, pottery kilns were also found outside the fortification walls of Halawa Tell A, dating to approximately the same time in the late EB as the kiln found at Habuba Kabira (Phases 4–5). On a slope in the northwestern part of the tell, four circular potter's kilns were revealed when the rising water from the lake of

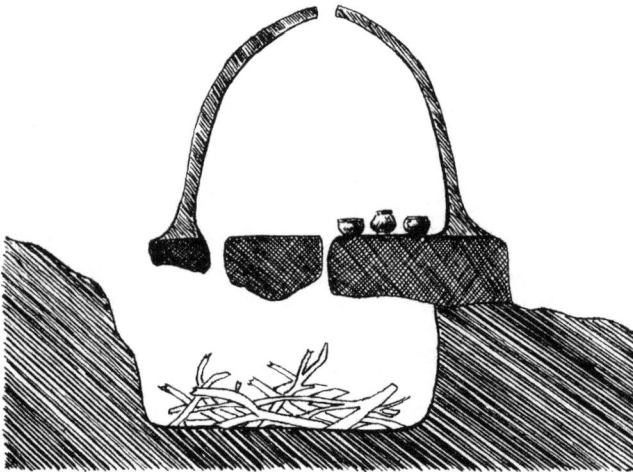

Figure 8.5 Drawing and schematic section of potter's kiln (level 10), Tell Habuba Kabira.

the Tabqa dam cut away part of the tell (Orthmann 1981: 61). One kiln was particularly well-preserved, since it had been filled entirely with gravel material and was subsequently topped by another 1.5 m of settlement debris after it had gone out of use (Orthmann 1981: 61). Each kiln, having a diameter of about 1.5 m, was made of mud brick and comprised a baking chamber set above the firebox. The two chambers were separated by a perforated platform that allowed the heat to rise from the lower space to the one

186

above. The walls of the baking chamber formed a tall beehive-like shape (Orthmann 1981: 61). Although no baked vessels were found within any of the kilns, the occurrence of ash mixed with numerous pieces of pottery and burned lumps of terra-cotta supports the installations' identification as pottery kilns (Orthmann 1981: 61).

One other ceramic kiln has been reported from Halawa Tell A, discovered in the last phase of Early Bronze Age occupation in the northern quadrant of the site in a sector of domestic housing (Figure 8.6) (Phase 6). The preserved parts of this horseshoe-shaped oven (3.5 m × 2 m) included parts of a firebox, stoke hole and domed roof. The interior walls of the kiln, made of mud bricks, had vitrified on account of the high temperatures in the firing chamber (Orthmann 1989: 55). Although this kiln is noteworthy because of its

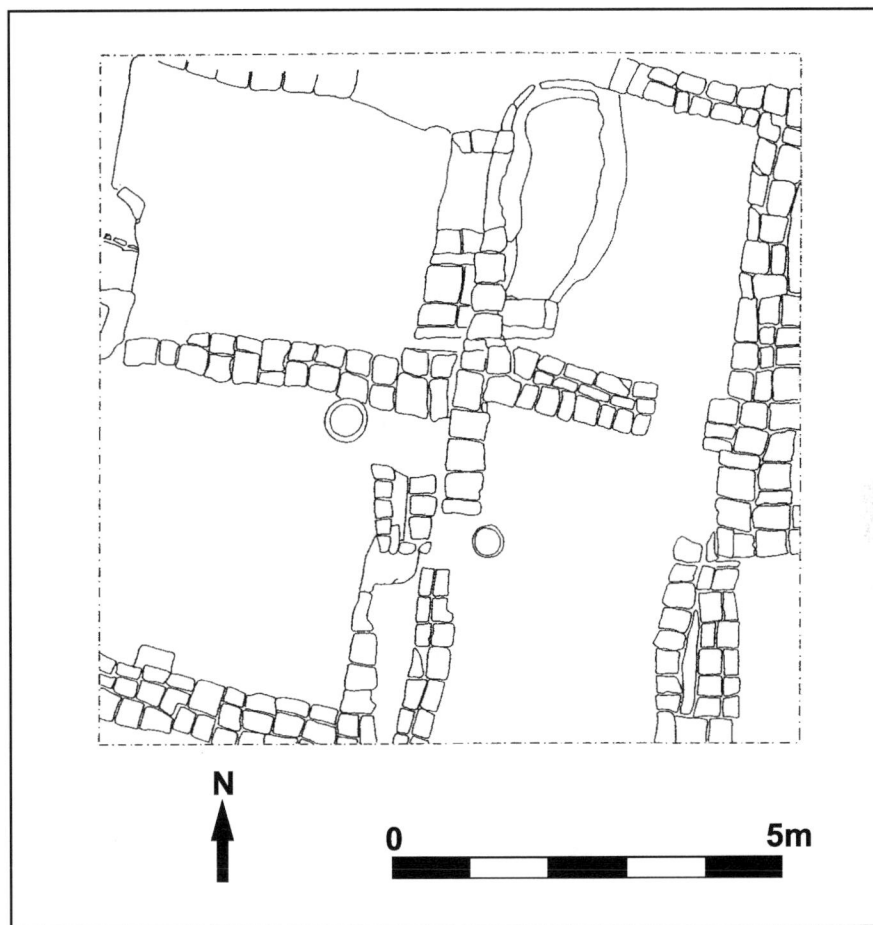

Figure 8.6 Horseshoe-shaped kiln at Halawa Tell A (Quadrant Q).

location in a house structure (House 12), it is significant that in this late phase of the EB, domestic occupation had become considerably impoverished. Many houses had ceased to be inhabited, and scattered installations, such as storage silos and working surfaces, appear to have replaced the more substantial architectural constructions of the earlier phases. In the case of the kiln, it would appear that the older walls of the house had actually been cut down to accommodate this installation, suggesting that this building may no longer have been the locale of domestic activities as before (Orthmann 1989: 55).

Potters' kilns found at Tell es-Sweyhat share similar contexts with the kiln location cited above from Halawa Tell A. At Sweyhat, kilns were located in the lower town, principally in its southeastern part. The kilns were dated to the end of the third millennium BC, at the same time as, or slightly later than, the period of Tell es-Sweyhat's greatest urban extent (late Phase 5) (Zettler 1997b: 47). The kilns were horseshoe-shaped, each possessing a firebox and stoke hole that was probably originally part of a two-chamber updraught kiln (Figure 8.7). The kilns measured about 2.40 m in length and had a maximum width of 1.40 m (Zettler 1997b: 47).

Although no stacks of fused bowls or jars were found in the kilns, plenty of wasters and fused sherds occurred in the excavations in the upper loci of

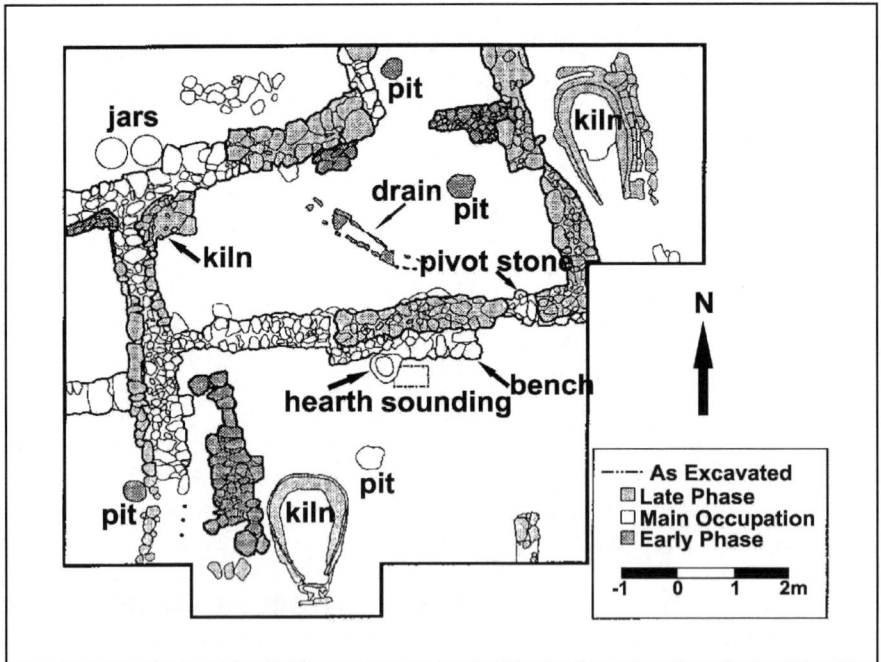

Figure 8.7 Horseshoe-shaped kilns in Op. 16, lower town, Tell es-Sweyhat.

the operation in the same stratigraphic position as the kilns, leaving no doubt that these ovens had been used for the firing of pottery (Zettler *et al.* 1996: 25; Zettler 1997b: 47).

Immediately to the southeast of the area where the horseshoe-shaped kilns were unearthed a circular kiln was excavated (Op. 23: Zettler 1997b: 47). The kiln, with a diameter of 2.5 m, does not appear to have been associated with any standing architecture. It was simply surrounded by stones which may have served as a kind of wind-shelter. The kiln was set in a bowl-shaped depression that had cut through earlier occupational debris and into virgin soil. It is likely that the kiln was a two-chamber updraught kiln. Although the floor between the firebox and baking chamber had not been preserved, traces of vents that had pierced the floor to allow heat into the upper chamber were found around the circumference of the firebox (Zettler 1997b: 48). Also found was a stoke hole on the kiln's southeastern side, while a semi-circular protrusion in the wall of the firebox may represent the remnants of a chimney (Zettler 1997b: 47–8). In size and form, this kiln compares favourably with those discovered outside the fortification walls at Halawa Tell A and Habuba Kabira (Heinrich *et al.* 1973: 56–8; Orthmann 1981: 61–2; Zettler 1997b: 47).

The strong magnetic signatures of the kilns at Tell es-Sweyhat were first detected while geomagnetic mapping was being performed in the lower town of the site (Peregrine *et al.* 1997: App. 4.1a, d). Their clustering in this one particular sector of the lower town suggests that this was an area specially designated for pottery production. At the same time, geomagnetic mapping in the area of the kilns to the east of the main mound detected traces of many room blocks, suggesting that at one time this area had been a rather densely built-up sector of the city (Peregrine *et al.* 1997: 78). With this information, one might posit that the kilns were located in areas of inhabited domestic units. As with Halawa Tell A, however, the archaeological evidence from the excavations in the lower town at Sweyhat reveals that in order to accommodate the kilns, the remnants of older houses' walls were cut away, or else their remnants were used as additional supports for the kiln structures (Zettler 1997b: 47). This implies that the kilns came into use only after the houses had ceased to function as inhabited domestic structures. In sum, rather than envisioning a densely settled urban neighbourhood with housing and production facilities existing side by side in this late phase of the EB, we should consider the possibility that this sector had now become an open area where only activities of an industrial nature were carried out.

The combined evidence of kilns from Tell Habuba Kabira, Halawa Tell A and Tell es-Sweyhat confirm that pottery was being manufactured at the local settlement level during the Early Bronze Age. This evidence, however, contributes only in small part to our understanding of the nature and scale of pottery production at these sites. If we disregard the presence of pottery production in the house from the early levels of Tell Habuba Kabira because of the equivocal nature of the evidence, we are left with potters' kilns whose contexts cannot be unambiguously connected with any identifiable domestic or public structures. The late EB kiln from Tell Habuba Kabira was discovered outside of the city walls in the high mound. The group of kilns from Halawa Tell A, likewise, were found outside of the city walls. Admittedly, some other kilns were encountered in household contexts within Halawa Tell A and the lower town of Tell es-Sweyhat, but these seem to have operated only after the houses had ceased to be inhabited. On the one hand, it is logical to assume from this evidence that the kilns were constructed in areas where the inhabitants of the settlement would not have been bothered by the intense heat and smoke that such installations would have generated. On the other hand, we are still uncertain about the identities of the users of the kilns and the type and degree of their specialization.

Another suggestion we can make is that potter's workshops may have existed in a special quarter somewhere within the settlements, but that potters chose to fire their vessels in open spaces outside of the city walls or in other disused spaces. In modern societies, ethnographic evidence for potting reveals that, although potters produced pottery vessels within household contexts, kilns were often located outside or on the edge of the settlement. These kilns were owned and used cooperatively among these households (Rice 1987: 156; Roux 2003: 769), just as cooperative baking ovens are used today in many Middle Eastern communities (Pollock 1999: 131). Cooperative use of kilns may have extended back as early as the fifth millennium in Syria, where production would have taken place at the household level with several households sharing the use and maintenance of the kilns (Akkermans and Schwartz 2003: 171).

Although these observations and also the locations of Euphrates kilns themselves do not allow us to define precisely the context of production (i.e. independent versus attached potters), we can probably rule out the notion that pottery production was a large-scale industry at these sites. If it were, we should probably expect to see production activities occurring in large, spatially segregated spaces where all stages of the manufacturing process, including firing, took place. It seems more likely, given the separation between workshop and kiln, that production was carried out on a less intensive scale, perhaps by small workshops or households. It might be significant that some kilns were found in clusters, as outside the walls at Halawa Tell A, and in the western lower town of Tell es-Sweyhat. Such a location may indicate a concentration of production in the hands of a group or guild of manufacturers in the settlements rather than an activity carried out by different individuals in widely dispersed workshops or households. The reconstruction of pottery production in some kind of nucleated, but still small-scale, workshop is also consistent with the manufactured pottery itself, which comprises well made and relatively uniform vessel types within each settlement.

Concerning elite, institutionalized involvement in ceramic production, it is significant that in most cases there is no clear-cut spatial relationship between kilns and either large-scale secular buildings or elite residences in any of the Syrian Euphrates sites under investigation. The possible exception may be the kiln located outside the walls of Tell Habuba Kabira, which occurs in a phase where all or much of the enclosed upper mound comprised public buildings and terraces rather than simple households. On the whole, however, kilns are widely separated from instances of fine architecture. It seems appropriate, then, to envision that the production of pottery, although a specialized activity, was largely in the hands of independent craftsmen who were neither controlled nor administered by a higher organization or authority.

Pottery production at Tell Banat: a unique case

Of all EB sites of the Syrian Euphrates Valley, Tell Banat offers the richest evidence for the production of pottery. By the sheer number of kilns, ash pits full of waste and associated work spaces, Tell Banat has generated more evidence for pottery production than any other site of the third millennium in the ancient Near East. It is thus very valuable for helping us to understand how pottery production was organized and administered within EB society.

Most evidence for pottery manufacture at Tell Banat comes from the western side of the mound, characterized by elevated, flat open terrain. Several areas have yielded evidence for pottery manufacture, namely Areas D, G, and A, which cover over 2 ha of the site (Porter and McClellan 1998: 18; McClellan 1999: 417; Porter 2002a: 12; 2002b: 158). Pottery found in these areas indicates that the manufacture of pottery took place during Phases 3–4, c. 2600–2300 BC (Porter 2002a: 12).

Area D, the most extensively investigated ceramic manufacturing area, yielded two main levels of use. Both levels are assigned to Phase 3 (2600–2450 BC) (Porter and McClellan 1998: 13). Ceramic production may also have taken place in Phase 4 in Area D (2450–2300 BC), as attested by a potter's kiln that seems to postdate the collapse or abandonment of the other installations in this sector (Porter and McClellan 1998:13 and 20). Phase 4 production activities have also been found in Areas G and A.

The earlier of the two Phase 3 levels in Area D is principally characterized by a large building, known as Building 12 (Figure 8.8) (Porter and McClellan 1998: 13–14). Although the mud brick walls of this structure are not entirely preserved because of later disturbances, it appears to have been a single building comprising at least seven rooms of roughly the same size and shape (Porter and McClellan 1998: 18). The function and significance of these rooms is uncertain, although the presence of a *tannour*, storage vessels, grinding stones and stone work platforms indicate that the rooms functioned as storage and work areas (Porter and McClellan 1998: 18). The building's

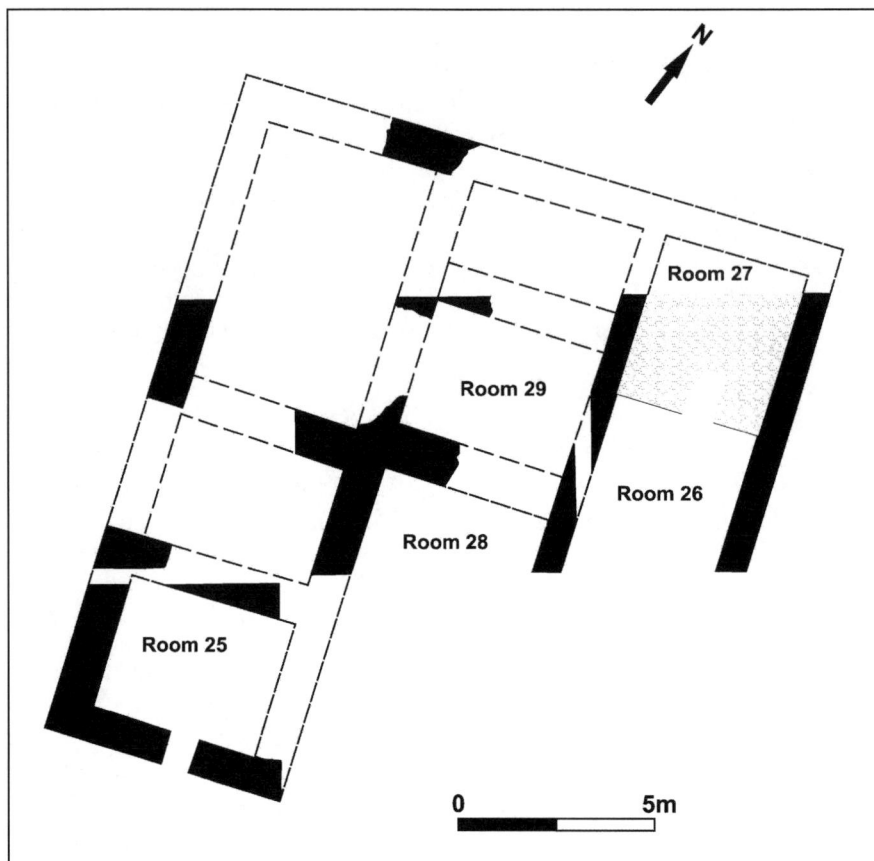

Figure 8.8 Potter's workshop (Level 2 Building 12), Area D, Tell Banat.

connection to pottery production is suggested by the discovery of the upper part of a tournette in one of the rooms (Room 27) and tools (Room 26), some of which have been interpreted as parts of bow-drills for fire-starting (Porter and McClellan 1998: 16, Figure 20: 10–12). Other tools, in combination with the work surfaces found in this room, may be connected to the preparation of ceramics, such as the grinding and mixing of paints, pastes and tempers (Porter and McClellan 1998: 16). Another well preserved room in the southwest corner of the excavated quadrant (Room 25), contained a series of pebbled surfaces and fire places, along with basalt grinders and other small stone tools (Porter and McClellan 1998: 19). The evidence here would suggest some kind of craft production space, although the presence of fire installa-tions, grinding stones and storage jars may indicate that the building was used for food storage and preparation as well (Porter and McClellan 1998: 16).

The combined evidence suggests that this workshop area served also as the living quarters of the craftsmen employed here (Porter 2002b: 158).

A strong functional connection can be made between Building 12 and the nearby potter's kilns. An ash dump full of pottery wasters and slag and the remains of a kiln, sealed by the walls and floors of the later phase of architecture, indicate that the dump was likely to be contemporary with the use of Building 12 of the earlier phase (Porter and McClellan 1998: 14). Further, the fact that the levels of the stacking chambers of two of the kilns (Kilns 2 and 4) are at the same elevation as the floors of two of the rooms of Building 12 supports the contemporaneity of these features (Porter and McClellan 1998: 16).

In the succeeding level of Phase 3, several changes were made to Area D. Rather than activities being confined to small work spaces within the well-built enclosed rooms of Building 12, they became spread out over a wide area. Many operations were now located in open, exterior or unroofed spaces (Porter and McClellan 1998: 16). The only discernible structures include Building 11, a single room with narrow stone walls and traces of a mud brick superstructure (Porter and McClellan 1998: 16, Figure 4), and Buildings 8 and 9, which are located to the north and west and appear to have been constructed somewhat later in level 1 (Porter and McClellan 1998: 17, Figure 5). These two latter buildings are characterized by flimsy walls, low room dividers of clay, and rubble foundations that could not have supported a roof (Porter and McClellan 1998: 19). Several installations are associated with this somewhat ephemeral architecture, including ovens, bins, benches, pebbled surfaces, storage vessels, post-holes and kilns (Porter and McClellan 1998: 16). Overall, the character of these spaces suggests the intensification of production, while household-related activities such as food preparation and cooking are now absent and seem to have been relegated to elsewhere at the site (Porter 2002a: 27).

Of the kilns, five were located in the immediate vicinity of the Area D buildings just described, while further investigations identified additional kilns extending some 200 m to the northeast of the buildings of Area D. Presumably, their location was partly chosen to take advantage of the prevailing winds, which blow from the northwest. Among the best preserved installations excavated in Area D is Kiln 2, a subterranean firebox surmounted by a brick stacking table pierced with flues through which the hot air passed into the baking chamber (Figure 8.9) (Porter and McClellan 1998: 20). The kiln was probably roofed with a mud brick dome, like that of Kiln 4 to the south, whose domed roof was found partially intact (Porter and McClellan 1998: 20).

Ceramic dumps consisting of slag, vitrified pottery and vessel discards were found around several of the kilns. Many of the discards featured distorted body shapes and irregular rims, or they were cracked from the firing process (Porter and McClellan 1998: 20–1).

Figure 8.9 Kiln 2, Area D, Tell Banat.

It is noteworthy that only a few types of vessels of Plain Simple Ware were obtained from the kiln refuse deposits. The types include deep, round-based bowls with everted modelled rims, round-based jars with flaring necks and everted rims, round-based cups with straight or slightly inturned walls, and round jars with narrow necks and two loop handles (Porter 1999: 312 and Figure 1). For the most part, these vessel types show uniformity in terms of their overall size, body shape, rim and base features. It was additionally observed that the paste and temper of the vessels is fundamentally the same throughout, with the exception of differences in the colour of the fired vessels, which would mainly be attributable to fluctuations in kiln temperatures during the firing process and the vessels' placement in the kiln stacking chamber (Porter and McClellan 1998: 21–3).

A few examples of Cooking Pot Ware were found in Area D, but rather than deriving from the kiln dumps, these cooking pots, along with pedestalled chalices and small lids, were found in the rooms of Buildings 11 and 12, often *in situ* in hearths or fireplaces (Porter 1999: 313). Very little in the way of Euphrates Banded Ware was recovered, except in the reconstruction debris of one of the kilns (Kiln 3: Porter 1999: 313).

Besides pottery or items related to the manufacture of pottery, other types of artifacts were recovered from the buildings of Area D. More than 70 fragments of baked clay animal figurines, representing a variety of animals such as sheep, goats, cattle and donkeys, as well as two equid figurines characterized by manes and short ears, were recovered from this quarter (Figure 8.10) (Porter and McClellan 1998: 24). The equid figurines are particularly noteworthy: one is characterized by an applied bridle, while the other has a squared-off and pierced muzzle, possibly intended for a rein ring (Figure 8.10 top right). These features may imply that such figurines are representations of domesticated horses. Together with the horse figurine from Sweyhat (Figure 8.10 top left), these figurines may represent some of the earliest representations of the domesticated horse in the ancient Near East. Whatever the case, the large quantity of these items suggest that terra-cotta animal figurines were also being manufactured in the Area D workshops.

Finally, as many as 50 ceramic wheels and/or spindle whorls were recovered from contexts in and around the buildings and kiln dumps of Area D. Their high number could also imply their manufacture in this workshop quarter. Alternatively, if such objects are regarded as spindle whorls, their presence, along with the existence of post-holes found in many parts of the complex (Porter and McClellan 1998: 16, 20), may suggest that textile manufacture was an activity carried out here (Porter 2002b: 158).

While Area G at Tell Banat almost certainly also constituted the locale of pottery production activities, specific details of its architecture and artifacts are still forthcoming (Porter 2002b: 163). Likewise, our knowledge of the southern end of Tell Banat in Area A is incomplete, although it is reported that EB ceramics were recovered in deposits of debris. Most of the vessels consist of small hemispherical cups and bowls, all in Plain Simple Ware (Porter and McClellan 1998: 31). The vessels show remarkable uniformity in terms of size and form, the cups all having plain rims and inturned walls, while the slightly larger bowls have beaded rims with plain or indented walls (Figure 8.11) (Porter and McClellan 1998: 31).

In addition to the discovery of unbaked vessels in Area A, a kiln separator was found along with considerable ashy material. This evidence suggests that here too was an area where pottery was formed and fired. Overall, the vessels found in Area A seem to correspond best with pottery dated to Phase 4 (Porter and McClellan 1998: 31), thus demonstrating, along with the evidence from Area G and the fragmentary evidence from Area D, that the production of pottery continued into this period at the site.

Based on the architectural and artifactual evidence from Areas D, G and A at Tell Banat, a number of conclusions can be offered about the nature and

Figure 8.10 Animal figurines from Tell es-Sweyhat (top left) and Tell Banat.

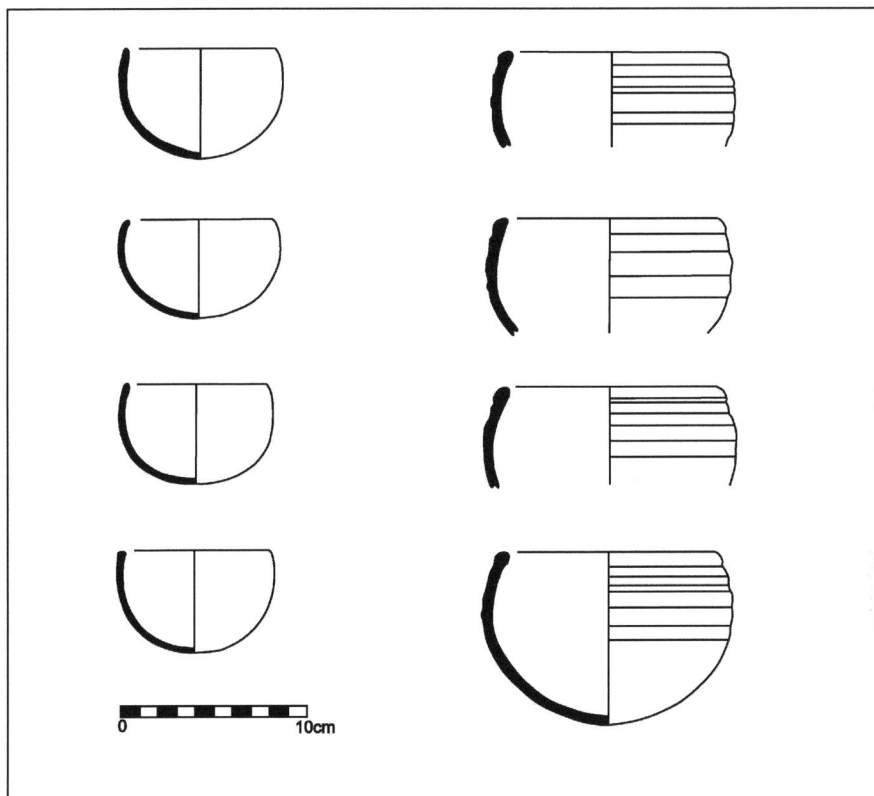

Figure 8.11 Cups from area of pottery production (Area A), Tell Banat.

organization of production within these areas. First, the high degree of morphological similarity among the vessels found in kiln refuse dumps suggests
that these pots were the product of specialists, sufficiently accomplished in
their craft to produce uniformly similar products many times over. We
would argue, therefore, that a relatively high degree of standardization was
attained, although further fine-grained studies of metric variability among
the vessel types and studies of technological and compositional features of the
pots will be necessary to determine the precise level of standardization and
intensity of production achieved (Roux 2003). Interestingly, it has been
persuasively argued elsewhere that third millennium northern Mesopotamian
pottery, while often manufactured by specialists, does not reflect especially
high rates of production, raising the possibility that vessels were not manufactured by full-time potters (Roux 2003: 780). In light of these findings,
we suspect that the Tell Banat pottery may have been manufactured in comparable conditions, the potters either working seasonally or as part-time
manufacturers. The latter proposition seems especially plausible given the

archaeological evidence for other production activities in Area D at Banat, which include terra-cotta figurines and textile production, implying that the craftsmen of this manufactory were engaged concurrently in a multiplicity of activities.

The restricted number of vessel types found in the kiln dumps around Buildings 11 and 12 suggests that these kilns and possibly the workshops associated with them were dedicated to the production of specific types within the overall pottery assemblage (Porter and McClellan 1998: 23). If these kilns and workshops produced only specific types of pottery, there may have been others at Tell Banat that produced different vessel types. Up until now, however, such facilities have not yet been excavated and identified. Given that scores of kilns were likely spread out across the western side of the site, it seems feasible that most vessels of the Period IV repertoire – including Euphrates Banded Ware whose presence in Area D is conspicuously low – were produced here.

The evidence from Tell Banat, with its massive expanse of kilns, waster deposits and workshop facilities, suggests clearly that pottery production was an important industry at this site during the third millennium BC. Yet we should probably not see Tell Banat as typical. The reason for this is that Tell Banat seems to have been a site with a specific function. In addition to pottery production, the remains at the site include many tombs and mortuary monuments but little domestic architecture. The site appears to have functioned as a massive funerary complex serving the needs of the dead on a scale not yet observed at other EB Euphrates settlements. The large facilities for the manufacture of pottery, therefore, might have been related to its intended use in funerary rituals and placement in tombs rather than for consumption by living members of the settlement or its environs.

Did Tell Banat's pottery production facilities have any attachment to individuals of importance or a centralized organization of some kind? Our evidence thus far does not suggest such an observable link. The vessels manufactured at Tell Banat appear to have been used in all funerary contexts, great and small. There is no discernible spatial relationship between this production area and the 'elite' structures found at Banat, if we are indeed correct to speak of such contexts in this way (Porter 2002b: 167–8). The rich Tomb 7 is a distance away, as are the 'public' Buildings 6 and 7. The excavators of Tell Banat observe some changes in the architecture and nature of craft production in Area D over time, in which living activities became relegated elsewhere (Porter 2002a: 27). Such changes could reflect a shift towards a more segmented, possibly increasingly stratified, society (Porter 2002a: 27). Nevertheless, even with such a transformation, it still remains difficult to see a clear link between production at Tell Banat and the presence of a few high-ranking individuals whose overall structuring of social and economic relationships among both the living and the dead included their control over and administration of craft activities.

DISCUSSION

When the evidence for craft production is viewed in its entirety, it becomes clear that the manufacture of metal objects, textiles, stone and shell jewellery and pottery was prevalent among many Syrian Euphrates communities of the Early Bronze Age. Even though excavations have yielded but a small fraction of the overall architecture and artifacts at these sites, enough work has taken place to confirm that craft activities were already established as early as the third millennium BC. By the latter part of the third millennium craft production is well represented in the material record, taking the form of tools and equipment used in the production processes, raw materials alongside the finished products, and sometimes the household spaces or workshop areas in which the manufacturing took place. Objects such as well-crafted metal weapons and tools, finely carved and polished beads and fine thin-walled ceramic vessels, indicate that many products were the work of specialists having the necessary skills to produce high-quality utilitarian or luxury items. Such a level of specialization attests to a high degree of organization within the cities in which such artisans lived and worked. Urban communities would have supported these artisans, releasing them from other forms of labour related to food procurement and processing long enough that their skills as artisans could be developed, and providing them with the necessities of life in exchange for their crafted goods.

Even with this level of specialization, however, the scale of production of the crafted goods must not have been exceptionally large or of a high intensity. Much of the equipment associated with the manufacture of pottery, jewellery, textiles and metals, for example, was found in association with other facilities, suggesting the use of shared work spaces for a variety of production activities. Even at Tell Banat, where many kilns, and other facilities attesting to pottery production were found, it is evident that this was but one of many manufacturing activities that artisans undertook within this craft quarter. Still other evidence for craft production has been found in domestic quarters, indicating that although some household members were trained as specialists in their craft, their work nonetheless did not disassociate them from their family units and domestic activities.

The context within which craft production took place was somewhat varied. By the middle of the third millennium, metal working seems to have been closely attached to the centres of the urban communities, either appearing within or in the vicinity of large public buildings. Metal working seems largely to have been sponsored by elite individuals, who owned the equipment, resources and artisans necessary to manufacture metal weapons and other items of personal adornment that enhanced and legitimated their status within society. Evidence for other crafts such as textile spinning and weaving, jewellery manufacture as well as pottery production, however, do not yet appear to have any strong connection with elite contexts. These crafts have a wider, more dispersed pattern, being located in various household contexts or scattered, isolated areas. We may postulate that although elite individuals may have occasionally commissioned the production of fine textiles, stone and shell jewellery and pottery from the artisans working in these contexts, the majority of items were manufactured to meet the requirements of commoners and were distributed throughout the urban settlements.

This picture of craft production that emerges for the Syrian Euphrates is vastly different from the kind of 'elite' controlled, institutionalized 'factories' that are attested in southern Mesopotamia and Ebla from the same time period. In these latter places, large land-owning institutions such as temples and palaces controlled and operated vast manufactories where the production of items such as precious stones, metals and textiles were undertaken at a high level of intensity by hundreds and sometimes even thousands of labourers. These workers, comprising many women and children, disassociated from their kin groups, both worked and lived under the auspices of these enormous governing institutions, receiving rations of food and clothing in return for their skills and labour. The products that they manufactured would have been consumed by the elites who were associated with these organizations, or else they were destined for state-controlled commercial ventures, to be exchanged for other fine products and raw materials across vast geographic distances.

Unlike these highly centralized systems, the Syrian Euphrates settlements have brought to light little evidence for large-scale industries, indicating that almost certainly such institutionalized, state-controlled activities did not exist in this region. These findings have important implications for our wider understanding of ways in which Euphrates urban communities were economically organized. Based on the available archaeological evidence, it is fair to say that locally crafted products, in general, were not a principal form of revenue during the third millennium. Although craft activities were clearly undertaken within Euphrates settlements, these activities do not appear to have generated a substantial surplus of goods used profitably in commercial exchanges on any significant scale.

This situation compels us to look for other forces that may have helped to drive the economy of this region. Profit was likely acquired through the administration and taxation of both foreign raw materials and crafted products flowing through the Euphrates region on their way to other destinations in the Near East. Although these products may not have been of local origin or manufacture, local commercial agents would have been required to oversee their safe and efficient conveyance through the region to other ports of trade. Revenue, therefore, was generated by those involved in such commercial enterprises. The second source of profit almost certainly came from the Euphrates' principal and most prized commodity: sheep and goats. These animals were extensively bred and pastured in the steppe lands beyond the valley and produced vital products in the form of milk, meat and especially fibres. Although we have seen that the actual production of these latter materials into finished textiles may not have been a principal industry, the raw materials themselves in the form of shorn sheep's wool and goat's hair were without question one of the region's biggest exports and generated a valuable source of revenue for many of the riverine communities.

9

DEATH, FUNERARY MONUMENTS AND ANCESTOR CULTS

INTRODUCTION: THE ARCHAEOLOGY OF DEATH IN THE EUPHRATES VALLEY

For human beings, death is a momentous, sobering and perplexing event. Death is inevitable, and no amount of coercion, coaxing, or begging of the gods, fate, or the forces of nature, can reverse its inescapable arrival. The people of ancient Mesopotamia were well aware of the certainty of death. Already by the third millennium BC, its sombre presence pervaded Mesopotamian literature, finding its way, for example, into the ageless poetry of the Gilgamesh Epic, whose hero, lamenting the untimely death of his beloved friend Enkidu, searches in vain for immortality.

Besides sharing anguish over the certainty of death, humanity universally is accustomed to treat this weighty event with reverence and ritual behaviour. By assisting the deceased to make the transformation from this life into the next through a prescribed set of solemn, ceremonial acts, human beings assure themselves of the safety and comfort of their departed loved ones. They also give closure and a sense of order to a most disturbing event in their lives. Death affects not only the person who dies but also those left behind, filling their lives temporarily with confusion, disorder and anxiety.

The inhabitants of the Euphrates Valley in Syria during the Early Bronze Age were strongly affected by death like other Near Eastern societies. Like their Sumerian neighbours in southern Mesopotamia, they held similar ideas about the causes and nature of death, about the gods' role in this event, and about what one could expect in the afterlife. The abundance of funerary artifacts and burials preserved in the archaeological record shows us that the ancient people of the Euphrates treated death with appropriate respect and ritual behaviour. We observe, for example, the careful way in which they prepared burials for their dead, and the ritual offerings and gifts which they placed within their tombs.

A large quantity of archaeological material has been recovered from the Euphrates Valley which sheds considerable light on northern Syrian funerary practices and the ancient people who developed these customs. The funerary record for the Early Bronze Age of the third millennium is especially rich, comprising a number of burial grounds, funerary monuments, artifacts and other associated mortuary installations.

The discovery of such remains began with the systematic excavations of Early Bronze Age sites in the Euphrates River Valley. Early in the twentieth century, when Sir Leonard Woolley and his British team excavated the northern ancient city of Carchemish, several Early Bronze Age pot and cist graves were located. These burials were found both at Carchemish itself and also at several cemeteries and burial grounds in the countryside around the site. T.E. Lawrence, then a student of archaeology, undertook the documentation of many of these burials. His responsibilities entailed keeping painstaking records of the minute and fragmentary remains of civilizations long vanished, but his passion for Syria perhaps exceeded his skills as a recorder of the past. What the Carchemish archaeological reports lack in consistency and completeness, however, they make up for by their colourful account of a fascinating and long-lived city-state and the richness of its mortuary practices.

In the 1930s, the French, working at Til Barsip, a site commonly called today by its modern Arabic name, Tell Ahmar, provided further knowledge about the burial practices of the ancient Euphrates inhabitants. While excavating the main acropolis mound of this extensive ancient settlement, they unearthed a grave structure which they named the 'Hypogeum'. Its enormous size, grandeur, and the abundance of its grave goods greatly surprised the excavators, unmatched as it was by any other third millennium monument found outside of southern Mesopotamia up to this time.

Construction of dams along the river, whose waters threatened to submerge thousands of years of human habitation in the river valley, prompted international teams of archaeologists to undertake the wide-scale exploration of ancient sites' burials and neighbouring cemeteries from the late 1960s up to the beginning of the new millennium. By today recovery work in this region is all but complete, the massive lakes of the dams having covered over many of the ancient sites.

In the 1990s, just before flood waters had encroached upon the river valley to the south of Carchemish, some of the most outstanding funerary monuments were uncovered. They include, for example, a spectacular stone-built tomb designated as Tomb 302. Discovered at Jerablus Tahtani in a prominent and visible location near the base of the settlement, this tomb surpasses the Hypogeum at Tell Ahmar in its size and the quality of its construction. Apart from this tomb, however, a most fascinating Early Bronze Age site was explored about 30 km to the south, at Tell Banat. This unique centre appears for much of its history in the third millennium to have functioned almost exclusively for mortuary purposes, complete with all the facilities necessary to prepare, equip, honour and bury the deceased. It seems also to have perpetuated the memory of dead ancestors through an elaborate funerary cult. These impressive remains at Tell Banat, representing a remarkable achievement of Early Bronze Age culture in the northern Euphrates Valley, attest to the singularity and richness of the region's ancient society and the complexity of its urban culture.

Archaeological approaches to death

Scholars have frequently studied ancient funerary practices and accompanying ritual actions, since both of these provide valuable information about past human behaviour and ideology. Funerary practices, for example, offer evidence of an ancient society's beliefs concerning death, the gods and the afterlife. Such studies of ancient religion are valid and important fields of inquiry, providing vital information about the fundamental ideologies of different societies that give shape to their distinctive traditions and customs.

Recently, studies have emphasized how mortuary remains can help us to understand how a society was organized. Grave types, ritual funerary practices, the selection of grave offerings and their placement within the burials, for example, can provide valuable insights into communities' social and economic structure. Studying practices related to death, therefore, help us to understand the behaviour of the living.

Lewis Binford, one of the first archaeologists to emphasize the value funerary remains have for understanding the living, argued that variability in a culture's burial practices was a direct function of social differentiation in that culture (Binford 1971). Some scholars have criticized Binford's failure to recognize that burials may be ideological representations of social relations rather than direct reflections of past social structures (Pollock 1999: 196). Despite this problem, however, Binford's work remains highly valuable for its presentation of a specific programme specifying the archaeological correlates of social organization and funerary deposits. Many archaeological investigations follow Binford's essential methodology, albeit cautiously. This chapter will do the same in certain contexts.

Today, in light of a richer understanding of funerary remains and their relation to ancient societies, studies with new perspectives have appeared. Many of these suggest the focus should be on the living survivors who were responsible for the deceased's interment, funeral and the burial's continued maintenance, and not on the social persona of the dead. Mourners may be concerned with the proper treatment of the dead, but they are also mindful of how funerary behaviour can re-model or re-structure social roles and responsibilities among themselves. J. Barrett, considering Early Bronze Age mortuary mounds in southern Britain, remarks that 'it is the mourners who are the active participants in the funeral ritual, and the practices are amongst those which continually bring the social system into being' (Barrett 1990: 182). The actions and ritual behaviour of the living actors in funerary rituals not only reflect the organization of a society but also give shape to and restructure it. Thus, material features such as burials, tomb markers, tomb offerings and the residues of ritual performances do not merely express funerary behaviour but they can also have transformative power, making and re-defining social roles and cultural identities. We will see below several concrete examples of the range of such materials in the case of the monumental mortuary remains of the Euphrates Valley during the Early Bronze Age. We will see that these monuments played a central, active role among the living inhabitants who created and maintained them.

Caveats and concerns about the Euphrates burial data

We can consider and analyse a multitude of variables within the archaeological record in our effort to reconstruct past social systems during the Early Bronze Age in northern Syria. Several weaknesses and gaps in the available data, however, will make the reconstructions that we derive from funerary remains tentative at best. One problem is the frequent, fragmentary nature of the archaeological record. At many sites, burials have been severely disturbed by thousands of years of the elements such as rain and erosion. The interiors of many graves that have often been found full of water-borne silt have destroyed funerary objects or displaced them within the tomb. The vissicitudes of time and nature have caused many tomb items to perish and decay. A wide range of tomb offerings within burials was made of organic materials. This fact is illustrated, for example, by the recurrent pattern of crossed copper pins found at the head, neck and feet of interred skeletons. These metal implements probably fastened the corpses' burial shrouds, the cloth having long since decayed. In another example, distinct impressions of wooden items, woven textiles and traces of basketry have been found on the soft bitumen floors of Tell Banat's Tomb 7, giving further evidence of grave items that once existed, but perished because of their organic composition (Porter 2002a: 20).

Tomb robbing has caused the greatest destruction to grave sites within the Euphrates Valley. While some of this robbing was done in antiquity, much of it occurred recently, just prior to the flooding of the valley in the late twentieth century. In many instances, excavators had to race to investigate a cemetery, fearing not only future flooding by water but also the stripping of graves by robbers eager to fetch a good price on the antiquities market for the burial artifacts they had looted.

Tomb robbing has undermined investigations of the precise layout of the deceased within the tombs since bones have been broken or unceremoniously shoved aside by looters desiring only items of value. These severely disturbed graves stand in marked contrast to well-preserved, intact burials such as those at Halawa, where the positions of the skeletons were carefully recorded, and where it was possible to determine the sex and age of individual corpses.

Sadly, no comparable data have been salvaged from contemporary cemetery sites such as Shamseddin and Tawi where information about the demographics of Euphrates society during the late Early Bronze Age could have been greatly augmented.

One other problem with the archaeological data concerns the way in which information was collected and recorded in the past. Since formal collection procedures were often missing at many excavation projects, the value of the data retrieved often came to depend on the skills of individual excavators and the number and accuracy of the observations that they chose to make. Unfortunately, archaeologists have been affected by their own particular interests and agendas. A project director's emphasis on the physical-anthropological study of the human remains in graves, for example, may have been done at the expense of a fine-grained study of the pottery and small finds associated with those remains. Alternatively, an excavator with an interest in chronology may have placed inordinate attention upon the pottery assemblages gathered from tomb contexts in an attempt to formulate a temporal cultural sequence, and in so doing, neglected to provide adequate information about the types of tomb structures that were found, their location within the cemetery, and specifics about their size and construction. Such flaws in reporting have been frequent among archaeological investigations, making the task of providing a comprehensive and accurate reconstruction of funerary practices, and the ideology and social behaviour that they reflect, a challenging one.

EARLY BRONZE AGE BURIALS IN THE NORTHERN EUPHRATES VALLEY

Important for an investigation of burial practices in the Euphrates Valley is a valuable article by E. Carter and A. Parker (1995), which describes a large quantity of archaeological burial data from third millennium contexts in northern Mesopotamia. This article attempts to test the effectiveness of pottery as a means of confirming the presence of different cultural zones that reflect specific political polities or ethnic groups. It tries to find correspondences between proposed ceramic horizons and contemporary burial types, proceeding on the assumption that mortuary traditions generally reflect the prevailing ideology of a social or cultural group. This article highlights factors important for our investigation. It shows that pottery best reflects technological and economic relationships that cross over political or ethnic boundaries. It also demonstrates the potential utility of burials in defining separate or overlapping cultural and social spheres of influence as well as aspects of social organization among living communities (Carter and Parker 1995: 109–10).

Carter and Parker present a valuable typology of graves in northern Syria and southern Turkey, one that has been largely adhered to in some of the most recent investigations of burial practices in the Euphrates (Porter 2002a: Table 2). This typology serves also as a basis for the discussion of burials in this chapter, although a few modifications have been necessary. These changes have been made in light of recent burial data published from cemetery sites in Syria such as Shamseddin, Djerniye, Wreide and Dja'de el Mughara (Meyer 1991; Orthmann and Rova 1991; Coqueugniot *et al.* 1998) as well as the impressive burials and mortuary monuments excavated at Jerablus Tahtani and Tell Banat (Porter 1995a; McClellan 1998; McClellan and Porter 1999; Peltenburg 1999b). The revised burial typology has also taken into account several recently explored EB sites on the Turkish side of the Euphrates, from which a significant amount of new burial data has been retrieved (Stein *et al.* 1997; Sertok and Ergeç 1999; Ökse 2002; Sertok and Kulaloglu 2002; Sertok in press). While most of our discussion focusses principally on Syrian burial data, we cannot ignore the Euphrates Turkish material since a number of burial patterns continue well up the river into this region.

Changes to Carter and Parker's grave typology are also the result of a careful re-examination of the data based on the tombs' location, size and construction. The most important changes include the addition of a new category of burial type, the tumulus, and an important distinction between two burial types where formerly only one type had been recognized. Together, these changes bring to light an interesting spatial pattern which may be related to the social-cultural composition of the population of the region.

In the following typology, we will briefly describe each of the known grave types along with pertinent information about their size, their presence at settlements and cemeteries within the Euphrates River Valley, and comments pertaining to the gender, age or unusual treatment of the dead found within. Our discussion will also include brief comments about the grave goods that accompanied such burials, and insights into their meaning and significance.

Pit burials[1]

The simplest graves are pit burials, which have a long history in the Syrian Euphrates Valley (Figure 9.1). They first appear in Phases 1 and 2, and persist until Phase 5 in the late third millennium. Pit burials are small, oval or rectangular pits dug into the ground to accommodate one, or sometimes two or three, individuals, and a small number of grave goods. The deceased in these burials have been usually laid out in the flexed position on their side. In most cases, the walls of the pit are not lined. The one known exception to this is the EB tomb found at Daj'de el Mughara, whose burial pit consisted of two long walls constructed of packed mud pisé, while the two ends were

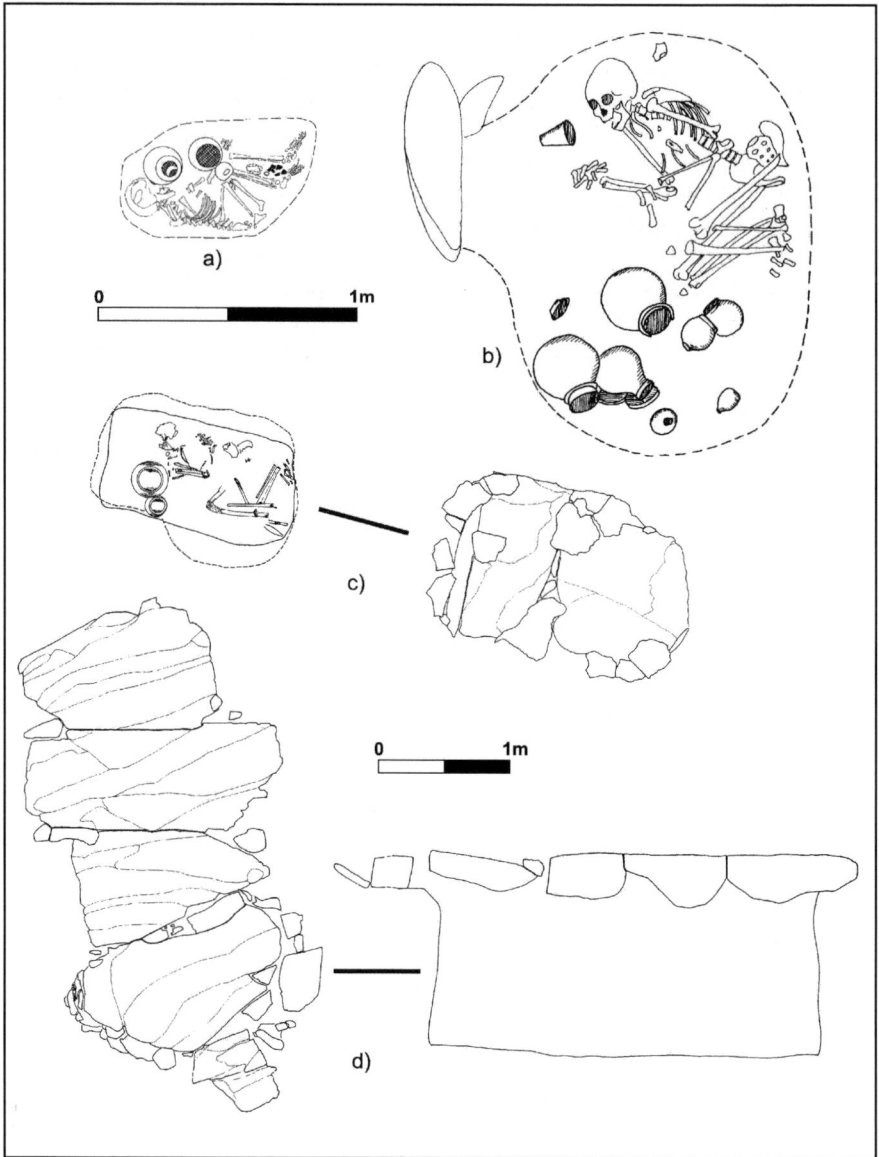

Figure 9.1 Pit burials. a: Q26 Tomb XII Selenkahiye; b: Q26 Tomb II Selenkahiye; c: Grave T63 Tawi; d: Grave T70 Tawi.

left unlined (Coqueugniot *et al.* 1998: 87). All pit burials were either covered over with earth or closed by one or more slabs.

Although listed under the same sub-heading as stone-walled 'dolmens' in Carter and Parker's tomb typology (1995: 107), the *Galeriegräbern* of the cemetery site of Tawi are more akin to pit burials since they consist of simple unlined pits that were dug into the ground and accessed from the top (Figure 9.1d).[2] The difference is that they are generally deeper, longer, and somewhat narrower than regular pit burials. Furthermore, they are covered with more than one stone slab. Nonetheless, they usually held only one, or at the very most, two deceased occupants, much like regular pit burials. To date, the cemetery of Tawi is the only place where such *Galeriegräbern* have been documented in the Euphrates Valley. It may be also significant to note that in Cemetery F at Tawi, a cluster of *Galeriegräbern* was surrounded by smaller, somewhat poorer pit burials, perhaps signalling the former burials' pre-eminence in the cemetery. Also, the graves' method of construction is somewhat unique, with the cover stones having been installed first before the pit underneath was dug (Kampschulte and Orthmann 1984: 31).

Pit burials have been reported at several sites up and down the Euphrates in Syria as far south as Selenkahiye and as far north as Jerablus Tahtani. At Halawa, it may be significant to note that unlike shaft burials, which are adjacent to Tell A at that site, the majority of pit burials are on the outer slopes of Tell B, which was inhabited earlier in the Early Bronze Age (Orthmann 1981: 54). Perhaps, then, a chronological development from pit burials to shaft graves can explain the presence of these two different grave-types at Halawa. Such a temporal development does not seem to hold true at other Euphrates sites, however, where pit burials appear contemporaneously with other grave types and frequently occurred with them in the same cemeteries.

Cist graves[3]

Like pit burials, cist graves also have a long history in the Syrian Euphrates, extending from Phases 1 and 2 up to Phase 4. Their presence in Phase 5 has not yet been confirmed. Cist graves consist of rectangular or square pits dug into the ground. They are distinguished from pit burials in that their walls are lined with flat stone slabs that have been set on edge (figs. 9.2–3). We include in this category graves with walls constructed of mud bricks set on edge instead of stones, as in one reported case from the site of Tell Ahmar (Thureau-Dangin and Dunand 1936: 109). Mud brick cist graves have also been reported on the Turkish side of the Euphrates River Valley at Gre Virike, Hacinebi and Gritille (Carter and Parker 1995: 106 n.61; Ökse 2002: 277). Stone-lined cist graves, in addition to those listed by Carter and Parker in cemeteries from Turkey (1995: 106), have now been located at Gre Virike, Şaraga Höyük, Hacinebi Tepe, Tilbes Höyük, and most prolifically, at the Birecik Dam Cemetery, where almost 300 EB cist tombs have been recorded (Stein *et al.* 1997; Sertok and Ergeç 1999: 89; Ökse 2002: 277–8; Sertok and Kulaloglu 2002: 375). By their sheer numbers, cist graves are a most prevalent burial-type in the Euphrates region of Turkey during the third millennium.

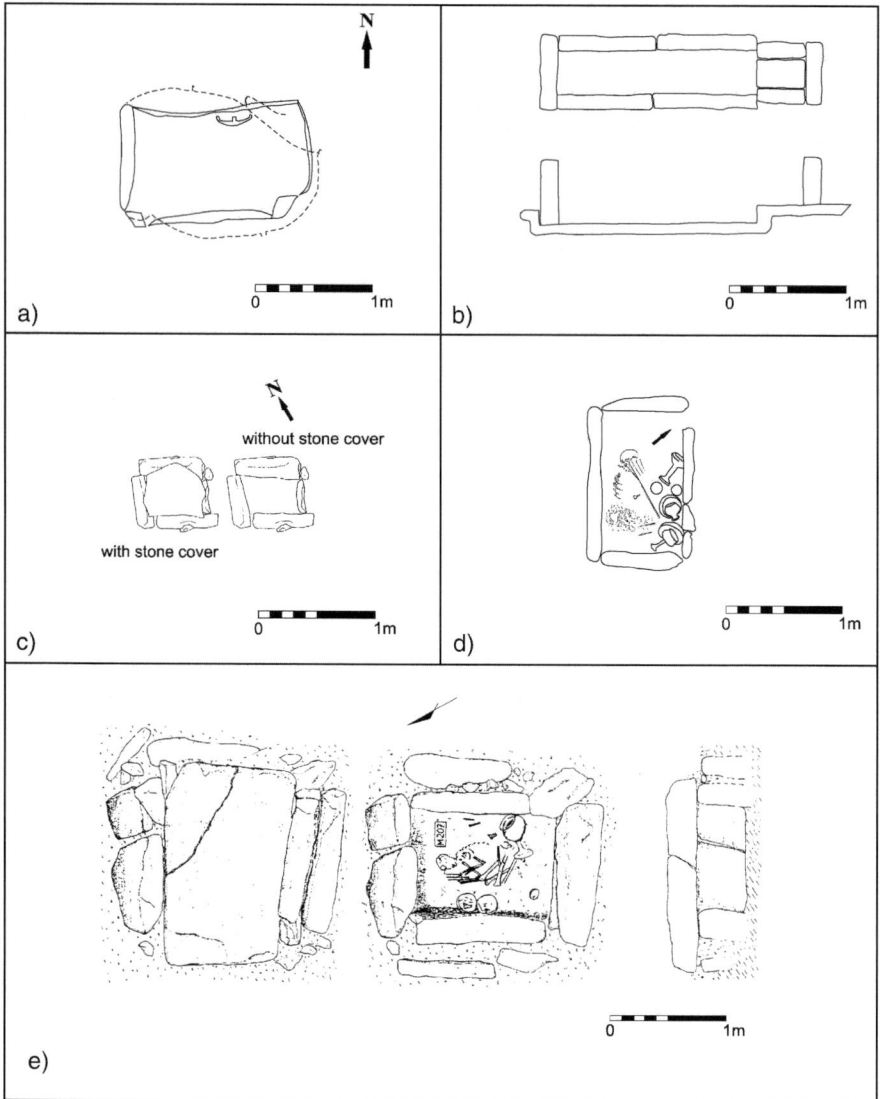

Figure 9.2 Cist graves. a: Grave T31 Tawi; b) Grave 41 Shamseddin; c) E401.1 Qara Quzaq; d) KCG 2 Carchemish; e) Birejik cist grave.

Cist graves were generally roofed over with a single flat slab, although few examples have been preserved. Many of these graves appear to have accommodated only one individual, the body having been placed in the flexed position. Multiple interments, however, have been reported at sites such as Tell al-ʿAbd, Jerablus Tahtani in Syria, and at Titris Höyük, and the Birecik

Figure 9.3 Cist tomb, Tell Ahmar.

Dam Cemetery in Turkey (Bounni 1979: 55; Algaze *et al.* 1995: 20, 28; Matney and Algaze 1995: 42; Sertok and Ergeç 1999: 90 Peltenburg *et al.* 1997: 8). At Carchemish, T.E. Lawrence reported the presence of three bodies in cist burial KCG 8, which was questioned by one of the expedition's directors (Woolley and Barnett 1952: 221 n.2). Lawrence also reported two skulls in cist-grave KCG 8, which Woolley himself queries (Woolley and Barnett 1952: 221 n.3). Given, however, that neighbouring sites such as Jerablus Tahtani have now positively identified multiple interments, it is no longer necessary to doubt the accuracy of Lawrence's observations.

In one grave at Titris Höyük, the skulls of earlier interments had been piled in the corner, and water-laid soil had accumulated between the skulls and grave goods, indicating that the grave had been reopened and reused for multiple occupants who had died at different times (Algaze *et al.* 1995: 20). There are a few instances where cist graves have been found empty of human remains, for example, in some of the burials at the Birecik Dam Cemetery, Şaraga Höyük and Carchemish (Sertok and Ergeç 1999: 90; Sertok and Kulaloglu 2002: 376). While in some cases, this phenomenon can be explained by tomb looting and destruction of bones due to natural causes, in other cases, it may indicate a multi-stage burial process, the bones having been moved and re-buried elsewhere. This practice has also been posited for some of the burials at the site of Tell Banat in Syria (Porter 2002b: 165).

Pithos burials[4]

Pithos burials are jars either buried horizontally or vertically in the soil, each accommodating the bones of one individual. Given that vertically-set jar burials are found in the earliest EB levels at Carchemish as well as the early pre-fort levels at Jerablus Tahtani (Woolley and Barnett 1952: 215–18; Peltenburg *et al.* 1997: 3), they belong to an earlier tradition than horizontally-placed jar burials, which, by contrast, are common in the later part of the EB, and which continue into the second millennium in Syria and elsewhere in the Near East (Dornemann 1979: 138). In a few places such as Titris Höyük and Oylum in Turkey, however, vertical pithos burials once again make a re-appearance at the very end of the EB and continue into the MB (Carter and Parker 1995: 106–7).

Pithos jar burials seem especially common in Turkey during the third millennium, having been recorded at a number of sites along the Euphrates, and most recently at Gre Virike and the Birecik Dam Cemetery (Sertok and Ergeç 1999: 89–90; Ökse 2002: 278). Nonetheless, they are also known from EB contexts in Syria along the Euphrates River, appearing at Jerablus Tahtani, Shiyukh Tahtani, Qara Quzaq, Tell Hadidi, and even as far south as Selenkahiye (Dornemann 1979: 138; Olávarri 1995a: 10; Peltenburg *et al.* 1995: 13–14; Falsone 1998: 31–2; Olavárri and Valdés Pereiro 2001: 20–1; Van Loon 2001: 4B.217). Taken together as a group, pithos jar burials in Syria extend from Phases 1 and 2 at the beginning of the EB, up to at least Phase 5.

While the majority of recorded pithos burials are those of children and infants, no doubt because of their small size, some of the horizontally-laid pithos burials at Jerablus Tahtani contained not only children, but also adolescents and adults (Peltenburg *et al.* 1995: 25).

Occasionally, one sees a close spatial relationship between cist graves and jar burials, as already noted by Carter and Parker (1995: 113). This is evident at the Hassek West cemetery at Hassek Höyük, where the pithos burials were located in and among the cist tombs (Behm-Blancke 1984: Abb. 9), and at the Birecik Dam Cemetery, where the jars were either found right against the cist tombs, or inside them (Sertok and Ergeç 1999: 89–90). Interestingly, this latter arrangement is also reported at Qara Quzaq in Syria (Olavárri and Valdés Pereiro 2001: 20, pl. VIII).

Stone chamber graves

Stone chamber graves are most prevalent during Phases 3 and 4 in the mid-third millennium. Carter and Parker refer to stone chamber graves as 'dolmens' or 'gallery graves' (Carter and Parker 1995: 107). Like the afore-mentioned pit and cist burials, many of these graves are accessed from the top (although there are exceptions, as listed below). They are distinct, however, in that their interior walls are constructed of horizontally-placed, roughly quarried stones, sometimes corbelling inwardly toward the top. The burials are capped by monolithic stone slabs. One stone chamber grave has been reported at Tawi, where it is referred to as a 'stone gallery grave' (Figure 9.4a) (Tawi T5: Kampschulte and Orthmann 1984: 9–12). With its unique stone corbelled-wall construction, however, it really should be distinguished from the other reported *Galeriegräbern* at this site, which, as discussed above, are not lined with stone and consequently have been classified above as elaborate pit burials.

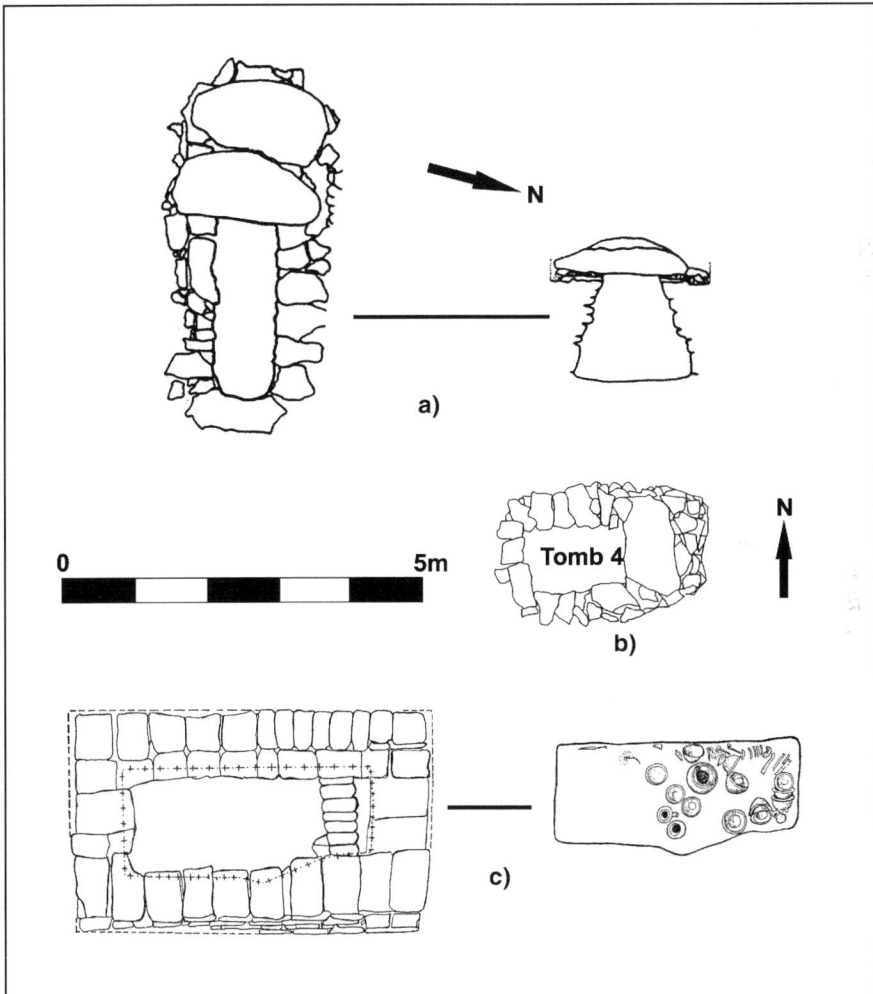

Figure 9.4 Chamber graves. a: Tawi Grave T5; b: Tomb 4 Tell Banat; c: brick tomb, Habuba Kabira.

Several stone chamber burials have been reported at Jerablus Tahtani, where they occur in a variety of intramural contexts (e.g. Tomb 787, Tomb 1036, and Tomb 1518: Peltenburg *et al.* 1996: 10–11; Peltenburg *et al.* 1997: 7). Another example of a stone chamber grave was found intramurally at Halawa Tell B, although it had been robbed entirely of its contents, and its capping stones were missing (H-600, Orthmann 1989: 50, 54). At Tell Banat, tombs that are described as stone cist graves by the excavators probably are better described as stone chamber graves since the stones of their walls have not been set on edge, a defining characteristic of cist graves (Figure 9.4b) (Tombs 3–5 and 9; Porter 2002a: 13, 17–20; McClellan and Porter 1999: 108, figs. 3–4). Also, in terms of their construction and dimensions, the Tell Banat graves are similar to the stone chamber graves found at other sites such as Tawi and Jerablus Tahtani. We must point out, however, that like several Euphrates cist graves which were found empty of human remains, some of the Banat chamber burials were also discovered without bones, suggesting a similar multi-stage burial process (Porter 2002b: 165).

An EB brick tomb from Habuba Kabira South which was dug into the house ruins of the earlier Uruk period might also be included in this group of chamber graves because its dimensions and overall appearance are similar to the other stone chamber graves listed above (Figure 9.4c) (Heinrich *et al.* 1973: 33–8).

As described above, many chamber graves discovered in the Euphrates Valley were accessed from the top. There are exceptions, however. A mid-EB tomb in one of Titris Höyük's extramural cemeteries, for example, comprised several courses of large cut stones sloping inward towards the top, a roof formed by large rectangular slabs, and an entrance on the western side that had been carefully closed by two standing stones (Algaze *et al.* 1995: 27). Similarly, an EB tomb reported at the site of Munbaqa in Syria was found with an entrance shaft at its southern end (Orthmann 1976: 38). Also part of this category are some of the single-chamber stone-built 'shaft' tombs reported by Carter and Parker at Lidar, Hayaz, Oylum, Gedikli in Anatolia, and at Tell Hadidi in Syria (Carter and Parker 1995: 108). These tombs are actually most similar in form to monumental stone-built shaft and chamber tombs (described below), although one could argue that their significantly smaller dimensions place them among the shaft-less chamber tombs of this category.

Stone chamber graves could accommodate one or several individuals. Multiple interments have been recorded in tombs both accessed from the top, and those accessed via an entrance shaft. The highest number of bodies comes from Tomb 1518 at Jerablus Tahtani, where at least five interments were recorded (Figure 9.5) (Peltenburg *et al.* 1997: 7).[5]

Figure 9.5 Chamber tomb 1518 from Area IV, Jerablus Tahtani.

Earth or rock-cut shaft graves[6]

One of the most frequent types of graves encountered in the northern Euphrates Valley of Syria are shaft graves, cut into the earth or bedrock. Although these graves are not attested in the earliest phases of the Early Bronze Age, they become numerous in Phases 3, 4 and 5.

The entrance shaft of this type of grave is a vertical or diagonal passageway cut from the surface. The shaft leads underground to one or two lateral chambers where the dead were laid to rest. Such burial chambers can be quite spacious, occasionally extending for several metres in length and having a height of more than 2 m. The entrances to the burial chambers were customarily sealed with a capping stone or the doorways were bricked up.

A slight variation of the shaft grave, identified so far only at the site of

215

Selenkahiye, is what is termed a Nodal Shaft Grave (Carter and Parker 1995: 107–8). Its vertical shaft is connected to one or more lateral chambers that have been cut at varying depths in the ground. The chambers are smaller than the burial chambers of the more common shaft graves, and were almost certainly intended to accommodate only one individual (Carter and Parker 1995: 108). According to Carter and Parker, the nodal shafts from Selenkahiye, which have similarities to one found at the site of Tell Chuera to the east, may predate the more widespread earth or rock-cut shaft tombs in the Euphrates (Carter and Parker 1995: 114). At the moment, this supposition is difficult to argue with certainty. One of the nodal shaft graves found intra-murally at Selenkahiye (V24) is dated just after the first phase of the site's occupation (Van Loon 2001: 3.60, 4A.177), probably during Phase 4 of the Early Bronze Age. On the other hand, a second nodal shaft grave (R26 Tomb 1) appears to have been constructed at a late period in the history of third millennium occupation at the site, and thus would be contemporary with other regular shaft graves found at Selenkahiye, the adjacent cemetery at Wreide and elsewhere in the Euphrates Valley (Van Loon 2001: 3.59).

Even though shaft graves are present at many Euphrates Valley sites, they show remarkable variability in size, layout and internal elements, from one site to the next. Such variation suggests the presence of a kind of local industry of grave construction, and site-specific burial traditions.

The simplest Syrian Euphrates shaft graves, discovered at Wreide and Selenkahiye in the south, and at Tell es-Sweyhat and el-Qitar to the north, are characterized by vertical shafts and one or two lateral chambers (Figure 9.6a). The burial chambers often have a rounded, oval appearance, but they lack symmetry and have no built-in features. In contrast are the shaft graves from Halawa Tell A, directly opposite Selenkahiye on the east bank of the Euphrates. While also single or double-chambered, the internal arrange-ments of these graves are distinguished by their well-cut interiors and built-in furniture (Figure 9.6b–c). Grave H-21, for example, is characterized by a horizontal shaft that descends to a single chamber by a series of cut steps (Orthmann 1981: Taf. 29). The chamber itself is distinguished by pilaster-like projections in both the side walls and the middle of the rear wall, which divide the interior space into smaller compartments. Within each of these compartments, the walls are lined with cut benches. On either side of the entranceway the benches feature pillow-like elevations for the head (Orthmann 1981: 51).

A slight variation of the standard Halawa shaft-grave plan is observed in grave H-35 (Figure 9.6b). In addition to a partitioned burial chamber with benches, this tomb has been fitted with an adjoining chamber that opened from the south wall of the principal chamber (Orthmann 1981: Taf. 30). The other distinguishing feature of the tomb are small trapezoidal niches, cut high up on the rear walls of both the main and adjoining chambers. They have a window-like appearance (Orthmann 1981: 52), which, together

216

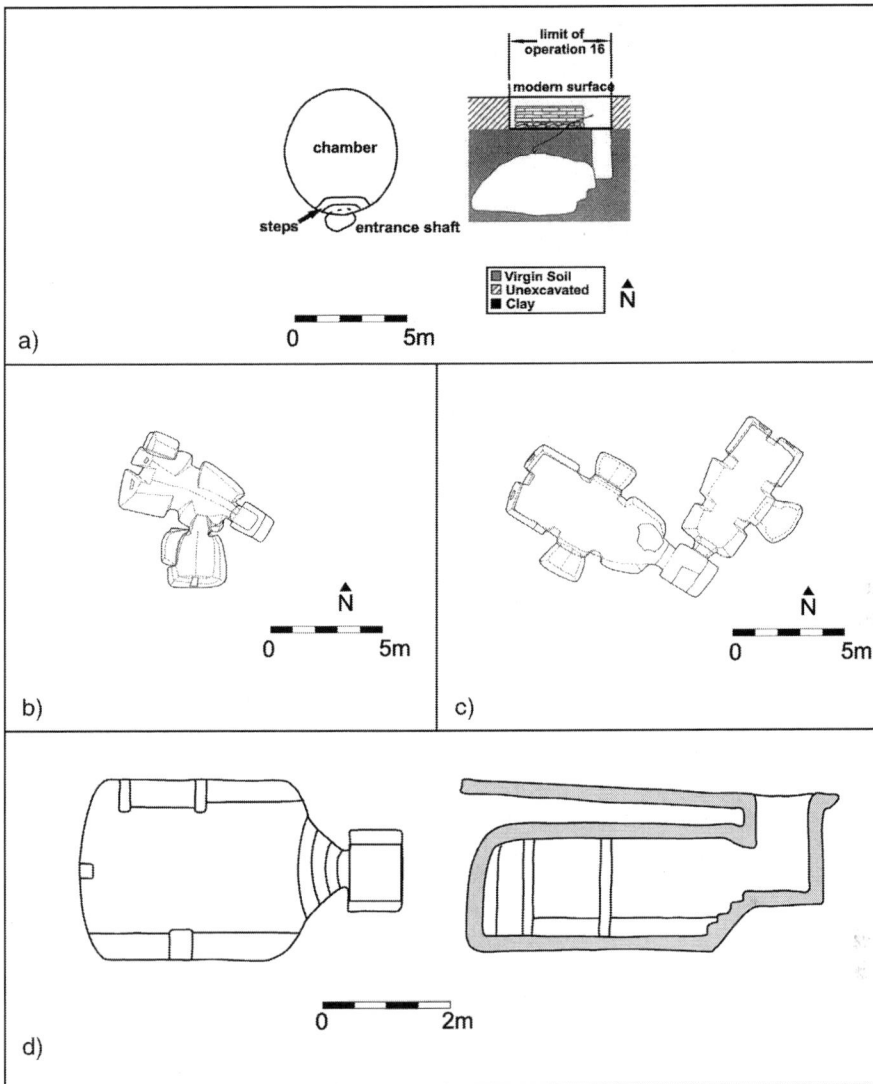

Figure 9.6 Shaft graves. a) Sweyhat Tomb 1; b) Halawa Grave H-35; c) Halawa Grave H-2; d) Shamseddin Grave 40.

with the pillowed benches, suggest that the grave was intended to imitate the interior of an subterranean bedroom or house (Carter and Parker 1995: 108). The presence of rear windows has been noted at a number of other shaft graves at Halawa, including the largest, grave H-2, which consists of two long chambers cut at right angles to one another from the vertical square shaft, and an interior arrangement of benches, niches and pilasters (Figure 9.6c) (Orthmann 1981: Taf. 33).

At no other sites are the shaft graves as elaborately accommodated. To the north of Halawa Tell A at the Tawi cemetery, where only one shaft grave has been extensively reported, the irregularly cut shaft leads to a chamber characterized by small bench-like fittings along the side walls, and a slightly projecting pilaster at the rear. This is a much impoverished version of the graves observed at Halawa (Kampschulte and Orthmann 1984: 14). At the site of Djerniye, the shaft graves are very rough and irregularly cut (Meyer 1991: 149–56). The numerous shaft graves from the cemetery site of Shamseddin are frequently distinguished by neat, rectangular or square burial chambers, which are often accessed from their well-cut vertical shafts by a descending set of stairs (Figure 9.6d). But, unlike the shaft graves at Halawa, these chambers do not feature any built-in furniture, except in a few instances, where the graves have been accommodated with deep-set niches (Graves 9 and 60 Meyer 1991: Abb. 10, 27), benches (Graves 34, 40 and 60: Meyer 1991: 56, Abb. 16, 27, 56), and in one grave, a low square platform and podium near the entranceway, possibly serving as places where grave offerings of food and drink were set (Grave 34: Meyer Abb. 16). An extramural shaft grave at Tell Banat (Tomb 2) was also found to contain two roughly cut niches in the rear wall of its burial chamber (Porter 2002a: 17).

An altogether different shaft grave is represented by Tomb 1 at the site of Tell Banat. Here the shaft (not explored) gives access to a narrow antechamber, which in turn branches into two more long, arched chambers (Figure 9.7). What is especially peculiar about this grave are the long, man-made tunnels cut in the rear walls of the burial chambers, which are small and impassable by adult humans. One of the tunnels, which was explored by sinking another excavation trench directly over it from the surface, proved to be empty and led nowhere (Porter 1995a: 2). The other tunnel remained unexplored, although the excavators do not exclude the possibility that it led to another chamber (Porter 1995a: 2). One wonders if the overall layout of this Tell Banat tomb has a similarity to the shaft tomb reported in Area EI at Tell Hadidi. While not illustrated, this latter grave is said to consist of a large chamber connected to numerous others in 'what seems to be an extensive catacomb-like installation' (Dornemann 1979: 118).

Earth or rock-cut shaft graves were intended to accommodate more than one deceased individual although the number of bodies varies tremendously from one site to the next, and even from one grave to another. At Selenkahiye and Wreide, one or two interments appear to be the norm for most shaft graves, but there are a few exceptions, in which up to five bodies were found (e.g. Wreide Tomb W011, Chamber B; Orthmann and Rova 1991: 10). The shaft graves at Halawa usually accommodated a greater number of individuals than those found at other sites. In tomb H-21, 11 bodies were found, H-37 contained 12 individuals, while tombs H-119 and H-30 contained the

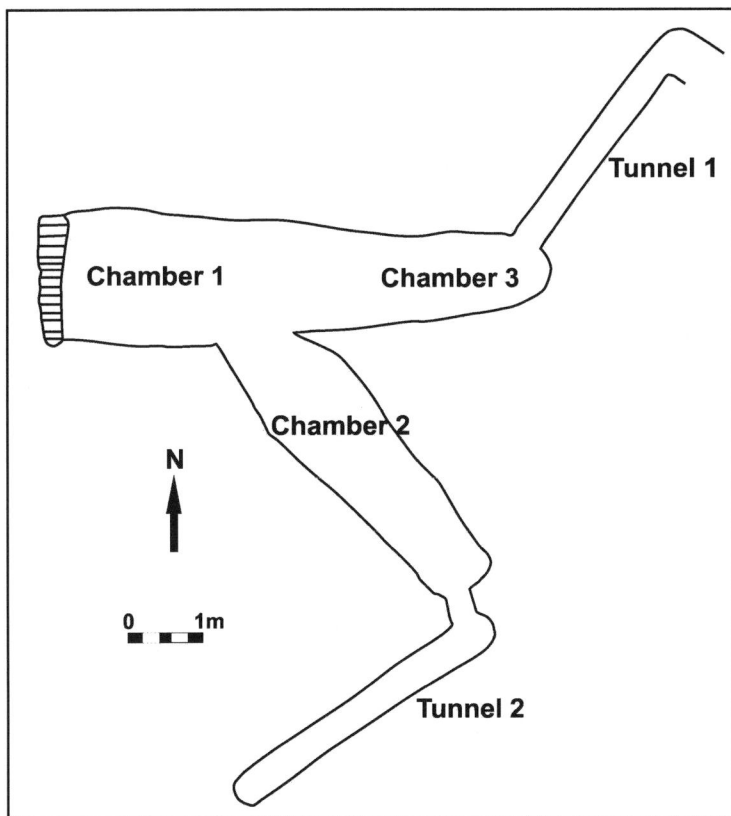

Figure 9.7 Sketch plan of Tomb 1, Tell Banat.

remains of 10 individuals (Orthmann 1981: 73). Shaft graves found at sites to the north of Halawa usually accommodated fewer than 10 individuals, with the exception of Tomb 5 at Tell es-Sweyhat, which held the remains of at least 10 bodies (Zettler 1997b: 54).

Shaft graves were used over an extended period, being closed and then later re-opened when other bodies were admitted. This continual re-use is indicated by the state of the bones found within the burial chambers. While some bodies were carefully laid out and their bones were found in an articulated state, older skeletons appear to have been pushed aside or tossed in order to make way for these new interments. In many instances, the bones of older skeletons were found spread across the entire length of the burial chamber. There are also cases, however, in which the older, disarticulated bones had been arranged into neat piles with the skulls placed on top (Wreide Tomb K; Van Loon 2001: 4A.157). Sometimes, pottery vessels were neatly stacked on top of the older bones. Alternatively, fragmentary bones and teeth were collected within jars (Porter 1995a: 5).

A curious observation was made at the cemetery of Shamseddin. In Grave 1 at that site, the bones of the deceased appear to have been intentionally smashed along with the grave inventory of ceramic vessels (Meyer 1991: 159). Many odd-looking stones were found within the tomb, suggesting that these were the items used for destroying the human remains and grave goods. The bones of the deceased were found entirely disarticulated, implying that this destructive act could not have taken place until after the flesh of the bodies had decayed, perhaps two to three years after the burial. Why such an act took place is a mystery, although given the almost complete lack of metal implements in the grave, the excavators suggest that ancient grave robbers, fearing retaliation from the dead for their theft, smashed the pots and bodies in an effort to render impotent any disturbed spirits (Meyer 1991: 160). Alternatively, this smashing may have been done for religious or ritual reasons, although why such a rite would have taken place in Grave 1 and possibly in only a few other shaft graves at Shamseddin, is unknown.

A fascinating observation was also made in H-35 at the site of Halawa Tell A. The interior of H-35's burial chamber is characterized by side and back projections as well as benches along the side and back walls. Of the 12 individuals found within this tomb, eight bodies, comprising seven males and one infant (probably also a male), were laid out on the floor, while the remaining four female bodies were placed on the back and side benches (Orthmann 1981: Taf. 35). This arrangement, in which a clear distinction has been made concerning the placement of males and females, may possibly reflect some existing social order within the living community at large, in which the men carried higher status or performed different duties from the women. Unfortunately, this pattern does not repeat itself in any other shaft tombs at Halawa. In other graves, males and females appear to have been laid out indiscriminately within the burial chambers, both on floors and benches, without any detectable pattern as to their placement.

Accompanying grave goods in earth and rock-cut shaft tombs

Of all the burial types of the northern Euphrates Valley, earth or rock-cut shaft graves have provided the richest assemblages of tomb offerings. These goods usually take the form of pots, metal weapons, stone, shell and silver jewellery, animal bones, stone statuettes, incised bone cylinders and clay models. While a comprehensive presentation and discussion of these artifacts merits a separate study of its own, for the purposes of this work here we offer only a few general statements about these objects, focussing in particular on their function and significance.

Pottery vessels constitute the most abundant of grave goods. All un-robbed shaft graves have yielded one or more pots. In some cases, numerous vessels filled the tombs. H-119 at Halawa had an assemblage of 99 pots (Orthmann 1981: Taf. 64–7), for example, while the shaft grave T6 at Tawi contained 110 vessels (Schwartz 1987: 241). Tomb 1 at Tell Banat contained a prolific assemblage of 163 vessels (Porter 1995a: 16). The fact that each of these tombs accommodated several deceased persons might account for the abundance of pots since each individual would have been provided with his or her own funerary set.

It is still uncertain how one should understand these tomb pottery assemblages. On the one hand we can accept the traditional interpretation that such pots were filled with food and drink that were intended to sustain the deceased in his or her afterlife or used as offerings for the gods of the underworld. An alternative interpretation, however, is that many or all of these vessels were used by living participants at a funerary feast that was held in honour of the deceased persons buried in the tomb (Peltenburg in press a). The fact that some pots were found stacked, indicating that they were empty when they were arranged in the tomb, may support the notion of a funerary feast (e.g. Wreide Tomb 2 and Selenkahiye Tomb 9: 4A.133, 4A.167). Pottery vessels and other tomb offerings found in levels of earth and debris high above the floors of the tombs may also be indicative of commemorative funerary feasts, these taking place on occasions well after the dead had been buried and the tombs had begun to fill with debris (Meyer 1991: 21; Zettler 1997b: 55; Peltenburg in press a).

Generally all vessel types are represented in the large grave assemblages. These include beakers, cups, bowls, small jars, and larger pots. Cooking pots are often present, although they are fewer in number than other vessel types. In Phases 3 and 4, one sees the preponderance of Euphrates Fine Ware, these consisting of bowls, jars and bottles decorated with spiral burnishing, corrugations and bands of red paint. Given the striking absence of such Fine Ware in non-funerary contexts, we conclude that this ware was specifically produced for use in burials.

A variety of metal weapons, namely daggers, spearheads and axes accompanied the dead in the shaft graves. Such weapons, when found *in situ*, were often placed near the shoulder or hips of specific individuals, indicating that they were the personal possessions of such individuals (e.g. Halawa H-70, Orthmann 1981: 54). Unfortunately, it is difficult to confirm an association between the presence of metal weapons and the gender of the deceased due to the infrequency with which sex determination has been performed on skeletal remains. Where such investigations have been carried out, as in the case of some of the Halawa shaft graves, there seems to be a strong association between weaponry and male individuals (Orthmann 1981: 54, 56).

Of all the metal artifacts, copper or bronze pins were the most numerous in shaft graves. Common were ball-headed pins with bent or straight shafts, these occurring mainly in Phase 3 graves (e.g. Porter 1995a: Figure 5; Zettler 1997b: Figure 3.20). Mushroom-headed pins with straight shafts appear usually in burials dated to Phases 4 and 5 (e.g. Orthmann 1981: Taf. 68; Van Loon 2001: Figure 4A.4A; 4A.11). These pins were often found in pairs, sometimes crossed, and frequently positioned above the head, at the area of the rib cage, or below the feet of a deceased individual.[7] It is possible that such pairs of pins were used to secure burial shrouds (Van Loon 2001: 4A.160, 4B.197). Alternatively, pairs of pins found near the shoulders or at the chest of some deceased individuals may have secured some short of shawl, similar to those seen in contemporary shell plaques from the site of Mari (Zettler et al. 1996: 20, Figure 9).[8] In Tomb 5 at Tell es-Sweyhat, the fact that such crossed pins were found in association with a decorated flat gypsum ring and a necklace of gypsum and carnelian beads supports the supposition that these were the personal adornments of the deceased and not shroud fasteners (Zettler 1997b: Figure 3.18).

Because of the number of plundered tombs, it is hazardous to make too many statements concerning wealth differentiation within the shaft graves of the Euphrates Valley. Some of the largest and most well-constructed tombs of the region, like the multi-chambered tombs at Halawa Tell A (e.g. H-2 and H-35) and Shamseddin (e.g. Grave 34) were found virtually empty of their contents. In shaft graves with intact offerings, grave goods do not stand out as being particularly precious or rare. A few burials containing several metal weapons and pins may indicate some economic success on the part of their owners. A deceased individual in a grave at Wreide (W066), for example, was buried with 13 metal implements (Orthmann and Rova 1991: 34). This abundance can be contrasted with other graves at Wreide (e.g. W011, W054) where significantly fewer metal implements were found, even though several individuals were interred (Orthmann and Rova 1991: 10, 18).

A few of the intramural burials found at Selenkahiye have yielded rich grave goods consisting of silver and bronze objects. The nodal shaft graves were accommodated with various bronze pins and weapons, as well as small silver items such as frontlets, earrings, and beads (Van Loon 2001: 4A.166–4A.177). Similarly the double shaft grave found in square W12/13 was also richly furnished with silver buckles, beads, pendants, ringlets, rings as well as other bronze adornments (Van Loon 2001: 4B.210–4B.213). Nonetheless, in terms of their size and construction these shaft graves were not large or lavish. They consisted of small, simple rock-cut oval chambers.

One final type of grave good will be described here. These are crudely shaped statuettes fashioned out of white limestone principally found in rock-cut shaft graves in the southern part of the Euphrates region considered in this study. The bodies of these statuettes are usually represented as simple rectangles, while the heads, which sit directly on the shoulders, are provided with little more than crude protrusions for noses and slight depressions for eyes (Orthmann and Rova 1991: 63). The lack of details makes it impossible to determine the sex of the figurines. Thus far, these statuettes have been found in shaft graves in the Wreide cemetery, both *in situ* and in the debris left behind by tomb robbers,[9] and at Selenkahiye.[10] Two stone statuettes of the same type were found in House 3–35 at the site of Halawa Tell A (Orthmann 1989: Abb.51:2; Meyer and Pruss 1994: 210; Hempelmann 2001: 159). Other instances of these stone figures have been reported at Tell Hadidi (Dornemann 1989: 75), to the south at Tell Bi'a (Strommenger *et al.* 1989: Abb. 16), and at Munbaqa, although the latter is rendered sitting on a throne and dates to the second millennium BC (Machule *et al.* 1987: Abb. 28).

The function of these unusual stone statuettes is uncertain. Their common association with burials indicates that they had a funerary function. It is possible that they were meant as representations of the deceased, and were used in ritual ceremonies that honoured the dead (Hempelmann 2001: 159). Support for this is the general correspondence between the number of statuettes found within the graves, and the number of persons laid to rest (Van Loon 2001: 4B.220). The statuettes' presence in a household context at Halawa Tell A is less unusual if one considers this the locale of rituals and mortuary feasts dedicated to dead ancestors, as has been proposed, based on its extraordinary repertoire of artifacts (Hempelmann 2001: 159).

The overall picture conveyed by shaft graves and their accompanying goods is that they were not intended to serve as ostentatious displays of wealth. In instances where precious offerings have been found, they are generally small and few in number, simply representing the personal effects of their deceased owners. These tombs and their goods hardly compare to the rich monumental shaft and chamber tombs of the region, which are finely constructed, visible, and contain a tremendous wealth of accompanying grave goods. While our data is severely incomplete due to issues of preservation and tomb looting, we cautiously conclude that unlike monumental tombs, shaft graves were not intended to reflect the economic status of their owners to any strong degree. The variable size and construction of these graves and the goods found within them are more likely reflecting issues relating to household or kin-related structures, age, occupation, gender, and local funerary beliefs and rituals, than serving as expressions of power and economic inequalities.

Monumental stone-built shaft and chamber tombs

This category includes the largest and the most visible tombs of the Euphrates Valley of the third millennium BC. Carter and Parker grouped these tombs with earth or rock-cut shaft tombs, since they are characterized by a passageway or shaft that provided access to the burial chamber (1995: 108). Moreover, such graves were intended for multiple burials. Nonetheless, there are several important differences that justify a typological separation between these tombs and earth or rock-cut shaft graves. One important distinction is the fact that their walls are built of massive blocks of unworked or worked stone. They are unlike shaft graves, therefore, which were simply cut into the rock or earth conglomerate of the ground.

Another notable feature of the tombs is their stonework, monumental in scale. Considerable expense and effort must have been involved in their construction, implying that they were particularly important graves, and that the people who commissioned them had considerable access to labour and resources. While stone is widely available in the Euphrates Valley, it would still have been a major logistical exercise to convey massive blocks of stone up to the burial site and set them in place. This is especially true of the capping stones of graves, which could often weigh up to a metric ton.

The following section provides a description of some of the most impressive monumental tombs in the Euphrates Valley.

Tell Qara Quzaq

Assigned to Phases 1–2 of the Early Bronze Age, the tomb at Qara Quzaq is the earliest of monumental graves documented in the Syrian Euphrates Valley (Figure 9.8). Although constructed of mud brick as opposed to stone, this funerary structure's prominent location and visibility, in our view, justifies its classification with the other tombs.

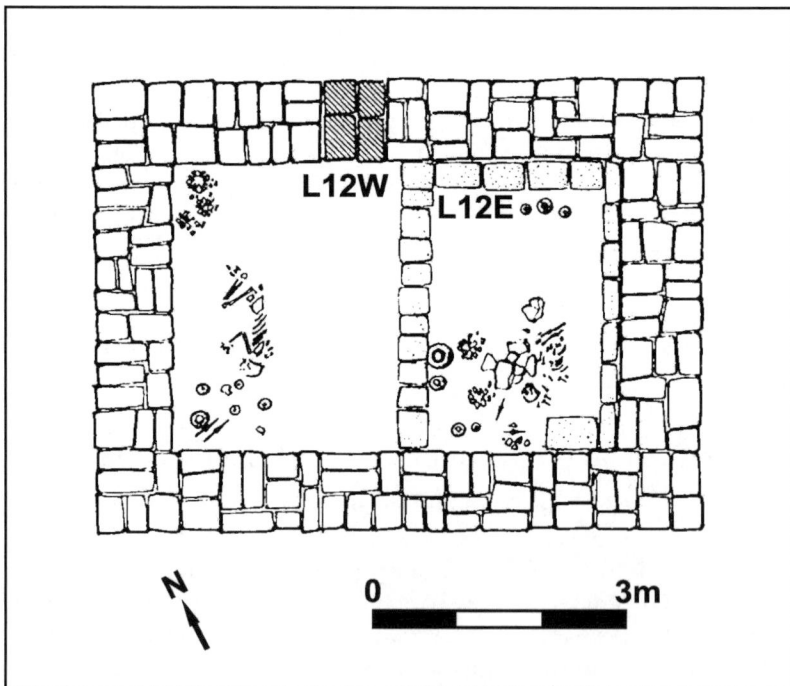

Figure 9.8 L-12 tomb, Qara Quzaq.

Constructed of red mud brick and covered with white limestone plaster, this square building, designated as L-12, may originally have served as a domestic house, but it was later used to accommodate the burials of two deceased individuals (Valdés Pereiro 1999: 120). The chamber was divided into two parts by a narrow partition wall, each room containing an individual lying on the floor in the flexed position and surrounded by a rich assemblage of funerary goods. These goods consisted of pottery, a great number of copper spearheads, bronze pins, and hundreds of crystal, frit and shell beads, most having been strung together to make necklaces and bracelets that were worn by the deceased. The bodies were those of a young adult female and a child. Traces of burning were detected on the bones of both skeletons, although no remains of ashes were found in either of the excavated chambers of the building. This evidence suggests that whatever burning activities took place, they occurred in a separate location (Olávarri 1995b: 16–17).

The funerary building L-12 was found in the vicinity of a large temple, L.247. Together, these structure formed a kind of cultic compound, separated from other domestic structures in the settlement by a brick temenos wall (Olávarri 1995b: 16).

Even though reports fail to say so, it is apparent that Grave L-12 at Qara Quzaq was situated above ground level when it was used as a funerary structure. This feature and the tomb's central position in the settlement make it akin to monumental stone-built tombs discovered elsewhere in the Euphrates Valley, which were also visible and prominently located. It is principally for this reason that the Qara Quzaq funerary structure has been grouped with these other tombs.

Tell Hadidi

Two such tombs dated to Phases 3 and 4 of the Early Bronze Age have been reported and illustrated at this site. The most impressive is the Area D tomb, which features a shaft with stairs leading down from the surface to a small rectangular chamber which had burial chambers on either side of it (Figure 9.9). Within each chamber, the walls were constructed of roughly shaped stones set in courses that narrowed to the ceiling in a corbelled fashion. Above the walls, massive stone slabs formed the roof (Dornemann 1980: 227). Impressively, the doorways to the chambers were built with large blocks of stone that were shaped and smoothed into jambs and lintels (Dornemann 1979: 118). Altogether, the length of the tomb was over 15 m. It is unfortunate that this particular tomb was found greatly disturbed. Not only had it been re-used in the Late Bronze Age, when much of its original contents were removed or thrown away, it had been subjected to extensive tomb robbing.

Another large stone-built tomb was found in Area LI. It is smaller than Tomb D, with a total length of just over 5 m, and a width of 1.6 m (Figure

Figure 9.9 Interior of Area D tomb, Tell Hadidi.

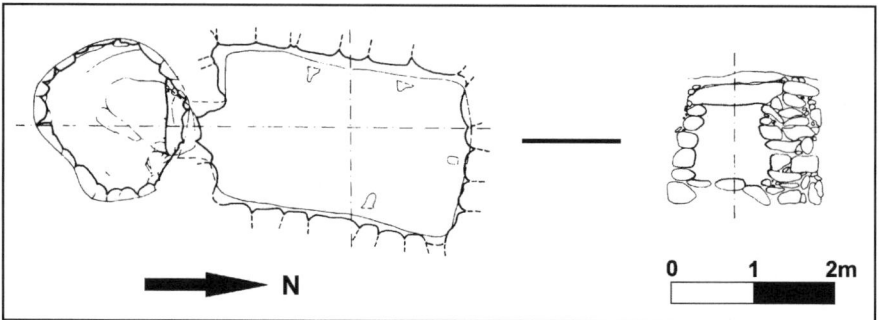

Figure 9.10 Plan and section of Area L I tomb, Tell Hadidi.

9.10). The oval shaft leads into a simple rectangular burial chamber whose stone walls are closer to the vertical than in the Area D tomb (Dornemann 1979: 118). Like the other grave, however, this one is roofed with massive slabs of stone. While in a fragmentary state, some tomb goods were salvaged from this tomb, which included broken pieces of pottery, fragmentary metal objects and hundreds of beads left behind by tomb robbers (Dornemann 1980: 227).

A monumental stone-built tomb was reported in Area LII, near the edge of the low tell. When it was discovered and excavated, this exceptionally large tomb, with a length of over 12 m, was dated to the Late Bronze Age (Dornemann 1979: 147). There is little doubt that it was used at that time. It is entirely possible, however, that this Hadidi tomb was built a millennium before its Late Bronze Age re-use because of the discovery of an impressive

Early Bronze Age stone-built tomb at Tell Banat, not unlike Tomb LII in form, size and construction, (McClellan and Porter 1999: 110).

Briefly, the Area LII tomb consists of a number of underground chambers accessed from a stairway at the north end. Particularly distinctive are the interior walls of the burial chambers, which consist of nicely worked stones that taper slightly towards the top. These chambers are roofed with massive stones worked into flat slabs about 3.5 m in length. At the rear of the tomb is a large rear chamber, with an internal measurement of 4.25 m, and a central column. Unlike the smooth, worked appearance of the interior walls of the other chambers, this room's walls are constructed of rough-worked stones, in keeping with those of the other EB Hadidi tombs just described (Dornemann 1980: 226).

Tell Banat

Tomb 7 at Tell Banat is one of the most intriguing and unique stone-built shaft and chamber tombs in the Euphrates Valley (Figure 9.11). Rather than allow it to be flooded along with the rest of Tell Banat by the rising waters of the Tishreen Dam, Syrian antiquities authorities chose to dismantle this tomb and move it to the National Museum in Aleppo, where it now resides. Tomb 7 appears to have enjoyed a long life, having first been constructed in Phase 3, and then subsequently re-used and modified in Phase 4 of the Early Bronze Age (Porter 2002a: 18).

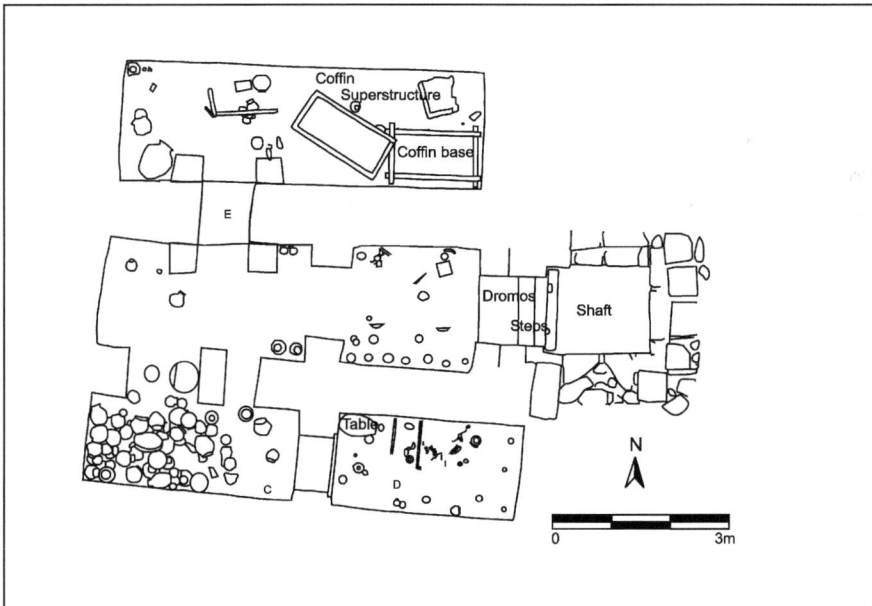

Figure 9.11 Tomb 7 plan and contents, Tell Banat.

The tomb was located in Area C at the site, where it cut into a large artificial gravel deposit (McClellan and Porter 1999: 109). The massive roofing slabs of this tomb may once have formed part of an open courtyard or outdoor area. Such a suggestion is supported by the existence of a white limestone plastered surface around the roofing slabs (Porter 2002b: 158). Later on, however, the tomb seems to have become an entirely subterranean and sequestered burial place (Porter 2002b: 161). A large building, tumulus and smaller burials were located in the vicinity of the tomb (McClellan and Porter 1999: 108). The strong funerary character of all of these features lends support to Banat's function as a massive funerary complex, Tomb 7 being one of the larger and richer graves within this complex.

Entered from the surface by a shaft and stepped dromos, the tomb interior contained several underground chambers accessed by connecting passageways. Many of the chambers had wall niches, and the passages were marked by the use of half-arches. The walls of the tomb were made of carefully dressed limestones, these having been additionally trimmed and smoothed on the inside after the walls had been constructed (McClellan and Porter 1999: 109). Each of the stones had been mortared with bitumen. Bitumen was also used to plaster the floors of the tomb chambers, which were made of set baked bricks. The roof of the tomb consisted of 10 massive, monolithic stone slabs, each weighing over a metric ton, the interstices of which were also filled with bitumen so as to create a watertight cover (McClellan and Porter 1999: 109; Porter 2002a: 18). In its finished state the interior had a fine, finished appearance, giving the impression more of a tomb from an elite cemetery in Egypt than from a settlement in northern Syria (Figure 9.12).

The fact that Tomb 7 was used over an extended period of time is indicated by several modifications and repairs made within. Breaks and chips in the stonework of the chambers were often patched with bitumen. The floors were also resurfaced with bitumen. Additional limestone supports, a pillar and a column were placed in the passageways between the chambers in an effort to maintain the structural integrity of the interior space (McClellan and Porter 1999: 109).

The earliest interment within the tomb was an individual who was laid in a wooden coffin in one of the tomb's chambers. Since coffins are not well attested outside of the Royal Cemetery at Ur in southern Mesopotamia, its presence here is quite extraordinary (Porter 2002a: 19). While the body and the coffin itself were not well preserved, many fragments of objects and other grave goods survived, attesting to the importance of the deceased individual who was buried here. Over a thousand gold beads of a variety of shapes were found strewn over the body. Noteworthy are the excellent parallels the beads have with those found at sites in Anatolia such as Poliochni, Alaca Höyük and the Treasure of Priam at Troy (McClellan and Porter 1999: 110). Other finds included eye and eyebrow inlays for statues, and a small stone wig or

Figure 9.12 Interior of Tomb 7, Tell Banat.

hairpiece. Small objects of lapis lazuli, mainly bottle stoppers, had been inlaid with gold. An ostrich egg inlaid with mother-of-pearl and lapis lazuli was also found in one of the niches in the coffin chamber, while several other shattered ostrich eggs were found on the floor (McClellan and Porter 1999: 109–10). Traces of inlaid wooden furniture were found, their remnants found adhering to bronze nails. Last, highly decorated wooden and organic pieces were found along with lines of simple gold studs. These may have originally have been attached to leather straps, long since decayed.

On the opposite side of the tomb, one of two chambers was filled with over 50 pots stacked on the floor. Near the doorway in the adjoining chamber a thin circular tabletop of alabaster that had been propped up against the wall. This chamber contained the bones of one individual, and while the bones show evidence of hard work and a poor diet, the body was accompanied by grave goods of considerable richness, including a bronze pin, two life-size fly beads of lapis lazuli and a gold pendant (Figure 9.13) (Porter 2002a: 19).

Considering all of its elements together, Tomb 7 at Tell Banat is a highly impressive structure. Not only is it the most finely constructed tomb discovered so far in the northern Euphrates Valley, its contents indicate that it was of considerable importance. The individuals buried in Tomb 7 must have held considerable status, wealth and authority within their communities during their lifetimes. The fact that the tomb and its contents have parallels

Figure 9.13 Gold pendant from Tomb 7, Tell Banat.

with southern Mesopotamia and Anatolia, and the fact that lapis lazuli must have been imported from distant Afghanistan surely attest to the extent of Tell Banat's far-reaching economic and cultural contacts during its apogee in the middle of the Early Bronze Age.

Tell Ahmar

One of the earliest tombs discovered in the northern Euphrates Valley of Syria in the twentieth century, the Hypogeum at Tell Ahmar is still considered one of the most impressive Early Bronze graves (Figure 9.14). Like Tomb 7 at Tell Banat, the contents of the Hypogeum can be assigned to Phases 3 and 4 of the Early Bronze Age.

The chamber of the Hypogeum is accessed from the surface by a rectangular shaft. The chamber itself is about 5 m in length, 3 m in width and over 2 m high. It is distinguished by a stone-paved floor and walls built of large stones left in a rough state, with little pieces of stones inserted in the gaps (Thureau-Dangin and Dunand 1936: 96). The walls curve towards the interior at the top in a slight corbelled fashion, resembling the modest batter of the walls observed in Tomb LI at Tell Hadidi. Five enormous limestone slabs were set transversely over the roof.

Large terra-cotta nails, stuck into the long and short walls of the chamber about 30 cm from the ceiling, represent an unusual feature of this tomb (Thureau-Dangin and Dunand 1936: pl. XX: 2). Their function is still undetermined. Bodies and grave goods were still found intact in the tomb. Two bodies, those of adults, had been laid side by side in the eastern part of the tomb, together with a large number of sheep bones. Just above their heads in the centre of the floor of the chamber were several bronze objects, while to the west, the remaining half of the chamber was filled with an enormous pile of pottery (Thureau-Dangin and Dunand 1936: pl. XX). In

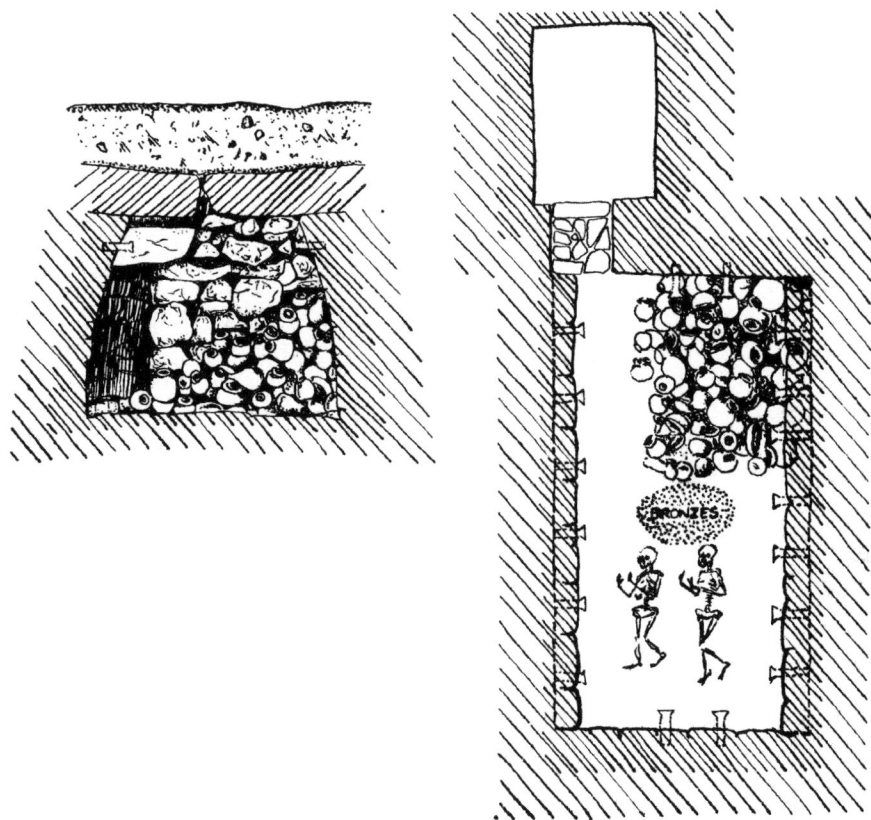

Figure 9.14 'Hypogeum' at Tell Ahmar: side and top views.

all, a total of 1,045 vessels were found in the Hypogeum, making it the richest tomb, ceramically, to be discovered in the Euphrates River Valley thus far.

When the University of Melbourne returned to Tell Ahmar in 1988 to re-open the area in which the Hypogeum had been discovered by the French some 58 years earlier, they noted some additional features which provide a unique context for this tomb. While the French had regarded the Hypogeum as an isolated structure, recent excavations unearthed two rooms directly to the north of the tomb which are clearly associated with it (Roobaert and Bunnens 1999: 164). In the earlier phase, the floors of these rooms were lower than the tops of the walls of the Hypogeum and higher than its floor. In the second phase, when the rooms were re-built, their floors corresponded roughly to the level of the covering slabs of the tombs (Roobaert and Bunnens 1999: 164). What this difference implies is that the Hypogeum was only partially sunk into the ground when it was first built, and that it was only in a second, later phase that it became a truly subterranean installation. One other significant observation was the discovery of stairs descending towards the north on the western side of the complex and possibly leading to another chamber tomb (Roobaert and Bunnens 1999: 165). Overall, this entire area of the tell appears to have been characterized by at least one and possibly several funerary structures and associated rooms. They formed a unique and visible complex in the settlement, possibly having an important role in the religious and social life of the Early Bronze Age community that lived there.

Jerablus Tahtani

Discovered at the Early Bronze Age settlement of Jerablus Tahtani, Tomb 302 stands out as a particularly distinctive funerary monument. The tomb is situated at the southern foot of the settlement, close to the river's edge. The fact that the structure was separated from other buildings by temenos-like walls underlines its importance. The tomb comprised a restricted dromos at the western side that was accessed only by a bent axis entrance-way (Figure 9.15). Beyond that entrance was a long walled passage that led towards the upper levels of the settlement, ascending the mound by a sloping, stone-paved floor and stairs (Peltenburg et al. 1996: 14). The area in which Tomb 302 had been constructed featured several pre-existing architectural features, and the tomb itself had been built directly over large storage silos, indicating its rather late date in the occupational sequence of this Early Bronze Age site (Peltenburg et al. 2000: 69–70). Based on the pottery found within Tomb 302, it should probably be assigned to Phase 4.

Tomb 302 is not unlike previous tombs described in that it too features an entranceway on the west which leads to a large rectangular burial chamber (6.6 m × 3.5 m), constructed of massive, transversely laid, undressed limestone blocks in six courses that corbel towards the top (Peltenburg et al. 1995: 7). Its western entrance is defined by a very large stone lintel and a threshold, while a rectilinear annex, whose purpose is unclear, was set at the rear of the chamber (Peltenburg et al. 1996: 13).

It is unusual that no intact or collapsed roofing or portal slabs were recovered from Tomb 302, begging the question of what happened to the roof, if it had existed at all (Peltenburg et al. 1995: 8). Moreover, the tomb itself appears to have been enclosed or revetted by a large mound which would have been visible at surface-level. In other words, the stone chamber was but one component of what was originally a visible, upstanding monument (Peltenburg et al. 1995: 7).

The encasing mound was made of bands of orange bricky constructional material interleaved with horizontal lenses of bone, pottery and pebbles. Tomb 302 and this surrounding mound would have covered an area of at least 8 m × 10 m in the latest phase (Peltenburg et al. 1995: 8). A thick

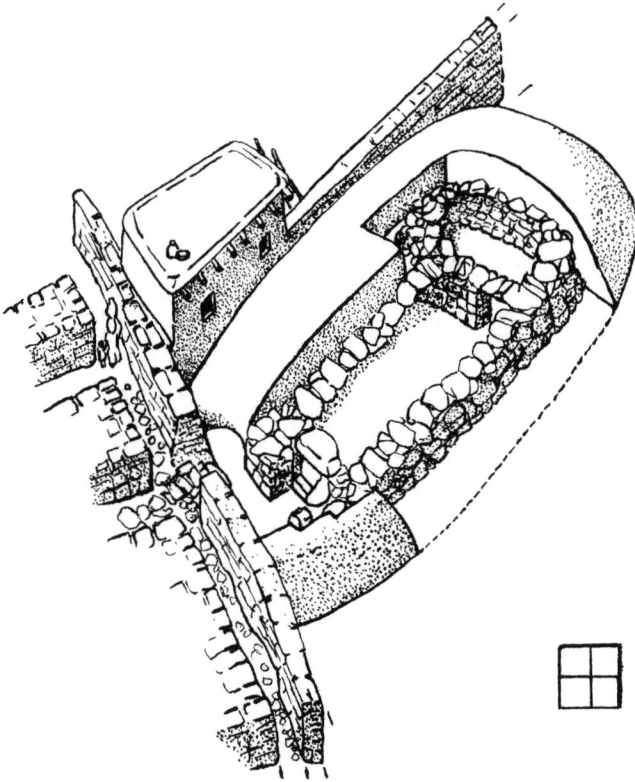

Figure 9.15 Reconstruction of Tomb 302, Jerablus Tahtani.

deposit of mound material constituted a major component of the fill inside the tomb, suggesting that at some point the roofing slabs were removed in order to envelop the entire structure in the mound. Alternatively, the mound was constructed around the roofed structure and at a late date, for some unknown reason, the roofing slabs were taken away, and the mound material simply eroded into the chamber (Peltenburg *et al.* 1995: 8).

The original tomb deposits were still present at the level of the floor even though the interior of the tomb had been looted and subjected to exceptional floods (Peltenburg 1999a: 102). The deposits near the floor of the chamber included several noteworthy items, including at least 100 examples of tall pedestalled 'champagne' vases, not unlike the footed vessels found in the burials at Carchemish and in the Tell Ahmar Hypogeum. They are rather cumbersome vessels, with stems that are often poorly attached to the vases, suggesting that they were not intended to be used over a long period of time. The vases' virtual absence in contemporary domestic contexts suggests that they were part of the funerary equipment of a deceased individual, possibly functioning as serving vessels for the deceased to be used in the afterlife, or alternatively, used during the funerary feasts or commemorative banquets by living participants (Peltenburg 1999b: 432; in press a).

Most importantly in the lower deposits were found the remains of 12 individuals. Studies of the bones of these individuals show that they included one infant, four children, two adults and five mature adults. On the basis of the presence of children in the tomb, it was suggested that Tomb 302 should be considered a family vault, possibly that of an important family in the settlement (Peltenburg 1999b: 431).

The deposits of exotic or luxury goods in the primary phase of this tomb are also notable, since besides pottery they included objects of gold, silver and rock crystal, ostrich eggshells and ivory plaques, and dagger pommels (Peltenburg 1999a: 102). Although the tomb was extensively looted, the remnants of these objects, comprising precious materials, testifies to the original wealth of the grave offerings.

Peltenburg has emphasized the importance of Tomb 302 at Jerablus Tahtani, drawing attention to the unusually large size of this funerary complex, the restricted and elaborate approach to it, and its prominent position at the foot of the settlement. In this location, it was visible not only to the inhabitants of the settlement but also to those approaching the site from the river (Peltenburg 1999b: 430). The tomb's monumental construction indicates a considerable investment of labour and planning (Peltenburg 1999b: 430). These aspects, along with the presence of precious grave objects and the fact that smaller, satellite burials were found in a cluster around this monument all underline the pre-eminence of the tomb and by extension the individuals buried within it, who almost certainly belonged to a family of elite status in the community (Peltenburg et al. 1995: 10).

The tomb objects and the stratigraphic relationship of the tomb in relation to the sequence of occupation and architectural construction at Jerablus Tahtani fix the tomb's date to Phase 4, around the mid-third millennium BC (Peltenburg 1999b: 429). As we have seen in our previous chapters, it is around this time that the processes of urbanism were intensifying in northern Syria, and when the manifestations of urbanism, such as increased social stratification and economic differentiation, were becoming more apparent. Tomb 302, an expensive and highly visible burial-place for one of the community's elite families, reflects well this growing social and economic differentiation among inhabitants of an increasingly complex society.

Significance of monumental shaft and chamber built tombs

In his discussion of Tomb 302 from Jerablus Tahtani, Peltenburg calls attention to the important role this funerary structure played among the living descendants of the dead who were buried here. He suggests that such individuals would have emphasized the continuing prominence and sacredness of this tomb of the dead ancestors as a means of perpetuating and reinforcing their own elevated status within society (Peltenburg 1999b: 427–8). Such a practice may have been especially important in this period of urban growth, when major changes in the old social order were occurring, tensions among new socio-economic groups were growing, and effective strategies were required among the existing elite to assure their continued prominence within this changing society (Peltenburg 1999b: 429; Schwartz *et al.* 2003: 339–40). It seems that a real or fabricated association with prominent symbols of traditional social order and power, such as monumental funerary structures dedicated to the ancestors, would have been effective tools in promoting and maintaining that privileged status.

The continuing significance of the tomb structure would have been especially emphasized if it came to be regarded as a place of ancestor veneration and remembrance, and if the potency of the monument required not only the appropriate funerary rituals at the time of the disposal of the dead, but also continuing visitations, offerings and feasts at the tomb long after the dead had been buried here. Interestingly, the performance of such death rituals is referred to in several ancient Near Eastern written sources found at Mari in southern Syria and cities in southern Mesopotamia. In such societies, offerings to dead kin often took place over the course of several generations after the death of a kin-member, and served to reinforce the status of the descendants by reference to the authority of the dead (Peltenburg 1999b: 428). While many of these textual sources pertain to royalty, it has been shown that death rituals were observed by other levels of Mesopotamian society as well (Peltenburg 1999b: 428, after Tsukimoto 1985).

In the case of Tomb 302, there is evidence that visitations and offerings continued to be made at this monument even after the roofing slabs had been removed and the earth of the surrounding mound had eroded into the interior of the tomb chamber. Above this eroded material were found several caches of objects such as pottery, terra-cotta bull figurines and metal weaponry. The lack of human remains among these caches of objects suggests that these deposits signify tomb visitations and not new episodes of corpse disposal (Peltenburg 1999b: 433). As with the cult of the dead kin known from texts in ancient Mesopotamian textual sources, such offerings served to establish the status of the donors by reference to the power of the dead and illustrious ancestors (Peltenburg 1999b: 433). The presence of such deposits, and the fact that their artifacts are also dated to the Early Bronze Age indicates the continuing significance of this tomb, even after its enclosing mound had begun to encroach into its roofless interior.

Considered as a whole, the monumental, stone-built burial chambers of the Euphrates Valley of northern Syria share several striking similarities. All are massively built. All accommodated several individuals, suggesting their probable function as family vaults. Where tomb offerings have been

preserved, they are numerous, exotic or precious. Their continued importance is signified by their maintenance or elaboration through time, and
repeated tomb offerings. Perhaps their most noteworthy feature is their visibility. Tomb 302 at Jerablus Tahtani was certainly a highly conspicuous
monument, with its location at the base of the mound and the fact that a
large mound enclosed it. As we have seen, recent investigations at Tell
Ahmar have shown that the Hypogeum may originally have been an above-
ground structure, and further, that it was attached to several other funerary
structures, forming a prominent, visible complex in the settlement. While
Tomb 7 at Tell Banat was subterranean, it is believed that its massive roofing
stones were in full view, serving as part of a large, freely accessible courtyard
(Porter 2002b: 158). The tombs at Tell Hadidi had grand entrances from
ground-level in what is thought to have been densely inhabited sectors of the
Early Bronze Age city. In sum, all of these monuments appear to have been
quite visible to members of the living community who had built and maintained them, thus distinguishing them from earth or rock-cut shaft graves,
which were largely hidden from view, and which had less prominent markers
on the surface to indicate their presence.

Monumental tombs are not restricted in their distribution to the northern
Euphrates Valley of Syria. Such tombs have also been reported at sites such as
Tell Bi'a, located further down the Euphrates River. In the southern part of
the central mound, a set of six above-ground mud brick elite tombs were
discovered (Strommenger and Kohlmeyer 2000). The Bi'a tombs are similar to
the stone-built shaft and chamber tombs further to the north in that they are
also monumental in scale. Further, with their above-ground construction, they
assumed a central and visible place within the settlement. The same can be said
for the monumental stone-built tombs discovered at Mari, located further
down the Euphrates River. Those found in the temple precinct of Ishtar, for
example, were also centrally located and visible (Jean-Marie 1990: 305–10).
Finally, to our list we can now add an Early Bronze elite stone-built tomb
found at an elevated level in the Acropolis Centre at Umm el-Marra, a site
located to the west of the Euphrates Valley in Syria (Schwartz *et al.* 2003).

Given the widespread geographical distribution of these monumental
stone-built graves, it seems unlikely that they are reflecting the spatial limits
of one socio-cultural territory or the political boundaries of an ancient city-
state. Rather, we should probably seek to explain the tombs' commonality as
strategies employed by ascendant elites as a means of illustrating and
enhancing their status, not only within their own cities, as has already been
conjectured, but also among their peers from other contemporary princi-
palities. These local elites were thus attempting to legitimate their status by
identifying themselves with elite behaviour elsewhere, even across political
and cultural boundaries (Peltenburg 1999b: 429). This would seem, therefore,
to be an instance of 'peer polity interaction' (Renfrew 1986: 7–8). In sum, the
distribution of monumental, visible tombs in northern Mesopotamia has a

greater relationship to issues of elite status and the perpetuation of power in Early Bronze Age societies than to the territorial limits of one political polity.

Monumental tumuli

This new category, which has been added to the Euphrates' burial typology, consists of artificially constructed mounds or tumuli. These structures have been positively identified at the site of Tell Banat, although it is possible that they are present at other sites during the third millennium BC, but have gone undetected. Alternatively, their presence has been noted, but their overall structure and third millennium date have not been verified (Peltenburg in press b, citing Roaf and Postgate 1981: 198; and Wilkinson 2003: 123).

A conical mound located about 200 m northeast of Tell Banat, otherwise known as the White Monument or Mortuary Mound I, is most impressive, exhibiting monumental scale, unique construction and a distinctive appearance. The structure, which actually comprises a series of successive mounds constructed over several centuries of the mid-third millennium BC (Phases 3 and 4), is known to have been composed of layers of packed earth, reddish gravel and chunky white marl (Figure 9.16). It forms a conical or elliptical freestanding structure that in its latest phase was over 100 m in diameter and stood over 20 m in height (McClellan 1998: 243). The exterior face of this structure was covered with thick coatings of white terra pisé plaster, corrugated in horizontal bands (Figure 9.17) (McClellan 1998: 244–5). Such an external finish no doubt gave the monument a dazzling white appearance from afar.

While no true burials or tomb chambers have been found inside or on top of the White Monument, several discrete deposits of human skeletal parts, some animal bones, and pottery were cut into or placed onto the sloping sides of the monument, and then encased within layers of earth and marl (Porter 2002b: 160–1). It has been conjectured that such bone deposits represent the

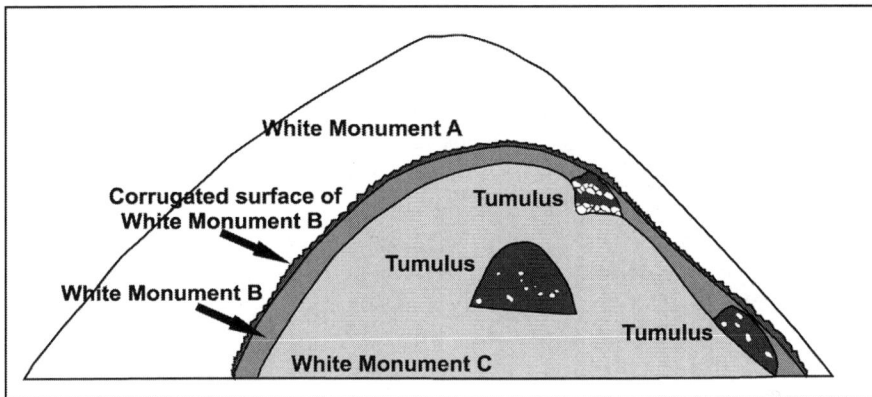

Figure 9.16 Schematic section of the White Monument, Tell Banat North.

Figure 9.17 Corrugations and white plastered surface, White Monument, Tell Banat North.

final stage of a multi-stage burial practice, in which the skeletal remains were taken away from their original burial place and returned with others in a collective, anonymous mass of bones. Such an act may have highlighted the corporate nature of the community, where primacy of descent and individual identities were de-emphasized in favour of the tribal collective, even among the dead (Porter 2002b: 170). Whatever the case, the fact that such bone deposits were found in this tumulus confirms that the monument had a mortuary function. We may also note, significantly, that the fields immediately surrounding the mound are peppered with burials, all of which date to the third millennium BC (McClellan 1998: 246). The concentration of graves around these mounds also surely supports the mound's mortuary character.

Besides the White Monument located to the east of Tell Banat proper, another earlier structure was identified within the site itself. Found underneath Buildings 6 and 7, this monument, designated Mortuary Mound II, consisted of a conical-shaped mound about 7.5 m in diameter, although it could have been much larger originally and had been subsequently truncated (Porter 2002a: 16). Although it had been badly disturbed by later activities, Mortuary Mound II was distinguished as a sloping surface constructed of layers of gravel and dirt, with a carefully white-plastered and hard-packed coating that also showed signs of being corrugated (McClellan 1998: 246; Porter 2002a: 16). At some point early on, the tumulus was covered by a massive artificial deposit of gravel. This formed the platform that was laid as preparation for the construction of Buildings 6 and 7. The removal of Mortuary Mound II from sight by this gravel layer may have been done in an effort to render it dysfunctional, or to de-sanctify it. For what purposes this gravel served, it was extensive, being at least 3.5 m thick. It clearly represents a massive earth-moving project.

Perhaps forming a sub-set of the monumental mortuary mound just described are smaller earth tumuli. The difference is that these smaller mounds almost always covered above-ground stone-built tombs. Tomb 302 at Jerablus Tahtani, for example, belongs to this category since it was encased in an earthen mound (Peltenburg 1999b: 431). Other such burial tumuli have been reported at the Bronze Age site of Baghouz, further south along the Euphrates River Valley near the Syrian/Iraqi border (Mesnil du Buisson 1948). Last, a series of above-ground megalithic monuments, or dolmens, have been reported at Rumeilah, about 20 km south of Tell Banat, although the earth tumuli that likely enclosed them have not survived (McClellan and Porter 1999: 108).

SPATIAL CONSIDERATIONS OF TOMB TYPES AND CEMETERIES

The grave typology formulated above has underlined the range and variability of burial practices existing in the Euphrates Valley of Syria during the Early Bronze Age. This general pattern of variability can also be observed in the graves' placement within or outside occupied settlements, as well as their spatial relationships to one another in individual cemeteries and sites. Despite this variability in tomb location, however, a few interesting patterns emerged in the data that appear to reflect specific social and economic behaviour among the inhabitants of the region.

Intramural graves

Early Bronze Age tombs were frequently sited within or very near to contemporary settlements. While the prevailing preference seems to have been for the burial of the dead in cemeteries just outside of occupied settlements, there are also a few notable instances of intramural graves. The inhabitants of Selenkahiye, for example, appear to have been buried in the area immediately to the south of the site at the Wreide cemetery, but many were also buried inside their city. Two nodal shaft graves were found within the settlement, one near the northern city wall under a floor in a domestic area of the city (Van Loon 2001: 3.59), and the other in one of Selenkahiye's principal streets, cut below its pavement (Van Loon 2001: 4A.177). Shaft graves were also found in a cluster in the west-central part of the settlement near a city gate (Van Loon 4B.198). One of the richest shaft tombs, W12/13, was located in a part of the central town area where it cut into domestic architecture belonging to an earlier occupation phase (Van Loon 2001: 4B.210). Neither tomb W12/13, nor the five other simpler burials that were located near it, however, have any structural connections with existing houses, suggesting that they belong to a phase of abandonment in this particular sector of the city (Van Loon 2001: 4B.210).

Intramural burials have been reported elsewhere too. The impressive stone-built shaft-and-chamber tombs investigated by Dornemann at Tell Hadidi were found in areas of the lower town, east of the main acropolis. It is reported that wall fragments and floor remains were found near these tombs, although the stratigraphic evidence documenting the placement of tombs under such buildings was difficult to ascertain (Dornemann 1979: 117).

All of the reported burials from the site of Qara Quzaq derive from contexts within the town (Olávarri 1995a: 10; Valdés Pereiro 1999: 120; Olávarri and Valdés Pereiro 2001: 20–1). The same goes for those found at Tell Ahmar and Carchemish. At Jerablus Tahtani, an abundance of pit, cist, stone chamber and pithos burials have been reported intramurally, although in addition to these, an area at the northern end outside of the fortification walls, where excavations exposed two EB graves, may have served as the location of an extramural cemetery (Peltenburg *et al.* 2000: 72–3).

The reasons for burying the dead within or close to places of the living is uncertain, although such practices are not unique to northern Syria. In Southern Mesopotamia during the third millennium, intramural burials were quite common. Bodies were interred in otherwise unused or abandoned parts of settlements, such as rubbish dumps, or else they were buried under the floors of inhabited houses (Pollock 1999: 206).

In her discussion of the co-existence of both intramural and extramural burials in southern Mesopotamia, Susan Pollock discusses the growing tension between household production and consumption on the one hand, and activities within the *oikoi*, the collective term for larger and wealthier estates belonging to important public officials, temples and palaces within the cities (Pollock 1999: 117–18). Unlike households whose membership consisted of nuclear or extended families living under one roof, these *oikoi* comprised large socio-economic units with a dependent workforce and managerial personnel who were not necessarily related to one another through kinship ties (Pollock 1999: 117–18). In this environment of competing levels of production, individuals may have felt pressure to connect themselves with the *oikos*-community through burial within a corporate cemetery, often located beyond the limits of the city. Alternatively, the continuing practice of burial within family houses may have underlined the continued strength of individuals' ties to this more basic level of organization. One wonders if a similar dynamic had developed in the northern Euphrates River Valley at the same time. As has been noted in the earlier chapters, the third millennium was a time of increasing social and economic complexity as cities in this region grew and prospered. Further, we have already seen considerable evidence for the development of larger secular buildings, temples and other public works requiring cooperation within the community beyond the simple domestic level of production. Perhaps then, the distinction between intramural and extramural burials is related to the presence of both household and *oikos* groups, one preferring to bury their dead within or near their own household complexes, while the other encouraged interment of its members in a specially designated cemetery located beyond the walls of the city.

As convincing as this reconstruction may sound, however, we should remain somewhat cautious about imposing the structure of one society onto that of another. The *oikoi* system may seem to be a good way of considering the socio-economic structure of southern Mesopotamia. But in the northern Euphrates Valley, the contradistinction between the household on the one hand and the state, entirely divorced from kinship ties on the other, does not work entirely well. This region continued to demonstrate a strong tribal character despite growing social and economic complexity and an increasingly urban environment. Thus, even within the most densely inhabited centres of the Euphrates Valley, many of the inhabitants still identified themselves with the tribal group to which they belonged, and performed many social obligations and economic activities along tribal lines within the wider community. When we consider the relationship between burial locations and social organization, we must be mindful of this unique situation. In light of this, perhaps we should see extramural cemeteries as the burial places of tribal members, while intramural burials were for those who did not wish to emphasize their tribal affiliation, either because they were outsiders or newcomers, or because they wished to highlight their role or influence in some other sphere of socio-economic activity.

If we now consider the practice of intramural versus extramural burials according to the different grave types that have been identified in the Euphrates Valley, do any other interesting patterns emerge? As observed in Table 9.1, in which the presence of different grave types within or outside an occupied settlement is indicated by an 'x', only monumental stone-built shaft and chamber tombs are absent from extramural cemeteries.

This spatial pattern is not surprising, given that the overall visibility of such monumental tombs, as previously discussed, assisted the tombs' role in structuring social relationships among the settlement's living inhabitants. By their intramural location, the potency of these funerary monuments would have been all the more emphasized. Not only were these tombs ostentatious by virtue of their large size, elaborate construction, and the fact they were above ground or otherwise well-marked, they were continually acknowledged because of their prominent location within the city. By their spatial centrality, they would have provided constant reminders to the city's inhabitants of the importance of the deceased who were buried within, and the deceased's descendants, who reinforced their connection to such monuments through regular and continued ceremonies and offering rites within and around these funerary locales.

Extramural graves

Several Early Bronze Age cemeteries have been found beyond the walls of the settlements to which they were associated. The cemeteries do not appear to have been located at a great distance from the settlements they served. Burials within the cemetery at Wreide, for example, began immediately at the foot of the mound of Selenkahiye and extended towards the south. The graves at the site of Tell Halawa were clustered in groups along the eastern, southern, southwestern and northwestern slopes of that settlement mound, some almost immediately outside of the ancient city-walls (Orthmann 1981: Taf. 80). While the ancient site of Tell Djefle has not been excavated and its EB occupation remains uncertain, it is significant that the associated cemetery (Tawi), consists of graves that were arranged in a semi-circle around it (Kampschulte and Orthmann 1984: Abb. 2). The same arrangement has also been observed at Shamseddin. Grave-clusters extended in many directions away from the centre at Tell Banat, occurring in the fields around and beyond the White Monument tumulus and along the slope of a hill that extends to the east of Tell Banat (McClellan and Porter 1999: 108). At Tell es-Sweyhat, a cemetery has so far only been identified on the edge of the Early Bronze Age settlement in the northwestern corner.

While several graves have been sited on flat ground, the majority of them appear to have been cut into the sides of slopes. Rather than this slope-location having any religious or social meaning, it may simply be that it was easier and less time-consuming to cut a burial, particularly a shaft grave, into the ground from the side rather than from the top. That natural conditions often dictated the layout of a grave is also evident in the orientation of the graves. At the cemeteries of Tawi, Halawa and Shamseddin, where such information is readily available, it is was observed that the long axis of the shaft grave was almost always placed at right angles to the contour of the

Table 9.1 Presence (x) of burial types within intramural and extramural contexts

Burial Type	Intramural	Extramural
Pit	x	x
Cist	x	x
Pithos	x	x
Stone Chamber	x	x
Earth or Rock-Cut Shaft	x	x
Monumental Stone-built		
Shaft and Chamber	x	
Monumental burial tumuli	x	x

hillside into which it was dug. In summary, most graves demonstrate a multiplicity of orientations depending upon the direction of the slope of the hills.

BURIAL TYPES AND THEIR GEOGRAPHICAL DISTRIBUTION

The map shown in Figure 9.18 represents an updated version of the map appearing in Carter and Parker's earlier article, incorporating revisions and additions to their original typology, and focussing in particular on burial types reported along the Euphrates River Valley of northern Syria and extending into southeastern Turkey. Each burial type is indicated by a unique pictorial symbol. While the map has generated several significant patterns, the most interesting is the geographical distribution of cist graves and earth and rock-cut shaft graves. For purposes of clarity, the geographical distribution of cist and shaft graves is also presented in a table in Table 9.2. In this table, the precise location of these graves, from north to south, is listed.

The pattern observable in this table was not clearly evident in Carter and Parker's earlier study because the authors had grouped earth and rock-cut shaft graves together with stone-built shaft and chamber tombs (Carter and Parker 1995: 108). When a distinction between these burial types is made, however, the distribution of earth and rock-cut shaft graves is seen to be limited, for the most part, to the southern part of the region under investigation, from the cemetery site of Wreide in the south, up to Tell Banat in the north. Except for the Anatolian site of Dibecik and tombs in the vicinity of Tilbes Höyük, northern Euphrates sites have failed to produce these distinctive rock-cut shaft tombs. On the other hand, the northern part of the study area contains an abundance of cist graves. The quantity of cist graves is particularly high at Anatolian sites such as Titris Höyük, the Birecik Cemetery, where almost 300 cist graves have been reported, and the site of Lidar, where no less than 200 cist graves have been recovered thus far (Carter and Parker 1995: 113). The northern orientation of the cist burials, therefore, appears very pronounced.

It is tempting to derive some meaning from the clear geographical distinction between the cist and earth or rock-cut shaft graves. One could suggest a number of factors to account for this interesting spatial pattern, including the possibility that the grave-types reflect the existence of two separate political territories. One could posit, for example, that the distribution of cist graves reflects the extent of an important Early Bronze Age polity such as Carchemish. Although archaeological investigations have failed to uncover significant exposures of that ancient city's EB occupation, third millennium textual sources certainly do report its existence and its importance along

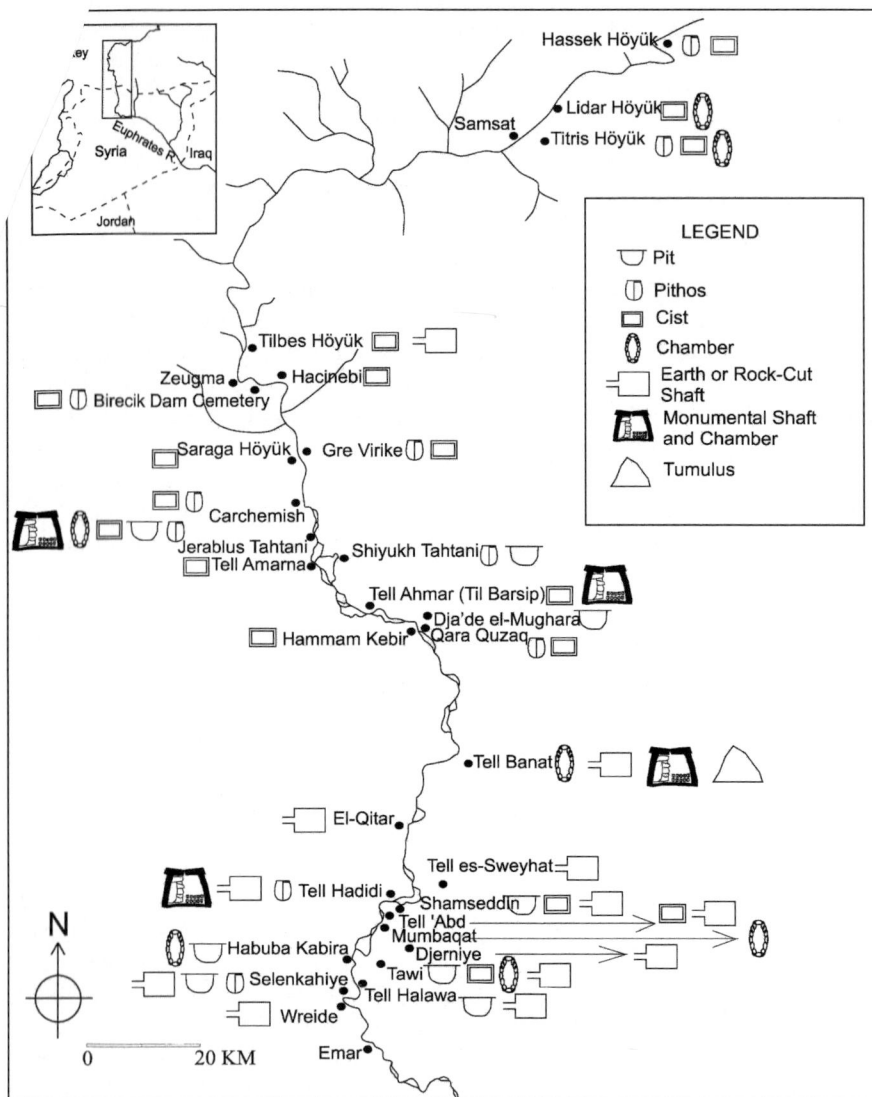

Figure 9.18 Geographical distribution of burial types in the northern Euphrates Valley.

the Euphrates River. In contrast, one might suggest that the southerly distribution of shaft graves reflects the territorial extent or influence of some other political polity such as Emar or Tuttul (Tell Bi'a). Both of these sites were also known to have been important EB cities along the Middle Euphrates River.

Unfortunately, cross-cultural studies demonstrating clear associations

Table 9.2 Presence of cist graves and earth or rock-cut shaft graves at Euphrates Sites of Anatolia and northern Syria

Euphrates Valley EB Site	Cist Grave	Earth or Rock-Cut Shaft Grave
Hassek Höyük	x	
Lidar Höyük	x	
Titris Höyük	x	
Tilbes Höyük	x	x
Hacinebi	x	
Birecik Dam Cemetery	x	
Şaraga Höyük	x	
Gre Virike	x	
Carchemish	x	
Jerablus Tahtani	x	
Tell Amarna	x	
Tell Ahmar	x	
Hammam Kebir	x	
Qara Quzaq	x	
Tell Banat		x
el-Qitar		x
Tell es-Sweyhat		x
Tell Hadidi		x
Shamseddin	x	x
Tell al-ʿAbd	x	x
Djerniye		x
Tawi	x	x
Halawa		x
Selenkahiye		x
Wreide		x

between grave types and political affiliations are lacking, casting suspicion upon the veracity of the relationship posited here along the Euphrates. Further undermining this proposal is the fact that at three sites in the region, Tell al-ʿAbd, Shamseddin and Tawi, both grave-types co-exist and appear to be roughly contemporaneous. If political boundaries are to be linked with the presence or absence of cist and shaft graves, it is difficult to explain their co-occurrence at these sites. To which political polity would these sites have belonged?

If we turn more closely to Shamseddin, Tell al-ʿAbd, and Tawi, is there anything about the presence of cist and shaft graves at these sites that may offer any additional clues about the significance of these burial types and their unique geographical distribution? Particularly suggestive are the burials' spatial relationships to one another. At the site of Shamseddin, for example, both cemeteries A and C have yielded the remains of stone-line cist graves and earth-cut shaft graves. In both cemeteries there is a clear spatial separation between the two types of burials. In Cemetery A at Shamseddin, while *c* graves appear in regularly spaced rows along the southern slope *c*ill, the stone cist graves are located at a distance at the northern end *c*emetery. The same kind of pattern is repeated in Cemetery C, where the *g*raves are located on a different hill upon which the cemetery is located, being spatially distinct from the shaft graves (Meyer 1991: 89–90).

At Tawi, a similar separation of burial types is evident. Shaft graves were *f*ound in a cluster in only one area of Area B, on the edge of a high hill *d*irectly to the east of the ancient settlement. In contrast, cist graves, which were more numerous, were found clustered in area A, at a healthy distance from the shaft graves (Kampschulte and Orthmann 1984: 75–80).

The absence of a final report from the first excavations at Tell al-ʿAbd makes it difficult to confirm the relation between the cist and shaft graves at this site. The excavator describes a cemetery of cist graves at the foot of the eastern slope of the mound (Bounni 1979: 55), while shaft graves are reported further to the east, on the slope of a small wadi (Orthmann 1980: 99). Although we cannot be sure because of the brief nature of this report, it would appear that here too was a spatial separation existing between cist and shaft burials.

Are there still other factors that might account for the unusual distribution of cist and shaft graves? Is time a factor? To be sure, cist graves do appear to have had a longer history in the northern Euphrates Valley than shaft graves. They extend even as far back as the earliest EB phases of settlement in the region (Phases 1 and 2). The cist graves of the Birecik Dam Cemetery, Carchemish and Tell Ahmar can be included among these early examples, judging by their pottery and metal artifacts (Thureau-Dangin and Dunand 1936: 108–10; Woolley and Barnett 1952: 218–22; Sertok and Ergeç 1999). On the other hand, cist graves continue to appear in later EB contexts, where they are approximately contemporary with earth or rock-cut shaft graves, the majority of which date from the mid-to-late EB (Phases 3–4). While much burial data are sadly lacking for the cist graves of Shamseddin because of poor preservation and tomb looting (Meyer 1991: 90), a few chronological conclusions can nonetheless be determined. At Cemeteries A and C, where scattered pot sherds around the looted cist tombs were collected, the vessel forms were found to match up precisely with the pottery that had been collected from shaft graves (Meyer 1991: 62–5; 99–102), indicating the two burial types' contemporaneity. At Tawi, the nine reported cist tombs from Area A were likewise heavily robbed (Kampschulte and Orthmann 1984: 75). Only Grave T31 yielded a single pot. Unfortunately the vessel is difficult to date, although accompanying it was a tanged crescentic axe, a type that is also known from the cemetery at Amarna to the north and dated to Phase 3 or 4, around the middle of the third millennium BC (Kampschulte and Orthmann 1984: Taf. 30; Tubb 1982: 9). A great deal of the pottery from other burials at Tawi can be similarly dated, as can shaft graves from other neighbouring sites such as Tell es-Sweyhat and Tell Banat (Kampschulte and Orthmann 1984: Taf. 18–28; Porter 1995a; Zettler 1997b: App. 3.1–3.3). In summary, the present evidence indicates that many cist burials can be dated earlier than shaft graves in the northern Euphrates Valley. Nonetheless, with their continuing presence in the region in the latter half of the EB, some would have been contemporary with earth or rock-cut shaft graves.

We exclude still other factors that might account for the different burial types. Differences in gender hardly match up with the marked north–south distribution of cist graves and shaft graves. Moreover, where studies of human skeletal material have been performed, such as at the shaft-grave cemetery of Halawa, they verify that both sexes could be buried in such graves (Orthmann 1981: 72). It is likewise difficult to correlate the unusual north–south configuration of the two burial types with differences in wealth or status within one population. In any event, the full range of wealth differentiation can be observed among the shaft graves alone – from the simplest small rock-cut tombs, to magnificently cut and elaborately furnished inhumations that contained a wealth of grave goods – such that searches for wealth distinctions based on different burial types are unwarranted.

Burial types and ethnic identity

One last possible explanation to justify a northern and southern distribution of cist and rock-cut shaft graves, and their co-existence at three sites but in separate locales, is the presence of two ethnic groups. Several factors would support such a proposition.

First, unlike the widespread lack of reported correspondences between political polities and mortuary remains in the anthropological literature, ethnic identity can sometimes be correlated with burial remains and practices. A survey of studies of the archaeological manifestations of ethnicity from around the world finds several examples of ethnic groups who are distinguished from other groups by the ways in which they bury their kinsmen and conduct funerary rituals. One example comes from the Mesoamerican centre of Matacapan, located in southern Veracruz. During the Middle Classic Period (AD 400–700), this centre appears to have supported enclaves of people from Teotihuacan, a large and important urban centre with tremendous influence throughout Mesoamerica. At Matacapan, distinct occupation zones or enclaves rich in Teotihuacan-style materials, such as cylindrical tripod bowls, candeleros, and Teotihuacan-inspired civic-ceremonial architecture were found. Also evident in these enclaves were distinctive burial practices, namely the flexed interment of the deceased below house floors within domestic structures, a custom practised at Teotihuacan, along with infant jar burials, another Teotihuacan mortuary custom (Santley et al. 1987). The combination of these funerary remains and the other artifacts, therefore, presents a strong case for a Teotihuacan ethnic presence at this site.

Closer in region and date to the mortuary remains described here are archaeological remains connected with the Hyksos, a population group that had settled in the Delta region of northern Egypt during the Second Intermediate Period of Egypt (c. 1648–1540 BC). The distinctive 'Asiatic' character of the Hyksos population is particularly evident in burials found at sites such as Tell el-Dab'a, Tell el-Maskhuta and Inshas, where vaulted mudbrick chamber tombs and the presence of donkey sacrifices clearly represent non-Egyptian funerary traditions and practices (Weinstein 1992: 345).

One can see by these examples, therefore, how the ethnic identities of particular human groups are marked by distinctive funerary remains and their accompanying rituals, for which material residuals have been preserved. Such examples support the notion that differences between cist and shaft burial types in the northern Euphrates Valley of the Early Bronze Age could also be attributable to the presence of two distinct ethnic groups in this region.

Second, although it is difficult to suppose a situation in which individuals were affiliated with different political polities co-existing at the same site, it is not hard to accept that more than one ethnic group resided together in the same settlement. Once again, a survey of the anthropological literature, which includes cross-cultural studies of ethnicity, produced many examples of such a phenomenon. In the modern world, the co-existence of two or more distinct ethnic groups residing in the same city is extremely common (Glazer and Moynihan 1965; Nagata 1974), while the same has been observed in many cities in the ancient world. In ancient Mesopotamia during the Ur III period, for example, Amorite groups were known to have co-existed with Sumerian populations in several southern Mesopotamian cities (Kamp and Yoffee 1980: 90). In light of these examples, therefore, we cannot exclude the possibility that cities in the Euphrates Valley of Syria and Anatolia during the EB also comprised mixed ethnic populations.

Which ethnic group, then, might be associated with the cist burials? Although Carter and Parker did not find such a clear spatial pattern among burials as observed here, their overall impression of the northern orientation of cist burials led them to suggest that such graves might be linked with Anatolian/Hurrian populations (Carter and Parker 1995: 113). This proposition seems quite plausible, given the textual evidence for the presence of small Hurrian states to the north and northeast of Akkad in the late third millennium BC (Carter and Parker 1995: 113). While the Hurrians seem to have been most numerous in the Habur region of northeastern Syria (at Nagar and Urkesh) as well as to the east of the Tigris River (Stein 1997: 127), it is not unlikely that smaller pockets of Hurrian groups settled along the Euphrates River in Anatolia, and further south in Syria, where they would have settled alongside the indigenous populations of this region. Interestingly, this proposition also finds support in geographical place names known from contemporary ancient sources, as will be discussed below.

On the other hand, can we ascribe an ethnic identity to the users of the earth or rock-cut shaft graves? In order to address this question, we need to survey the entire geographical region in which such graves have been found. Shaft graves are abundant not only in the area of the 'Big Bend' of the Euphrates region, they are present further to the south at Tell Bi'a (Strommenger and Kohlmeyer 1998). Further, they cross over into western Syria, and the Levant, where they are reported in Palestine and Transjordan. Shaft graves occur throughout the EB period in the Levant, but become especially prevalent in the Early Bronze IV period, in the last centuries of the third millennium BC. This is also the period in which shaft graves are the most numerous in the Syrian Euphrates Valley. Given this distribution, perhaps we can propose a Semitic identity for the owners of the shaft graves. We know that Semitic groups such as the Amorites were present in northern and western Syria, especially during the end of the Early Bronze age, so perhaps we are looking at the kinds of burials that the Amorites, or possibly, proto-Amorites, used for the interment of their dead.

As a last word on the discussion of ethnic variability in the northern Euphrates Valley, one can turn to Marco Bonechi's recent study of Pre-Sargonic geographical names. His study, which utilizes third millennium textual sources from Ebla and Mari, focusses in particular on place names from the region along the Euphrates up to the modern border between Turkey and Syria, including the toponymy of the area around Carchemish (Bonechi 1998). While Bonechi ascertains that the majority of place names in this region are Semitic, originating some time at the beginning of the third millennium BC, some Hurrian place names are also detectable, appearing in greatest numbers in the northernmost part of the area, namely in the foothills just north of the present-day Syrian-Turkish border in the regions of the Euphrates and Balikh Rivers (Bonechi 1998: 236). As is common of border zones, Bonechi is not surprised to find small enclaves with a Hurrian toponymy present relatively far from the Anatolian foothills (namely to the south, in Syria), while at the same time he conjectures that small enclaves with Semitic toponymy also existed far from the plains, e.g. in the Anatolian highlands (Bonechi 1998: 237). This type of pattern, detectable among geographical place names in ancient textual sources, is very tantalizing as it mirrors precisely the pattern that we have observed among cist and earth or rock-cut shaft graves. Thus, just as pockets of Hurrian place-names can be recognized within a region dominated by Semitic toponymy, so too can cist graves be detected among the prevalent shaft grave types of northern Syria. At the same time, a few scattered rock-cut shaft graves in Anatolia parallel the presence of occasional Semitic toponyms in the north. In sum, the convergence of textual and archaeological data, as noted here, offers considerable validity to the notion that two separate ethno-linguistic populations co-existed in the Euphrates valley of northern Syria and southern Anatolia, and that they can be distinguished from one another in the funerary record.

It is clear that much still needs to be done to account for the interesting spatial distinction between shaft and cist graves in the northern Euphrates Valley and their equation with two ethnic populations, possibly Hurrians and Amorites. The examination of other aspects of the burials, such as the way in which the dead were treated and accompanying grave goods, might yield further differences that can be correlated to ethnic distinctions.

TELL BANAT: AN EXTRAORDINARY MORTUARY CENTRE

Although many of the excavated sites along the Euphrates River Valley of northern Syria have produced evidence for Early Bronze Age burials, the site of Tell Banat stands apart from these by its extraordinary assemblage of mortuary monuments and associated funerary installations (Figure 9.19). When considered as a whole, Tell Banat has parallels with no other Euphrates' site, nor any other Bronze Age site in the Near East investigated thus far. For this reason we chose to discuss the mortuary evidence from Tell Banat separately here.

The following discussion will describe the chief characteristics of this site. It will also summarize some of the principal conclusions of the Banat's excavators, who have not only carefully recorded Tell Banat's monuments, but have also tried to resolve important issues regarding the remains' temporal

Figure 9.19 View of Tell Banat (area of modern village) and Tell Banat North behind.

sequence, their spatial connections with other funerary installations, and their function and ideological character. The researchers' thoughtful considerations of the diversity of mortuary remains and their significance have underlined the myriad of overlapping, conflicting and congruous social relationships and ideology existing among the inhabitants of this intriguing settlement. Such relationships indicate a culture and society that was far more complex than originally perceived, and defined by more than simple socio-economic status disparities (Porter 2002b: 158). Further, these multiple social relationships 'did not simply reflect the nature of life in the third millennium', they 'actively produced it' (Porter 2002b: 158).

Our typology of graves has already provided a description of Tomb 7 at Tell Banat, an impressive stone-built shaft and chamber tomb. We also described other burials uncovered at Tell Banat or in its immediate environs. These included stone-walled chamber tombs and earth-cut shaft tombs, located both within (Tomb 1) and outside of the ancient settlement (Tomb 2). Last, we provided a description of the Mortuary Mounds, which are impressive, artificially constructed tumuli. Deposits of human bones found within these monuments suggest that they had some mortuary significance, as does the fact that lesser, contemporary burials were found in the fields around them.

The strong funerary character of Tell Banat is indicated by other remains besides burials and mortuary mounds. In Chapter 6, we described two large-scale structures, Buildings 6 and 7. These buildings' association with mortuary activities is supported by their close spatial relation to a variety of graves, including Tomb 7, as well as their location on the enigmatic thick gravel layer that covered Mortuary Mound II in its entirety.

The extensive manufacturing sector of Tell Banat should also be considered. This area contained kilns and a sequence of buildings which functioned as the workshops of craftsmen engaged in the mass manufacture of pottery. The ubiquity of pottery in all of the third millennium BC graves at Tell Banat, and the fact that many of the grave vessels duplicate those produced in the site's pottery manufactories, suggest that the principal function of these workshops was to fabricate large quantities of pottery for funerary consumption.

When considered as a whole, Tell Banat represents a remarkable settlement. It is significantly different from other sites along the Euphrates River from the same period which are invariably characterized not only by cemeteries and graves, but also blocks of houses and places of domestic activity. While these other sites served primarily as settlements for living inhabitants, the primary purpose of Tell Banat was the accommodation of the dead. Those who did reside at the site seem to have been there for the purpose of maintaining or serving this mortuary centre in some capacity. Nevertheless, this 'city of the dead' must not be construed as having functioned exclusively for the comfort and sustenance of the dead, with little connection or social relevance to living persons. On the contrary, in their constituent parts, the remains at Tell Banat were potent symbols, communicating strong messages about society, tradition, and appropriate behaviour among the living.

It is tempting to regard the remains of Tell Banat, which comprise elaborate and monumental architecture, extensive industrial installations, and at least one impressive tomb with rich and abundant burial gifts, as reflecting a socio-political system dominated by an elite (Porter 2002b: 165). In this light, the individuals buried in Tomb 7 could have been members of a local royal family, while other less impressive graves belonged to the subordinate population who were controlled by this elite (Porter 2002b: 165). Textual evidence from sites like Ebla might support this picture, since that city was marked by the presence of the king and his royal family. At Ebla, the distinction between royal and commoner was perpetrated not only by certain norms and practices within daily life, but also through funerary practices. Royal burials were clearly marked and segregated from the rest of the settlement. Regular pilgrimages were made to such tombs of the royal ancestors, and rituals at these funerary locales served to sanctify and legitimate the authority of the living kings who were descended from them (Porter 2002a: 5; 2002b: 168).

Despite this evidence, however, one should remember that Early Bronze Age society in the Euphrates River Valley, unlike Ebla to the west, was not widely defined by instances of status differentiation, either in burial practices and burial goods, or in other aspects of the region's urban culture. It would surely be erroneous to deny the presence of elite groups in the region, as testified by visible stone-built tombs like those at Tell Banat, Jerablus Tahtani and Tell Ahmar. These types of tombs, however, represent only a small fraction of the total range of burials present in the Euphrates Valley. Moreover, few other graves reflect status differentiation through their size, layout, and tomb artifacts. While there are certainly many variations of burials and burial objects from site to site, and from grave to grave, it can be argued that factors such as ethnic distinctions, economic relationships, and tribal versus household affiliations account for this diverse array of graves and furnishings. Thus, to place an inordinate emphasis on status differentiation at Tell Banat would seem incongruous with mortuary remains elsewhere in region. We can also add, as a last remark, that too many anomalous burial practices exist at Tell Banat itself to be convincingly explained by status differentiation alone.

One interesting observation concerns the degree of individual identity that appears to have been erased in the act of burial at many of Banat's funerary contexts. All of the burials contained within the White Monument, for example, are disarticulated and have few grave goods. These mortuary practices do not appear to express the individuation of specific members of the group, their status or position. On the contrary, they highlight the corporate nature of the deceased, all of whom were buried in a similar, unostentatious manner in a single locale (Porter 2002b: 166). It is suggested that this amorphous mass of dead ancestors was the result of a multi-stage burial practice, in which the body was taken away from its original burial place and individual funerary goods, and disarticulated in a individual-less mass of anonymity. There is much evidence in the form of empty graves and second-ary graves of disarticulated skeletons at Banat to testify to this practice. Through the creation of this amorphous mass of ancestors, primacy of descent and individual identities were lost in the collectivity (Porter 2002b: 170).

In her interpretation of the enigmatic White Monument at Banat, Porter attributes to them the place of the cult of the ancestors. In contrast to other world cultures, however, in which ancestors are named individuals who establish rights, relationships and positions in descent hierarchies among the living, the ancestors at Banat are an unnamed amorphous group (Porter 2002b: 167). Their anonymity is suggested by the encompassing nature of the tumulus itself, which encases earlier tumuli, and the characterless nature of the burials within it.

Porter argues that the way in which the ancestors are perceived as such has implications for the living society at Banat, whose own social behaviour is informed and reinforced by the manner in which they see their ancestral community behaving:

> The society of ancestors forms a blueprint for the nature of social relationships among the living, which may be adhered to or deviated from in the real world, but which nevertheless has impact upon the nature of that world. That the ancestral community of the White Monuments portrays a corporate society by virtue of their nebulous treatment of their remains is integrally related to the notion of corporation in the world of the living.
>
> (Porter 2002b: 167)

Such ancestral monuments, then, whose funerary message is that of integra-tion and corporation, would have encouraged the same type of behaviour among the living inhabitants.

It should be noted that this ideology of corporation appears to be similar to that held by other ancient Mesopotamian communities. Textual sources from the city of Mari to the southeast, for example, speak of rites such as the so-called *kispum*, a regularly performed communal meal at which the living and the dead are present. Such a ritual was intended to perpetuate and affirm the role of a generalized class of the dead in the realm of the living (Porter 2002a: 5). While this ritual seems to have been central to the legitimation of the king, it nonetheless placed emphasis on the importance of incorporation among those who participated in it, and in so doing, affirmed an ideal tribal unity.

This kind of corporate social structure is entirely in keeping with what has already been conjectured about Euphrates society from the point of view of settlement subsistence, social organization, architecture and artifacts. Further, we can add how this corporate society fits very well with the proposed tribal aspect of Syrian Euphrates society. Despite the overall trend towards larger and more densely populated urban centres and greater political and economic complexity among sites over the course of the third millennium BC, the basic structure of society remained tribal, and individuals continued to identify themselves according to the kin-based tribal group to which they belonged. The continuing tribal character of the Euphrates region may have been the result of the continuing importance of pastoralism. As we have already related, mobile pastoralists flourished throughout the Early Bronze Age, and they constituted a very important aspect of the economic and social character of the region.

The kin-based tribal-based structure of Euphrates society is accepted also by the Tell Banat researchers, who note that in such a society, while elites or rulers may have been present, they were linked to the rest of the community through kinship ties that permeated many types of social interaction (Porter 2002b: 168). Further, they note that 'kin structures were not negated by the state, nor annulled by increasing sizes of settlement and polity . . . but were actively productive of the state and arrogated by it' (Porter 2002b: 168). Altogether, this form of kin-based structure would have served to 'perpetuate at least a degree of parity among different sectors of society and allowed greater access to decision-making and power-sharing' (Porter 2002b: 168). Such a model of a corporate society, derived from the mortuary remains of Tell Banat, is truly elegant. One wonders how many future funerary findings in the northern Euphrates Valley and perhaps elsewhere, will lend further support to this compelling notion.

DISCUSSION

This overview of the archaeology of death has emphasized a number of important issues that are critical to our understanding of settlement and society in the northern Euphrates River Valley during the Early Bronze Age. We have tried to show how funerary remains not only offer information about this ancient society's beliefs about death and the afterlife, they also help us to understand how Euphrates' society was organized, particularly in terms of its social structure and economy. We have also seen how in some cases the material remains of burials, tomb offerings and the residues of ritual performances did not merely express funerary behaviour. They had transformative power among the living, making and re-defining social roles and cultural practices.

It is clear that a myriad of issues influenced how a deceased individual was to be interred and the kinds of funerary rituals taking place in his or her honour. These issues, which were related to social organization, ethnic identities, economic differentiation, peer polity interaction, age, gender differences and religious beliefs, influenced the types, sizes, layout, and location of tombs. They also had a bearing on the quantity and quality of grave offerings laid inside of the tombs. Together, this variety of burial evidence strongly underlines the complexity of society during the Early Bronze, with its multiplicity of overlapping, competing or complementary relationships, all existing together within densely inhabited urban communities and their surrounding territories.

Tremendous variability occurred in funerary practices from one Euphrates site to another. Thus, no two cemeteries were exactly alike in terms of their burial types, the location of their tombs and the ways in which the dead were interred within them. Even with sites in close proximity to one another, we see tremendous differences in funerary remains and the accompanying mortuary rites they reflect. Such differences stress yet again the independent character of the settlements within this region. While all Euphrates settlements were no doubt bound together by common social and economic structures, as well as beliefs about religion, the gods and the afterlife, the ways in which they specifically interpreted these notions and ideologies and acted upon them were unique and distinctive.

One of the most interesting observations derived from our investigation of Euphrates funerary practices is the notion of the corporate polity, possibly engendered by the strong pastoral, tribal background of many of the region's inhabitants. As we have discussed, this corporate ideology finds reflection in the mortuary remains of Tell Banat, where people's individual identities were removed after they died, to be subsumed within a collective mass of unnamed ancestors. This ancestral worship was focussed primarily on the Mortuary Mounds, these being impressive, white monuments that towered high above the river valley at Tell Banat. By their monumentality they served to strengthen the notion of shared traditions and common kin descent. Although such tumuli at Tell Banat have been the only ones to be positively identified, it is likely that several other such mounds existed, and that these funerary markers and the theme of corporate belonging that they reflect, were well known in the Euphrates Valley.

At the same time as such potent symbols of unity and social parity existed, there was a concurrent tendency within Euphrates society that favoured the growth of social-economic hierarchies, characterized by wealthy and powerful elites. These individuals asserted their prominent status by building impressive tombs for themselves and filling them with a rich assortment of rare and precious grave goods. Monumental shaft and chamber tombs, observed at Tell Banat, Tell Ahmar, Jerablus Tahatani and Tell Hadidi, stand out as excellent examples of elite tombs, and confirm that Euphrates society was not completely immersed within an ideology of collectivity and inclusion. There existed a strong, contrasting element of social inequality in the region as well. This development seems to have reached a peak around Phase 4 (*c.*2450–2300 BC), at precisely a time when settlements were experiencing urban growth, and monumental tombs were most numerous. We cannot be certain of the precise factors that favoured this elite growth, although it is likely that people's increased contact with other regions, made accessible by riverine communications and trade, encouraged this development. The fact that many tomb offerings in the large tombs comprised precious and rare goods obtained from distant lands further supports the strong association between elite growth and far-reaching contacts.

The excavators of Tell Banat, who also recognize the growth of elite power in the Euphrates Valley in the mid-to-late third millennium, have proposed a theory to explain this development, while at the same time acknowledging the continued persistence of a corporate ideology. They argue that to legitimate their claims to power, the elite would have continued to utilize the traditional symbols of social relations, such as the White Monument, in order to emphasize a communal imagery of the idealized past (Porter 2002a: 28). In other words, the elite endeavoured to make their power more palatable by presenting the imagery of community and the continuity of a long-established social system even when such a system was being strongly undermined (Porter 2002b: 170). If this is truly the operating principle at Tell Banat, one can see how potent symbols of community and a corporate social system were used and manipulated, and also how they carried transformative power. These symbols not only reflected social relationships and community ideologies, but actually served to create, perpetuate and transform them.

However fascinating and significant these mortuary practices and funerary traditions were, they eventually came to an end. By Phase 6 at the end of the Early Bronze Age, precious little evidence exists for graves and funerary monuments in the northern Euphrates Valley. The site of Tell Banat had long ceased to be occupied and its mortuary mounds were neglected. By the onset of the Middle Bronze Age in the early second millennium, nearly all of the rich and potent funerary symbols of the dead had been extinguished and forgotten.

10

THE END OF THE EARLY BRONZE AGE: EUPHRATES SETTLEMENT IN DECLINE

Understanding urban collapse in the ancient Near East

The last centuries of the third millennium BC mark an intriguing time in the Near East. Areas that once had flourishing cities and had thrived under effectual political and economic systems, declined dramatically. States succumbed to internal disorder, cities were destroyed or abandoned, and populations were uprooted and displaced. The great empires of southern Mesopotamia and Egypt, which had powerful royal dynasties and far-reaching trade contacts, now fell precipitously. In other areas of the Levant and Northern Mesopotamia, where urban states were smaller and less structurally complex, collapse also occurred. Here cities that had controlled extensive tracts of agricultural and pastoral lands, and had prospered under stable, productive economies, crumbled and eventually disappeared.

Tumultuous upheavals mark this period of collapse, although little is known about the actual events that led up to and took place during this troubled time. The small number of surviving inscriptions that have been recovered give few clear clues about this period of recession. Moreover, obscure or unspectacular architectural and artifactual remains characterize much of this period's archaeological record. It is no wonder that the Near East at this time is frequently referred to as a 'dark age', since the fragmentary and ambiguous nature of the evidence give the period an overall enigmatic and murky quality.

Despite the difficulties presented by this obscure evidence, we should not exclude this period of decline from our study of Bronze Age urban settlement and society. An examination of the ways in which cities experienced collapse contribute as significantly towards our understanding of the settlements' complex and distinctive nature as do studies of their growth and success. It is valuable, therefore, to attempt to comprehend more fully the circumstances that led to urban demise in the Near East. It will be useful to see how cities responded to factors that threatened to weaken their social or economic structures, and how they were able to revive after serious political disruptions. Once we understand these topics, we will be able to understand

and appreciate more fully the true character of an urban settlement. They will shed light on the special attributes that give a settlement its unique cultural distinctiveness, and the mechanisms that enable it to persevere through periods of both prosperity and recession.

Settlement in the Euphrates River Valley of Syria, the main focus of this work, provides an especially interesting and unique example of the rise and demise of Bronze Age urban society. Although human settlement in this region was not immune to the social and economic upheavals that affected many other parts of the Near East at the end of the third millennium BC, it stands out as an interesting example of a society in which several earlier Bronze Age institutions and cultural traditions managed to survive and continued to shape the essential character of Euphrates culture throughout the period of decline and after. Further, although some settlements within the Euphrates Valley were abandoned during this period, several others continued to be inhabited. Finally, only a short time period passed before these communities revived, growing once more into flourishing cities, taking part in brisk trade along the river, and effectively exploiting the agricultural and pastoral potential of their hinterlands.

This chapter will present the archaeological evidence that demonstrates the region's character of continuity and resilience. It will also present explanations of why settlement in the Euphrates River Valley differs from that of other contemporary Near Eastern societies. It will discuss as well the region's environment and the nature of its social, political and economic institutions. This chapter overall will show that an understanding of the essential fabric of an ancient city is facilitated not only by looking at the optimal conditions that led to its growth and prosperity, but also by comprehending its responses to negative forces that weakened its foundations and threatened to bring an end to its very existence.

Near Eastern regions affected by late third millennium collapse

As noted above, we find that several regions of the Near East experienced some form of decline at the end of the third millennium BC. We will now summarize the nature of this decline in each area and briefly describe the form that settlement and society took in the wake of these disruptions.

In the alluvial plains of the Tigris and Euphrates Rivers of southern Mesopotamia, two great empires fell in succession during this period. The house of Akkad, the first imperial power in southern Mesopotamia to consolidate political control over a mosaic of competing city-states and to establish trading opportunities over a vast area of the Near East, came to an end around 2150 BC. This Akkadian Empire was replaced shortly afterwards by the Third Dynasty of Ur, although this state too, characterized as it was by an extremely centralized bureaucracy and overstretched economy, rapidly crumbled around 2000 BC. The once-great capital city of Ur was overrun by foreigners, and the whole empire was thrown into a state of internal chaos and political fragmentation (Yoffee 1988: 46–51).

North of the Tigris-Euphrates flood plain, the region of the *Jezireh* of Upper Mesopotamia, essentially comprising the Khabur Plains of north-eastern Syria and the Sinjar Plain of northern Iraq, underwent a similar crisis towards the end of the third millennium BC. Up to this point in time, the area had been pursuing a regime of agricultural maximization, no doubt precipitated by the growth of large urban settlements. Extensive manuring (evidenced by widespread sherd scatters) and a multitude of linear hollows, interpreted as roadways radiating out from settlements to the fields, are believed to reflect the intensity of agricultural production that took place during this period (Wilkinson 1994: 492–3). Around 2200 BC, however, the area experienced a dramatic reduction in this intensified dry-farming agricultural regime, about the same time that Akkadian imperial control in this region began to weaken (Weiss and Courty 1993). While recent archaeological evidence at sites like Tell Brak and Tell Mozan indicate that some urban settlements survived after this time (Oates *et al.* 2001: 393[1]), overall an appreciable reduction in the number of occupied sites, in addition to a pattern of contracting settlement, appear as the prevailing trend in the *Jezireh* between 2200–1900 BC (Weiss and Courty 1993: 141; Peltenburg 2000: 164–5). This change may have been brought about by a large-scale population emigration, in which human groups moved towards southern Mesopotamia via the Euphrates River valley in their quest for reliable food and pasturage (Weiss and Courty 1993: 144). Alternatively, it is possible that many of the inhabitants adapted successfully to pastoralism, and that such a transformation left sparse remains in the archaeological record (Peltenburg 2000: 180).

Still other regions of the Near East were affected by collapse at the end of the third millennium. In Egypt, this period is marked by the end of the prosperous Old Kingdom, and its replacement by the First Intermediate Period, a time of political fragmentation and decentralization (Morris in press). In most areas to the west of the Jordan River in Palestine, as early as 2300 BC, the Early Bronze III urban centres were destroyed or abandoned, and the stable productive subsistence systems, based on intensified agriculture, industry and trade, ceased to operate (Richard 1987: 34; Dever 1989: 228). In the Early Bronze IV period that followed, the region experienced a kind of 'ruralization', in which a diversified subsistence economy based on small-scale farming and pastoral nomadism prevailed for several centuries (Palumbo 2001: 237).

Several reasons for the collapse of urban centres have been put forward by those studying archaeological and textual data from different parts of the ancient Near East, two of which are examined here. One of these theories takes into account the impact of the natural environment on the growth or deterioration of an ancient human society. The other hypothesis, which concerns a Near Eastern 'world economy', emphasizes the multi-dimensional, interactive character of most human societies. In these 'general systems' perspectives, changes or disruptions that take place in one part of an interconnected network of political and economic systems can seriously affect other parts of that network as well.

Climatic change

The first hypothesis put forth to explain why the Near East became engulfed in a 'time of troubles' in the late Early Bronze period is climatic change. This is described as consisting specifically of increased aridity, decreases in available sources of water and drops in flood levels along major rivers. Such changes may have had a sufficiently debilitating effect to bring about catastrophe to Near Eastern political systems, especially in environmentally fragile regions where a constant and stable climate was essential if agricultural regimes were to survive and flourish.

Several people who study the collapse of the Old Kingdom and the following two centuries of instability of the First Intermediate Period in Egypt support this hypothesis. B. Bell (1971), drawing heavily from existing palaeo-climatic data and historical texts from Egypt, argues that a 'Great Drought' took place between 2200–2000 BC. She refers to the work of K. Butzer, who reported the end of a moist interlude in Egypt around 2350 BC, after which increasing aridity set in. Bell also refers to textual evidence surviving from the First Intermediate Period, which includes no less than 20 references to famine. The texts describe not only people dying of hunger, but also provincial governors dispensing grain to the hungry, sending shipments to assist neighbouring polities and modifying irrigation canals in order to convey water to otherwise parched and useless agricultural fields (Morris in press). It is significant too, that during this period, artistic representations in Egyptian tombs no longer illustrate desert fauna and trees, perhaps suggesting that desert life had become depleted by this time (Kemp 1983: 179).

There has recently been both questioning of and support for the hypothesis of a change in climate. First, Butzer's most recent consideration of the geological, climatic and historical data has weakened the significance of climatic change, at least in the case of the Old Kingdom of Egypt (Butzer 1997). His study draws on evidence of water levels at Lake Turkana in Kenya, the source of the Blue Nile. The lake dropped in level between 2750–2200 BC, rose again abruptly around 2150–2050, dipped again and rose once more around 1600 BC. This pattern is complemented by findings based on lake cores taken from both Lake Turkana and the northeastern Nile Delta, that point to a lower water level towards the end of the third millennium. Interesting data also appear in the Fayum Depression to the west, which was linked to the nearby Nile floodplain by a secondary channel. There lakes were supported by an influx of Nile flood waters, with recessions during periods of lower floods. Analyses of these lake levels show that the floods were high between 3100–2900 BC, then lower, with a short-lived minimum around 2200 BC.

These convincing data might suggest climatic deterioration at the end of the third millennium BC (c. 2200 BC). Butzer, however, points out that the lowest flood levels are contemporary with the First Intermediate Period of the eighth and ninth dynasties, but not with the dynasties of the Old Kingdom some two centuries earlier (Butzer 1997: 258). It was at this time that Egyptian civilization actually began its dramatic collapse. Thus Butzer, seeking an explanation other than climatic change, suggests that internal factors in Egypt, such as the increasing territorial holdings and the wealth of the temple estates that were exempt from taxation, and greater administrative autonomy within the provinces, served to weaken the centralized government. The final fatal blow may have come from the over-long reign of the last pharaoh of the sixth dynasty, Pepi II (c. 2330–2240 BC). At his death, the Egyptian state promptly disintegrated, with power devolving to strong local families in the provinces, and pharaonic authority dissolving completely (Butzer 1997: 258). Destabilizing factors of this kind within Egyptian society itself were sufficient to account for the country's decline, in Butzer's view.

But the climatic theory still has its adherents. They include Harvey Weiss and his colleagues, whose analyses of soil deposition in archaeological contexts in northeastern Syria have been especially influential in promoting climatic change as a prime cause of urban collapse (Weiss *et al.* 1993). Micromorphological soil studies of excavated strata from the site of Tell Leilan in the Khabur Plains and elsewhere in the *Jezireh* of Upper Mesopotamia have isolated late third millennium desertion levels containing tephra fallout along with other soil profiles that point to marked environmental deterioration. From these data, Weiss argues that, in addition to a dramatic volcanic event occurring at the end of the Akkadian occupation of Tell Leilan, an abrupt climatic change occurred, bringing about a rapid intensification of wind circulation, an increase in atmospheric dust and the establishment of arid conditions (Weiss and Courty 1993: 143). Weiss believes that this change in climate was not a local phenomenon, but was of global proportions, affecting many regions of the Old World. In the case of Greater Mesopotamia, he argues that such climatic severity not only brought about the abandonment of the North Mesopotamian Plain but also the fall of the Akkadian Empire in the south and synchronous political collapse in adjacent regions. He also finds compelling support for this dramatic event in contemporary Mesopotamian literature in the form of references to 'drought, harvest failure, decreased Euphrates flow, wind turbulence, and a variety of atmospheric aberrations that suggest volcanic activity, including "flaming" potsherds raining from the sky' (Weiss 2000: 209).

Weiss' assumptions, however, have been challenged. Critics have pointed out anomalies and inconsistencies in his climatic data, questioning in particular his suggestion of an association between a volcanic eruption and a global climatic change. Such an explosive event finds little support in published ice corings from Greenland and deep-sea cores in the eastern Mediterranean (Butzer 1997: 250). The latest research by M.-A. Courty on micromorphological studies of soil layers elsewhere in the Khabur Plains of the *Jezireh* has further undermined this argument (Courty 2001). In her study of dust fallout in third millennium BC contexts at the site of Tell Brak, Courty has pushed back the date of some sort of cataclysmic occurrence to 2350 BC. The original, erroneous date of 2200 BC for this event, based on her study of Tell Leilan dust levels, is now explained as the result of the soil having been recovered from secondary fills instead of primary contexts. Further, she emphasizes that this remarkable event was more likely to have been caused by some cosmic impact, possibly the explosion of a bolide in the atmosphere, rather than by fallout from a volcano. Whatever the nature of the event, it cannot be seen to be related to the dramatic climatic change that is argued to have taken place around 2200 BC.

The discussion above shows that climatic data obtained from Egypt and Upper Mesopotamia fails to provide an agreed-upon date for a climatic change. Its significance as a factor causing urban decline in this period has also been questioned. Other factors within the society may more convincingly account for increased instability and decline at this time.

What extensive climatic data from both Egypt and Upper Mesopotamia all agree upon, however, is that some form of climatic deterioration occurred in the Near East between approximately 2350 and 2200 BC. This period of 150 years coincides well with the time during which upheavals in many parts of the Near East occurred. Although we hesitate in light of this evidence to make climatic change the major cause of collapse, we can suggest that climatic fluctuations, occurring simultaneously with other debilitating elements in an urban society or state, had the effect of worsening an already-weakened system. Future studies may add confirmation to climatic change as significant at this time.

Collapse of a 'world economy'

A second hypothesis put forth to explain the major changes we are discussing is essentially an economic one. Butzer emphasizes the importance of inter-regional connections in both the rise and decline of political economies during the third millennium BC. He speaks of a form of 'world economy' existing at this time, which consisted of a web of inter-related polities and economies. When this web was strong, centres flourished around the Near East, but when it weakened, the centres declined and outlying rural communities grew in their place (Butzer 1997: 280–7).

With such a network of interconnecting systems, regions like Palestine and Egypt could have been affected simultaneously. Events in both areas suggest possible changes of this sort. During the Old Kingdom in Egypt, the pharaohs' insatiable desire for luxury goods led to a monopoly of foreign trade with Palestine. Their demand was for wine and oil, and also timber, fir resin and Dead Sea asphalt. In face of such a demand, Palestine increased its production of the sought-after commodities. Intensification of agriculture and the growth of populations and cities ensued, especially where trade networks were particularly strong (along the coast, for example). But when this strong economic link was severed as the result of Egyptian militarism and its misguided decision to enforce hegemony over Palestine at all costs, Palestinian towns collapsed. As they ceased to flourish, synchronous economic turmoil arose in Egypt, with its already-faltering monarchy. Since Egypt's trade monopoly and profits had ended, the pharaohs were now deprived of the currency of power just when they needed it the most (Butzer 1997: 260).

At the same time elsewhere in the Levant, Butzer suggests that the destruction by the rulers of Akkad of the important coastal city of Byblos precipitated even further economic decline in Egypt. Since Byblos was the country's most profitable port of trade in the Near East, its fall would have cut off the country completely from the Near Eastern exchange network and possibly even from points further afield, such as the Aegean and Anatolia. The Akkadian conquest of Byblos, as well as of the rest of Syria, would have inevitably led to an inability on the part of Akkad itself to generate capital, leaving it economically weakened as well (Butzer 1997: 282).

We can see that damage to any part of the Near Eastern exchange network would have led to the breakdown and collapse of most or all of the regions that belonged to this interconnected web. In our view, this hypothesis offers a most compelling explanation for the decline of urban society that can be observed at the end of the third millennium BC.

While the hypotheses we have described can never be proven, their value is still considerable, particularly for the study of the Euphrates Valley of Syria, the principal focus of this work. They assist, for example, in underlining the impact that climatic and environmental stresses may have on the essential livelihood of a society. They also highlight the need to understand both the social and economic structures of societies and the nature and degree of these polities' economic and political interconnections with other regions and states. It may never be possible to explain what led to significant decline in the Near East, but awareness of factors that may affect settlement histories and human culture can help us to understand more fully a region's development and demise. We can formulate ways in which a region may have responded and adapted to such factors. We can then suggest why a region either collapses entirely under the weight of destabilizing or disruptive forces, or alternatively, how it is able to withstand these forces and successfully regenerate itself.

Northern Euphrates valley settlement

We turn now to the developments and alterations that took place within ancient settlements in the northern Euphrates River Valley of Syria in the last centuries of the third millennium BC. Archaeological records provide much of the evidence for these transformations. This section will consider how these changes compare with those experienced in other parts of the Near East in decline at the same time. It will suggest factors that may be responsible for some of the differences or similarities observed within these regions. Our argument will be that while urban decline existed as a Near East-wide phenomenon at the end of the third millennium, it took many different forms in individual regions. The Euphrates Valley of Syria stands out as an intriguing and noteworthy example of this variegated phenomenon. We will highlight how an awareness of the environmental, socio-political and economic elements of the Euphrates River Valley, forming the fabric of human society and giving shape to its unique cultural character, help to evaluate this region's responses, successful or not, to the forces of time and change.

Settlement abandonment, discontinuity and decline

During the last centuries of the third millennium BC, several large towns or cities along the river, which had once supported sizeable populations and were often characterized by fortification systems, large-scale secular build-ings, funerary monuments and densely inhabited domestic quarters, were abandoned. The site of Jerablus Tahtani, for example, which in the mid-Early Bronze Age had a city wall and protective rampart, textile and metal manufacturing installations, grain processing and storage facilities, as well as a prominent burial monument in the form of a tomb enclosed by a tumulus, was abandoned. The tell was not re-occupied again until the Late Iron Age (Peltenburg *et al.* 1995: 14–15). While the excavators of Jerablus Tahtani do not posit a date for this abandonment, a comparison of the late Early Bronze pottery from this site and other Euphrates' sites whose relative dates are reasonably secure, suggests that its final occupation was around 2200 BC, or sometime during Phase 5 according to our Euphrates sequence.

Another instance of abandonment is the great mortuary centre of Tell Banat on the eastern bank of the Euphrates River. Even as early as 2300 BC at the end of Phase 4, this site, which had once supported several large tombs, a related large-scale building, and associated pottery manufactory, was des-erted. Around the same time, the nearby monolithic tumulus known as the White Monument ceased to be maintained (Porter and McClellan 1998; Porter 2002a: 12).

The site of Selenkahiye, which possessed an elite residence as well as housing, workshops and a city wall, seems to have survived somewhat longer than Jerablus Tahtani and Tell Banat. It appears to have been deserted around 2100–2000 BC, during Phase 5, judging by its latest pottery (Van Loon 2001).

It is significant that an even greater number of other sites along the Euphrates River were not abandoned, although they too appear to have been affected by the widespread tide of collapse. Such sites are characterized by a considerable diminishment in their settlement size, and/or the disuse of large-scale buildings and fortifications, and accompanied in some cases by destruction by fire. At the site of Tell Kabir, for example, the Early Bronze long-roomed temple *in antis*, went out of use, and after a time its walls collapsed (Porter 1995b: 130). Dug into this bricky collapse were four large storage pits, in which were found good examples of late third millennium pottery (Phase 5: 2300–2100 BC). Following this, and dating to Phase 6, only domestic architecture characterized this sector of the settlement (Porter 1995b: 143–52).

At the site of Halawa Tell A, the Early Bronze Phases 3c and 3b at that site (equivalent to Phases 3–5) featured a sizeable residential district, a city wall and a long-roomed temple *in antis*. In contrast, the succeeding phase 3a, which dates to Phase 6 at the very end of the Early Bronze Age, was characterized by an absence of fortifications and monumental architecture. The remains of flimsy walls, or re-used older walls defined the nature of occupation. Associated with these modest architectural features were storage silos, small fireplaces, *tannours*, and irregular working surfaces made of clay, pebbles and plastered material (Orthmann 1989: 55).

The settlement history of Tell es-Sweyhat presents a similar picture of decline. This site had actually enjoyed its fluorescence quite late in the third millennium, even after other centres such as Tell Banat and Jerablus Tahtani had ceased to be occupied. During this time, which corresponds to Phase 5, the site was composed of a fortified citadel on the central mound, and a large lower town enclosed by a wall (Zettler 1997a: 4). The site may have reached a size as large as 40 ha (Danti and Zettler 1998: 213). Consequently, however, this settlement shrank dramatically in size, continuing to exist now only on the central mound, while the important elite function of the citadel buildings appears to have been discontinued after they were abandoned or destroyed by fire (Holland 1976: 51; Armstrong and Zettler 1997: 27). The last phases of the late third millennium occupation at Sweyhat (Phase 6 according to our Euphrates sequence) are represented by layers of ash and flimsy architectural remains, largely the remnants of domestic dwellings (Armstrong and Zettler 1997: 27–8).

Tell Hadidi had been an impressive Early Bronze Age site along the Euphrates, characterized by both an extensive lower town composed of tightly spaced houses along a long street, and a central acropolis mound (Dornemann 1979: 116). Elite individuals at the settlement were buried in monumental chamber tombs located in various sectors of the lower town

(Dornemann 1979: 117–18). During its zenith in the Early Bronze Age, Tell Hadidi grew in size to around 56 ha, making it one of the largest known settlements in the northern Euphrates Valley of Syria (Dornemann 1979: 116; McClellan 1999: 413). The presence of smaller EB villages in the vicinity of Tell Hadidi as well as several roadways radiating out from the site and even crossing over to the other side of the Euphrates, testify further to Tell Hadidi's prominence in the third millennium (Wilkinson 2004: 133). Around 2000 BC during Phase 6, however, the settlement appears to have undergone a dramatic diminishment of size after a major destruction. The lower town was abandoned altogether, and occupation became limited to the area of the main acropolis mound only (Dornemann 1985: 50–1). There is no evidence that Tell Hadidi was characterized by anything other than simple domestic housing during this period of 'collapse'.

In sum, archaeological evidence testifies to a region-wide collapse of settlements at the end of EB, marked by the complete abandonment of sites, or a dramatic reduction in site size and settlement complexity. Along with this, urban centres and their dependencies of farming and pastoral communities no longer flourished from economic exchanges with one another or through the intensive agricultural and pastoral exploitation of their hinterlands. By the end of the third millennium, the northern Euphrates region had devolved into a ruralized landscape of small self-sufficient village-size settlements. Each community functioned at a very simple political and economic level of organization. Settlements were now composed chiefly of domestic housing, and simple food-producing and food-processing activities now served to meet the needs of those small communities only.

While the decline in settlement in the Northern Euphrates Valley in Syria at the end of the third millennium cannot be overlooked, however, one must also take note of the success with which this region was able to regenerate itself at the beginning of the Middle Bronze Age in the early second millennium. It was only a short period of time, perhaps no more than a century, before this region once again featured large settlements strung out along the banks of the river, each growing in prosperity through the successful exploitation of the natural resources of their surrounding territory and taking part in the brisk commercial trade which had resumed along the river from north to south, and overland, from east to west. What is even more striking is that considerable cultural continuity appears to have existed throughout, with many aspects of the material culture from the Early Bronze Age developing smoothly into the subsequent Middle Bronze period, despite the interval of collapse that separated these two periods. Further, combined archaeological and textual evidence suggests that the same fundamental aspects of Euphrates urban government and economic structures re-surfaced after the period of collapse. In summary, in spite of widespread turmoil and weakness that gripped many parts of the Near East at the end of the Early Bronze Age, the culture of the Northern Euphrates Valley shows itself to be remarkably resilient, being able to withstand successfully considerable stresses to its political fabric and subsistence economy, regenerating itself smoothly and changing little in its essential core over an extended period of time.

Resiliency and cultural continuity

The following observations provide details of the evidence that supports an overall trend of resiliency and cultural continuity from the Early to Middle Bronze Ages.

As mentioned above, several sites, although experiencing some diminishment in size and the discontinuation of public buildings, elite tombs, industrial manufactories and fortifications at the very end of the Early Bronze Age, show no signs of having been completely destroyed or abandoned. On the contrary, these sites appear to be characterized by a continuous and unbroken sequence of occupational phases that carry through from the end of the Early Bronze Age into the Middle Bronze Age. Sites with such settlement continuity include Tell Amarna (Tunca 1999: 130–1; Pons 2001: 41–2),[2] Shiyukh Tahtani (Falsone 1998: 25; 1999: 138), Tell Ahmar (Roobaert and Bunnens 1999: 164–6), Qara Quzaq (Valdés Pereiro 1999: 118–19, 2001: 120), Tell Kabir (Porter 1995b), Tell es-Sweyhat (Holland 1976: 49–63; 1977: 37–43; Armstrong and Zettler 1997: 19–28; Cooper 1997: 24–6), Tell Hadidi (Dornemann 1979; 1985: 50–6), Munbaqa (Werner 1998: 38–48), Halawa Tell A (Orthmann 1981; 1989), Tell Habuba Kabira (Heusch 1980: 168–77), and Emar (Finkbeiner 1999–2000; 2002: 128–30).[3]

The time between the demise of the urban polities at the end of the EB during Phase 6 and their regenerated forms in the Middle Bronze Age appears to have been very short, perhaps no more than 100 years. This is evidenced, for the most part, by the fact that many of the new foundations of MB structures were set directly on top of the remnants of earlier EB buildings. One can note this phenomenon at Halawa Tell A, for example, where the MB inhabitants even re-used the foundations of the earlier EB buildings, integrating the remains into the foundations of their own new houses (Orthmann 1989: 23). It is also interesting to note that at Halawa, in the case of at least one sector of the city, the function of that quarter remained the same. Quadrant Q, which in the EB was the principal domestic area of the settlement, continued in that capacity into the Middle Bronze Age, implying that the later inhabitants were well aware of the configuration of the earlier settlement, and retained that layout (Orthmann 1989: 22).

At Habuba Kabira, the continued existence and use of several mudbrick walls through occupational phases attributed to both the end of the EB and the early MB have been noted, indicating that a short period had passed between these periods (Heinrich et al. 1969: 48). Continuity in architecture can also be observed in the form of part of Habuba Kabira's fortification walls, which feature a distinctive inset-offset pattern of buttresses and recesses in the latest EB levels (Heusch 1980: 174–5). This type of wall construction may also have existed along the northern fortification walls of the EB settlement of Selenkahiye, where short bastions or small buttress-like jumps have been observed (Van Loon 2001: 3.87). Interestingly, this architectural features manifests itself again in the regenerated settlement of Munbaqa, where the long, well preserved stretch of the MB town wall features a strikingly similar pattern of alternating buttresses and recesses (Machule *et al.* 1993: 76–7).

As a last example of EB–MB continuity, a long-roomed temple *in antis* structure at the site of Munbaqa (Steinbau 1) was excavated on the summit of the mound. Its original foundations appear to have been constructed back in the Early Bronze Age, when the building featured a small cult room with stepped podium (Orthmann and Kühne 1974: 59–65). Consequently the temple remained as an important religious centre through the Middle and Late Bronze Ages, indicated by the number of alterations and restorations performed in subsequent building phases (Heinrich *et al.* 1974: 11–45). Again, such evidence highlights the degree of occupational and architectural continuity, not to mention an unbroken sequence of religious-cultural traditions.

Cultural continuity is readily observable in the pottery assemblages from the Early to Middle Bronze Ages. Rather than revealing a sharp and abrupt break in stylistic traditions and technology between these two periods, the Euphrates ceramic sequence indicates a smooth, unbroken development of vessel types from one cultural phase to the next. To be sure, there is evidence that many of the finer, thin-walled and highly fired wares of the assemblage, such as caliciform cups, experience a dramatic drop in frequency in the last centuries of the third millennium BC, concurrent with Phase 6, the last phase of the EB (Cooper 1999: 324). Still other decorated Euphrates Fine Wares, characterized by red painted bands and spiral burnishing, cease to exist altogether in Phases 5 and 6 of the EB. These wares are absent, for example, in the assemblage of the Area IV 'Burned Building' at Tell es-Sweyhat, which can be dated later than 2150 BC, in Phase 5 (Holland 1976; 1977; Armstrong and Zettler 1997: 25). They are also absent in the Period II 'pit' phase at Tell Kabir, which is contemporary with or slightly later than the Area IV occupation at Tell es-Sweyhat (Porter 1995b: 139–43). Last, one can observe that MB vessels are somewhat thicker walled and coarser than EB pots. The MB assemblage also possesses fewer ware categories and fewer varieties of surface decoration.

Despite these changes, however, one can still observe that several EB vessel forms continue throughout the last years of the collapse at the end of the Early Bronze Age and persist or evolve gradually into the subsequent regenerated occupation phases of the Middle Bronze Age (Chapter 1 above, Cooper 1998: figure 1–2). Some technological aspects of the Euphrates pottery also exhibit considerable continuity. Cooking pots – which in Phase 6 of the EB were carefully finished on the wheel and characterized by simple out-turned rounded rims and a calcite tempered fabric – continued to be produced with the same technological and morphological character-istics well into the Middle Bronze Age, where they persist as the standard northern Euphrates cooking vessel (Cooper 1999: 324). We see, therefore, that the developments observed in the pottery assemblage of the Northern Euphrates Valley demonstrate the same degree of change, whether by evolu-tion or transformation, that would characterize any ceramic tradition of a continuously occupied region over an extended period of time.

Yet other evidence for continuity in the Bronze Age is found in the politi-cal make-up of settlements in the Euphrates Valley. The archaeological data show that the political configuration of settlements in the Euphrates Valley was quite similar before and after the period of collapse that separated the EB and MB. In the Early Bronze Age, the region comprised a number of autonomous cities, characterized by rather densely populated centres that were surrounded by tracts of agricultural fields and grazing land and some-times featured smaller satellite communities. Each of these urban polities would essentially have been politically and economically independent of one another. Few of these sites have yielded more than a small number of administrative artifacts and other material evidence that indicate any signifi-cant authority or influence from the important yet distant urban centres of Ebla and Mari, constantly vying, according to inscriptions, for control of this particular stretch of the river (Astour 1992: 26–51). To be sure, the dearth of archaeological evidence for control from Ebla and Mari should caution us from positing too many historical reconstructions through these textual sources alone. What may have been perceived as definite military and eco-nomic successes in this region among the authorities of these two great centres, may have actually been regarded as something quite different by the local inhabitants of the region in question.

During the Middle Bronze Age, the same configuration of urban settle-ments appears to have re-emerged, each with its own control over land and other resources. To date, no archaeological evidence suggests that any one settlement exercised political and economic authority or control over the others. Again, however, contemporary cuneiform sources from Mari may dis-tort this picture somewhat. These texts suggest that this stretch of the Euphrates River may have formed the border between the states of Mari, Yamhad and Carchemish, and that settlements and populations along its banks were firmly under the control of one of these polities. Nonetheless, archaeological investigation of these sites has failed to produce any tangible evidence for such political configurations (for a full discussion, see Cooper 1997: 332–47; 2001: 79–86).

What we see thus far is that while some Euphrates urban settlements were abandoned, contracted in size and diminished in complexity at the end of the Early Bronze Age, the region did not collapse and wither altogether. On the contrary, several features testify to a strong, unbroken cultural continuity and the persistence of social and political structures across several centuries of urban fluorescence, decline and regeneration. This phenomenon becomes especially striking when it is compared to the developments that have been documented in other regions of the ancient Near East from the same time period, such as Palestine and the Khabur Plains of northeastern Syria, where severe and long-lasting settlement disruptions and cultural discontinuities occurred.

What accounts for this high degree of continuity and resilience in the Euphrates Valley of Syria? What factors existing within this region and among its inhabitants could have prompted these trends, setting the region apart from other areas of the Near East? While there are almost certainly a multitude of factors bearing on this issue, three key, somewhat inter-related features, can best account for this unique situation.

Environment

First, the environment played an important role in the way in which the settlements developed in the Northern Euphrates Valley. As we have already discussed, studies indicate this region falls at the southern limit of the semi-arid transitional zone between the desert steppe and the better-watered lands of northern and western Syria. This particular stretch of the Euphrates Valley was, therefore, something of a marginal land, in which dry framing, although possible, was precarious, and where pastoralism as well as other forms of food production, constituted critical parts of the subsistence economy (Zettler 1997a: 2). Thus, for successful survival in this marginal environment, a diversified subsistence economy was necessary. Recent palaeobotanical and faunal analyses confirm this assumption.

In and around the site of Tell es-Sweyhat, for example, there is ample evidence for the herding of sheep and goats in the steppe behind the river valley, even during the flourishing of Sweyhat's urban phase in the twenty-second century BC. Moreover, the percentage of wild animal remains, particularly onager and gazelle, reaches a maximum when the population of the city was at its highest (Weber 1997: 141–2). Both types of evidence, therefore, underline the varied subsistence in this region, even in times of stability and relative prosperity. As a result of this varied, flexible economy, when the Euphrates Valley was faced with the disintegration of a centralized urban authority or climatic deterioration, the diversity of its subsistence base enabled the remnant population to adapt itself accordingly. Consequently, the return to a more prosperous economy and stable political system would have occurred swiftly and smoothly. This situation appears in marked con-trast to the agricultural regimes that appear to have characterized Western Palestine in the Early Bronze III period and the Khabur Plains of Upper

Mesopotamia. These areas had concentrated intensively on one form of subsistence (namely agriculture) over any others. As a result, when negative forces came into play, either in the form of climate change or political instability, these regimes lacked the flexibility to withstand such stresses, and rapidly withered. This lack of flexibility might then explain why these regions experienced long 'dark ages' in the last centuries of the third millennium before their eventual rejuvenation in the Middle Bronze Age.

Site autonomy

Second, the fact that the settlements of the Euphrates Valley were largely autonomous, never under the rigid control of a greater political authority over the duration of the Early and Middle Bronze Ages, may also help to explain their high degree of resilience and cultural continuity. Individual settlements or city-states were not intimately tied to the fate, successful or otherwise, of a higher, centralized power. Again, the Khabur Plains region provides an interesting counterpoint to this situation. Since this region had come under the control of the expanding Akkadian empire, it enjoyed increased prosperity and grew in complexity (Weiss and Courty 1993: 139–41). But this very dependence may have led to its downfall. When the Akkadian Empire broke apart, settlement in the Khabur Plains crumbled along with it. In contrast, in the environment found in the Euphrates Valley, where settlements were autonomous and economically self-sufficient, their ability both to withstand stresses and to encourage growth was much greater. They depended heavily on the abilities of their individual inhabitants. This feature of the Euphrates settlements may help to explain why they managed to bear the hardships of the period and to adapt themselves accordingly.

Tribal character

A third important feature of these settlements is their persistent tribal character throughout the Early and Middle Bronze Ages. While Euphrates settlements expanded into large centres at times of stability and prosperity, they never adopted what can be considered full state systems, typically characterized by the presence of recognizable economic, political and ritual hierarchies, and dominant ruling strata, as opposed to commoner strata, within a closed, urban environment. On the contrary, the population appears to have been continuously defined by loosely organized confederacies of both agrarian and pastoral nomadic kin-groups. Membership in these groups transcended the boundaries of individual centres or specific places of residence. Their political relationships encouraged the dissemination of power across the community rather than being concentrated in the hands of a few elite individuals.

As we have described earlier (Chapter 2 above), the type of political

271

organization posited here agrees well with what Blanton and his colleagues call a 'corporate' political system which is more group-oriented, with power being shared across different groups and sectors of society (Blanton *et al.* 1996: 2; Fleming 2004: 177). This system seems to have co-existed with the more well known 'exclusionary' system that centres on individual leadership and the absolute control of sources of power. Turning to the archaeological record, convincing evidence among Euphrates settlements of Syria during both the Early and Middle Bronze Age supports this social-political configuration in which both 'exclusionary' and 'corporate' power co-existed. The third millennium monumental stone tombs and tumuli of Jerablus Tahtani, Tell Ahmar and Tell Banat, for example, surely testify to the presence of elites, whose wealth and labour resources no doubt assisted in the construction and accommodation of these lavish funerary monuments. But, as Anne Porter has observed among the graves and mortuary mounds of Tell Banat, many interments contained disarticulated human bones in secondary burials, and the lack of differentiation between burials and groups of burials do not 'express the individuation of specific members of the groups, their status or position, but rather highlight the corporate nature of the deceased' (Porter 2002b: 166).

Although archaeological investigations at Euphrates' sites have uncovered considerable architectural evidence for the Early and Middle Bronze Ages, few excavations have uncovered large buildings that can be considered true 'royal' residences. In the Early Bronze Age, we have already noted that only three sites have revealed the presence of secular elite buildings of any kind. These consisted of Buildings 6 and 7 at Tell Banat, the Southern Mansion at the site of Selenkahiye (Van Loon 2001: 3.35–3.42), and the 'Burned Building' and associated 'building complex' on the central mound at Tell es-Sweyhat (Holland 1977: 36–43; Danti and Zettler 2002: 39). In these cases it is hard to connect such buildings to the presence of an overarching royal dynasty within the community. Buildings 6 and 7 at Tell Banat were not overly imposing structures within the settlement. Because the buildings were not located on high ground or an acropolis, they did not dominate the site (Porter 2002b: 167). Neither of the elite structures at Selenkahiye or Tell es-Sweyhat are especially monumental or palatial in plan. The excavators suggest that Selenkahiye's central authority was probably limited in power. Not only does the town wall show a haphazard layout with changes in orientation and building technique from one sector to another, its actual construction was also left to individual quarters or blocks of the settlement (Van Loon 2001: 3.110). At Tell es-Sweyhat, the large, multi-roomed warehouse comprises evidence for grain storage, metalworking and an administrative artifact (an inscribed weight). But, as we have discussed, while this building reflects the presence of a wealthy elite in the city, none of its features necessitates the presence of a superordinate authority with highly centralized, absolute control over the surrounding city and hinterland. It has also been noted that the layout and furniture of the recently excavated 'building complex' on the high mound at Tell es-Sweyhat suggest that this structure may have served as a gathering place for the elders of the city, not the residence of a royal individual (Danti and Zettler 2002: 39).

In the case of the Middle Bronze Age, excavations to date have failed to uncover any elite structures that might be connected with a centralized authority or king. Although there is evidence of substantial fortifications (Tell Hadidi, Munbaqa and Emar), quarters of domestic housing (Halawa Tell A, Tell Habuba Kabira, and Emar) and storage facilities (Qara Quzaq) at these regenerated Middle Bronze Age sites, no palatial-style residences have yet been unearthed.

Textual sources also provide evidence that kingship was absent or strongly limited. We have already mentioned the presence in the letters of the Mari Archives of a collective decision-making assembly of elders called the *tahtamum* that prevailed in cities such as Tuttul and Emar on the Euphrates River (Chapter 2 above). It would appear that in some cities these elders served as the official governing body that decided town affairs in the absence of a local individual chief or king (Fleming 2004: 195–200). The *tahtamum* are well attested in the Euphrates region during the Middle Bronze Age (Durand 1989: 27–44), while the occurrence of the term *tahtamum* at third millennium Ebla seems to support the existence of this institution in the earlier Early Bronze Age too (Fleming 2004: 214).

Other textual sources provide indications that a strong tribe-based society characterized the Euphrates region. From the Mari tablets of the Middle Bronze Age, we learn that even the urban leaders identified themselves not only with the city over which they ruled, but with the tribal family to which they belonged. Zimri-Lim, for example, titled himself not as 'king of Mari' but also as 'king of the Haneans', thus stressing his nomadic tribal affiliation (Schwartz 1995: 255). While this inscriptional material derives mostly from the Euphrates Valley further downstream at Mari, the fact that the territorial limits of these tribal groups are known to have extended well to the north, suggests that such tribal ascriptions may have been prevalent among the populations of the northern Euphrates Valley as well.

There is, therefore, compelling archaeological and textual evidence for the persistence of a tribal-based socio-political structure among the Euphrates communities of the Early and Middle Bronze Ages. This tribal organization probably had the effect of curbing or hindering the growth of highly centralized urban polities characterized by ruling dynasties and rigid social hierarchies. Although the existence of such strong decentralizing forces meant that this region never enjoyed the heights of political power and economic prosperity, it probably also meant that it would never experience the kinds of precipitous or violent collapses to which tightly structured and rigidly organized state systems are highly susceptible.

This phenomenon may be both analogous and somewhat related to the region's adaptation to its environment, as described above. The Euphrates' subsistence economy was flexible and varied, and enabled its communities to adapt successfully to prevailing environmental conditions in difficult times. So the same can also be said for the socio-political structure of such communities, whose loosely organized and heterarchical political relationships gave them a highly elastic character, thus enabling them to modify their social and political structures to suit the conditions in which they found themselves. In the conditions prevailing at the end of the third millennium BC, therefore, the local communities of the Euphrates River, despite experiencing forces that threatened to bring an end to their economies and way of life, were able to develop strategies which ensured their continued existence and carried them through them to more stable times, making the task of rebuilding and revitalizing their communities a relatively straightforward process.

Jordan: a parallel instance?

The findings and conclusions for the Euphrates Valley of Syria seem to parallel closely those recently proposed for the Transjordan during the Early Bronze IV period (c. 2350–2000 BC). Like the Euphrates Valley, we do not see in the Transjordan a complete and dramatic shift from an urban landscape with an intensified agricultural economy to a complete absence of cities and few sedentary, farming communities, as has sometimes been posited for Western Palestine (Dever 1995: 291). On the contrary, the Early Bronze IV period of the Transjordan comprised a myriad of small sedentary sites, a few villages and at least one fortified 'town' (Palumbo 2001: 240–6). Furthermore, technological and provenience studies of the material cultural assemblages from several of these sites have highlighted the degree of specialized production and technological innovations that developed at the village level during this time, despite the absence of large towns or cities and the kinds of complex production processes and exchange nodes they might be expected to facilitate (Falconer 1994; Palumbo 2001: 253–7).

Essentially, what is highlighted in the Transjordan for the Bronze Age is the persistence and resilience of human settlement at the village level, which is seen as the strongest and most enduring socio-economic entity in this region. In this ruralized landscape of autonomous villages, a diversified, flexible economy was prevalent, and it gave the population the adaptive ability to shift from one type of productive strategy to another, as circumstances dictated (Marfoe 1979: 8; Palumbo 2001: 260). As for cities, in this 'heartland of villages' (Falconer 1987), they are to be viewed as exceptional entities on a fundamentally rural system, and, while economic complexity and social stratification become more pronounced during periods of urbanism, the underlying village core, with its kin-based structure and diversified, flexible economy, remained essentially stable and intact.

Overall the conclusions reached for the Transjordan parallel quite favourably the Syrian Euphrates River Valley, especially when one considers the strong continuity that is manifested in the Euphrates throughout the periods of urban fluorescence, decline and regeneration. This phenomenon of continuity reflects the stable, adaptive capabilities of a largely rural-based economic system that existed in the northern Euphrates region. This model fits very well also with the suggested tribal character of the Euphrates communities, since such a social structure would have been more likely to have been born from a landscape of small, loosely organized confederacies of kinship groups spread out across village communities than a landscape perennially characterized by urban polities and their more hierarchically structured socio-economic systems.

Reasons for regeneration in the Middle Bronze Age

We now must ask a further question. Even if we accept that the Euphrates landscape was like its Jordanian neighbour in that it was essentially 'rural' and 'tribal' at its base, why did this region experience a transformation towards larger, more densely populated settlements, some characterized by considerable defences and other public works, at the beginning of the Middle Bronze Age (c.2000–1900 BC)? Most of these Middle Bronze Age settlements, as we are aware, were founded directly upon earlier Early Bronze settlements and display considerable cultural continuity from the earlier periods. Further, many of the same basic social structures appear to have remained intact, and the basic subsistence economy, although intensified, was never radically altered. Thus, this transformation cannot easily be credited to an influx of new people implanting their radically different urban ways on the region. Rather, the growth in size and scale of the Euphrates settlements at the beginning of the Middle Bronze Age appears to have happened within the existing communities.[4]

Should we look for the cause of growth from the outside? Is increased trade a factor? At the start of the second millennium, there was a consolidation of power by a number of powerful Amorite groups in Mesopotamia, some of the most influential locating themselves along the Euphrates River at sites such as Mari, or in southern cities such as Larsa and Babylon (Kuhrt 1995: 78–80, 95–8, 108–9). These new centres, eager to validate and to enhance their power and prestige, energetically pursued their quest for such valuable materials as precious metals, stone, and timber, and in so doing, revitalized trade routes. The Euphrates River was one of the most profitable of these routes, providing access to the rich resources of the Taurus to the north, and the active ports of the Mediterranean to the west (Klengel 1983: 25–32). In this light, therefore, perhaps the regeneration of settlements along the northern Euphrates River can be attributed to this resumption of trade and exchange. Such settlements would have benefited economically from the establishment of commercial relationships with foreign merchants and caravans. They could have intensified their own levels of production to participate in this active commerce, and may also have received tariffs from shipments of goods passing through their territories (i.e. Burke 1964: 67–103; Durand 1990: 81). This growing prosperity and increased contact with the wider world may explain in large part the growth in size and complexity of their settlements.

This possibility is, at the moment, only conjecture, and before it can be verified, archaeological and textual evidence will have to prove that the growth of urban life and the resumption of long-distance trade began earlier in the Middle Bronze Age at other settlements like Mari, and then spread to points further northwest along the Euphrates. Further archaeological investigations will be needed, especially a fine-tuning of the relative chronologies of Middle Bronze Age sites in Syria. But these deeper enquiries may be able to provide information that could produce the critical key to unlocking this very intriguing period of urban decline and consolidation.

If trade was a factor in revitalizing new centres along the Euphrates, was its decline a possible reason for a concurrent decline of urban centres at least a century earlier? A collapse of trade relations can have a resounding impact, just as Butzer suggested for the Near East as a whole. Was this the case too for the Euphrates settlements? Thus, just as the introduction of long-distance trade brought improved fortunes to an existing, essentially stable and resilient society, the withdrawal of trade could have had the opposite effect, removing the extra economic benefit to the region, forcing it to withdraw to a more basic and simplified form of economic and political existence. In archaeological terms, such a decline could be manifested by diminishment of settlements, impoverishment in material cultural assemblages, and possibly the abandonment of some of the region's large centres, especially those in which commercial activities had become a critical component of their internal socio-economic structure and which were essential for their continued existence and prosperity.

Such a proposition seems highly compelling, especially when we consider that the breakdown of commercial exchanges and long-distance trade was a persuasive hypothesis for the collapse of states and urban society elsewhere in the Near East at this time. Moreover, in the case of Euphrates settlements, trade and commercial exchange may well have had significant implications since the Euphrates River itself is the most prominent natural feature of this unique landscape. This river had served for millennia as the essential life-line for the communities strung out along its banks, bringing sustenance to its inhabitants and acting as the principal avenue along which cultural exchanges and communications were conducted. Cuneiform sources emphasize time and time again the importance of this river in conveying materials to the resource-poor regions of southern Mesopotamia and contributing in no small way to that land's continuing prosperity and economic complexity. That trade along this important waterway was a vital ingredient in shaping and altering the human societies that grew up along its banks seems altogether a clear and appropriate proposition. It remains now for future investigations to prove the possible strength of this suggestion.

CONCLUSION

Settlement data from the Euphrates River Valley of Syria at the end of the third millennium BC in the Bronze Age have provided useful information about the form that urban demise took in this intriguing area of the Near East. It has suggested how this demise differed from other regions experiencing similar forms of collapse. It has also suggested explanations for why ancient settlements of the Euphrates Valley stand out in their capacity to withstand and adapt to changing and sometimes disruptive forces. This chapter has especially highlighted how such factors as the environment, subsistence economy, and the socio-political character of the region's population greatly affected the degree to which such processes were experienced. We see that for the Near East as a whole, two hypotheses may explain urban collapse: climatic change, and the collapse of a 'world economy'. In the case of the Euphrates settlements these may well have been operative. A climatic change may have had a negative influence. Trade may have decreased. But these settlements' flexible economies and autonomous, tribal, political structures seem to have had a definitive impact. In the northern Euphrates region, successful adaptations to the marginal natural environment, in combination with the political character of decentralization, greatly reduced the extent to which the area suffered from periods of dramatic decline. These same factors along with the presence of revitalized trade, enabled its communities to recover with success and rapidity.

11

CONCLUSIONS

The vast quantity of archaeological data presented in the chapters of this book clearly emphasize the rich cultural composition of the communities which developed and flourished along the banks of the Euphrates River during the Early Bronze Age. Although each riverine settlement exhibits a considerable degree of variability and individuality in terms of its overall layout, artifactual assemblage and architectural history, it is possible to discern overarching themes and common cultural developments among these diverse sites which give rise to general conclusions about the populations of the northern Euphrates region and the progress of urbanization during this intriguing ancient period.

Early EB complexity

One important finding concerns the high level of cultural complexity in existence during the early phases of the Early Bronze Age. When we consider all of the archaeological evidence of this period as a whole, we see that settlements were not only numerous and well-established within the Euphrates Valley during this period, but that several communities already show clear signs of socio-economic sophistication. In terms of settlement abundance, archaeological surveys and excavations in the Tell es-Sweyhat embayment on the left bank of the Euphrates River have positively located a high number of small, early EB farming and pastoral communities. Of the 12 sites with evidence for third millennium occupation in this area, nine were already settled during Phases 1–2 of the Early Bronze Age. Although these settlements cannot be fitted into any discernible hierarchical settlement structure in which they were linked to larger, common centres, their individual economies appear to have been well consolidated. Excavated sites such as Tell Hajji Ibrahim indicate that communities were well aware of the pastoral and agricultural potential of their marginal, yet diversified environment, and made effective use of its resources.

Not all early EB settlements were small. Across the river from the Sweyhat embayment, Phases 1–2 pottery found across the wide expanse of the upper and lower tell at Hadidi indicate that even in this early stage of the Early Bronze Age, a settlement larger than 50 hectares could have developed (Dorneman 1985: 50). We have already conjectured that Tell Hadidi's economic success was based not only on a successful exploitation of the land and its natural resources, but also its exposure to and participation in long-distance commercial exchanges, afforded by its location on an important crossing point over the river.

Elsewhere, excavations carried down to early EB levels have frequently revealed unexpectedly large or well-planned architectural constructions. These include, for example, the solid lines of defence at Tell Habuba Kabira and Tell Halawa B and the large mud brick citadel at Tell es-Sweyhat. Early indications of town planning are attested at Shiyukh Fouqani, where its houses were set along one side of a long street. The temple complex at the site of Halawa Tell B is perhaps the most grand and impressive of early EB constructions. Only shortly after the earliest phases of occupation at this site, the entire central sector of housing was transformed into a sacred precinct featuring a series of stepped platforms which supported a monumental temple with architectural embellishments similar to those found on Sumerian temples of southern Mesopotamia. Such evidence confirms not only that the inhabitants of the Euphrates region were exposed to southern Mesopotamian cultural developments, but that they possessed the organizational abilities and access to wealth necessary to plan and build these structures and to maintain them over a extended period of time.

In view of this evidence for the abundance and complexity of early EB settlements, it is difficult to accept the argument that in the centuries following the withdrawal of the Late Uruk colonies and intensive economic contacts with southern Mesopotamia, the whole of the Euphrates Valley of northern Syria experienced a dramatic 'ruralization' in which the region diminished to only a few scattered farming villages and low-order political and economic systems (Akkermans and Schwartz 2003: 211). The reasons for the Euphrates' enduring socio-economic complexity can be attributed to several factors, perhaps the most important being the region's continuing participation in the trade of precious resources originating in the highlands of Anatolia. The Near Eastern demand for important raw materials from Anatolia, especially copper, continued in strength during the Early Bronze Age. Euphrates settlements, in their location on one of the major trade routes between Anatolia and the thriving markets of the south, would have taken advantage of their position as intermediaries on this route to reap the benefits of this flourishing commerce in metals. The rich array of copper and bronze objects found in Phases 1–2 tombs such as Qara Quzaq and Carchemish well attest to the continued importance of the metals trade, and the metals' presence in the Euphrates Valley confirms that local settlements profited from this commercial network.

Settlement variability

A second general observation about Euphrates settlement during the Early Bronze Age concerns the variable character of Euphrates Valley communities, even from their earliest inception in the first phases of the Early Bronze Age. Despite being united by a relatively homogenous regional culture, attested by common material attributes of pottery, metalwork and other artifacts, individual sites exhibited considerable individuality in terms of their site layout and architectural traditions. We have observed, for example, that both Halawa Tell B and Qara Quzaq were home to important sacred temple complexes in Phases 1–2 of the early EB, but that the physical arrangement of these sacred spaces and the central focus of their cults appears to have differed considerably. The overall layout of Euphrates sites was also tremendously variable, some featuring high central acropolis mounds, like the site of Tell es-Sweyhat, while other sites, like the roughly contemporary late EB settlement at Halawa Tell A, possessed different configurations where none of the buildings of the settlement were elevated above other structures.

We can summon many other physical features that highlight the considerable diversity of EB architecture features and site planning. In many cases, these features reflect the varying function of the settlements. We have highlighted, for example, the principal role of the site of Tell Banat as a large mortuary centre, where a cult of dead ancestors constituted a strong focus of the religious traditions practised there. In contrast, the small site of Tell Kabir nearby, with its temple *in antis*, probably had as its central cult focus a very different religious tradition. Extensive domestic neighbourhoods at sites such as Halawa Tell A and Selenkahiye indicate that these sites served primarily as places of residence, while other sites may have served as storage facilities for agricultural and pastoral surpluses, trading depots along the river, or fortified military outposts.

In regard to the issue of site variability in the Early Bronze Age, we have also noted that differences between sites and their respective functions have no discernible relation to their size. Sites characterized by monumental structures are not only found at the largest of sites. We have seen, for example, that both Jerablus Tahtani and Tell Ahmar featured monumental tombs of great wealth even though their overall site size did not exceed more than a few hectares. In contrast, the comparably large 12-ha site of Selenkahiye possessed many tombs, although none were inordinately large or rich.

All of this evidence, combined with the apparent lack of relationship to site size, indicates that we are dealing with an unusual configuration of settlements whose function and layout cannot be explained in straightforward hierarchical terms. Thus, one does not see here large central places which controlled and co-ordinated the religious, political and economic activities of smaller, simpler, satellite sites in their hinterlands. In contrast, what emerged in the Early Bronze Age was a more dispersed, heterarchical pattern featuring sites bound to one another in a complex system of overlapping economic networks and interconnecting socio-political relationships. In this system, no single settlement emerged as a regional nucleus or the centre of a state polity. The reasons for the growth and success of this unusual pattern of settlement in the Early Bronze Age are somewhat obscure, although the environment emerges as an important factor. The topographically fragmented and limited territorial space available in the Euphrates Valley would have constrained the growth of large regional polities while it promoted the development of smaller, autonomous communities and their own distinctive cultural traditions. We must also factor in the highly divergent economic base of the Euphrates settlements, which ranged from agricultural pursuits, to large-scale pastoralism and hunting activities, to trading ventures along the river. The geographical location of each Euphrates site and its participation in these economies would have affected the settlement's function and the nature of its relationship to other neighbouring communities.

Dual socio-economic character

We must also consider the variable social structures and ways of life that such diverse economic systems promoted. On the one hand, the growth of elites and material wealth may have developed in the wake of successful commercial riverine contacts and exposure to foreign cultural systems. The presence of large-scale secular buildings such as the Southern Mansion at Selenkahiye and Tell es-Sweyhat's acropolis complex, as well as the large, richly furnished tombs at Jerablus Tahtani, Tell Ahmar, Tell Banat and Tell Hadidi, certainly attests to the wealth and high status acquired by some individuals. Several of these elites may have wielded considerable power and control over the religious, social and economic institutions of the communities in which they resided. This trend towards elite growth seems particularly apparent in the second half of the third millennium BC, the period which saw the greatest influx of large-scale secular structures and monumental tombs. We suspect that increased cultural and commercial contacts with other areas of Syria and the wider Near East were largely responsible for this development.

On the other hand, the archaeological evidence reveals an equally pervasive inclination towards the limitation of elite growth. The presence of central acropolis mounds, where large secular buildings served as the residence and headquarters of elites, are not widely attested, except in a few cases. The lack of centralized control may also be seen in the variable nature of city fortifications, suggesting that local neighbourhoods, rather than city-wide, centralized powers, were responsible for the construction and maintenance of communities' defensive systems. A similar pattern is reflected in the organization of production, in which most craft industries were not managed or controlled by a central, elite institution. On the contrary, evidence for craft production is dispersed throughout the settlement, suggesting the presence of independently organized craftsmen who gained a livelihood through their own economic initiatives and organizational abilities.

Regarding the burial of the dead, with the exception of the largest tombs, one sees little economic differentiation among the graves of most Euphrates inhabitants. Variability in tomb design and grave offerings were usually the function of other factors relating to social structure, ethnic identity, age and gender, rather than to unequal access to wealth. The most potent symbols of social equality and a collective as opposed to exclusionary ideology were the massive mortuary mounds of Tell Banat. There is no evidence that individual elite persons or families were associated exclusively with these highly visible monuments. If such persons were buried here, their individual identities had been deliberately removed after they died, this was attested by the anonymous, disarticulated nature of the burials made into the sloping sides of the White Monument at Tell Banat, and the paucity of associated grave goods. The White Monument was a potent symbol of the dead ancestors, but rather than commemorating the greatness of past, prominent individuals, it served to reinforce collective traditions and strengthened the notion of corporate belonging and common kin descent.

The dual socio-economic character of the population of the Euphrates Valley of northern Syria, in which one sees a concurrent dynamic of both elite growth and collective, heterarchical relationships, is an especially distinctive feature of this region. We have suggested that the roots of this opposing dynamic can be found in the divergent economies and ways of life of the inhabitants of the Euphrates River Valley and their environs. On the one hand, the region's strong pastoral livelihood, encouraged by the abundance of pastureland in the open steppe lands beyond the river valley, ensured that people would retain a rural, tribal character in which collective decision-making and corporate organizational structures were highly favoured. On the other hand, wealth acquired by individuals with ties to the profitable trade networks along the river, and their exposure to the cultures of other cosmopolitan regions of the Near East would have promoted the growth of social and economic inequalities and the attendant development of elites. The dualistic character of these two opposing socio-economic systems were sometimes in tension with one another, while at other times they operated in a balanced system of complementarity. To the best of our knowledge, the development and persistence of this unusual dynamic is not well attested among other Near Eastern regions during the Early Bronze Age.

Future directions

While this book has endeavoured to emphasize the abundance of archaeo-logical material for the Euphrates region and significant developments discerned from these rich data, a number of important issues still require further consideration. One issue concerns the degree to which foreign powers impacted the Euphrates Valley, and the nature of their presence in the region. As we have discussed, textual sources make it certain that the Syrian states of Mari and Ebla had tremendous commercial and political interests in the Euphrates River Valley, but since unequivocal archaeological evidence for these polities' presence is very scant, it remains difficult to understand what kind of control, if any, they wielded here. Further refinements to the chronological sequence of the Euphrates region and the detection of clear synchronisms with the Ebla and Mari cultural assemblages may help at least to establish the precise moments in time when these states and polities interacted. From thence it may be possible to detect additional, more subtle developments linked to increases in long-distance trade, settlement complexity and economic intensification that affected the internal structure of Euphrates' settlements and confirm their relationship to outside polities. It should also be important to consider the effects of the withdrawal of control and influence from Ebla and Mari after around 2200 BC, and the impact that the decline of the Akkadian Empire of southern Mesopotamia had on existing trade networks and political systems.

Landscape studies in and around archaeological sites have proved tremendously useful in understanding issues relating to the subsistence economy of the river valley and uplands. They have shown how factors such as the climate, soil quality, access to water and other topographical features of the landscape affected the level of agricultural potential and sustainability of different regions of the river valley. Observations recording the distances between contemporary ancient sites, their size and population estimates relative to one another has also made possible statements about the presence or absence of settlement hierarchies and insights into local economic and political structures. Research within and beyond the Tell es-Sweyhat embayment on the left bank of the Euphrates, in tandem with paleobotanical and faunal studies in that area, have been among the most conclusive of such studies (Miller 1997a; Weber 1997; Danti 2000; Wilkinson 2004). They clearly underline the value of multi-disciplinary research in generating full information about the success and decline of settlement in antiquity. This form of research, when carried out elsewhere in the river valley in the future, should elucidate additional patterns about land-use and settlement that will provide an even fuller picture of the Early Bronze Age and the progress of urbanism through time than what is currently known.

While considerable efforts must focus on local environmental factors and their role in the development of urban societies in the Euphrates Valley of northern Syria, researchers must also consider the impact that riverine trade had on shaping the culture and socio-economic complexity of Early Bronze Age communities within this region. Evidence in the form of imported tomb goods at a number of Euphrates sites, shared artistic and architectural traditions with southern Mesopotamia and other regions, as well as the frequent location of sites along the banks of the river indicate that riverine commerce was a vital part of the economy in the region during the Early Bronze Age. No doubt, many individuals played active roles as intermediaries in this commercial network, facilitating trade links between Syro-Mesopotamian polities and the resource-rich highlands of Anatolia (Algaze 1999: 546). Further fine-grained studies of the material cultural assemblages of EB sites should underline even further the importance of this trade system. They may even identify specific settlements whose economies were particularly invested in such commercial ventures, and how their political and economic structures were affected by such activities.

Many of the Early Bronze Age sites described in this book now lie under several metres of water, resting within the artificial lakes created when the valleys behind the massive Tabqa and Tishrin hydro-electric dams were flooded. Although these sites' archaeological remains are now inaccessible, other unexplored ancient tells remain beyond the limits of the submerged valley and in the surrounding uplands. We are certain that future investigations of these sites will bring to light additional evidence for the rich antiquity of this region and reveal the striking complexity of the ancient Early Bronze Age cities that once developed here during what was a fascinating and eventful period of ancient urban growth.

NOTES

1 INTRODUCTION

1 Extract of letter by T.E. Lawrence is quoted by permission of the Trustees of the Seven Pillars of Wisdom Trust. The letter is part of the correspondence and papers of T.E. Lawrence at the Bodleian Library, Oxford. Shelfmark reference: MS. Eng. c. 6739, folios (fols.) 159–60.

2 Sites providing well-illustrated examples of pottery from Phases 1–2 include Carchemish (Woolley and Barnett 1952: pls. 57–9); Shiyukh Tahtani (Falsone 1998: figs. 4–5); Tell Ahmar (Area A: Jamieson 1990: figs. 19–48); Qara Quzaq (Level V: Valdés Pereiro 1994: figs. 35–6; 2001: 31–47); Tell Hadidi (Area RII Str. 1 and Str. 2 level 1: Dornemann 1988: figs. 4–7; 1990: pls. 20–1); Tell es-Sweyhat region (Wilkinson 2004: figs. 6.3–6.5); Hajji Ibrahim (Phases A-B: Danti 2000: 169–85); Tell es-Sweyhat (Area II, Phases A–F: Holland 1976: figs. 4–5; Operations 1, 20 and 12: Armstrong and Zettler 1997: App. 2.1); Munbaqa (Orthmann and Kühne 1974: Abb. 4–6); and Halawa Tell B (Orthmann 1981: Taf. 56–7).

3 Sites providing well-illustrated examples of Phase 3 pottery include Shiyukh Tahtani (Falsone 1998: Figure 7); Dja'de el-Mughara (Coqueugniot et al. 1998: figs. 4–8); Qara Quzaq (level IV: Valdés Pereiro 1994: figs. 23–34; 2001: figs. 17–22, 29–30); Tell Banat (period IV: Porter 1995a; Porter and McClellan 1998: figs. 9–12); Tell es-Sweyhat (tombs 1, 2 and 5: Zettler 1997b: App. 3.1–3.3); Tell Hadidi (early Tomb LI: Dornemann 1988: figs. 13–8); Shamseddin (early burials, especially Grave 19: Meyer 1991); Djerniye (Meyer 1991); Tawi (early burials, especially Graves T1, T4, T19–22, T70–1: Kampschulte and Orthmann 1984: Taf. 1–2, 18–28, 33–4); and Halawa Tell A (Graves H–64 and H–70: Orthmann 1981: Taf. 58–62).

4 Sites providing well-illustrated examples of Phase 4 pottery include Jerablus Tahtani (Peltenburg et al. 1995: figs. 19–20, 22, 27–8; 1996: figs. 18–19; 1997: figs. 8 and 14); Shiyukh Tahtani (Falsone 1998: figs. 6 and 8); Tell Ahmar (Hypogeum: Thureau-Dangin and Dunand 1936: figs. 29–32, and pls. 20–7); Qara Quzaq (level III–2: Valdés Pereiro 1994: figs. 17–22); Tell Banat (period III: Porter and McClellan 1998: figs. 13–19; Porter 1999: figs. 3–4; and Porter 2002a: Figure 11; also the bulk of the pottery found on the surface of the White Monument: McClellan 1998: 14–19); el-Qitar (grave found near the site: Sagona 1986: figs. 2–3); Tell Hadidi (Tombs EI, LI and 1972: Dornemann 1979: figs. 12–14; 1988: figs. 19–20; 1990: pls. 18–19); Tawi (especially Graves T5–6, T16: Kampschulte and Orthmann 1984: Taf. 3–11, 14–15); Halawa Tell A (older phase of level 3: Orthmann 1989: Abbs. 42–3); Selenkahiye (Van Loon 2001: pls.

285

5.A1–A31); Selenkahiye and Wreide tombs (Van Loon 2001: figs. 4A.1–9, 12A; 5B, 39A–B; Orthmann and Rova 1991: Abbs. 11–18, 25–9). Also, the Phase 4 pottery from Tell Amarna has recently been published by P. Sconzo, along with other vessels in the Carchemish region that were collected by L. Woolley and T.E. Lawrence during their investigations of Carchemish and its environs in the early 1900s (Sconzo in press a).

5 Note that we have pushed the terminal date for Phase 5 forward to 2100 BC, from Porter's date proposed date of 2150 BC (Porter in press). This is largely on account of radiocarbon dates obtained from good floor contexts in the Area IV 'Burned Building' on the main mound at Tell es-Sweyhat. This structure is clearly dated to Phase 5 on account of its pottery. The radiocarbon dates indicate that the building was probably occupied later than 2150 BC (Armstrong and Zettler 1997: 25).

6 Sites providing well-illustrated examples of pottery from Phase 5 include Tell Amarna (especially phase V: Pons 2001); Qara Quzaq (level III–1: Valdés Pereiro 1994: figs. 13–16; 2001: Figure 12); Tell Kabir (= Banat Period II: Porter 1995b: Figure 9; Porter, in press: Figure 6); Tell es-Sweyhat (Area IV 'Burned Building': Holland 1976: figs. 7–14; 1977: figs. 2–10); Tell Hadidi (Areas C and M: Dornemann 1979: 16–19); Munbaqa ('Kuppe' levels 1–5: Machule et al. 1986: Abb. 12–17); Shamseddin (Grave 1: Meyer 1991); Tawi (Grave T9: Kampschulte and Orthmann 1984: Taf. 12–13); Halawa Tell A (Level 3: Orthmann 1981: Taf. 54–5; 1989: Abb. 23–5); Selenkahiye (Van Loon 2001: 5A.244–6 and associated plates; Figure 5B.40–42); Wreide (Tomb N: Van Loon 2001: Figure 4A.10; and possible also Grave W 054: Orthmann and Rova 1991: Abb. 19–24); and Emar (Finkbeiner 2002: Abb. 13–14; 2003: Abb. 20–5).

7 The pottery of Phase 6 is the least well-illustrated of EB assemblages in the Euphrates Valley. The most complete published assemblage comes from level 6 at Tell Kabir (Porter 1995b: figs. 14–20). The latest EB occupation phase at Halawa Tell A, level 3a, almost certainly should belong to this phase (Orthmann 1989: 54–6). At Tell Amarna, Phases IV and III correspond to Phase 6 (Pons 2001). Last, recent excavations on the main tell at Tell es-Sweyhat have uncovered two settlement phases (5 and 6) that postdate the late third millennium city. The pottery from these phases has not yet been published but it has a clear transitional EB–MB character, and should belong, therefore, to Phase 6 as well.

4 DEFENCE OF EARLY BRONZE AGE CITIES

1 City walls built entirely of mud brick include those found at Halawa Tell B (Orthmann 1989: 87), and Tell Habuba Kabira, levels 2–7 (Heusch 1980: 162–3).

2 Mud brick city walls with stone foundations have been uncovered at Jerablus Tahtani (Peltenburg et al. 1996: 8), Tell es-Sweyhat (Zettler 1997b: 49), Tell al-'Abd (Finkbeiner 1994: 116), Tell Habuba Kabira, levels 10–15 (Heusch 1980: 168), Halawa Tell A (Orthmann 1989: 13) and Selenkahiye (Van Loon 2001: 3.51).

5 HOUSING AND HOUSEHOLDS

1 Terra-cotta wheeled vehicles have been found in Tomb 5 at Tell es-Sweyhat (Zettler 1997b: Figure 3.22), and in Tomb 2 at Tell Banat (Porter and McClellan 1998: 33 and Figure 23:1).

2 Figurines have been found at Tell Ahmar, Qara Quzaq, Tell Banat, Tell Kabir, Tell es-Sweyhat, Tell Hadidi, Tell Munbaqa, Tell al-ʿAbd, Tell Habuba Kabira, Halawa Tell A, and Selenkahiye.

6 LARGE-SCALE SECULAR BUILDINGS

1 Pots with unusual forms are illustrated, for example, in Holland 1976: figs. 10–13 (esp. Figure 10: 2, 4–5; 12:1, 13:1).

9 DEATH, FUNERARY MONUMENTS AND ANCESTOR CULTS

1 Pit burials have been found at Jerablus Tahtani (Peltenburg *et al.* 1996: 11; 1997: 8; 2000: 71–2), Shiyukh Tahtani (Falsone 1998: 30–2), Shamseddin (Meyer 1991: 15), Tawi (Kampschulte and Orthmann 1984: 63–105; Schwartz 1987: 241), Habuba Kabira (Heinrich *et al.* 1973: 33), Halawa Tell B (Orthmann 1981: 53–5), and Selenkahiye (Van Loon 2001: Chapters 4A and 4B, numerous examples).

2 Examples of these graves include T16, T19, T20–22, T70–71 at Tawi (Kampschulte and Orthmann 1984: 26–9, 33–62, 93–102).

3 Cist graves have been reported at Carchemish (Woolley and Barnett 1952: 218–22), Jerablus Tahtani (Peltenburg *et al.* 1997: 8; 2000: 71), Tell Amarna (Woolley 1914: 91), Tell Ahmar (Thureau-Dangin and Dunand 1936: 108–10), Hammam Kebir (Woolley 1914: 90), Qara Quzaq (where an infant had been placed in a jar inside of the cist: Olávarri and Valdés Pereiro 2001: 20, Lam. VIII), Shamseddin (Graves 41–9 in Cemetery A, and Graves 94–120 in Cemetery C: Meyer 1991: 58–61 and 99), Tell al-ʿAbd (Bounni 1979: 55) and Tawi, (but only in Cemetery A, Kampschulte and Orthmann 1984: 7). Cist tombs are also reported from Tell Banat, although they appear more akin to chamber tombs (Porter 2002a: 17–21).

4 Horizontal pithos burials have been reported at Jerablus Tahtani, where they occur in a cluster to the south of the paramount stone-built tomb Tomb 302, and are believed to be either contemporary or slightly later than that important tomb (Peltenburg *et al.* 1995: 13–14). Pithos burials have also been reported at Shiyukh Tahtani (Falsone 1998: 31–2), Qara Quzaq (where one of the three was found inside a cist grave: Olávarri 1995a: 10; Olávarri and Valdés Pereiro 2001: 20–1), Tell Hadidi (Dornemann 1979: 138), and at Selenkahiye, just inside the northern city wall (Van Loon 2001: 4B.217).

5 At Jerablus Tahtani, stone chamber graves are often referred to as stone chamber burials, and include Tomb 787 found in Area IV intramurally, with corbelled walls (Peltenburg *et al.* 1996: 10), Tomb 1036, also found in Area IV (Peltenburg *et al.* 1996: 11), and Tomb 1518 in the extension of the Area IV step trench to the south, from the latest EB levels (Peltenburg *et al.* 1997: 7). Still other corbel-wall chamber tombs are reported but not described or pictured (Peltenburg *et al.* 1997: 8; 2000: 71).

6 Shaft graves are too numerous to name individually. They have been found at Tell Banat (Porter 1995a), el-Qitar (Sagona 1986), Tell es-Sweyhat (Zettler 1997b), Tell Hadidi (Dornemann 1979), Shamseddin (Meyer 1991), Tell el-ʿAbd (Bounni 1979), Djerniye (Meyer 1991), Tawi (Kampschulte and Orthmann 1984), Halawa Tell A (Orthmann 1981), Selenkahiye (Van Loon 2001) and Wreide (Van Loon 2001 and Orthmann and Rova 1991).

7 At the Wreide Tombs D, G and H, a crossed pair of pins were found near the rib cage (Van Loon 2001: 4A.140, 4A.149, 4A.152). At Wreide Tomb L, two pins

were lying near the ankles (Van Loon 2001: 4A.160), whereas in Tomb VII in the Old Canal Cut at Selenkahiye, two pins were found above the skull (Van Loon 2001: 4B.197).

8 Also at Halawa H–119, several of the mushroom-headed pins were found in pairs in the vicinity of the shoulders of the deceased, perhaps serving as fasteners for the deceased's clothing (Orthmann 1981: 56).

9 W 054 Chamber C (Orthmann and Rova 1991: 21, 63; Abb. 30–4) and Tombs K and N (Van Loon 2001: figs. 4A.9A and 4A.10).

10 Tombs P, Q26 Tomb I, U22 Tomb IX, and W13 Tomb I (Van Loon 2001: 4A.12A, 4B.201, 4B.208, 4B.210).

10 THE END OF THE EARLY BRONZE AGE: EUPHRATES SETTLEMENT IN DECLINE

1 See also the recent findings at Chagar Bazar, which indicate post-Akkadian occupation, although the scale and extent of this settlement are still largely undetermined (McMahon *et al.* 2001: 205–10).

2 While it is difficult to verify from the published reports of the architectural remains that Tell Amarna has an uninterrupted stratigraphic sequence from Early to Middle Bronze Ages, this is clearly borne out in the pottery from the site, which has been carefully studied by Nina Pons (Pons 2001: 23–76). In particular, the pottery of Phase III in Area A possesses some of the same 'transitional EB-MB' forms as exist at other Euphrates sites. Moreover, my own research on Middle Bronze Age tombs at the site has confirmed the existence of a well-developed Middle Bronze Age assemblage at Amarna. In summary, Tell Amarna's pottery assemblage, comprising all periods under scrutiny in this investigation (EBIV, EB-MB, MB), supports settlement continuity.

3 The absence of fine-tuning in the relative ceramic chronology, and still-incomplete or uncertain stratigraphic sequences at some sites (namely Tell Ahmar, Qara Quzaq, and possibly Munbaqa) leave open the possibility that these sites experienced occupational hiatuses at the very end of the Early Bronze or beginning of the Middle Bronze (e.g. Werner 1998: 45; Valdés Pereiro 1999: 120). Nonetheless, any such disruptions do not appear to have been very long in duration.

4 This argument has important implications concerning the ethnic identity of the inhabitants of the Euphrates settlements during the Early and Middle Bronze Ages. From textual sources from the early second millennium BC, we know that most of Syria came to be dominated by population groups who were ethnically Amorite (Klengel 1992: 39–43; Nichols and Weber in press). There was a powerful Amorite dynasty at the city of Mari (Kuhrt 1995: 95–8). Amorite kingdoms also developed in other parts of Syria, namely at Yamhad, Qatna and Carchemish (Klengel 1992: 44–74).

Given that the northern Euphrates Valley of Syria was surrounded on all sides by Amorite polities, it is logical that this region would have been inhabited by Amorites as well. If we are to insist, however, that there was considerable continuity in traditions, material culture, social structure and subsistence strategies from the end of the Early Bronze Age through to the Middle Bronze Age, then we must conclude that the Early Bronze Age inhabitants of this region were themselves Amorites, or 'proto-Amorites'. At the very least, they belonged to a Semitic group whose ethnic affiliation to the Amorites was very close. In this light, the proposition that Amorites swept in, supplanted the older population, and established a new Middle Bronze Age culture must be discarded, at least for this particular region of the Near East. Past studies emphasize not the dichotomy between one ethnic group and another, but rather the degree to which one group comprised a diversity of lifestyles and economic strategies, i.e. nomadic, sedentary, farming, pastoralist, urban and rural (Kamp and Yoffee 1980). Given this ethnic diversity, I submit that almost all of the differences/discontinuities that can be observed between the Early Bronze period and the regenerated Middle Bronze period in northern Syria can be explained by the differing degree and duration to which parts of one and the same group of people had become sedentary and fully immersed in urban life with all of its complex trappings and institutions. Further studies which explore the true archaeological correlates of Amorite ethnicity will no doubt help to resolve this very important issue beyond what is argued here.

BIBLIOGRAPHY

Akkermans, P. and Schwartz, G. (2003) *The Archaeology of Syria. From Complex Hunter-Gatherers to Early Urban Societies (c.16,000–300* BC), Cambridge: Cambridge University Press.

Algaze, G. (1999) 'Trends in the Archaeological Development of the Upper Euphrates Basin of Southeastern Anatolia during the Late Chalcolithic and Early Bronze Ages', in G. Del Olmo Lete and J.-L. Montero Fenollós (eds) *Archaeology of the Upper Syrian Euphrates. The Tishrin Dam Area. Proceedings of the International Symposium Held at Barcelona, Jan. 28th–30th, 1998*, Barcelona: Editorial Ausa, pp. 535–72.

Algaze, G., Breuninger, R. and Knudstad, J. (1994) 'The Tigris-Euphrates Archaeological Reconnaissance Project: Final Report of the Birecik and Carchemish Dam Survey Areas', *Anatolica* 20: 1–97.

Algaze, G., Goldberg, P., Honça, D., Matney, T., Mısır, A., Rosen, A.M., Schlee, D. and Somers, L. (1995) 'Titris Höyük, A Small EBA Urban Center in SE Anatolia. The 1994 Season', *Anatolica* 21: 13–64.

Algaze, G., Dinckan, G., Hartenberger, B., Matney, T., Pournelle, J., Rainville, L., Rosen, S., Rupley, E., Schlee, D. and Vallet, R. (2001) 'Research at Titris Höyük in southeastern Turkey: The 1999 Season', *Anatolica* 27: 23–106.

Andrae, W. (1922) *Die archaischen Ischtar-Tempel in Assur*, Leipzig: Hinrich.

Archi, A. (1985) 'Circulation d'objets en métal précieus de poids standardisé à Ebla', in J.-M. Durand and J.-R. Kupper (eds) *Miscellanea Babylonica, Mélanges Offerts à Maurice Birot*, Paris: Editions Recherche sur les civilisations, pp. 25–34.

—— (1990) 'Imar au IIIe millénaire d'après les archives d'Ebla', *MARI* 6: 21–38.

—— (1992) 'The City of Ebla and the Organization of its Rural Territory', *Altorientalische Forschungen* 19: 24–8.

Armstrong J.A. and Zettler, R.L. (1997) 'Excavations on the High Mound (Inner Town)', in R.L. Zettler (ed.) *Subsistence and Settlement in a Marginal Environment: Tell es-Sweyhat, 1989–1995 Preliminary Report*, MASCA Research Papers in Science and Archaeology 14. Philadelphia: Museum Applied Science Center for Archaeology, University of Pennsylvania Museum of Archaeology and Anthropology, pp. 11–32.

Aruz, J. (ed.) (2003) *Art of the First Cities. The Third Millennium* B.C. from the Mediterranean to the Indus, New York: Metropolitan Museum of Art.

Astour, M.C. (1992) 'An Outline of the History of Ebla (Part 1)', in C.H. Gordon and

G.A. Rendsburg (eds) *Eblaitica: Essays on the Ebla Archives and Eblaite Language, Volume 3*, Winona Lake, Indiana: Eisenbrauns, pp. 3–82.

—— (1995) 'Overland Trade Routes in Ancient Western Asia', in J.M. Sasson (ed.) *Civilizations of the Ancient Near East*, New York: Scribner, pp. 1401–20.

Bachelot, L. (1999) 'Tell Shiuokh Faouqani (1994–1998)', in G. Del Olmo Lete and J.-L. Montero Fenollós (eds) *Archaeology of the Upper Syrian Euphrates. The Tishrin Dam Area. Proceedings of the International Symposium Held at Barcelona, Jan. 28th–30th, 1998*, Barcelona: Editorial Ausa, pp. 143–62.

Badre, L. (1980) *Les figurines anthropomorphes en terre cuite à l'Age du Bronze en Syrie*, Paris: Bibliothèque Archéologique et Historique.

Barrett, J.C. (1990) 'The Monumentality of Death: The Character of Early Bronze Age Mortuary Mounds in Southern Britain', *World Archaeology* 22: 179–89.

Behm-Blancke, M.R. (1984) 'Hassek Höyük. Vorläufiger Bericht über die Ausgrabungen in den Jahren 1981–1983', *Istanbuler Mitteilungen* 34: 31–149.

Bell, B. (1971) 'The Dark Ages in Ancient History I. The First Dark Age in Egypt', *American Journal of Archaeology* 75: 1–26.

Bell, G.L. (1910) 'The East Bank of the Euphrates from Tel Ahmar to Hit', *Geographical Journal* 36: 513–37.

Besançon, J. and Sanlaville, P, (1985) 'Le milieu géographique', in P. Sanlaville (ed.) *Holocene Settlement in North Syria*, Oxford: B.A.R. publications, pp. 7–40.

Bier, C. (1995) 'Textile Arts in Ancient Western Asia', in J.M. Sasson (ed.) *Civilizations of the Ancient Near East*, New York: Scribner, pp. 1567–88.

Biga, G. (1988) 'Frauen in der Wirtschaft von Ebla', in H. Waetzoldt and H. Hauptmann (eds) *Wirtschaft und Gesellschaft von Ebla*, Heidelberg: Heidelberger Orientverlag, pp. 159–71.

Binford, L. (1971) 'Mortuary Practices: their Study and Potential', *American Antiquity* 36: 6–29.

Blackman, M.J., Stein, G. and Vandiver, P.B. (1993) 'The Standardization Hypothesis and Ceramic Mass Production: Technological, Compositional, and Metric Indexes of Craft Specialization at Tell Leilan, Syria', *American Antiquity* 58: 60–80.

Blanton, R., Feinman, G.M., Kowalewski, S.A. and Peregrine, P.N. (1996) 'A Dual-Processual Theory for the Evolution of Mesoamerican Civilization', *Current Anthropology* 37:1–14.

Boileau, M.-C. (2005) *Production et distribution céramique au IIIe millénaire en Syrie du nord-est. Une étude technologique des céramiques de Tell ʿAtij et Tell Gudeda*, Paris: Maison des sciences de l'homme.

Bonechi, M. (1998) 'Remarks on the IIIrd Millennium Geographical Names of Syrian Upper Mesopotamia', in M. Lebeau (ed.) *About Subartu. Studies devoted to Upper Mesopotamia. Vol. 1 – Landscape, Archaeology, Settlement* (Subartu 4) Turnhout: Brepols, pp. 219–41.

Bounni, A. (1979) 'Preliminary Report on the Archeological Excavations at Tell al-ʿAbd and ʿAnab al-Safinah (Euphrates) 1971–72', in D.N. Freedman (ed.) *Archaeological Projects from the Tabqa Dam Project – Euphrates Valley, Syria*, (AASOR 44) Cambridge, MA: American Schools of Oriental Research, pp. 49–61.

Braidwood, R.J. and Braidwood, L.S. (1960) *Excavations in the Plain of Antioch 1: The Earlier Assemblages, Phases A–J*, Chicago: University of Chicago Press.

Buccellati, G. and Kelly-Buccellati, M. (1988) *Mozan 1. The Soundings of the First Two Seasons*, (Bibliotheca Mesopotamica 20) Malibu: Undena.

Bunnens, G. (ed.) (1990) *Tell Ahmar. 1988 Season*, Leuven: Publications of the Melbourne University Expedition to Tell Ahmar.

—— (in press) 'Site Hierarchy in the Tishrin Dam Area and the Geographical Horizon of the Ebla Texts', in E. Peltenburg (ed.) *The Carchemish Region in the Early Bronze Age: Investigating the Archaeology of Boundaries*, Oxford: Oxbow Books.

Burke, A.A. (2004) 'The Architecture of Defense: Fortified Settlements of the Levant during the Middle Bronze Age', unpublished PhD dissertation, University of Chicago.

Burke, M.L. (1964) 'Lettres de Numušda-Nahrâri et de trois autres correspondants à Idiniatum', *Syria* 41:67–103.

Butzer, K.W. (1997) 'Sociopolitical Discontinuity in the Near East, *c.*2200 B.C.E.: Scenarios from Palestine and Egypt', in J.N. Dalfes, G. Kukla and H. Weiss (eds) *Third Millennium BC Climate Change and Old World Collapse* (NATO ASI Ser. I 49), Heidelberg: Springer Verlag, pp. 245–96.

Carter, E. and Parker, A. (1995) 'Pots, People and the Archaeology of Death in Northern Syria and Southern Anatolia in the Latter Half of the Third Millennium BC', in S. Campbell and A. Green (eds) *The Archaeology of Death in the Ancient Near East*, Oxford, Oxbow Books, pp. 96–116.

Clason, A.T. and Buitenhuis, H. (1978) 'A Preliminary Report on the Faunal Remains of Nahr el Homr, Hadidi and Ta'as in the Tabqa Dam Region in Syria', *Journal of Archaeological Science* 5: 75–83.

Cooper, E.N. (1997) 'The Middle Bronze Age of the Euphrates Valley, Syria: Chronology, Regional Interaction and Cultural Exchange', unpublished PhD dissertation, University of Toronto.

—— (1998) 'The EB-MB Transitional Period at Tell Kabir, Syria', in M. Fortin and O. Aurenche (eds) *Espace Naturel, Espace Habité en Syrie du Nord (19e–2e millénaires av. J-C.)*, Lyon: Maison de l'Orient Méditerranéen, pp. 271–80.

—— (1999) 'The EB-MB Transitional Period at Tell Kabir, Syria', in G. Del Olmo Lete and J.-L. Montero Fenollós (eds) *Archaeology of the Upper Syrian Euphrates. The Tishrin Dam Area. Proceedings of the International Symposium Held at Barcelona, Jan. 28th–30th, 1998*, Barcelona: Editorial Ausa, pp. 321–32.

—— (2001) 'Archaeological Perspectives on the Political History of the Euphrates Valley, during the Early Second Millennium BC', in M. Fortin (ed.) *Canadian Research On Ancient Syria*, Québec: Musée de la civilisation à Québec, pp. 79–86.

Copeland, L. and Moore, A. (1985) 'Inventory and Description of Sites', in P. Sanlaville (ed.) *Holocene Settlement in North Syria*, Oxford, B.A.R. publications, pp. 41–98.

Coqueugniot, É., Jamieson, A.S., Montero Fenollós, J.-L, and Anfruns, J. (1998) 'Une tombe du Bronze ancien à Dja'de el Mughara (Moyen-Euphrate, Syrie)', *Cahiers de l'Euphrate* 8: 85–114.

Costin, C.L. (1991) 'Craft Specialization: Issues in Defining, Documenting, and Explaining the Organization of Production', in M.B. Schiffer (ed.) *Archaeological Method and Theory, vol. 3*, Tuscon: University of Arizona Press, pp. 1–56.

Courty, M.-A. (2001) 'Evidence at Tell Brak for the Late ED III/Early Akkadian Air Blast Event (4 kyr BP)' in D. Oates, J. Oates and H. McDonald (eds) *Excavations at Tell Brak. Vol. 2: Nagar in the Third Millennium BC*, Cambridge and London:

McDonald Institute for Archaeological Research and the British School of Archaeology in Iraq, pp. 367–72.

Courty, M.-A. and Roux, V. (1995) 'Identification of Wheel Throwing on the basis of Ceramic Surface Features and Microfabrics', *Journal of Archaeological Science* 22: 17–50.

Culican, W. and McClellan, T.L. (1983–84) 'El-Qitar: First Season of Excavations, 1982–83'. *Abr-Nahrain* 22: 29–63.

Danti, M.D. (1997) 'Regional Survey and Excavations', in R. Zettler (ed.) *Subsistence and Settlement in a Marginal Environment. Tell es-Sweyhat, 1989–1995 Preliminary Report*, MASCA Research Papers in Science and Archaeology 14. Philadelphia: Museum Applied Science Center for Archaeology, University of Pennsylvania Museum of Archaeology and Anthropology, pp. 85–94.

—— (2000) 'Early Bronze Age Settlement and Land Use in the Tell es-Sweyhat Region, Syria', unpublished PhD dissertation, University of Pennsylvania.

Danti, M. and Zettler, R. (1998) 'The Evolution of the Tell es-Sweyhat (Syria) Settlement System in the Third Millennium B.C.' in M. Fortin and O. Aurenche, *Espace Naturel, Espace Habité en Syrie du Nord (19e–2e millénaires av. J-C.)*, Lyon: Maison de l'Orient Méditerranéen, pp. 209–28.

—— (2002) 'Excavating an Enigma. The latest discoveries from Tell es-Sweyhat', *Expedition* 44: 36–45.

Del Olmo Lete, G. and Montero Fenollós, J. (1998) 'Du temple à l'entrepôt. Un exemple de transformation de l'espace urbain à Tell Qara Quzaq en Syrie du nord', in M. Fortin and O. Aurenche (eds) *Espace Naturel, Espace Habité en Syrie du Nord (19e–2e millénaires av. J-C.)*, Lyon: Maison de l'Orient Méditerranéen, pp. 295–304.

Delougaz, P., Hill, H. and Lloyd, S. (1967) *Private Houses and Graves in the Diyala Region*, (OIP 88) Chicago: University of Chicago Press.

Dever, W. (1989) 'The Collapse of the Urban Early Bronze Age in Palestine – Toward a Systemic Analysis', in P. de Miroschedji (ed.) *L'urbanisation de la Palestine à l'âge du Bronze ancien*, Oxford: B.A.R. publications, pp. 225–46.

—— (1995) 'Social Structure in the Early Bronze IV Period in Palestine', in T. Levy, *The Archaeology of Society in the Holy Land*, London: Leicester University Press, pp. 282–96.

Dolce, R. (1988) 'Some Aspects of the Primary Economic Structures of Ebla in the Third and Second Millennium BC: Stores and Workplaces', in H. Waetzoldt and H. Hauptmann (eds) *Wirtschaft und Gesellschaft von Ebla*, Heidelberg: Heidelberger Orientverlag, pp. 35–46.

Dornemann, R. (1979) 'Tell Hadidi: A Millennium of Bronze Age City Occupation', in D.N. Freedman (ed.) *Archaeological Projects from the Tabqa Dam Project – Euphrates Valley, Syria*, (AASOR 44) Cambridge, MA: American Schools of Oriental Research, pp. 113–51.

—— (1980) 'Tell Hadidi: An Important Center of the Mitannian Period and Earlier', in J.-C. Margueron (ed.) *Le Moyen Euphrate*, Leiden: E.J. Brill, pp. 218–34.

—— (1985) 'Salvage Excavations at Tell Hadidi in the Euphrates River Valley', *Biblical Archaeologist* 48: 49–59.

—— (1988) 'Tell Hadidi: One Bronze Age Site among Many in the Tabqa Dam Salvage Area', *Bulletin of the American Schools of Oriental Research* 270: 13–42.

—— (1989) 'Comments on Small Finds and Items of Artistic Significance from Tell

Hadidi and Nearby Sites in the Euphrates Valley, Syria', in A. Leonard and B. Williams (eds) *Essays in ancient Civilization presented to Helene Kantor*, Chicago: Oriental Institute of University of Chicago, pp. 59–75.

—— (1990) 'The Beginning of the Bronze Age in Syria in Light of Recent Excavations', in P. Matthiae, M. Van Loon and H. Weiss (eds) *Resurrecting the Past: A Joint Tribute to Adnan Bounni*, Leiden: Nederlands Historisch-Archaeologisch Instituut te Istanbul, pp. 85–100.

—— (1992) 'Early Second Millennium Ceramic Parallels between Tell Hadidi–Azu and Mari', in G.D. Young (ed.) *Mari in Retrospect. Fifty Years of Mari and Mari Studies*, Winona Lake, Indiana: Eisenbrauns, pp. 77–112.

Dunham, S. (1993) 'A Wall Painting from Tell al-Raqa'i, North-East Syria', *Levant* 25: 127–43.

Durand, J.-M. (1989) 'L'assemblée en Syrie à l'époque pré-amorite', in P. Fronzaroli (ed.) *Miscellanea Eblaitica*, vol. 2, Florence: Università di Firenze, pp. 27–44.

—— (1990) 'Le Cité-État d'Imâr a l'époque des rois de Mari', *MARI* 6: 39–92.

Edzard, D.O. (1981) 'Neue Erwägungen zum Brief des Enna-Dagan von Mari (TM.75.G.2367)', *Studi Eblaiti* 4: 89–97.

—— (1997) *Gudea and His Dynasty*, (The Royal Inscriptions of Mesopotamia. Early Periods vol. 3/1) Toronto: University of Toronto Press.

Eichler, S., Frank, D.R., Machule, D., Mozer, G. and Pape, W. (1984) 'Ausgrabungen in Tall Munbaqa 1983', *Mitteilungen der Deutschen Orient-Gesellschaft* 116: 65–93.

Falconer, S.E. (1987) 'Heartland of Villages: Reconsidering Early Urbanism in the Southern Levant', unpublished PhD dissertation, University of Arizona.

—— (1994) 'Village Economy and Society in the Jordan Valley: A Study of Bronze Age Rural Complexity', in G.M. Schwartz and S.E. Falconer (eds) *Archaeological Views from the Countryside*, Washington: Smithsonian Institution Press, pp. 121–42.

Falsone, G. (1998) 'Tell Shiyukh Tahtani on the Euphrates. The University of Palermo Salvage Excavations in North Syria (1993–94)', *Akkadica* 109–110: 22–64.

—— (1999) 'Tell Shiyukh Tahtani', in G. Del Olmo Lete and J.-L. Montero Fenollós (eds) *Archaeology of the Upper Syrian Euphrates. The Tishrin Dam Area. Proceedings of the International Symposium Held at Barcelona, Jan. 28th–30th, 1998*, Barcelona: Editorial Ausa, pp. 137–42.

Finet, A. (1979) 'Bilan provisoire des fouilles belges du Tell Kannâs', in D.N. Freedman (ed.) *Archaeological Projects from the Tabqa Dam Project – Euphrates Valley, Syria*, (AASOR 44) Cambridge, MA: American Schools of Oriental Research, pp. 79–95.

Finkbeiner, U. (1994) ʿAbd, in H. Weiss (ed.) 'Archaeology in Syria', *American Journal of Archaeology* 98:116–17.

—— (1995) 'Tell el-ʿAbd', *Damaszener Mitteilungen* 8: 51–83.

—— (1997) ʿAbd, in H. Weiss (ed.) 'Archaeology in Syria', *American Journal of Archaeology* 101: 97–100.

—— (1999–2000) 'Emar and Balis 1996–1998: Preliminary Report of the Joint Syrian-German Excavations with the Collaboration of Princeton University', *Berytus* 44: 5–34.

—— (2002) 'Emar 2001 – Bericht über die 4. Kampagne der syrisch-deutschen Ausgrabungen', *Baghdader Mitteilungen* 33: 109–46.

—— (2003) 'Emar 2002 – Bericht über die 5. Kampagne der syrisch-deutschen Ausgrabungen', *Baghdader Mitteilungen* 34: 10–100.

Fleming, D.E. (2004) *Democracy's Ancient Ancestors. Mari and Early Collective Governance*, Cambridge: Cambridge University Press.

Fortin, M. (1990) 'Rapport préliminaire sur la seconde campagne de fouilles à tell 'Atij et la première à tell Gudeda (automne 1987), sur le moyen Khabour', *Syria* 67: 219–56.

—— (1999) *Syria, Land of Civilizations*, Québec: Musée de la Civilisation.

Frangipane M. (1998) 'Arslantepe 1996. The Finding of an E.B. I "Royal Tomb"', *Kazı Sonuçları Toplantısı* 19: 291–310.

Frayne, D. (1993) *Sargonic and Gutian Periods (2334–2113 BC)*, (The Royal Inscriptions of Mesopotamian Project, Early Periods vol. 2) Toronto: University of Toronto Press.

Freedman, D.N. (ed.) (1979) *Archaeological Projects from the Tabqa Dam Project – Euphrates Valley, Syria* (AASOR 44), Cambridge, MA: American Schools of Oriental Research.

Garnett, D. (ed.) (1938) *The Letters of T.E. Lawrence*, London: Jonathan Cape.

Gasche, H., Armstrong, J., Cole, S. and Gurzadyan, V. (1998) *Dating the Fall of Babylon: A Reappraisal of Second-Millennium Chronology*, Chicago: University of Ghent and the Oriental Institute of the University of Chicago.

Glazer, N. and Moynihan, D.P. (1965) *Beyond the Melting Pot*, Cambridge, MA: Harvard University Press.

Goren, Y. (1996) 'The Southern Levant during the Early Bronze IV: The Petrographic Perspective', *Bulletin of the American Schools of Oriental Research* 303: 33–72.

Greenberg, R. and Porat, N. (1996) 'A Third Millennium Levantine Pottery Production Center: Typology, Petrography and Provenance of the Metallic Wares of Northern Israel and Adjacent Regions', *Bulletin of the American Schools of Oriental Research* 301: 5–23.

Hawkins, J. (1976–80) 'Karkamiš', *Reallexikon der Asssyriologie* 5: 425–46.

Heinrich, E., von Schuler, E., Schmid, H., Ludwig, W., Strommenger, E. and Seidl, U. (1969) 'Bericht über die von der Deutschen Orient-Gesellschaft mit Mitteln der Stiftung Volkswagenwerk im Euphrattal bei Aleppo', *Mitteilungen der Deutschen Orient-Gesellschaft* 101: 28–67.

Heinrich, E., Ludwig, W., Strommenger, E., Opificius R. and Sürenhagen (1970) 'Zweiter vorläufiger Bericht über die von der Deutschen Orient-Gesellschaft mit Mitteln der Stiftung Volkswagenwerk in Habuba Kabira und in Mumbaqat unternommenen archäologischen Untersuchungen (Herbstkampagne 1969), erstattet von Mitgliedern der Mission', *Mitteilungen der Deutschen Orient-Gesellschaft* 102: 27–85.

Heinrich, E., Schmid, H.J., Kara, H-C., Strommenger, E., Sürenhagen, D., Hecker, G., Seidl, U., Machule, D. and Rentschler, D. (1971) 'Dritter vorläufiger Bericht über die von der Deutschen Orient-Gesellschaft mit Mitteln der Stiftung Volkswagenwerk in Habuba Kabira und in Mumbaqat unternommenen archäologischen Untersuchungen (Herbstkampagne 1970), erstattet von Mitgliedern der Mission', *Mitteilungen der Deutschen Orient-Gesellschaft* 103: 5–58.

Heinrich, E., Strommenger, E., Frank, D.R., Ludwig, W., Sürenhagen, D., Töpperwein, E., Schmid, H., Heusch, J.-C., Kohlmeyer, K., Machule, D., Wäfler, M. and Rhode, T. (1973) 'Vierter vorläufiger Bericht über die von der Deutschen

Orient-Gesellschaft mit Mitteln der Stiftung Volkswagenwerk in Habuba Kabira (Habuba Kabira, Herbstkampagnen 1971 und 1972 sowie Testgrabung Frühjahr 1973) und in Mumbaqat (Tall Munbaqa, Herbstkampagne 1971) unternommenen archäologischen Untersuchungen, erstattet von Mitgliedern der Mission', *Mitteilungen der Deutschen Orient-Gesellschaft* 105: 5–68.

Heinrich, E., Strommenger, E., Frank, D.R., Ludwig, W., Sürenhagen, D., Töpperwien, E., Schmid, H., Heusch, J.-C., Kohlmeyer, K., Machule, D., Wäfler, M. and Rhode, T. (1974) 'Vierter vorläufiger Bericht die von der Deutschen Orient-Gesellschaft in Habuba Kabira und in Mumbaqat', *Mitteilungen der Deutschen Orient-Gesellschaft* 106: 5–52.

Hempelmann, R. (2001) 'Menschen- und tiergestalitige Darstellungen auf frühbronzezeitlichen Gefässen von Halawa A', in J.-W. Meyer, M. Novák and A. Pruss (eds) *Beiträge zur vorderasiatischen Archäologie. Festschrift W. Orthmann*, Frankfurt am Main: Johann Wolfgang Goethe-Universität, pp. 150–69.

Herzog, Z. (1997) 'Fortifications', in E.M. Meyers (ed.) *The Oxford Encyclopedia of Archaeology in the Near East*, New York: Oxford University Press, pp. 319–26.

Heusch, J.-C. (1980) 'Tall Habuba Kabira im 3. und 2. Jahrtausend: Die Entwicklung der Baustruktur', in J.-C. Margueron (ed.) *Le Moyen Euphrate*, Leiden: E.J. Brill, pp. 159–78.

Holland, T.A. (1975) 'An Inscribed Weight from Tell Sweyhat in Syria', *Iraq* 37: 75–76.

—— (1976) 'Preliminary Report on Excavations at Tell Sweyhat, Syria, 1973–4', *Levant* 8: 36–70.

—— (1977) 'Preliminary Report on Excavations at Tell es-Sweyhat, Syria 1975', *Levant* 9: 36–65.

—— (1993–94) Tall as-Swehat, in H. Kühne (ed.) 'Archäologische Forschungen in Syrien', *Archiv für Orientforschung* 40/41: 275–85.

Holland, T. and Zettler, R. (1994) Sweyhat, in H. Weiss (ed.) 'Archaeology in Syria', *American Journal of Archaeology* 98: 139–42.

Jamieson, A. (1990) 'Area A – The Pottery', in G. Bunnens (ed.) *Tell Ahmar. 1988 Season*, Leuven: Publications of the Melbourne University Expedition to Tell Ahmar, pp. 25–105.

—— (1993) 'The Euphrates Valley and Early Bronze Age Ceramic Traditions', *Abr Nahrain* 31: 36–92.

Jean-Marie, M. (1990) 'Les tombeaux en pierres de Mari', *MARI* 6: 303–36.

Joffe, A.H. (1993) *Settlement and Society in the Early Bronze Age I and II, Southern Levant*, Sheffield: Sheffield Academic Press.

Kamp, K.A., and Yoffee, N. (1980) 'Ethnicity in Ancient Western Asia during the Early Second Millennium BC: Archaeological Assessments and Ethnoarchaeological Perspectives', *Bulletin of the American Schools of Oriental Research* 237: 85–104.

Kampschulte, I. and Orthmann, W. (1984) *Gräber des 3. Jahrtausends im syrischen Euphrattal. 1. Ausgrabungen bei Tawi 1975 und 1978*, Bonn: Dr. Rudolf Habelt.

Kemp, B.J. (1983) 'Old Kingdom, Middle Kingdom and Second Intermediate Period c. 2686–1552 BC', in B.G. Trigger, B.J. Kemp, D. O'Connor and A.B. Lloyd (eds) *Ancient Egypt, A Social History*, Cambridge: Cambridge University Press, pp. 71–182.

Kepinski-Lecomte, C. and Ergeç, R. (2000) 'Tilbeshar 1999. Occupations de la vallée du Sajour de la fin du Chalcolithique au Bronze Moyen', *Anatolia Antiqua* 8: 215–25.

Klengel, H. (1983) 'The Middle Euphrates and International Trade in the Old Babylonian Period', *Les Annales archéologiques arabes syriennes* 34: 25–32.

—— (1992) *Syria, 3000–300 B.C.* Berlin: Akademie Verlag.

Kuhrt, A. (1995) *The Ancient Near East, c.3000–330 BC*, London: Routledge.

Lacambre, D. and Tunca, Ö. (1999) 'Histoire de la vallée de l'Euphrate entre le barrage de Tišrin et Karkemiš aux IIIe et IIe millénaire av. J.-C.', in G. Del Olmo Lete and J.-L. Montero Fenollós (eds) *Archaeology of the Upper Syrian Euphrates. The Tishrin Dam Area. Proceedings of the International Symposium Held at Barcelona, Jan. 28th–30th, 1998*, Barcelona: Editorial Ausa, pp. 587–603.

Liebowitz, H. (1988) *Terra-Cotta Figurines and Model Vehicles* (Bibliotheca Mesopotamica 22) Malibu: Undena.

McCarthy, A. (in press) 'Is there a Carchemish Region Glyptic Style? Reflections on Sealing Practices in the Northern Euphrates Region', in E. Peltenburg (ed.) *The Carchemish Region in the Early Bronze Age: Investigating the Archaeology of Boundaries*, Oxford: Oxbow Books.

McClellan, T.L. (1998) 'Tell Banat North: The White Monument', in M. Lebeau (ed.) *About Subartu. Studies devoted to Upper Mesopotamia. Vol. 1: Landscape, Archaeology, Settlement*, (Subartu 4) Turnhout: Brepols, pp. 243–69.

—— (1999) 'Urbanism on the Upper Syrian Euphrates', in G. Del Olmo Lete and J.-L. Montero Fenollós (eds) *Archaeology of the Upper Syrian Euphrates. The Tishrin Dam Area. Proceedings of the International Symposium Held at Barcelona, Jan. 28th–30th, 1998*, Barcelona: Editorial Ausa, pp. 535–72.

McClellan, T.L. and Porter, A. (1999) 'Survey of Excavations at Tell Banat: Funerary Practices', in G. Del Olmo Lete and J.-L. Montero Fenollós (eds) *Archaeology of the Upper Syrian Euphrates. The Tishrin Dam Area. Proceedings of the International Symposium Held at Barcelona, Jan. 28th–30th, 1998*, Barcelona: Editorial Ausa, pp. 107–16.

—— (in press) 'Archaeological Surveys of the Tishreen Dam Flood Zone', *Les Annales Archéologiques Arabes Syriennes*.

McCorriston, J. (1997) 'The Fiber Revolution. Textile Extensification, Alienation, and Social Stratification in Ancient Mesopotamia', *Current Anthropology* 38: 517–49.

McMahon, A., Tunca, Ö. and Bagdo, A.-M. (2001) 'New Excavations at Chagar Bazar, 1999–2000', *Iraq* 63: 201–22.

Machule, D., Karstens, K., Klapproth, H.-H., Mozer, G., Pape, W., Werner, P., Mayer, R., Mayer-Opificius, R. and Mackensen, M. (1986) 'Ausgrabungen in Tall Munbaqa 1984', *Mitteilungen der Deutschen Orient-Gesellschaft* 118: 65–93.

Machule, D., Benter, M., Boessneck, J., von de Driesch, A., de Feyter, T.C., Karstens, K., Klapproth, H.-H., Koelling, S., Kunze, J., Tezeren, Ö. and Werner, P. (1987) 'Ausgrabungen in Tall Munbaqa 1985', *Mitteilungen der Deutschen Orient-Gesellschaft* 119: 73–134.

Machule, D., Benter, M., Czichon, R., Luciani, M., Miftah, M., Pape, W. and Werner, P. (1993) 'Ausgrabungen in Tall Munbaqa/Ekalte 1991', *Mitteilungen der Deutschen Orient-Gesellschaft* 125: 69–101.

Marfoe, L. (1979) 'The Integrative Transformation: Patterns of Sociopolitical Organization in Southern Syria', *Bulletin of the American Schools of Oriental Research* 234: 1–42.

Margueron, J.-C. (1980) 'Emar: Un exemple d'implantation hittite en terre syrienne', in J.-C. Margueron (ed.) *Le Moyen Euphrate*, Leiden: E.J. Brill, pp. 285–313.

—— (1982) *Recherches sur les palais mésopotamiens de l'age du bronze*, Paris: Librairie Orientaliste Paul Geuthner.

—— (1990a) 'La salle aux piliers du palais de Mari de l'époque agadéenne', *MARI 6:* 385–400.

—— (1990b) 'Une tombe royale sous la salle du trône du palais des Shakkanakku', *MARI* 6: 401–22.

Marro, C., Tilbet, A. and Bulgan, F. (2000) 'Fouilles de sauvetage de Horum Höyük (province de Gaziantep): quatrième rapport préliminaire', *Anatolia Antiqua* 8: 257–78.

Masuda, S.-I. (1983) 'Terracotta House-Models Found at Rumeilah', *Les Annales Archéologiques Arabes Syriennes* 33: 153–60.

Matney, T. and Algaze, G. (1995) 'Urban Development at Mid-Late Early Bronze Age Titris Höyük in Southeastern Anatolia', *Bulletin of the American Schools of Oriental Research* 299/300: 33–52.

Matthews, R. (2003) *The Archaeology of Mesopotamia, Theories and Approaches*, London: Routledge, 2003.

Matthews, W. (1995) 'Micromorphological Characterisation and Interpretation of Occupation Deposits and Microstratigraphic Sequences at Abu Salabikh, Southern Iraq', in A.J. Barham and R.I. Macphail (eds) *Archaeological Sediments and Soils, Analysis, Interpretation and Management*, London: Archetype Books, pp. 41–76.

Matthiae, P. (1977) *Ebla: An Empire Rediscovered*, London: Hodder and Stoughton.

—— (1997) 'Ebla', in E.M. Meyers (ed.) *The Oxford Encyclopedia of Archaeology in the Near East*, Oxford: Oxford University Press, pp. 180–3.

Matilla Séiquer, G. and Rivera Nũ ez, D. (1994) 'Estudio paleoetnobotánico de Tell Qara Quzaq-I', in G. Del Olmo Lete (ed.) *Tell Qara Quzaq – I. Campañas I–III (1989–1991)*, Barcelona: Editorial AUSA, pp. 151–82.

Mazar, A. (1995) 'The Fortification of Cities in the Ancient Near East', in J.M. Sasson, *Civilizations of the Ancient Near East*, New York: Scribner, pp. 1523–37.

Mazzoni, S. (1985) 'Elements of the Ceramic Culture of Early Syrian Ebla in Comparison with Syro-Palestinian EBIV', *Bulletin of the American Schools of Oriental Research* 257: 1–18.

Meijer, D.J.W. (1980) 'The Excavations at Tell Selenkahiye', in J.-C. Margueron (ed.) *Le Moyen Euphrate*, Leiden: E.J. Brill, pp. 117–26.

Mesnil du Buisson, Le Comte du (1948) *Baghouz: L'ancienne Corsôte*, Leiden, E.J. Brill.

Meyer, J-W. (1991) *Gräber des 3. Jahrtausends v. Chr. im syrischen Euphrattal. 3. Ausgrabungen in Šamseddin und Djerniye*, Saarbrücken: Saarbrücker Dr. und Verlag.

—— (1996) 'Offene und geschlossene Siedlungen', *Altorientalische Forschungen* 23: 132–70.

Meyer, J-W. and Pruss, A. (1994) *Die Kleinfunde von Tell Halawa A*, Saarbrücken: Saarbrücker Druckerei und Verlag.

Milano, L. (1995) 'Ebla: A Third Millennium City-State in Ancient Syria', in J.M. Sasson (ed.) *Civilizations of the Ancient Near East*, New York: Scribner, pp. 1219–30.

Miller, N.F. (1997a) 'Sweyhat and Hajji Ibrahim: Some Archaeobotanical Samples from the 1991 and 1993 Seasons', in R. Zettler (ed.) *Subsistence and Settlement in a Marginal Environment. Tell es-Sweyhat, 1989–1995 Preliminary Report*, MASCA

Research Papers in Science and Archaeology 14. Philadelphia: Museum Applied Science Center for Archaeology, University of Pennsylvania Museum of Archeology and Anthropology, pp. 95–122.

—— (1997b) 'Farming and Herding Along the Euphrates: Environmental Constraint and Cultural Choice (Fourth to Second Millennia B.C.)', in R. Zettler (ed.) *Subsistence and Settlement in a Marginal Environment. Tell es-Sweyhat, 1989–1995 Preliminary Report*, MASCA Research Papers in Science and Archaeology 14. Philadelphia: Museum Applied Center for Archeology, University of Pennsylvania Museum of Archaeology and Anthropology, pp. 123–32.

Montero, J.-L. (1995) 'Estudio provisional del ajuar metálico del conjunto funerario de los *loci* 12 E y 12 W. Tell Qara Quzaq (Siria). Campaña 1992', *Aula Orientalis* 13: 25–30.

Montero Fenollós, J.-L. (1999) 'Metallurgy in the Valley of the Syrian Upper Euphrates during the Early and Middle Bronze Ages', in G. Del Olmo Lete and J.-L. Montero Fenollós (eds) *Archaeology of the Upper Syrian Euphrates. The Tishrin Dam Area. Proceedings of the International Symposium Held at Barcelona, Jan. 28th–30th, 1998*, Barcelona: Editorial Ausa, pp. 443–69.

Moortgat, A. (1960) *Tell Chuera in Nordost-Syrien: Vorläufiger Bericht über die Grabung 1958*, Köln and Oplanden: Westdeutscher Verlag.

—— (1962) *Tell Chuera in Nordost-Syrien: Vorläufiger Bericht über die dritte Grabundgskampagne 1960*, Köln and Oplanden: Westdeutscher Verlag.

Moortgat, A. and Moorgat-Correns, U. (1976) *Tell Chuera in Nordost Syrien. Vorläufiger Bericht über die siebente Grabungskampagne 1974*, Berlin: Gebr. Mann.

Morris, E. (in press) ' "Lo, Nobles Lament, the Poor Rejoice", Social Order Inverted in First Intermediate Period Egypt', in G.M. Schwartz and J. Nichols (eds) *After Collapse: The Regeneration of Complex Societies*, Tuscon: University of Arizona Press.

Nagata, J.A. (1974) 'What is a Malay? Situational Selection of Ethnic Identity in a Plural Society', *American Ethnologist* 1: 331–50.

Nichols, J. and Weber, J. (in press) 'Societal Collapse and Regeneration at Early and Middle Bronze Age Umm el-Marra, Syria', in G.M. Schwartz and J. Nichols (eds) *After Collapse: The Regeneration of Complex Societies*, Tuscon: University of Arizona Press.

Novák, M. (1995) 'Die Stadtmauergrabung', in W. Orthmann (ed.) *Ausgrabungen in Tell Chuera in Nordost-Syrien*, Saarbrücken: Saarbrücker Druckerei und Verlag, pp. 173–82.

Oates, D., Oates, J. and McDonald, H. (2001) *Excavations at Tell Brak. Vol. 2: Nagar in the Third Millennium BC*, Cambridge and London: McDonald Institute for Archaeological Research and the British School of Archaeology in Iraq.

Ökse, T.A. (2002) 'Excavations at Gre Virike in 2000', in N. Tuna and J. Velibeyoğlu (eds) *Salvage Project of the Archaeological Heritage of the Ilisu and Carchemish Dam Reservoirs: Activities in 2000*, Ankara: Middle East Technical University, pp. 270–85.

Olávarri, E. (1995a) 'Excavaciones en Tell Qara Quzaq. Informe provisional: campañas tercera y cuarta (1991–92). Misión arqueológica de la Universidad de Barcelona en Siria', *Aula Orientalis* 13: 5–14.

—— (1995b) 'Dos tumbas del Bronce Antiguo de Qara Quzaq', *Aula Orientalis* 13: 15–23.

Olávarri, E. and Valdés Pereiro, C. (2001) 'Excavaciones en Tell Qara Quzaq:

Campañas IV–VI (1992–1994)', in G. Del Olmo Lete, J.-L. Montero Fenollós and C. Valdés Pereiro (eds) *Tell Qara Quzaq II. Campañas IV–VI (1992–1994)*, Barcelona: Editorial Ausa, pp. 13–76.

Oppenheim, A.L. (1964) *Ancient Mesopotamia. Portrait of a Dead Civilization*, Revised Edition Completed by Erica Reiner. Chicago: University of Chicago Press.

Orthmann, W. (1976) 'Mumbaqat 1974. Vorläufiger Bericht über die von der Deutschen Orient-Gesellschaft mit Mitteln der Stiftung Volkswagenwerk unternommenen Ausgrabungen', *Mitteilungen der Deutschen Orient-Gesellschaft* 108: 25–44.

—— (1980) 'Burial Customs of the Third Millennium BC in the Euphrates Valley', in J.-C. Margueron (ed.) *Le Moyen Euphrate*, Leiden: E.J. Brill, pp. 97–105.

—— (1981) *Halawa 1977–1979*, Bonn: Dr. Rudolf Habelt.

—— (1985) 'Art of the Akkade Period in Northern Syria and Mari', *MARI* 4: 469–74.

—— (1989) *Halawa 1980–1986*, Bonn: Dr. Rudolf Habelt.

—— (1990) 'L'architecture religieuse de Tell Chuera', *Akkadica* 69: 1–18.

Orthmann, W. and Kühne, H. (1974) 'Mumbaqat 1973. Vorläufiger Bericht über die von der Deutschen Orient-Gesellschaft mit Mitteln der Stiftung Volkswagenwerk unternommenen Ausgrabungen', *Mitteilungen der Deutschen Orient-Gesellschaft* 106: 53–97.

Orthmann, W., Klein, H. and Lüth, F. (1986) *Tell Chuera in Nordost-Syrien. Vorläufiger Bericht über die neunte und zehnte Grabungskampagne 1982–1983*, Berlin: Mann.

Orthmann, W. and Rova, E. (1991) *Gräber des 3. Jahrtausends v. Chr. im syrischen Euphrattal. 2. Ausgrabungen in Wreide*, Saarbrücken: Saarbrücker Druckerei und Verlag.

Özbal, H., Adriaens, A. and Earl, B. (2000) 'Hacinebi Metal Production and Exchange', *Paléorient* 25: 57–65.

Palmieri, A. Sertok, K. and Chernykh, E. (1993) 'From Arslantepe Metalwork to Arsenical Copper Technology in Eastern Anatolia', in M. Frangipane (ed.) *Between the Rivers and Over the Mountains. Archaeologica Anatolica et Mesopotamica Alba Palmieri dedicata*, Rome: Dipartimento di Scienze Storiche Archeologiche e Antropologische dell'Antichità, Università di Roma 'La Sapienza', pp. 573–99.

Palumbo, G. (2001) 'The Early Bronze Age IV', in B. MacDonald, R. Adams and P. Bienkowski (eds) *The Archaeology of Jordan*, Sheffield: Sheffield Academic Press, pp. 271–89.

Parr, P. (1968) 'The Origin of the Rampart Fortifications of Middle Bronze Age Palestine and Syria', *Zeitschrift des Deutschen Palastina-Vereins* 84: 18–45.

Peltenburg, E. (1999a) 'Tell Jerablus Tahtani 1992–1996: A Summary', in G. Del Olmo Lete and J.-L. Montero Fenollós (eds) *Archaeology of the Upper Syrian Euphrates. The Tishrin Dam Area. Proceedings of the International Symposium Held at Barcelona, Jan. 28th–30th, 1998*, Barcelona: Editorial Ausa, pp. 97–105.

—— (1999b) 'The Living and the Ancestors: Early Bronze Age Mortuary Practices at Jerablus Tahtani', in G. Del Olmo Lete and J.-L. Montero Fenollós (eds) *Archaeology of the Upper Syrian Euphrates. The Tishrin Dam Area. Proceedings of the International Symposium Held at Barcelona, Jan. 28th–30th, 1998*, Barcelona: Editorial Ausa, pp. 427–42.

—— (2000) 'From Nucleation to Dispersal. Late Third Millennium BC Settlement Pattern Transformations in the Near East and Aegean', in O. Rouault and M. Wäfler (eds) *La Djéziré et l'Euphrate syriens de la protohistoire à la fin du IIe millénaire av. J.-C: tendances dans l'interprétation historique des données nouvelles*, (Subartu 7) Turnhout: Brepols, pp. 163–86.

—— (in press a) 'Feasting and Funerary Offerings in the Syrian Early Bronze Age: Evidence from Jerablus Tahtani', in J.-C. Margueron, P. de Miroschedji and J.-P. Thalmann (eds) *Proceedings of the Third International Congress on the Archaeology of the Ancient Near East*, (Paris, April 14–19, 2002) Winona Lake, Indiana: Eisenbrauns.

—— (in press b) 'Intra-site Burial Variation at Jerablus Tahtani: a Regional Perspective', in E. Peltenburg (ed.) *The Carchemish region in the Early Bronze Age: Investigating the Archaeology of Boundaries*, Oxford: Oxbow Books.

Peltenburg, E., Bolger, D., Campbell, S., Murray, M.A. and Tipping, R. (1996) 'Jerablus-Tahtani, Syria, 1995: Preliminary Report', *Levant* 28: 1–25.

Peltenburg, E., Campbell, S., Croft, P., Lunt, D., Murray M.A. and Watt, M.E. (1995) 'Jerablus-Tahtani, Syria, 1992–4: Preliminary Report', *Levant* 27: 1–28.

Peltenburg, E., Campbell, S., Carter, S., Stephen, F. and Tipping, R. (1997) 'Jerablus-Tahtani, Syria, 1996: Preliminary Report', *Levant* 29: 1–18.

Peltenburg, E., Eastaugh, E., Hewson, M., Jackson, A., McCarthy, A. and Rymer, T. (2000) 'Jerablus Tahtani, Syria, 1998–9: Preliminary Report', *Levant* 32: 53–75.

Peregrine, P.N., Bell, A., Braithwaite, M. and Danti, M. (1997) 'Geomagnetic Mapping of the Outer Town', in R. Zettler (ed.) *Subsistence and Settlement in a Marginal Environment: Tell es-Sweyhat, 1989–1995 Preliminary Report*, MASCA Research Papers in Science and Archaeology 14. Philadelphia: Museum Applied Science Center for Archaeology, University of Pennsylvania Museum of Archaeology and Anthropology, pp. 73–84.

Petty, A. (2004) 'Bronze Age Figurines from Umm el-Marra, Syria: Style and Meaning', unpublished PhD dissertation, Johns Hopkins University.

Pfälzner, P. (1998) 'Eine Modifikation der Periodisierung Nordmesopotamiens im 3. Jtsd. v. Chr.' *Mitteilungen der Deutschen Orient-Gesellschaft* 130: 69–71.

—— (2001) *Haus und Haushalt. Wohnformen des dritten Jahrtausends vor Christus in Nordmesopotamien*, Mainz am Rhein: von Zabern.

Philip, G. (1989) *Metal Weapons of the Early and Middle Bronze Ages in Syria-Palestine*, Oxford: BAR International Series.

—— (1995) 'Warrior Burials in the Ancient Near Eastern Bronze Age: the Evidence from Mesopotamia, Western Iran and Syria-Palestine', in S. Campbell and A. Green (eds) *The Archaeology of Death in the Ancient Near East*, Oxford: Oxbow Books, pp. 140–54.

—— (2001) 'The Early Bronze I-III Ages', in B. MacDonald, R. Adams and P. Bienkowski (eds) *The Archaeology of Jordan*, Sheffield: Sheffield Academic Press, pp. 163–232.

—— (in press) 'The Metalwork of the Carchemish Region: Distinctive or Derivative?' in E. Peltenburg (ed.) *The Carchemish region in the Early Bronze Age: Investigating the Archaeology of Boundaries*, Oxford: Oxbow Books.

Pollock, S. (1991) 'Of Priestesses, Princes and Poor Relations: the Dead in the Royal Cemetery of Ur', *Cambridge Archaeological Journal* 1: 171–89.

—— (1999) *Ancient Mesopotamia. The Eden that Never Was*, Cambridge: Cambridge University Press.

—— (2001) 'The Uruk Period in southern Mesopotamia', in M. Rothmann (ed.) *Uruk Mesopotamia and its Neighbours. Cross-Cultural Interactions in the Era of State Formation*, Oxford: James Currey, pp. 181–231.

Pons, N. (2001) 'La poterie de Tell Amarna (Syrie) au BA IV et au BM I', *Akkadica* 121: 23–75.

Porter, A. (1995a) 'Tell Banat – Tomb 1', *Damaszener Mitteilungen* 8: 1–50.

—— (1995b) 'The Third Millennium Settlement Complex at Tell Banat: Tell Kabir', *Damaszener Mitteilungen* 8: 125–63.

—— (1999) 'The Ceramic Horizon of the Early Bronze in the Upper Euphrates', in G. Del Olmo Lete and J.-L. Montero Fenollós (eds) *Archaeology of the Upper Syrian Euphrates. The Tishrin Dam Area. Proceedings of the International Symposium Held at Barcelona, Jan. 28th–30th, 1998*, Barcelona: Editorial Ausa, pp. 311–20.

—— (2002a) 'The Dynamics of Death: Ancestors, Pastoralism, and the Origins of a Third-Millennium City in Syria', *Bulletin of the American Schools of Oriental Research* 325: 1–36.

—— (2002b) 'Communities in Conflict. Death and the Contest for Social Order in the Euphrates River Valley', *Near Eastern Archaeology* 65: 156–73.

—— (in press) 'The Ceramic Assemblages of the Third Millennium in the Euphrates Region', in M. al-Maqdissi, V. Matoïan and C. Nicolle (eds) *La céramique de l'âge du Bronze en Syrie*, Damascus: IFAPO.

Porter, A. and McClellan, T. (1998) 'The Third Millennium Settlement Complex at Tell Banat: Results of the 1994 Excavations', *Damaszener Mitteilungen* 10: 11–63.

Postgate, N. (1992) *Early Mesopotamia. Society and Economy at the Dawn of History*, London: Routledge.

Reade, J. (1968) 'Tell Taya (1967): A Summary Report', *Iraq* 30: 234–64.

—— (1971) 'Tell Taya (1968–69): A Summary Report', *Iraq* 33: 87–100.

—— (1973) 'Tell Taya (1972–73): A Summary Report', *Iraq* 35: 155–87.

Reichel, C. (2004) 'Appendix B: Site Gazeteer', in T.J. Wilkinson *On the Margin of the Euphrates: Settlement and Land Use at Tell es-Sweyhat and in the Upper Lake Assad Area, Syria*, Chicago: Oriental Institute of the University of Chicago, pp. 223–60.

Renfrew, Colin (1986) 'Peer Polity Interaction and Socio-Political Change', in C. Renfrew and J. Cherry (eds) *Peer Polity Interaction and Socio-Political Change*, Cambridge: Cambridge University Press, pp. 1–18.

Richard, S. (1987) 'The Early Bronze Age: The Rise and Collapse of Urbanism', *Biblical Archaeologist* 50: 22–43.

Rice, P. (1987) *Pottery Analysis: A Sourcebook*, Chicago: University of Chicago Press.

Rivera-Nũ ez, D., Matilla, G. and Obón de Castro, C. (1999) 'Paleoethnobotanical Approach to the Upper Euphrates', in G. Del Olmo Lete and J.-L. Montero Fenollós (eds) *Archaeology of the Upper Syrian Euphrates. The Tishrin Dam Area. Proceedings of the International Symposium Held at Barcelona, Jan. 28th–30th, 1998*, Barcelona: Editorial Ausa, pp. 245–56.

Roaf, M. and Postgate, J.N. (1981) 'Excavations in Iraq, 1979–80', *Iraq* 43: 167–98.

Roobaert, A. and Bunnens, G. (1999) 'Excavations at Tell Ahmar – Til Barsib', in G. Del Olmo Lete and J.-L. Montero Fenollós (eds) *Archaeology of the Upper Syrian Euphrates. The Tishrin Dam Area. Proceedings of the International Symposium Held at Barcelona, Jan. 28th–30th, 1998*, Barcelona: Editorial Ausa, pp. 163–78.

Routledge, B. (1998) 'Making Nature Human: Small-Scale Production and Specialization at Tell Gudeda in the Middle Khabour Valley', in M. Fortin and O. Aurenche (eds) *Espace naturel, espace habité en Syrie du Nord (10e–2e millénaires av. J-C.)*, Lyon: Maison de l'Orient Méditerranéen, pp. 243–56.

Roux, V. (2003) 'Ceramic Standardization and Intensity of Production: Quantifying Degrees of Specialization', *American Antiquity* 68: 768–82.

Rye, O.S. (1976) 'Keeping your Temper under Control: Materials and the Manufacture of Paluan Pottery', *Archaeology and Physical Anthropology in Oceania* 11: 106–37.

Sagona, A. (1986) 'An Early Bronze Age IV Tomb at el-Qitar, Syria', *Abr Nahrain* 24: 107–19.

Santley, R., Yarborough, C. and Hall, B. (1987) 'Enclaves, Ethnicity, and the Archaeological Record at Matacapan', in R. Auger, M.F. Glass, S. MacEachern and P.H. MacCartney (eds) *Ethnicity and Culture*, Calgary: Dept. of Archaeology at the University of Calgary, pp. 85–100.

Schneider, G. (1989) 'A Technological Study of North-Mesopotamian Stone Ware', *World Archaeology* 21: 30–50.

Schwartz, G.M. (1987) Review of Kampschulte, I. and Orthmann, W. 'Gräber des 3. Jahrtausends im syrischen Euphrattal. 1. Ausgrabungen bei Tawi 1975 und 1978' (Bonn: Dr. Rudolf Habelt), *Bibliotheca Orientalis* 44:1/2, 239–43.

—— (1995) 'Pastoral Nomadism in Ancient Western Asia', in J.M. Sasson (ed.) *Civilizations of the Ancient Near East*, New York: Scribner, pp. 249–58.

—— (2000) 'Perspectives on Rural Ideologies: the Tell al-Raqa'i "Temple"', in O. Rouault and M. Wäfler (eds) *La Djéziré et l'Euphrate syriens de la protohistoire à la fin du second millénaire av. J.-C.: tendances dans l'interprétation historique des données nouvelles*, (Subartu 7) Turnhout: Brepols, pp. 163–82.

Schwartz, G., Curvers, H., Dunham, S. and Stuart, B. (2003) 'A Third-Millennium BC Elite Tomb and Other New Evidence from Tell Umm el-Marra, Syria', *American Journal of Archaeology* 107: 325–61.

Schwartz, G.M. and Nichols, J. (eds) (in press) *After Collapse: The Regeneration of Complex Societies*. Tucson: University of Arizona Press.

Sconzo, P. (in press a) 'The Bronze Age Pottery from the Carchemish Region. The Woolley-Lawrence Collections at the British and Ashmolean Museums', in J.-C. Margueron, P. de Miroschedji and J.-P. Thalmann (eds) *Proceedings of the Third International Congress on the Archaeology of the Ancient Near East*, (Paris, April 14–19, 2002) Winona Lake, Indiana: Eisenbrauns.

—— (in press b) 'Plain and Luxury Wares of the Third Millennium BC in the Carchemish Region: Two Case-Studies from Tell Shiyukh Tahtani', in E. Peltenburg (ed.) *The Carchemish Region in the Early Bronze Age: Investigating the Archaeology of Boundaries*, Oxford: Oxbow Books.

Serrat, D. and Bergadà, M. (1999) 'Geomorphological Study of the Upper Syrian Euphrates Basin', in G. Del Olmo Lete and J.-L. Montero Fenollós (eds) *Archaeology of the Upper Syrian Euphrates. The Tishrin Dam Area. Proceedings of the International Symposium Held at Barcelona, Jan. 28th–30th, 1998*, Barcelona: Editorial Ausa, pp. 239–44.

Sertok, K. (in press) 'May Fruitstands Define a Cultural Area?' in E. Peltenburg (ed.) *The Carchemish region in the Early Bronze Age: Investigating the Archaeology of Boundaries*, Oxford: Oxbow Books.

Sertok, K. and Ergeç, R. (1999) 'A New Early Bronze Age Cemetery: Excavations Near the Birecik Dam, Southeastern Turkey. Preliminary Report (1997–98)', *Anatolica* 25: 87–107.

Sertok, K. and Kulaloglu, F. (2002) 'Şaraga Höyük 2000', in N. Tuna and J.

Velibeyoğlu (eds) *Salvage Project of the Archaeological Heritage of the Ilisu and Carchemish Dam Reservoirs Activities in 2000*, Ankara, Middle East Technical University, pp. 370–81.

Squadrone, F.F. (2000) 'Metals for the Dead. Metal Finds from the Birecik Dam Early Bronze Age Cemetery in the Middle Euphrates Area, near Carchemish (Turkey)', in P. Matthiae, A. Enea, L. Peyronel and F. Pinnock (eds) *Proceedings of the First International Congress on the Archaeology of the Ancient Near East, Rome May 18th–23rd, 1998*, Rome: Università degli Studi di Roma 'La Sapienza', pp. 1541–56.

Stager, L. (1991) 'The Massive Middle Bronze Fortifications – How did they Work?' *Biblical Archaeology Review* 17: 30.

Stein, D.L. (1997) 'Hurrians', in E.M. Meyers (ed.) *The Oxford Encyclopedia of Archaeology in the Near East*, Oxford, Oxford University Press, pp. 126–30.

Stein, G., Boden, K., Edens, C., Pearce Edens, J., Keith, K., McMahon, A. and Özbal, H. (1997) 'Excavations at Hacinebi, Turkey 1996: Preliminary Report', *Anatolica* 23: 111–71.

Stol, M. (1983) 'Leder(industrie)', *Reallexikon der Assyriologie* 6: 527–43.

Strommenger, E. (1976) 'Fünfter vorläufiger Bericht über die von der Deutschen Orient-Gesellschaft mit Mitteln der Stiftung Volkswagenwerk in Habuba Kabira unternommenen archäologischen Untersuchungen (Kampagnen 1973, 1974, 1975)', *Mitteilungen der Deutschen Orient-Gesellschaft* 108: 5–22.

—— (1980) *Habuba Kabira. Eine Stadt vor 5000 Jahren. Ausgrabungen der Deutschen Orient-Gesellschaft am Euphrat in Habuba Kabira*, Mainz am Rhein: Von Zabern.

—— (1997) Bi'a/Tuttul, in H. Weiss (ed.) 'Archaeology in Syria', *American Journal of Archaeology* 101: 112–16.

Strommenger, E. and Kohlmeyer, K. (1998) *Tell Bi'a/Tuttul – 1: Die Altorientalischen Bestattungen*, Saarbrücken, Saarbrücker Druckerei und Verlag.

—— (2000) *Die Schichten des 3. Jahrtausends v. Chr. im Zentralhügel E (Ausgrabungen in Tall Bi'a/Tuttul 3)*, Saarbrücken, Saarbrücker Druckerei und Verlag.

Strommenger, E., Böhme, S., Brandes, M.A., Hemker, C., Kohlmeyer, K., Ludwig, W., Schulze-Wischeler, H., Selz, G. (1989) 'Ausgrabungen eu Tall Bi'a 1987', *Mitteilungen der Deutschen Orient-Gesellschaft* 121: 5–64.

Suleiman, A. (2003) 'The Northern Stratigraphical Sounding (Field G)', in M. Lebeau and A. Suleiman (eds) *Tell Beydar 1995–1999 Seasons of Excavations. A Preliminary Report*, (Subartu 10) Brepols: Turnhout, pp. 301–13.

Thureau-Dangin, F. and Dunand, M. (1936) *Til-Barsib*. Paris: Librairie Orientaliste Paul Geuthner.

Tsukimoto, A. (1985) *Untersuchungen zur Totenpflege (kispum) im altern Mesopotamien*, (AOAT 216) Neukirchen-Vluyn: Neukirchener Verlag.

Tubb, J. (1982) 'A Crescentic Axehead from Amarna (Syria) and an Examination of Similar Axeheads from the Near East', *Iraq* 44: 1–12.

—— (1985) 'Some Observations on Spearheads in Palestine in the Middle and Late Bronze Ages', in J.N. Tubb (ed.) *Palestine in the Bronze and Iron Ages: Papers in Honour of Olga Tufnell*, London: Institute of Archaeology, pp. 189–96.

Tunca, Ö. (1992) 'Rapport préliminaire sur la 1ère campagne de fouilles à Tell Amarna (Syrie)', *Akkadica* 79–80: 14–38.

—— (1999) 'Tell Amarna. Présentation sommaire de sept campagnes de fouilles (1991–1997)', in G. Del Olmo Lete and J.-L. Montero Fenollós (eds) *Archaeology of the Upper Syrian Euphrates. The Tishrin Dam Area. Proceedings of the International Symposium Held at Barcelona, Jan. 28th–30th, 1998*, Barcelona: Editorial Ausa, pp. 129–36.

Valdés Pereiro, C. (1994) 'La cerámica de la Edad del Bronce de Tell Qara Quzaq. Campaña de 1991', in G. Del Olmo Lete (ed.) *Tell Qara Quzaq – I. Campañas I–III (1989–1991)*, Barcelona: Editorial Ausa, pp. 35–143.

—— (1999) 'Tell Qara Quzaq: A Summary of the First Results', in G. Del Olmo Lete and J.-L. Montero Fenollós (eds) *Archaeology of the Upper Syrian Euphrates. The Tishrin Dam Area. Proceedings of the International Symposium Held at Barcelona, Jan. 28th–30th, 1998*, Barcelona: Editorial Ausa, pp. 117–27.

—— (2001) 'La cerámica de Tell Qara Quzaq. Campañas 1992–94', in G. Del Olmo Lete, J.-L. Montero Fenollós and C. Valdés Pereiro (eds) *Tell Qara Quzaq II. Campañas IV–VI (1992–1994)*, Barcelona: Editorial Ausa, pp. 119–254.

Van der Mieroop, M. (1987) *Crafts in the Early Isin Period*, Leuven: Departement Oriëntalistiek.

—— (1997) *The Ancient Mesopotamian City*, Oxford: Clarendon Press.

Van Loon, M.N. (1967) *The Tabqa Reservoir Survey 1964*, Damascus: Direction Générale des Antiquités et des Musées.

—— (1979) '1974 and 1975 Preliminary Results of the Excavations at Selenkahiye near Meskene, Syria', in D.N. Freedman (ed.) *Archaeological Projects from the Tabqa Dam Project – Euphrates Valley, Syria*, (AASOR 44) Cambridge, MA: American Schools of Oriental Research, pp. 97–112.

—— (2001) *Selenkahiye. Final Report on the University of Chicago and University of Amsterdam Excavations in the Tabqa Reservoir, Northern Syria, 1967–1975*, Istanbul: Nederlands Historisch-Archaeologisch Instituut.

Van Zeist, W. and Bakker-Heeres, J.A.H. (1985) 'Archaeobotanical studies in the Levant, 4. Bronze Age site on the North Syrian Euphrates', *Palaeohistoria* 27: 247–316.

Vandiver, P. (2003) 'A Preliminary Study of Ninevite 5 Pottery Technology at Tell Leilan', in E. Rova and H. Weiss (eds) *The Origins of North Mesopotamian Civilization: Ninevite 5 Chronology, Economy, Society*, (Subartu 9). Turnhout: Brepols, 429–53.

Veenhof, K.R. (1977) 'Some Social Effects of Old Assyrian Trade', *Iraq* 29: 109–18.

Voigt, M. (1991) 'The Goddess from Anatolia', *Oriental Rug Review* 11/2: 33–9.

Waetzoldt, H. (1972) *Untersuchungen zur neusumerischen Textilindustrie*, Rome.

Wattenmaker, P. (1994) 'Political Fluctuations and Local Exchange Systems in the Ancient Near East: Evidence from the Early Bronze Age Settlements at Kurban Höyük', in G. Stein and M. Rothmann (eds) *Chiefdoms and Early States in the Near East: The Organizational Dynamics of Complexity*, Madison, WI: Prehistory Press, pp. 193–208.

—— (1998) *Household and State in Upper Mesopotamia*, Washington: Smithsonian Institution.

Weber, J.A. (1997) 'Faunal Remains from Tell es-Sweyhat and Tell Hajji Ibrahim', in R. Zettler (ed.) *Subsistence and Settlement in a Marginal Environment. Tell es-Sweyhat, 1989–1995 Preliminary Report*, MASCA Research Papers in Science and Archaeology 14. Philadelphia: Museum Applied Science Center for Archaeology, University of Pennsylvania Museum of Archaeology and Anthropology, pp. 133–68.

Weinstein, J.M. (1992) 'Hyksos', in D.N. Freedman (ed.) *Anchor Bible Dictionary vol. 3 H–J*, New York, Doubleday, pp. 344–8.

Weiss, H. (1983) 'Excavations at Tell Leilan and the Origins of North Mesopotamian Cities in the Third Millennium B.C.', *Paléorient* 9/2: 39–52.

—— (2000) 'Causality and Chance. Late Third Millennium Collapse in Southwest Asia', in O. Rouault and M. Wäfler (eds) *La Djéziré et l'Euphrate syriens de la protohistoire à la fin du IIe millénaire av. J.-C: tendances dans l'interprétation historique des données nouvelles*, (Subartu 7) Turnhout: Brepols, pp. 207–17.

Weiss, H. and Courty, M.-A. (1993) 'The Genesis and Collapse of the Akkadian Empire: The Accidental Refraction of Historical Law', in M. Liverani (ed.) *Akkad, the First World Empire*, Padua: Sargon, pp. 131–55.

Weiss, H., Courty, M.-A., Wetterstrom, W., Guichard, F., Senior, L., Meadow, R. and Curnow, A. (1993) 'The Genesis and Collapse of Third Millennium North Mesopotamian Civilization', *Science* 261: 995–1004.

Werner, P. (1998) *Tall Munbaqa. Bronzezeit in Syrien*, Neumünster: Wachholtz Verlag.

Wilkinson, T.J. (1976) 'The Ancient Landscape of the Tell es-Sweyhat Plain', Appendix III in T.A. Holland, 'Preliminary Report on the Excavations at Tell es-Sweyhat, Syria, 1973–74', *Levant* 8: 67–70.

—— (1994) 'The Structure and Dynamics of Dry-Farming States in Upper Mesopotamia', *Current Anthropology* 35: 483–520.

—— (2000) 'Regional Approaches to Mesopotamian Archaeology: The Contribution of Archaeological Surveys', *Journal of Archaeological Research* 8: 219–67.

—— (2003) *Archaeological Landscapes of the Near East*, Tucson: University of Arizona Press.

—— (2004) *On the Margin of the Euphrates: Settlement and Land Use at Tell es-Sweyhat and in the Upper Lake Assad Area, Syria*, Chicago: Oriental Institute of the University of Chicago.

Wilkinson, T.J. and Tucker, D.J. (1995) *Settlement Development in the North Jazirah, Iraq: A Study of the Archaeological Landscape*, Warminster, UK: Aris and Phillips.

Woolley, C.L. (1914) 'Hittite Burial Customs', *Annals of Archaeology and Anthropology, University of Liverpool* 6: 87–98.

—— (1921) *Carchemish II. The Town Defences*, London: British Museum Publications.

Woolley, L. and Barnett, R.D. (1952) *Carchemish III. The Excavations in the Inner Town*, London: British Museum Publications.

Yoffee, N. (1988) 'The Collapse of Ancient Mesopotamian States and Civilization', in N. Yoffee and G. Cowgill, *The Collapse of Ancient States and Civilizations*, Tucson: University of Arizona Press, pp. 44–68.

Zagarell, A. (1986) 'Trade, Women, Class and Society in Ancient Western Asia', *Current Anthropology* 27: 415–30.

Zeder, M.A. (1998) 'Environment, Economy, and Subsistence on the Threshold of Urban Emergence in Northern Mesopotamia', in M. Fortin and O. Aurenche (eds) *Espace naturel, espace habité en Syrie du Nord (10e–2e millénaires av. J-C.)*, Lyon: Maison de l'Orient Méditerranéen, pp. 55–67.

Zettler, R.L. (1997a) 'Introduction', in R. Zettler (ed.) *Subsistence and Settlement in a Marginal Environment: Tell es-Sweyhat, 1989–1995 Preliminary Report*, MASCA Research Papers in Science and Archaeology 14. Philadelphia: Museum Applied Science Center for Archaeology, University of Pennsylvania Museum of Archaeology and Anthropology, pp. 1–10.

—— (1997b) 'Surface Collections and Excavations in the Lower Town and Lower Town South', in R. Zettler (ed.) *Subsistence and Settlement in a Marginal Environment: Tell es-Sweyhat, 1989–1995 Preliminary Report*, MASCA Research Papers in Science and Archaeology 14. Philadelphia: Museum Applied Science Center for Archeology, University of Pennsylvania Museum of Archaeology and Anthropology, pp. 35–72.

Zettler, R., Miller, N.F., Weber, J.A., Peregrine, P. and Danti, M.D. (1996) 'Tell es-Sweyhat, 1989–1995. A City in Northern Mesopotamia in the Third Millennium B.C.', *Expedition* 38: 14–36.

INDEX